A view of Bala from the south, showing the source of the River Dee.

THOMAS CHARLES'S SPIRITUAL COUNSELS

Y PARCH. THOMAS CHARLES, B.A., BALA.

THOMAS CHARLES'S SPIRITUAL COUNSELS

*Selected from His Letters and Papers
by Edward Morgan*

With an Introduction

by

Iain H. Murray

THE BANNER OF TRUTH TRUST

THE BANNER OF TRUTH TRUST

Head Office
3 Murrayfield Road
Edinburgh, EH12 6EL
UK

North America Office
PO Box 621
Carlisle, PA 17013
USA

banneroftruth.org

© The Banner of Truth Trust 2021
First Published 1836 as
Essays, Letters and Interesting Papers of the late Thomas Charles
First Banner of Truth edition 1993
This (retypeset) edition 2021

*

ISBN
Print: 978 1 80040 185 3
Epub: 978 1 80040 105 1
Kindle: 978 1 80040 118 1

*

Typeset in 11/14 Adobe Garamond Pro
at The Banner of Truth Trust, Edinburgh

Printed in the USA by
Versa Press Inc.,
East Peoria, IL

The publishers wish to express their appreciation to Dr John Aaron
for his assistance in the preparation of this volume.

CONTENTS

Biographical Introduction	xi
Preface	xxxi

ESSAYS

1.	Spiritual Pride	1
2.	Humility	20
3.	The Operations of the Holy Spirit	34
4.	Sanctification	51
5.	Affliction – Its Use and Benefits	62
6.	The Tares and the Wheat	65
7.	Divine Guidance	70
8.	Spiritual Appetite	74
9.	God Affording Seasonable Help	79
10.	The Gift and Objects of God's Love	82
11.	The Sin of Grieving the Spirit	85
12.	The Infinite Greatness of the Son of God	89
13.	On Walking with God	94
14.	God Our Light	100
15.	Natural and Renewed Conscience	103
16.	Conformity to the Image of God	107
17.	Realizing Faith	114
18.	The Ground of Faith – The Testimony of God	117
19.	The Object of Faith – The Promises of God	122
20.	Enmity against God	127
21.	The Leadings of Mercy	133
22.	The Means of Mortifying Sin	138

23. The Divine Witnesses	143
24. The Two Witnesses	149
25. The Case of Judas	154
26. The Saviour's Unchangeableness	157

LETTERS

To Mr David Charles, of Carmarthen

1. How the Convinced of Sin May Obtain Peace	161
2. The Means to be Used for Obtaining Peace	168

To Miss Sarah Jones, of Bala, afterwards Mrs Thomas Charles

1. Remedy for All Complaints	176
2. Christ Dying for the Ungodly	177
3. The Fears and Doubts of a Gracious Soul	178
4. The Difference between Unbelief and Holy Jealousy	180
5. The Christian's Treasure – 'It Is Well'	183
6. Safety in God – Hopeful and Hopeless Death	184
7. Indwelling Sin – Growth in Grace	185
8. The Best Friend – Recovery from Illness	187
9. All Events under God's Direction	188
10. Spiritual Communion	189
11. Human Counsel Not Safe	191
12. The Happy Effects of Real Humility	191
13. The Infallible Physician	193
14. The Goodness and Love of God	194
15. Fear and Love – The Love of Christ	194
16. The Furnace and the Refiner	196
17. The Spiritual Contest	198
18. Zeal – Resignation – Heaven – Christ Our Rest	201
19. Walking with God	202
20. An Overhasty Spirit – Worldly Cares	205
21. The Guidance of the Holy Spirit	206
22. The Single Eye	208
23. Trusting the Lord – His Promise to Be with Us	209

Contents

24.	Clouds and Storms Necessary	210
25.	Review of the Past – Christ the Only Refuge	211

To His Wife

1.	The Gospel, the Power of God – Success Expected	214
2.	God Nigh – Communion with Him	215
3.	Blessings Received through Trials	217
4.	Faith, an Enemy to Sin	219
5.	Doubts Injurious to the Progress of Piety	220
6.	The Sabbath	222
7.	Humbling Views of One's Self	223

To Miss Wright, of Tarvin, Chester

1.	Consolations to the Afflicted	225
2.	Forgiveness Connected with Penitence, etc.	226

To Mr Richard Jones, of Wrexham

Man's Nothingness – Need of Christ – Spiritual Blessing — 228

To Mrs Ann Jones, of Wrexham

1.	Living to God – Kind Thoughts of Him	229
2.	The Necessity and Benefits of the Bible Society	230

To Mr Robert Jones, Rhos-lan, Lleyn, Caernarvonshire

A Welsh Letter Respecting the Trysorfa, etc.	232
The Same Translated	235

To Mrs Thomas Colley, of Cefngwifed, Near Newtown, Montgomeryshire

1.	Condolence on Her Husband's Death	238
2.	The Education of Children, etc.	239

To Miss Eliza Colley, of Cefngwifed

Thoughts Respecting Schools, etc. — 242

To Mr John Walker, of Chester

Christ Our Peace – The Hope of Glory — 243

To Mr and Mrs John Walker, of Chester

1.	Congratulations on Their Marriage	245
2.	Fellowship with God, etc.	246

To Mr and Mrs William Astle, of London
- 1. The Difference between Conscience and Grace — 247
- 2. The Gospel Comforts — 250
- 3. Children, God's Gifts, to be Devoted to God — 250
- 4. An Unworthy Sinner and a Pardoning God — 253
- 5. God in Christ Receiving Sinners — 255
- 6. The Fullness of Christ is Our All — 256
- 7. God's Mercies – His Promises to Sinners — 258
- 8. God's Gifts – Christ Our All – Spirituality in Ministers — 260

To the Rev. Mr John Mayor, of Shawbury
- 1. Gratitude to God and Man — 262
- 2. Dependence on God – Marriage – Trial — 262
- 3. Watchfullness – God a Present Help — 264
- 4. Afflictions Necessary — 264
- 5. Divine Teaching – Support in Affliction, etc. — 265
- 6. Reflections on Mr Lucas's Death — 267
- 7. The Religious State of North Wales — 268
- 8. Welsh Bibles – Mrs Charles's Illness – Mr Scott's Writings — 268
- 9. On the Death of an Infant — 270
- 10. Strength for Duty – Sin and Self — 271
- 11. Mr Charles's Experience during His Illness — 271

To Miss Mary Ashwell, of Milborne Port, Somerset
- 1. Humility and Thankfullness — 275
- 2. God's Care of His Children — 277
- 3. The Hope of Meeting Above – Revivals — 278
- 4. Wesleyan Methodists – Unceasing Labours — 280
- 5. Romaine's Death – Dress — 281

To Mr R. D —, of Liverpool
- The Honour of Promoting God's Cause — 283

To Edward Morgan (A Young Clergyman)
- 1. Guidance of Providence, etc. — 285

2.	Present Faithfullness	285
3.	Extempore Preaching – Davies's and Walker's Sermons – Old German Divines – Learning Hebrew	286
4.	Liverpool Bible Society, etc.	287
5.	Activity – the Sinner's Encouragement	288
6.	Directions for Studying, etc.	288
7.	The Want of Activity in Ministers and Others	290
8.	Consciousness of Defects – Faith Described – Success of Sunday Schools	291
9.	Animation in Preaching – Zeal – Boldness	293
10.	Different Modes of Preaching, etc.	295
11.	Regeneration and Faith	296
12.	No Abstruse Things in Sermons, etc.	297

To Miss Mary Foulks, of Machynlleth
    The Excellency of the Bible   298

To Miss Mary Hughes, of Liverpool
    The Duty of Working for God   300

To Mrs E — , C — n
1.	The Importance of Knowing God in Youth	301
2.	Consolation under Bereavements	301

To the Rev. Henry Grey, of Stenton, Haddington, Scotland
1.	Preaching Excursions – Progress of the Schools	304
2.	Illness – Sunday Schools – Ministry – Innovation	306

PAPERS

Preface to the Rev. Mr Oliver's Hymn Book   309

Sunday Schools

1. General Address, March 1809   313
2. A Letter to the Teachers and Scholars of a Sunday School at Blaenannerch, Cardiganshire, 1809   317
3. Address to the Teachers of Sunday Schools, 1811   322

THOMAS CHARLES'S SPIRITUAL COUNSELS

MINUTES OF QUARTERLY MEETINGS

1. Minutes of an Association, at Llanrhwst, January 1-2, 1795 — 325
2. Minutes of an Association, at Machynlleth, April 15-16, 1795 — 330
3. Minutes of an Association, at Bala, June 15-16, 1795 — 337
4. Minutes of an Association, at Llanfair, April 11-12, 1796 — 343
5. Minutes of an Association, at Bala, June 13-14, 1797 — 350

BIOGRAPHICAL INTRODUCTION

ALTHOUGH the Principality of Wales is a comparatively small region, the spiritual conditions in the north and the south of that country in the mid-eighteenth century presented a striking contrast. From the 1730s the south and the west experienced a spiritual awakening which had begun to make the population a Bible-loving people. Clergymen of the Church of England, led by Daniel Rowland and William Williams, together with unordained exhorters such as Howell Harris, drew hundreds and thousands from the world and set them on a joyful course for heaven. Given the name of 'Methodists' (to which was soon added 'Calvinistic' to distinguish them from the Wesleyan movement in England[1]), these people nevertheless remained a part of the Church of England though their fellowship and organization in 'societies' existed apart from the parish system.

In the north it was entirely different. Not a single clergyman favoured the preaching which had brought such change elsewhere; on the contrary, most were like Dr Edwards, the Vicar of Machynlleth, who would refer to Rowland and his brethren as 'those wicked Methodists.' Edward Morgan, himself a clergyman, could speak of his colleagues in north Wales as 'rich, self-indulgent and idle.' Those outside the Established Church – the Nonconformist successors of the Puritans – had ceased to provide any challenge in this situation and in 1736 they could number only six chapels in the whole area, including one at Bala, a wool-manufacturing town in the heart of north Wales. When Howell Harris preached in a

---

[1] James Hutton, reporting something of the spiritual conditions in England to Count Zinzendorf in March 1740, wrote: 'In Wales some thousands are stirred up. They are an exceedingly simple and honest people, but they are taught the Calvinistic scheme.'

private house in Bala in 1741 the service was disrupted and he was nearly killed by a mob. In later years an older citizen of that town recalled the conditions which then prevailed: 'Bibles were very scarce; hardly any of the lower ranks could read at all. ... Gluttony, drunkenness, and licentiousness like a torrent overran the land. ... From the pulpit the name of the Redeemer was hardly ever heard; nor was there much mention made of the natural sinfullness of man, nor of the influence of the Holy Spirit.'[1]

But Harris's fearless preaching in Bala was not without fruit and one who passed from death to life under its influence was Jane Jones who, with the husband she married in 1737, became one of the leading shopkeepers of the town. David and Jane Jones would have remained unknown to posterity if it had not been for their one child, Sarah, who was born in 1753, sixteen years after their wedding. Twenty-five years later 'Sally' Jones, still unmarried, was famed in Merionethshire for her personality, her looks and her earnestness in religion. It seems that news of her certainly played a part in drawing a student at Oxford by the name of Thomas Charles to accept the invitation of a fellow Welsh student to visit north Wales in the summer of 1778. Upon just such seemingly small issues great matters often turn.

Thomas Charles, born near Carmarthen two years after his future wife, was a stranger to the north and until 1773 he was also a stranger to the experience which made Sally different from so many of her contemporaries. In that year, on January 20, the seventeen-year-old Carmarthen schoolboy heard Daniel Rowland preach and his 'mind was overwhelmed and overpowered with amazement' at the truth. He could say: 'The change a blind man who receives his sight experiences doth not exceed the change I at that time experienced.' So, with the Christian ministry in view, Charles settled into a course of study at Jesus College, Oxford, in February 1776. The summer vacation of the following year he spent with John Newton at Olney from where he wrote to a friend:

[1] *Trysorfa Ysprydol* (*Spiritual Treasury*), 1799, pp. 30-31. Quoted in *Life of Howell Harris*, J. Hughes (Newport and London, 1892), p. 75.

Having a Newton to be instructed by, both by edifying discourses in the pulpit, and by conversation in the closet, what place or situation can I be in, more pleasing and delightful? I had formed in my mind great expectations of him, but really he has exceeded my most sanguine expectations. ... Had I the strongest constitution and the best advantages of human literature, yes, of all learning, both sacred and profane, yet I am perfectly convinced that all this would be much too little to make me a gospel preacher. One may speak a great deal, and that very orthodox; but unless he has a little of the unction of the Holy Spirit, he might, for aught I know, as well be silent. That is what I want in my prayers, studies and meditations.[1]

In 1778, the year when Charles first saw Sally Jones at Bala, Charles was ordained in the Church of England and settled in a curacy at Shepton Beauchamp in Somerset. No one could have then anticipated that these facts were going to collide with each other, nor did they at the outset. Sally remained on his mind, he even refers to her in a letter, to the former student friend who had introduced them, as 'My Dear Sally,' but he had no further contact with her until a first letter was posted on December 28, 1779. It began:

> My Very Dear Friend – Such an unexpected address from a person who never saw you but once, and that at such a long interval of time, will I suppose at first not a little surprise you ...

Such was the beginning of a courtship which ended in their wedding at the parish church of Llanycil, Bala, on August 20, 1783. For Charles that period seemed a great deal longer than three-and-a-half years. Sarah's letters, often written from the shop counter in Bala, show that she had been slow to reciprocate the feelings he expressed and when at last she did, and marriage was discussed, it

---

[1] *The Life of Thomas Charles of Bala*, D. E. Jenkins (Denbigh, 1910), vol. 1, pp. 50-51. Future references to this title will be given as *Thomas Charles*.

[xiii]

was only to encounter a new problem. The thought of Sally being as remote from home as Somerset was more than her parents could bear or allow. John Newton entered into the problem and obtained a curacy for Charles in south Wales but even that location was unthinkable to her mother and step-father.[1] Sorrowfully, Charles explained in a letter to a friend:

> She is an only child of tender and affectionate parents. ... It would be worse than death for her to be removed, whilst they live, to a considerable distance. ... I would not for the world be the means of bringing their grey hairs with sorrow to the grave. Everything, therefore, must remain as it is, till I meet with a situation within a convenient distance of the place where they live in North Wales.

Such was the background to the momentous decision that Charles finally reached. The reception to his preaching evangelical Christianity had been far from encouraging in Somerset; all the indications were that it would be far worse if he found himself settled in a parish in Merionethshire. Even so, he tried without success to find an appointment in north Wales. 'Is it not the easiest and safest way to put an end to our acquaintance than to be perplexed with it?' Sally asked in a letter of February 1781. After further disappointments in the way of finding a curacy (and therefore a source of support) near her home Charles gave up Somerset, where he had recently been offered a 'perpetual curacy,' and married Sally in Bala in the summer of 1783 without any sure source of future income. He had still, at that date, not given up all hopes of finding a place among his clerical colleagues and soon after his marriage we find him with an opening at Llangynog, a parish twelve miles from Bala. This lasted for only two Sundays. The nearest evangelical ministerial friend was probably John Mayor of Shawbury, Shropshire, and as he was in poor health Charles left Sally at Bala and gave help in Mayor's two churches in the autumn

---

[1] David Jones died when Sally was about six or seven years old, and her mother remarried.

Biographical Introduction

of 1783. He was also rejected in the parish of Llandegla, where he preached for his friend, Simon Jones. He wrote to Mayor:

> Last Sunday, the whole parish, with two or three of the principal inhabitants at their head, came and accosted me in a rougher strain than I have ever been used to before. They insisted on my preaching no more in their church; for they added, 'You have cursed us enough already.' I took care that nothing but the plain simple truth should give offence …

Back in Bala, where Sally's mother said he would 'make an excellent shopkeeper,' Charles found another invitation, to the curacy at Llanymawddwy, fourteen miles from Bala and over a wild, mountainous track. From January 25, 1784, Charles made that journey, usually by foot, in all weather; but in March, and for the third time, he was given a dismissal. It was his last curacy.

John Newton, for one, was apprehensive about Charles's course of action, and his likely inaction, as far as his future in the Established Church was concerned. Probably word had reached him that Charles was 'at times nearly resolved to lay aside all thoughts of the Church.' 'For aught I can tell,' Newton wrote to him, 'the reason why the Lord has permitted you to be silenced in Wales, may be, that he has a work for you to do in Yorkshire or Northumberland.' Was it right, he went on to ask, to leave the Church of England 'entirely on considerations of a temporal nature, and your own personal apparent interest?' (i.e., Charles's wish that their home should be in Bala). Commenting on these words, D. E. Jenkins, Charles's biographer, writes:

> Mr Charles was as convinced as his good and distinguished friend of God's leading and blessing; the point now was, Why had God led him to Bala? and why did the surrounding mountains refuse to lower their heads in order to expand his horizon? The Church offered him nothing, and God offered him (1) Bala (2) Merionethshire, and (3) North Wales.

But Jenkins writes with all the advantages of hindsight. That was certainly not the choice as Charles saw it in 1784. The most he could say in the summer of that difficult year was, 'I feel myself much inclined to take Wales, as I did my wife, "for better, for worse, till death do us part."'

Judged by the appearance of things, Sally and her parents were the reason why he was unemployed and to be found at times behind a shop counter. But behind the appearance there was in Charles the constraint of a prayerful faith. Uncertain of the future though he was, he had learned more necessary things in all the sore trials of the years following his ordination. His disappointments in Somerset and elsewhere, the long wait for Sally, and, worst of all, his conscious incapacity and the small influence for good which seemed to attend his work, had all worked for good. It is significant that the first chapters in this book are on 'Spiritual Pride' and 'Humility.' He was brought low. In the words of D. E. Jenkins, 'God had appointed him to plough a field of virgin soil, as far as Evangelicalism was concerned, and was sharpening his ploughshare with the hone of tribulations and the grit of tested faith.'[1] And, more fully, Edward Morgan comments:

> When God intends a person for some great work, he prepares him for it. He makes him know and feel what he is in himself, sinful, depraved, weak, devoid of every spiritual good, and full of every evil. ... Mr Charles was destined by heaven for great and glorious services. He was now undergoing a course of hard discipline, to fit him for his work. The success he met with in after life, and the honour to which he attained, would have found in the pride of the heart too ready a combustible, and might have proved his ruin, had not that pride been previously mortified. ... The foundation of his humility was deeply laid: and it was laid, no doubt, during the first years of his ministry, by the realizing views he had of his own sin and unworthiness.[2]

[1] *Thomas Charles*, vol. 1, pp. 415-16.

[2] *A Brief Memoir of the Life and Labours of the Rev. Thomas Charles*, Edward Morgan, second edition (London, 1831), pp. 198-200. This same lesson Charles urged on others. While writing to the Countess of Huntingdon in 1791 about the need of London he says, 'Let us go in humble, humble faithfullness, we shall certainly sow if not reap the harvest.'

Biographical Introduction

The course of action which Charles finally took to end his enforced idleness, unsurprising though it sounds to us, was one which for some time, he tells us, he 'never thought of.' In spite of the connection of his parents-in-law with the despised Methodists (Sally's step-father preached among them), Charles never seems to have been at their meetings in Bala. He certainly never preached among them, yet here, unlike the congregations as dead as 'so many stocks or stones' which he had faced elsewhere, were people eager to hear the word of God. With the local clergy declining to use even his unpaid services, Charles went to the Society meeting in Bala in July 1784. Soon he began to preach among them and within a few months he was to be found as an itinerant preacher among the Calvinistic Methodists in north Wales – the first clergyman in the north ever to cast his lot among them. At twenty-nine years of age he was a comparative youngster among older believers. John Evans, one of the Calvinistic Methodists in Bala, recalled the coming of Charles into their midst in a conversation which occurred many years later when Charles was questioning a woman seeking church membership. Evans was present but, being elderly and deaf, was unable to follow the conversation. At length Charles turned to his old friend with the words, 'I find her very uninformed, John Evans, what do you think ought to be done with her?' 'Well,' replied the Christian of long experience, 'you were uninformed yourself when you came to us.'[1]

A new chapter had opened in Charles's life and experience. In April 1785 we find him writing:

> I am just this moment come home from three weeks' tour through Caernarvonshire and Anglesey. The fields here all over the country are white for the harvest. Fresh ground is daily gained. Whole neighbourhoods where the word has been heretofore opposed call aloud for the gospel. Thousands flock to hear and many in different parts of the country, we have good reason to believe, are effectually called.'

---

[1] *Thomas Charles*, vol. 3, p. 607.

When the aged Daniel Rowland heard Charles at Llangeitho later that summer he was in no doubt why the young man had been shut up to Bala: 'Charles is the Lord's gift to North Wales.'

In this same eventful year, 1784–85, another form of service had opened for Charles. Impressed by the utter ignorance of the children and youth of the town he began to invite some of them to the home he and Sally shared with her parents above and behind the shop. Whether this was done on a Sunday or weekday is not clear, but the numbers grew so that before long the gathering had to be moved to the building used by the Methodists. As Charles began to travel about the north he was soon convinced that the need of children could not be met without a much wider effort. Charity Schools had been instituted many years earlier and had become valuable spiritual agencies. His initial experiment in Bala now led to a parallel development in the north. In a letter of March 24, 1787, he writes:

> When I came a little acquainted with the country, I was surprised and grieved to find so many totally illiterate and not able to read a word in the Bible in their Mother's tongue. I have attempted and succeeded far beyond my expectations in setting up charity schools, with a view only to teaching poor children and young people to read the Bible in a language they understand, and teach them the principles of the Christian religion by catechizing them. We had seven school-masters last year in employ, and we think of increasing the number to twelve this ensuing summer … I visit all the schools myself as often as I can. The money is raised by voluntary subscriptions among our societies. … I have been often, in my journeys through different parts of the country, questioned, whether I knew if a Welsh Bible could be bought for a small price? And it has hurt my mind much to be obliged to answer in the negative.

These were circulating schools, that is to say, schools set up in a district for about nine months (which Charles believed was the time needed to teach young people to read the Scriptures), and then the schoolmasters moved on to other places. By 1789 there were fifteen such teachers and by 1794 the number had reached twenty. Simultaneously the Calvinistic Methodist Societies, under Charles's leadership, were developing Sunday schools. There can be no question that he had an unusual aptitude for this work, coupled with much affection for children. In his own home their first child, a son, was born in June 1785, to be followed by a daughter two years later who was only to live for twelve months in this world: 'How free was the grace which saved her and took her to glory! It came to her unthought of, unsought for, and undesired.'[1] In the instruction of children supreme attention was given to the memorisation of Scripture and Charles found that, with the right help, children of only five years old were capable of memorizing many chapters of the Bible.

Remarkable effects sometimes followed this practice. Edward Morgan speaks, for instance, of one area where it seemed as though no spiritual impression could be made upon the low moral standards of a particular neighbourhood. Sexual promiscuity, associated with dancing and drunkenness, was widespread. Wakes arranged to watch over a corpse before burial often became occasions for this kind of behaviour and an 'annual wake' had long assumed the character of a revel. One year, about two months before the annual wake, Charles sent word to the teachers of Sunday Schools in this district:

> Requesting them to get the children to search the Bible for texts which prohibit directly or indirectly such evil practices as dancing, drunkenness, fornication etc., and to commit them to memory, saying that they might expect him there at the feast to catechise the children. The young people set to work and there was a great deal of talk in the town and neighbourhood about the subject. When the time arrived, Mr Charles went there, and most of the people of the place, led by curiosity perhaps in a great measure, went to hear what the children had to say on these subjects. The meeting

[1] See below, p. 272.

began as usual with singing and prayer. Then Mr Charles began to ask some questions on the points given them to learn. 'Is dancing, my dear children, a sin?' 'Yes,' said one emphatically, 'it was owing to dancing that the head of John the Baptist was cut off.' 'Is drunkenness set forth as bad and sinful in the Scriptures?' 'Yes,' answered another, and repeated these words: 'Woe unto them that follow strong drink, that continue till night till the wine inflame them, and the harp and the viol, the tabret and the pipe are in their feasts; but they regard not the work of the Lord, neither consider the operations of his hands.' Isaiah 5:11, 12. In this way he proceeded with them concerning the other sins and the answers were given with great propriety and seriousness. The people began to hold down their heads, and appeared to be much affected. Observing this, he addressed them in the kindest manner and exhorted them by all means to leave off their sinful practices, and to learn the word of God after the example of the children, and to try to seek superior pleasures and a better world. The effect was so great that all went home and the houses of revelling were completely forsaken.

This anecdote is a reminder that the spread of the gospel in north Wales was not without much hard work and organisation but the main emphasis was always upon prayerful dependence upon God. When he was among Mayor's indifferent hearers at Shawbury in January 1784, Charles wrote to his wife:

> Help me, my dear, with your fervent prayers. I long to see past times of the outpouring of the Spirit returning again, when the voice of God by his ministers was terrible, powerful and full of majesty.

Three years later, in March 1787, after speaking about a new chapel at Dolgellau, he could report:

> In the mountainous country surrounding that little town the gospel spreads powerfully, and those who never heard the sound of the gospel till within these few years are

brought by its power under the yoke of Christ. Indeed, it is wonderful to see and pleasing to think of the amazing change effected in different parts of this hitherto dark country, by its power alone. The outpouring of the Spirit has been and still continues at times so abundant and powerful among those who made the utmost opposition to it, that we see with our eyes an evident fulfilment of the promise of the Father to the Son – 'the Lord shall send the rod of his strength out of Zion: rule thou in the midst of thine enemies' (Psa. 110:2).[1]

Four years after this, Bala itself saw a great awakening. Charles wrote to a minister in London on December 7, 1791:

Here, in our town of Bala, for some time back, we have had a very great, powerful, and glorious outpouring of the Spirit of our God on the people in general, especially young people. The state and welfare of the soul is become the general concern of the country. Scores of the wildest, and most inconsiderate of the people, have been awakened. … This glorious work began on a Sunday afternoon, in the chapel, where I preached twice that day, and cannot say that there was anything particular in the ministry of that day, more than what I had often experienced among our dear people here. But, towards the close of the evening service, the Spirit of God seemed to work in a very powerful manner on the minds of great numbers present who never appeared before to seek the Lord's face; but now, there was a general and loud crying, 'What must I do to be saved?' and, 'God be merciful to me a sinner.' And, about nine or ten o'clock at night, there was nothing to be heard from one end of the town to the other but the cries and groans of people in distress of soul. And the very same night, a spirit of deep conviction and serious concern fell upon whole congregations, in this neighbourhood, when calling upon the name of the Lord.

[1] *Thomas Charles*, vol. 1, pp. 565-66.

In the course of the following week we had nothing but prayer meetings, and general concern about eternal things swallowed up all other concerns. And the spirit of conviction spread so rapidly that there was hardly a young person in the neighbourhood but began to enquire, What will become of me? The work has continued to go on with unabated power and glory, spreading from one town to another, all around this part of the country. New conquests are gained every week and new captives brought in. A dispensation so glorious, I never beheld, nor indeed expected to see in my day. ... Whilst it stirs up the dormant enmity and rage of some, who continue the determined enemies of our Lord; yet the coming of the Lord amongst us has been with such majesty, glory, and irresistible power, that even his avowed enemies would be glad to hide themselves somewhere from the brightness of his coming. ... It is an easy and delightful work to preach the glorious gospel here in these days; for many are the fervent prayers put up by the people for the preacher; and they hear the word for eternity. Divine truths have their own infinite weight and importance in the minds of the people. Beams of divine light, together with irresistible energy, accompany every truth delivered. I bless God for these days, and would not have been without seeing what I now see in the land – No; not for the world.[1]

This year 1791 proved to be of the greatest importance in many respects. It marked the beginning of revivals which continued in several districts of north Wales over the three following years and, more occasionally, similar scenes were to be seen there repeatedly over the next forty years. The moral change was immense and permanent for several generations to come. In 1795 the Calvinistic Methodist Association at Bala (which brought together the leaders from many Societies) could record that while family worship had been virtually unknown sixty years earlier, 'now, by the grace of

[1] *Thomas Charles*, vol. 2, pp. 88-91.

heaven, there are hundreds of families worshipping God in every county.'¹ In 1811 we find Charles writing:

> The whole country is in a manner emerging from a state of great ignorance and barbarity, to civilization and piety. ... Bibles without end are called for, are read diligently, learned by heart, and searched into with unwearied diligence and care. Instead of vain amusements, dancing, card-playing, interludes, quarrelling, and barbarous and most cruel fightings; we have now prayer meetings, our congregations are crowded, and public catechizing is become pleasant, familiar and profitable.²

The year 1791 also marked the beginning of a passing of spiritual leadership to the north and to Charles. Daniel Rowland had died in 1790, to be followed by his close associate, William Williams, on January 11, 1791. In the year preceding, Williams wrote a long letter to Charles on the importance of purity of doctrine and of maintaining the creedal statements of the reformed churches. Another long letter from his hand followed, written only a few days before is death.³ He told the younger man that though he had 'travelled nearly three thousand miles every year for over fifty years' he could now only move between his fireside and his bed. More than anyone else, Williams had been the penman among the preachers of the Awakening in Wales and perhaps he correctly surmised that Charles would be his successor in this respect as in others. What was needed at this later date was a work of preservation and consolidation. Charles was prepared by God for that role. A lesser leader in his position might have supposed that, given the expanding evangelistic opportunity in the country, this was no time to think of anything else. That was not Charles's view. Only a few months after Williams' death, we find him involved in examining errors alleged in the teaching of one of the best-known

---

¹ See below, p. 343.
² *A Brief Memoir*, Morgan, p. 368.
³ See below, pp. 275-77, where extracts of Williams' letters of May 28, 1790 and of January 1, 1791 are conflated.

men among the Calvinistic Methodists, the Rev. Peter Williams, and it was at an Association meeting at Bala that the expulsion of Peter Williams from the connexion was confirmed.

Few men have held the objective contents of the faith – for which we are to contend – in better balance with experimental Christianity, than did Charles. He knew that knowledge and piety belong together and understood the danger of making emotion and excitement the primary characteristics of Christianity – a danger which is too easily forgotten in times of revival. Much though he loved itinerant preaching, from about this date he gave increasing time to putting the means of acquiring clearer biblical knowledge into the hands of the people. With this in view he published a catechism in 1789 which immediately established his theological reputation. A second edition was called for in 1791. In 1799 he originated an influential quarterly magazine, *Trysorfa Ysprydol* (*The Spiritual Treasury*)[1] and early in the 1800s he began work on what became his magnum opus, *Y Geiriadur Ysgrythyrol* (*Scriptural Dictionary*) which occupied him over many years. In January 1809 he could at last write to a friend: 'I have finished the *Geiriadur*. It really had well nigh finished me.' Edward Morgan believed that, next to the Bible, the *Scriptural Dictionary* was 'by far the best book in the Welsh language.' Besides his own literary work, Charles superintended the reprinting of older books. In 1803 he established a printing press – 'the Lord's Press' – at Bala and became responsible for supervision and proofreading. In the next eleven years the Bala press issued 55 editions of elementary school books.

All these and other efforts, however, were subsidiary to an overriding consideration – the giving of the Bible itself to the people. As already noted, the primary purpose of the circulating schools was to enable people to read the Bible. But the very success of these schools only underlined a more basic problem, namely, where were cheap copies of the Scriptures in Welsh to be obtained? Charles

---

[1] See below, p. 237.

Biographical Introduction

was concerned with that question as early as 1787.[1] Through the 1790s his chief hope of a supply lay in the 'Society for Promoting Christian Knowledge' in London. In 1792 Charles urged the Society to print 10,000 copies of the Welsh Bible, and promised to pay for 5,000 copies as soon as they were printed. The board of the SPCK was so hesitant and desultory that the asked-for edition of 10,000 did not appear until 1799. This supply had scarcely reached Wales before it was sold out. In the opinion of one observer, 'Not one fourth part of the country was supplied.' Back in 1787, writing of the Bible, Charles had supposed he could put '1,000 or 2,000 to very good use.' Twelve years later such had been the success of the gospel that 10,000 copies were not enough for a quarter of the country! The meaning of the statistics was perhaps best embodied in the story of sixteen-year-old Mary Jones who, after careful saving, walked barefoot the thirty miles to Charles's home in Bala to buy a Bible in the year 1800. She succeeded, though others who followed must have found the stocks entirely gone.

Despite such demand, astonishingly, the SPCK relapsed into its former inaction and so, convinced that other steps were necessary if the need of Wales was to be met, Charles gave a lead which set in motion events that secured the formation of the British and Foreign Bible Society. The impression made by Charles's pleas for Wales, accompanied by news of what was happening there, played a major part in bringing evangelical leaders in London and elsewhere to see what a flow of cheap Bibles might do for the whole world. Thus, in 1804, one of the most important agencies of the nineteenth century was born.

When the first Welsh New Testament from the Society was published in 1806, and the whole Bible the following year, the expectations of further large sales in Wales were more than fulfilled. In the words of one report: 'The young people were to be seen consuming the whole night in reading it. Labourers carried it with them to the fields, that they might enjoy it during the intervals of their labour and lose no opportunity of becoming

[1] See below, pp. 270-71.

acquainted with its sacred truths.' One testimony to the truth of this quotation comes from the one-time notorious English atheist, William Hone. Travelling in Wales, Hone was surprised to see a girl at a cottage door reading a Bible. 'Oh! the Bible!' he said to her as he stopped. 'Yes,' answered the girl, 'It is the Bible.' 'I suppose you are performing your task?' the Englishman enquired. 'Task?' responded the girl, 'What do you mean "task"?' 'I suppose your mother has set you so much to read,' Hone said confidently. 'Surely you would not otherwise read the Bible?' 'Not at all,' was the answer, 'I only wish I could read it all day long.'

Where there is true love of Christ and Scripture there will always be a wide catholicity of interest and concern. Charles was never preoccupied with his own work. He had valuable correspondence with Christians in Scotland and America; he visited Ireland and was often in London. He longed for the Bible to go to 'all the inhabitants of our globe'.[1] It was in that same spirit that the generally poor Christians of north Wales were among the most generous supporters of the Bible Society. Commenting on that point, Charles wrote: 'There are none of our poor people willing to live and die without contributing their mites towards forwarding so glorious a design. Their zeal and eagerness in the good cause surpass everything I have ever before witnessed. On several occasions we have been obliged to check their liberality, and take half of what they offered, being what we thought they ought to give. Great joy prevails universally at the thought that poor heathens are likely soon to be in possession of the Bible; and you never hear prayer put up without petition for the Bible Society and the heathen nations.'

Considering the extent of Charles's labours and travels, one is inclined to think that he was a man of unusually strong physique. That was not the case as his letters show. In 1800 his health was particularly low and a thumb had to be amputated on account of frostbite which he had suffered on an urgent winter journey in the mountains of Snowdonia. It was long remembered in Bala how,

---

[1] See below, p. 232.

when his illness looked most serious, an old man named Richard Owen thrilled a prayer meeting with the earnestness of his petition, 'Fifteen, Lord; wilt Thou not give him to us for fifteen years? For my brethren's sake, this prayer is made, and for my neighbours too.'

Charles lived to within six weeks of the time asked for in 1800. He died on October 5, 1814, in his fifty-ninth year, and his beloved Sarah (of whom he said, 'I bless the Lord that I have had a praying wife') followed him just nineteen days later. Edward Morgan concludes his *Brief Memoir* with comments on what he saw as the four outstanding characteristics of his subject. They were his love and benevolence; his spirituality of mind; his great popularity despite the fact that he did not have 'popular talents' as a preacher; and his humility. The year before his death Charles wrote:

> I feel ashamed when I think how little I have done, compared with what I ought to have done – with what was wanted to be done. 'O God, be merciful to me a sinner,' is the language of my heart daily.[1]

Today Charles's statue stands silent outside the large Calvinistic Methodist Chapel in Bala and his old home is rarely noticed by the passing tourists. Perhaps no man was the means of bringing more blessing to his native land and yet no volumes by him or upon his life have been available for a long time.[2] Too often, if he has been thought about at all, his life and writings have been adjudged to have little significance for modern times. The records of revival are considered as examples of primitive emotionalism and the impact of the Bible is explained in terms of a simple, uneducated people. But if, on the contrary, we believe that Christ is risen and that in history he has been pleased to show his power and presence through the preaching of the gospel, then this period of history both raises serious questions and gives us great encouragement. To

---

[1] See below, p. 293.
[2] A new biography of Charles has been published by the Trust: John Aaron, *Thomas Charles of Bala* (Edinburgh: Banner of Truth Trust, 2021).

know 'the Holy Ghost sent down from heaven' is not the prerogative of any one century. Our contemporary poverty is the poverty of ignorance and unbelief. We have lost truth and in so doing we have lost experience. The writings of Thomas Charles reveal nothing original but they can renew in us clearer convictions about the extent of man's fall and rebellion against God, and the amazing plan of redemption. This alone is the message which has changed and can change the world.

Charles was no party man and it was only slowly and reluctantly that the connexion to which he belonged became a separate denomination. But he believed the truths commonly designated 'Calvinistic' to be bound up with the very life and existence of the church. The supreme reason why there is any salvation at all is that there might be a people 'to the praise of the glory of his grace' (Eph. 1:6). He did not preach 'Calvinism,' but he and his associates preached the gospel in a way that unashamedly upheld those truths that humble man and display the sovereignty of divine grace. Far from thinking that such preaching inhibits evangelism, he believed it was the very means in the hands of God for conviction of sin and that wherever such conviction is found the truths called 'Calvinistic' are instantly relevant to man's condition: 'Everything in the councils of heaven favours a returning sinner – election, particular redemption, vocation, justification, etc. – all, all are in his favour.'[1] These same truths, joyfully believed, were at the heart of his daily living. In one of his early letters, he writes:

> I find it daily indispensably necessary to have a clear apprehension of the eternity, unchangeableness, freeness and independency of God's love, to enable me to walk forward with any degree of confidence and comfort. God's love depends upon nothing outside of himself, but upon his sovereign will and pleasure only. Christ did not die for us to cause God to love, but God's love alone was the cause of Christ's propitiation. ... I want nothing but to know

[1] See below, p. 290.

Biographical Introduction

more experimentally the power of this love, more effectually influencing my heart and life.[1]

When Charles drew near his end, like William Williams before him, he urged the maintenance of these truths upon the rising generation of ministers. A fine example of that will be found on pages 291-92 of the present volume. Not surprisingly, when a few generations after him had passed away, Charles's writings were set aside along with all the older authors who had once been household names in Wales.

This volume is not re-issued with the conviction that it provides all the best that can be gained from Charles. It contains only a comparatively brief collection of material in the format in which it was first published by his first biographer, Edward Morgan (1783–1869). Morgan's biography of Charles was printed in 1828 and this followed in 1836.[2] The first four articles were prepared by Charles himself for the press. The pages which follow, pp. 62-160 were extracted by Morgan from Charles's diary and they appear to belong exclusively to the earlier period of his life. As will be seen, the majority of the volume is taken up with letters. These suffer somewhat from defects for which Morgan is responsible. In the first place, in the fashion of the time, references to persons and places are frequently deleted. Where we have been able to ascertain the names of his correspondents these have been added. More seriously, Morgan has abridged the letters so that nearly all personal matters and details of that kind have been omitted. Our loss here is probably greatest in the letters to Sarah Jones, who became Mrs Charles. As an editor Morgan could never have brought himself to include such words as 'reams of paper could not tell you how much I love you.' D. E. Jenkins says that Charles had a 'supramundane

---

[1] *Thomas Charles*, vol. 1, p. 264.

[2] Writing to Morgan on April 8, 1835, John Elias said: 'As for printing a volume of Mr Charles's Letters, that also would be most acceptable. Whatever proceeds from him is excellent.' *John Elias: Life, Letters and Essays* (Edinburgh: Banner of Truth Trust, 1973), p. 329.

notion of what an autobiography ought to be,'[1] and he certainly thought that Morgan erred still more in that direction in his work as Charles's biographer and editor. Fuller copies of Charles's letters can be found in Jenkins' *Life of Thomas Charles*, and had Jenkins not fallen into a fault of a very different kind (and magnitude!) in the near 2,000 pages which make up those volumes, his work might have made the best starting point for the rediscovery of Charles today. Instead the Jenkins' biography, though loaded with magnificent detail, operates with the weight of a tombstone. Further, though Morgan has the faults already mentioned, he has one supreme factor in his favour in his handling of Charles and his materials: he was in thorough sympathy with the whole outlook and doctrinal commitment of the Welsh leader. This present volume is proof of that fact and for the spiritual inspiration it provides it would be hard to think of a volume that is easily ahead of these pages in spiritual value. 'Supramundane' it may be but it speaks to our souls and it speaks for eternity.

In 1788 the Rev. Thomas Jones (of Creaton) wrote to Charles:

> O! highly favoured country! I believe that you have more of the spirit and simplicity of the primitive Christians, among the rocks of Wales, than there is anywhere else at this day throughout the whole world.[2]

The statement was probably too strong but we rise from the reading of these pages at least understanding why it could be made.

IAIN H. MURRAY
July 1993, Edinburgh

---

[1] *Thomas Charles*, vol. 1. p. 85.
[2] *Thomas Charles*, vol. 1, p. 597.

PREFACE

The Memoirs of the late Mr Charles having been extensively approved by the religious public, it has been thought advisable to publish this volume: and it is given to the world under the fullest conviction of its being highly calculated to *do good*. Its materials are quite equal, and some even superior, in value to those in the 'Memoirs of his Life and Labours.' They contain the same evangelical doctrines, partake of the same heavenly spirit, and are calculated to impart the same godly instruction and spiritual consolation. Doing good seems to have been the main object of all that he wrote, and that promoted by exhibiting divine things according to Scripture, in a manner plain, yet interesting, and in a style remarkably simple and easy, and at the same time, dignified and forcible. There is sometimes no small degree of vigour displayed, a grasp of mind by no means common. The ideas, if not original, are at times truly grand and even sublime. The thoughts are occasionally, not only striking, but of a very superior order, especially when the subject is any of the perfections of God, or of the glorious offices of the Redeemer.

But what he seems to excel in, is on the subject of Christian experience; and on this he does greatly excel. His writings contain materials on this point that are truly valuable, calculated in a high degree to be useful. The tried, the doubting, and the tempted, will find in this volume what may by God's blessing be of great service to them. The self-deceived, the formal, and the self-righteous, may also learn here what may be of vital consequence for them to know. And there is no true Christian in any stage of his progress, who may not meet with some things in this volume, which may materially assist him in his holy warfare and arduous contest.

If there be a peculiarity in this good man's writings, it is this – he speaks as one *really acquainted* with what he has in hand, and *deeply impressed* with its importance. Many write good things and great things in a manner very striking and in a style most elegant, but betray no real acquaintance with what they speak of, nor any deep interest in what they so beautifully express. Their painting is not that of a man who had really viewed the scene. The whole, though correct, is as it were but copied; and though expressed forcibly, finely, and elegantly it is yet but the work of mind and imagination, and not the actual description of what has been seen and felt. But as we read the contents of this volume, the matter seems quite different. The writer appears to know and feel what he says. He speaks as one who has really seen what he describes, and has as it were touched and handled what he sets forth. It is the testimony of an eyewitness, and of one who has himself tried the experiment, and comes and tells us the result. When he speaks of God, he does so like one who has *seen* him who is invisible. When he describes the deceitfullness of the heart and the evil of sin, he does so as one who had known both by sad experience, and had found how injurious they are and what misery they bring. When again he delineates the glory and sufficiency of the Saviour, and the value of his word, he does so as one who had seen his glory, experienced his sufficiency, and found how precious he is. We cannot peruse his writings without observing that this is their character in a degree more than common, and constitutes a peculiar excellence.

The *four* first Essays were written as such by the author himself. Those which follow have been extracted from his *Diary*; and their dates have been appended to them. He seems to have made his diary the repository not so much of passing thoughts on subjects which occurred to him, as of such thoughts as had for some time engaged his attention. The subjects must have been maturely considered and written upon with much care; and they were afterward copied probably into his diary. The way in which it is written, it having scarcely any corrections or inter-lining, cannot well be accounted for in any other way.

Preface

The LETTERS that are to be found here are on a great variety of subjects, and were written on various occasions. Some are short, and some are of considerable length. The two first to his brother are peculiarly valuable – very clear, express, and satisfactory on two points, which people often find it difficult both in theory and practice to reconcile – the entirely free and full salvation of Christ – and the duty of incessant labour for the attaining of spiritual things. But without attempting further to describe the character of particular letters, it may be added, that they all contain some useful and interesting remarks, and prove the writer to be not only a wise and prudent counsellor, but also a sympathizing and affectionate friend, and above all, a holy man of God, mainly and intensely anxious for the honour of his name, the success of his gospel, and the present, and more especially the future and eternal good of mankind.

There are added some PAPERS which are in a considerable degree interesting. The first is a *part of a preface* to an edition of the Rev. Mr Oliver's Hymn book, intended for the Chapel at Chester, to which Mr Charles was left a Trustee. It is valuable as it contains counsels and doctrines to which it would be well for all Christians to attend. Then follow some *addresses* to Sunday Schools, in which are to be found many very useful remarks, and wise admonitions. The last papers are some *minutes* of discussions held at quarterly meetings, or as they are called 'Associations,' of the Welsh Calvinistic Methodists. They were drawn up by Mr Charles, and published in the magazine which he edited. There is a considerable number of them published, and many unpublished. Those given here are but a portion of those that are published; and they have been given not only for their own excellence, but also as a specimen of the important subjects discussed at those meetings, and of the excellent spirit which did, and probably still does, prevail in them. The observant reader, in perusing especially the minutes II and III, cannot fail to notice how *efficient* is the system adopted by this connection. The whole machinery is such, that whatever is proposed and approved at the Association is easily conveyed to every church or congregation within its limits. It is introduced from the Association into the *Monthly* Meetings by the preachers, and by the elders, deputed by those meetings to the Association. Then from the monthly, it is carried to the weekly meetings of each individual congregation by its own elders who attend the monthly meetings. All this is mostly done by word of mouth, and perhaps more effectually than by writing. A deep impression is produced in the higher assembly, is reproduced in the middle, and also in the lower. At the Association, the preachers, elders, and many of the people, sit in conclave, and discuss doctrinal, practical, and experimental subjects in a plain, familiar and conversational manner. The moral and spiritual state of the whole connection is the main object of their deliberations; and the spirit which animates the higher court, descends to every branch or church connected with it. Could anything of this kind be introduced into our National Church? The *Addresses* and *Minutes* have been translated from the originals in the *Trysorfa*, a magazine edited by Mr Charles.

May the perusal of this volume be attended by the blessing of *him*, who often deigns to make his word, conveyed through the writings and instrumentality of man, subservient to the promotion of his great and gracious designs, and who has frequently blessed the 'speaking' of his faithful servants, after they have gone to their rest, for the awakening of sinners and the edification of his people. *The Memoirs* of this good man, according to credible evidence, has been already owned to the conversion of some, and as it is generally admitted by those acquainted with them, to the spiritual instruction and comfort of many. May the following pages be made to answer the same great purposes, to the glory of God and the extension of the Redeemer's kingdom.

ESSAYS

I

Spiritual Pride

Ye shall be as gods, knowing good and evil. Gen. 3:5.

THE temptation by which Satan ruined our first parents, he too successfully applies daily to us, their wretched posterity. 'God doth know,' said he, 'that in the day ye eat thereof, then your eyes shall be opened; and ye shall be as gods, knowing good and evil.' It seems as if this were verified in the event; for 'the Lord God said, "Behold, man is become as one of us, to know good and evil."' Before the fall man knew nothing, as to good, but the will of his Creator; and it was enough for him implicitly to follow that. But since that direful event, he is become independent of God, and chooses for himself; 'He is become like one of us,' saith God, 'to know good and evil.' Instead of being a child, provided for by his Father, under his care and protection, he is become his own master, and his own physician, choosing good and rejecting evil, according to his own inclination. Thus he set up, as it were, for himself; a spirit of independency had taken possession of his soul.

This is the spirit which constitutes essentially the character of Satan himself. 'Whence comest thou?' said the Lord to him. His answer was, 'From going to and fro in the earth, and from walking up and down in it'; boldly intimating, that he acknowledged no superior, and was his own master, going where he would, and doing what he pleased, yea, even boasting as if the earth was his own, and that here none could control him, or at least had a right to do so. We, as his children, faithfully bearing his image, and exactly copying his example, are under the influence of the same independent spirit. And were the Lord to put the same question to us, our answer, if according to truth, must be similar – we go to and fro, live to ourselves, and do what we please, as independently of God as if there were no such Being. Thus we are like Satan. We are practical atheists, seeking for sufficiency and comfort in ourselves, and not in God – in the creature, and not in the Creator. No temper or frame of mind can be more opposite to God than this, or further from true godliness.

Whilst this self-sufficiency influences the heart, there is an utter impossibility of any reconciliation between us and God. 'God resisteth the proud.' And hence our Saviour saith, 'Except ye be converted, and become as little children, ye shall not enter into the kingdom of heaven.' We must be 'converted,' and become what man was at his creation, 'as little children,' that is, dependent on God, submissive to his will, seeking all our happiness in him only, being contented, that he should forever be the source of all our happiness, and that he should communicate it in the time, way, and degree he pleases. When thus converted, we, as the creatures of God, become humble in spirit, and, as sinners, we become contrite in heart. And in this frame we are to walk with God, and he will dwell in us: 'for thus saith the high and lofty One that inhabiteth eternity, whose name is Holy; I dwell in the high and holy place, with him also that is of a contrite and humble spirit, to revive the spirit of the humble, and to revive the heart of the contrite ones.' Here the religion of Christ begins; and our progress in the divine life is always safely estimated by our progress in humility. Humility is the strength and ornament of all other graces; it is the food that nourisheth them; the soil in which they grow.[1]

Though the whole scheme of gospel salvation in every view of it, and all the different providential dispensations of God towards

---

[1] 'Do you come to your joy and peace by humility and self-denial and mortification, and by becoming little children and servants of all? If not, take heed lest you nourish a changeling, an imp of hell, a selfish brat, instead of that fruit of the Spirit, the peace and joy of the Holy Ghost' (RICHARD BAXTER).

us, are directly calculated to hide pride from man; yet so deeply rooted is this spirit of independence and self-sufficiency in our hearts, that nothing but the effectual operations of the Holy Spirit can bring us to possess the humility of creatures, and the contrition of sinners. As creatures, we would possess all-sufficiency for happiness in ourselves; and, as sinners, we would be even our own Saviours, sufficient to rescue ourselves from sin and guilt, from destruction and misery. This seems to be intimated by the words, 'Behold man is become as one of us, to know good and evil' – as one of *us*, in the plural number, as if the whole Trinity, in themselves essentially considered, and also in their various relations to us, as Creator, Redeemer, and Sanctifier, were rejected, and man sought for sufficiency, relief, and happiness in himself only. And this seems farther intimated in the latter part of the verse – 'And now, lest he put forth his hand, and take also of the tree of life, and eat and live forever;[1] therefore the Lord God sent him forth from the garden of Eden to till the ground from whence he was taken.' These words plainly set forth a total rejection of God and his will, and a strange and a wilful propensity to seek a remedy for his misery, the consequence of his disobedience, in a way of his own finding out. He would still live, though he had sinned; and he thought he had sagacity sufficient to provide effectual means to prevent the execution of the threatening. But how vain were his contrivances, and how miserably was he disappointed! Cherubim, and a flaming sword, which turned every way, were placed at the east of the garden of Eden, to keep the way of the tree of life. Nothing, therefore, but renouncing his own wisdom and strength, and submitting wholly to God, and embracing the way he is pleased to provide, can save him from the threatened ruin. He turned himself from God to seek his comfort and his happiness in the creature: but behold, the whole earth, and all things in it, are cursed for

---

[1] This sentence seems incomplete, there appears to be a word or an expression wanting after 'now,' such as, 'let care he taken,' or 'let us take heed.' Junius and Tremellius supply the word, *videndum*. The verse would then be complete, and would run thus: 'And now let us take heed, lest he put forth,' etc. (Ed.)

man's sake: and its productions were to be thorns and thistles. To prevent death, man would eat of the tree of life: but behold, the cherubim and a flaming sword stop his way. What then can he do, but miserably perish, except his wilful and independent spirit be broken down, his pride humbled, and he be brought to lie at the foot of divine mercy?

Here is the difficulty: man has, as it were, set up for himself, and his whole nature as corrupted is wholly bent on seeking happiness for and in himself, separate from God – he knows not how to deny his own will, or discard his own wisdom and his own strength, or oppose his worldly lusts, which wholly lead him from God – besides, the way which God has provided for his happiness and salvation in Christ, is so extremely humiliating, that nothing but a total renunciation of himself in every view can ever enable him to embrace it. But how can the pride and independent spirit of man stoop to this? Here is the main controversy between man and God. Man would still be as God, knowing good and evil; and God cannot but unchangeably determine to bring down this idol, that he may be all in all. And if God saves man at all, it is inconsistent with his very nature, and opposite to all his holy perfections, to save him, but in a way, which effectually hides pride from man. He must cast down πᾶν ὕψωμα, every high thing that exalteth itself against the knowledge of God, and bring πᾶν νόκμα, every thought to the obedience of Christ; so that he that glorieth shall glory only in the Lord. We see this independent spirit working in various and opposite ways, but all leading further from God, and *directly calculated to set up this idol, man.*

I. We see the *great body of mankind with their faces universally set towards the world,* and their vigour exerted in one general race after the things *of the world.*

And what is this strong principle, which universally prevails, and actuates the whole mass? Everyone seems as if he would have the whole world to himself: and were the whole in his possession, it would be too little to satisfy his eager desires. To what purpose is this bustle and striving? Why are all these contentions and jarrings?

Spiritual Pride

Is it not, because man would have something to depend on, and to support himself by independently of God? He would be *as God*, able to supply himself with the means of comfort and happiness. He will not depend on God; but he would prove for himself good and evil.

That this is the principle, which so vigorously operates within, must appear abundantly evident to us, if we for a moment consider why it is that we desire so earnestly to have our comforts and safety in our own hands. Is it not, because we think them not so sure, or so satisfactorily placed as we wish they should be, in the hands of God? What would the carnally-minded give, could he but have his life and health at his own disposal, to keep and enjoy them at his own pleasure? When he is sick or poor, how far preferable does it appear to him, to be able to be his own physician, or to supply his own wants, than to receive both from the Almighty. But why does he think so? Is it not, because he likes not to depend on God? Is it not, because he would be independent of him? And as worldly things are the means, which bid fairest to help him in his ungodly pursuits, he thinks that he never can have enough. But, alas! all is insufficient. He is still disappointed; and therefore he is full of impatience, murmurings, and complaints. The support that he seeks, independently of God, is still wanting: and pride being disappointed, impatience corrodes his vitals, of which murmurings and complaints are the natural expressions and effects. We would be as gods, possessing all fullness and sufficiency in ourselves: and when we cannot be what we would – not so rich, not so great, not such gods as we wish and attempt to be, pride bursts forth in impatience, discontent, rage, and misery.

But when God brings us to himself, he effectually teaches us to deny this ungodliness, and our worldly lusts, crucifies us to the world, and brings us to forsake all that we have, in which we put confidence, and from which we seek any happiness. What he will take away, he will again restore suddenly and unexpectedly, and thereby convince us that we have all every moment from him. He will embitter every blessing, and make us know and feel the misery of departing from him; and convince us, that there is no happiness to be found but in himself only. And when he giveth us all things richly to enjoy, he will teach us at the same time to use all, not for ourselves, but for him – 'for whom, through whom, and to whom are all things.' In short, he will be our God, and will act in everything as such towards us, and will bring us to live upon him, and to him; and not upon the creature, and to ourselves. And when we become possessed of the humble frame and temper of dependent creatures, murmurings and complaints, impatience and disquietude, will all be banished: and we shall receive all good and evil, with holy submission and humble thankfullness, being abundantly satisfied, that the Lord is our God.

II. The same spirit that exerts itself in opposition to God's providential dispensations as to our state and circumstances in this world is found *quarrelling also with God's gracious dealings* with our souls, especially in young converts.

Sensibly feeling the heavy load of guilt on their consciences, they become impatient in their distress, and cannot bear the yoke which the Lord hath put upon them: but as Rachel said, 'give me children, or I die,' so they cry, 'give us peace, or we perish.' They being in a degree unhumbled, a secret but a stubborn rising of self-righteous pride will manifest itself in various ways – such as secret anger at heart, because they are thus and thus – a sullenness, like a person disappointed, because they cannot be as they would – a desperate wilfulness in complaining and in refusing comfort – and an aptness to fly in the face of God, and say, 'why has he thus dealt, or why does he thus deal with us?' And with these peevish and violent workings of pride, the devil joins at the same time with all his force, setting forth everything in the most discouraging light, and insinuating that there is little or no prospect of things being better. In the mean time, unbelief is also raging; deliverance seems hardly possible; all the means of it seem insufficient; so many things stand in the way; such corruptions within, such difficulties without, and such guilt remaining. The soul is ready to sink under the burden, being almost determined to give up all for lost.

In such inward workings of our minds, there is more of pride, and of an unhumbled spirit, dissatisfied with the sovereign pleasure of God respecting our condition, than we are apt to imagine. Being in such a spirit, do we not seek, and as it were, demand peace and comfort, as if they were our right, rather than the free and undeserved gifts of God? If not, why are we fretful and uneasy under delays? Why do we presumptuously expostulate, 'Why is he so long in coming?' If we narrowly examine our deceitful hearts, I doubt not, but that we shall find unhumbled pride at the bottom of all this impatience.

In proportion as this spirit prevails, is our utter unfitness to receive any gospel-blessing or comfort from the Lord. He never bestows his blessings, until he has previously brought us into a suitable frame to receive them. 'God giveth grace to the humble' – to those whom he hath previously emptied of their pride and self-sufficiency. When effectually humbled, they are easily satisfied with his dealings with them. Then every mercy bestowed appears, as truly it is, great and undeserved: and the language of the soul is, 'I am less than the least of all thy mercies.' We would be as gods; but the Lord will make us know, if we are truly his, that he is the Being to whom in everything absolute sovereignty belongs; that he cannot be limited, nor have his time prescribed to him, but will have us to exercise absolute submission and acquiescence in all his dealings and dispensations towards us. 'O Lord,' said David, 'thou art my God; my times are in thine hands'; his time of trouble and of peace, of darkness and of light, he acknowledged, with acquiescence and thankfullness, to be in the hand and at the disposal of God, and that it was his place humbly to wait the Lord's time and season for the enjoyment of his comforts and for the light of his countenance. Nothing indeed can succeed well with us, till we are brought to this frame of mind, till we are satisfied, that the Lord should carve for us both in temporal and spiritual things, till we are willing to bear his chastisements and thankfully to receive his comforts – when, and howsoever he is pleased to send either the one or the other. But when we are made willing, that the Lord should in everything be God to us, we cannot but succeed in the end; and though we may have to wait for the vision, yet it will assuredly come, and will not tarry, and will fully answer our largest expectations. 'Sorrow may endure for a night; but joy cometh in the morning.' 'Ye have heard of the patience of Job, and have seen the end of the Lord, that the Lord is very pitiful, and of tender mercy.'

Hence we see, how this spirit of pride and independency operates, with respect to spiritual as well as earthly things, and that it can feed on one as well as on the other. It is indeed changed in its form, and pursues its end in a different course; but it is the old man still, setting up for himself, though he wear the appearance of the new man in Christ. It is still Satan, though he be transformed into an angel of light.

III. Often when this spirit ceases to seek worldly riches, it tries to be supported, if possible, by *religious wealth*: and the man, if he cannot be a God to himself, will at least be his own Saviour.

The young man in the gospel who went away from Christ very sorrowful because he was very rich, and the Pharisee in the parable, were influenced by the same spirit, equally opposite to and distant from God. The one was rich in temporal things, and the other, as he thought, in spiritual things; each being a God to himself, possessing in himself all fullness and sufficiency. 'I thank thee, I am not as other men,' are the words of the Pharisee's lips; and 'I am rich and increased with goods, and have need of nothing' is the language of his heart. Well might the Lord say, 'Behold man is become as one of us': for who but God has such a fullness and sufficiency in himself, as to have need of nothing. But here, in religion, this spirit is of all things the most detestably odious in the sight of God. There is no creature in the universe so abominable to him, who 'raiseth up the poor from the dust, and lifteth up the needy from the dunghill,' as he is, who tries to support his own pride and independency by a mask of religion and a form of godliness.

But alas! this is the spring and life, if it has any: the sum and substance of the religion of many showy professors. Influenced by this principle, they will go about, for many years, seeking, with no small labour and pain, to establish their own righteousness, unwilling through the pride of their hearts to submit to the righteousness of God provided by Christ Jesus. 'They have not submitted,' saith the apostle, 'to the righteousness of God.' They were religious, yea, eminently zealous in religion; but they had not, and they would not, submit to the humbling scheme of the gospel. Such are, through the pride of their hearts, unwilling to be convinced, that they are altogether unprofitable, and wholly destitute of all strength to do any part of God's will, this being so totally and so directly opposite to the principle of independency within. But if they fancy that they can be saved by establishing a righteousness of their own, and live independently of God, without being beholden to his mercy – this persuasion sets at once all the springs of the soul in motion; and this flattering but vain hope drives them about in an endless round of religious performances, to establish their own righteousness. To submit to a righteousness purely without them, on the mere testimony of God, they know not how; a proud heart is unwilling, and savours it not. But to establish their own righteousness is a way of being saved, which appears highly rational, requires no great degree of self-denial, and is consistent with the utmost vanity of their hearts: they may thus still be *as gods*, knowing; and possessing good in and for themselves. And thus, while in the midst of the utmost poverty and misery, they would fancy themselves rich and increased with goods, and live, as to any dependence of heart upon God for spiritual blessings, 'without God in the world.'

IV. Even in those who have submitted to the righteousness of God, and put on Christ in sincerity, this spirit of pride and independency will still exert itself.

It will strive in various ways to keep them from simply relying, as altogether guilty, on him, who is made of God unto us righteousness: and it is not without the greatest difficulty that they are brought, in the face of sin and guilt, to rejoice wholly in the Lord their righteousness. When led to see their own righteousness as filthy rags, and driven from placing any confidence in the flesh – in their own doings – they are still anxious to possess something in themselves, on which to depend and build their hopes of acceptance with God; they will be tempted to look to the *work of the Spirit* in the heart, and make it the foundation, which can never be anything but the superstructure.

Christ, in his obedience and death, is the only sure foundation for sinners, as to pardon and acceptance with God. 'Other foundation can no man lay, than that which is laid, which is Christ Jesus.' The holiest saint stands in equal need of it, with the most profligate sinner; and to eternity it must be the alone stay and support of the spirits of just men made perfect. The *building* on this foundation is holiness and obedience. But if care be not taken, the natural pride of man will place the superstructure in the room of the foundation, or at least will attempt to put partly as the foundation some of those materials which are fit only for the construction of the building. 'Thus known holiness is apt to degenerate into self-righteousness; and what God gives for sanctification we are in danger of applying for justification.'[1] We are such Pharisees by nature, that we know not how to feel grace, and at the same time, believe, as if we had none – to rest simply on Christ's righteousness, without the addition of anything in us, either of outward performances or of inward grace; but we are still found mixing something of our own with the foundation; if we lay and fix it, it must be with some cement of our own graces, duties or endeavours. But the attempt is utterly fruitless. These things are wholly distinct in themselves, and must be distinctly managed by the soul in its dealings with God. The confounding of them by pride will only dishonour the grace of God, disturb our peace, and weaken our strength for obedience, as well as keep us from that humble posture which at all times becometh us as sinners. This principle of self-righteousness must be mortified, before we can walk humbly with God, and before we can be brought from everything without or within us, to rest simply for favour and acceptance with God, on him in whom the Father

---

[1] Dr Owen.

is well pleased. Not only is the foundation laid in mere grace, but the top-stone will be brought forth with shouting, 'Grace, grace!' The Lord alone must and shall be exalted; and we shall be brought to count *all* things but loss and dung for the excellence of the knowledge of Christ. Not only shall nothing be exalted for our justification before God *besides* him; but nothing shall be exalted *with* him; for 'the Lord *alone* shall be exalted in that day.'

To correct this self-righteous spirit, the Lord often plunges his own people into the ditch, and causes their own clothes to abhor them, when, it may be, they have washed themselves in snow-water, and thought their hands clean. He takes off the restraint from some one or another of their corruptions, suffers the world and the devil, with their temptations to assail them, till feeling still more their sinfullness and misery, they abhor themselves and repent in dust and ashes, and are more frequent and earnest in their applications to his blood which cleanseth from all sin, and are brought to exalt 'the Lord alone' in their hearts, and to rejoice in 'the Lord their righteousness.'

V. Are we not become as gods to ourselves, when in our *own strength* we address ourselves to our work, face difficulties, and encounter temptations?

Is it not natural to us thus to act independently of the Almighty? Do we not, even the best of us, find ourselves every day, almost in everything, acting as if we had an all-sufficiency of might and power in ourselves, and as if our own arms were to bring us salvation? And in this case may not the Lord well say, 'Behold man is become as one of us?' We are in a manner become insensible, that 'in *him* we live, move, and have our being,' but act as if we had everything in ourselves. In *him* only we can live comfortably and usefully. Whatever we do in life that is great and is profitable to ourselves or others, we have all our strength and abilities for it, in every view, from him. If we resist the devil, overcome the world, subdue the flesh, or live to God, we *live* in every sense *in him*. In him also we *move*; all the motions of the soul and body are from him entirely every moment. Not one motion of any single part of the body can we for an instant command without his permission – without his aid. Nor can there be in our minds, in the least degree, any spiritual motions of our thoughts, or any holy workings of our affections towards God, but what proceed every moment, in every degree, from him. In him we live, move, and have our being, both temporally and spiritually.

But in what heart dwells the practical belief of this? Are we not living, in this sense also, without God in the world? Where are they who are practically sensible, that, without continued influences and aids from above, we have, the best of us, wisdom for no work, strength for no duty, success under no trial, and victory over no enemy? Are we not found making weak attempts for duties, fruitless struggles against temptations, till almost overcome; before we are made truly sensible of our own weakness, and apply to the Lord for strength? What wonder is it, if in this case we hear people complaining, that they cannot do this work, or overcome that temptation. If they could, would they not set up the idol man, and 'sacrifice to their own net?' God is determined in everything to bring man out of himself. So far therefore as we depend on ourselves, so far we are sure to be disappointed.

It is our pride and self-sufficiency, and not our weakness, which gives any inward or outward enemy the victory over us. In proportion as we are truly humble, God giveth effectual grace to help us in every time of need. If denying ourselves, our own schemes, contrivances, and our own strength, we steadfastly look to him for deliverance under trials, difficulties and temptations, we shall infallibly obtain effectual relief, and experience his grace alone to be sufficient for us. But if, on the contrary, we forsake the Lord, and confidently rely on ourselves, what wonder is it, if, falling like Peter, when in a similar frame of mind, we be woefully taught how weak we are. 'I am ready,' said Peter, 'to follow thee, not only to prison, but to death; and though all should forsake thee, yet will not I.'[1] This was talking at a very high rate indeed; and it was a

---

[1] 'This presumptuous spirit is an infallible sign of pride. When Peter was truly humble, he could say, 'Is it I?' But he who feared, when he was humble, lest he

Spiritual Pride

language very unsuitable in the mouth of one who had been told, a little time before, that without Christ he 'could do nothing.' He was ready, it seems, and had everything necessary in himself, to endure trials, enter dungeons, and face death in its most terrible forms. Yes, he had more strength than all the rest – 'Though all should forsake thee, yet will not I.' Surely he had forgotten what and who he was. Peter doubtless had, on many former occasions, stood up boldly in the face of Christ's enemies, and preached the gospel in his name with success wherever his Master had sent him. What! *he* fall, who had stood so long and done so much! *he* deny Christ, who had so often owned and confessed him before man – before enemies! But he forgot the hand that supported him, and the grace that strengthened him, otherwise he would have said, as on a former occasion, 'Lord, save, or I perish.' Pride blinded his eyes, so that he saw not the invisible hand that had hitherto kept him from falling. Secretly puffed up, he thought that there was no doubt of his acquitting himself well. But in proportion to his dependence on himself, was his dreadful fall: for in this case, as he would seek none, so he could receive no help from above to keep him from falling.

Whoever, like Peter, thinketh he standeth, let him, above all others, take heed lest he fall. The everlasting arms being in this case neglected, and he confiding in a bruised reed, a fall is the sure consequence. 'Cursed be the man that trusteth in man' – in himself or in any other creature – 'and maketh flesh his arm; and whose heart departeth from the Lord.' The issue and event of things will assuredly prove him to be cursed, and awfully convince him, that in departing from the Lord, he forsaketh his own safety, exposeth himself to every evil, and becomes a prey to every enemy. God is determined in everything to bring man out of himself. As he is

---

should be the traitor, could not think so bad of himself when under the influence of pride, that he should ever deny his Master. What! 'I?' No; though all should forsake him, he should not. ... Spiritual pride and self-confidence will show itself by the neglect of those means, through the use of which the graces and comforts of the saints are continued to them.' (WILLIAM GURNALL)

not to live *to* himself, neither is he to live *upon* himself; but to live to and upon God, that the comfort may be ours, and the glory entirely the Lord's.

VI. Are we not become as gods, when we take and *keep to ourselves the praise and glory* due to God only?

Everything that is good, done in us or by us, every good thought, desire, word, or work, proceeds immediately from God; and to him all the glory is due. But are our hearts freely disposed to render to God the things that are God's? Or are we not secretly prone to value and commend ourselves, as if we had done something? 'They sacrifice to their own net,' saith the Prophet, 'and burn incense to their drag.' Instead of seeing the hand of God in them, they ascribe their successes, victories, and prosperity to their own schemes and contrivances – to their own diligence and power. But see the contrary spirit of unfeigned humility, conspicuously shining in the whole of St Paul's conduct. Whatever good was found in him, or done by him, he ascribes the glory and praise of all to God, 'the giver of every good and perfect gift.' He styles himself 'less than the least of all saints' and 'the chief of sinners,' no doubt feeling inwardly at the same time what he expressed. Though his whole life was one continued exertion in the Lord's service, though he laboured more abundantly than all the rest of the Apostles, yet the genuine language of his heart at all times was, 'By the grace of God I am what I am' – 'not I, but the grace of God which was with me.' Here we see him where he ought to be, as a creature and as a sinner – he is nothing, and God is all in all, and must have all the glory.

To make use of the Apostle's expressions is easy, but it is not so easy to feel what he felt, and to lie down in the same dust and ashes in which he lay. Often a great show of humility in speech and behaviour covers the rankest and most diabolical pride:[1] but the veil is so thin, that its motions are easily seen by those who have

---

[1] 'You little think, what humble carriage, what exclaiming against pride, what mournful self-accusing, may stand with this devilish sin of pride.' (RICHARD BAXTER)

their senses exercised to discern between good and evil. But how many deceive themselves in this matter, being unable or unwilling to distinguish between the shadow and the substance! Many think themselves most humble, when at the same time they are wholly devoid of the humble air and deportment of those who are guided and led to a behaviour becoming humility, by the vigour of a lowly spirit within; but are filled, it may be, with the glory of their own humility, and exalted to heaven with the high opinion of their self-abasement. Their humility is swelling, self-conceited, confident and assuming, without one spark of gratitude to God, or any disposition to give him the glory.

The deceitfullness of the heart and the subtlety of Satan, in no one thing appears so great, as in the workings of this sin: nor have we in anything more cause for continual watchfullness. Nothing is so subtle, so secret, so insinuating.[1] It often surprises us at an unexpected hour, and is in actual possession of us, before we are aware of his approach. It will take occasion to arise from everything; it will feed on the ashes of other sins, and gain strength by the exercise of real grace and of true humility. And though nothing so effectually tends to mortify pride and bring us to our proper place, as creatures and as sinners, as a great degree of the Divine presence, and much communion with God, yet great temptations to pride do also hence arise. Though the experience of such favours effectually mortifies pride in one way, yet it affords an occasion to it in another. We are in danger of worshipping ourselves as saints, when we have denied ourselves as sinners: so apt are we to forget ourselves, and overlook our unworthiness, through the enjoyment of distinguishing blessings!

The circumstances and situation of the angels who fell, most directly tended to suppress pride in every shape; yet, though they

---

[1] 'Pride is the most dangerous of all sins; for it is both more insinuating, having crept into heaven and paradise, and more dangerous where it is. For where all other temptations are about evil, this alone is conversant only about good things: and one dram of it poisons all measures of grace. I will not be more afraid of doing good things amiss, than of being proud, when I have well performed them.' (BISHOP HALL)

had no principle of pride in them, their high honours and privileges wholly overset and eternally ruined them by this temptation. The Apostle Paul also, though, as we have seen, so eminent for humility, was not without great danger from this spiritual enemy. After his admission into the third heaven, where doubtless he had such glorious discoveries of the Divine majesty, as tended most effectually to make and keep him humble, yet even then he needed a 'thorn in the flesh, lest through the abundance of revelations he should be exalted above measure.'

Reflecting upon, and talking about, former experiences, without the grace of those experiences in exercise, is what pride would be continually engaged in, and is often the beginning of our ruin, and the first step towards our downfall. In this case God himself is out of sight; and the effects of his presence and power are only contemplated: and thus we are effectually turned from the Creator to the creature, and are as great idolaters, as if we worshipped stocks and stones. It is no greater idolatry to worship the devil, than it is to worship an angel; nay, to be as gods to ourselves, when renewed by grace, is more abominable and detestably odious in the sight of God, than it was in our natural state of blindness and alienation from him; because our motives to humility must be clearer, more powerful and more numerous, and because we are returning to the place whence we were taken, in opposition to all the light, knowledge, undeserved goodness and mercy, which have been bestowed upon us.

To talk much about ourselves, of our own experiences and discoveries, though under pretence of giving glory to God, is a sure proof that we are as gods to ourselves, and that we would have others filled with admiration of the distinguishing favours we enjoy, and have them know what eminent saints we are. This was the very spirit of the Pharisee in the parable. In *words* he gave glory to God, for making him to differ, 'God, I thank thee, that I am not as other men.' He was not as other men; he was distinguished with divine favours, and was far more eminent in holiness and piety than all others. It is true, he acknowledges that God made him to differ; but then his mind dwells on the difference itself, till he is swollen bigger than all mankind put together. To ascribe all in *words* to the mere grace of God in Christ, in no degree prevents our thinking highly of our attainments and holiness; nor is it any proof that we are emptied of the pride and vanity of our natural minds.

Were we under the continual influence of an humble spirit, our attainments in religion would not be so apt to glitter in our own eyes; nor would we be so forward in admiring and talking about our own comeliness and beauty: but we should be more apt to consider ourselves as little children in grace, and our attainments to be those of babes in Christ; we should be daily ashamed of, and sorely lament, our great blindness and ignorance of God, our astonishing ingratitude, and the coldness of our love to him. Until we are brought to this state of true humility, taking shame to ourselves, and giving glory to God in and for everything, we cannot possibly enjoy communion with God, and growth in grace cannot possibly take place. Real humility takes nothing to itself, but sin and shame; and it gives all the glory to God, who is the Giver of every good and perfect gift.

From what has been said, it appears that the spirit of pride and independence is eminently the work of the devil within our souls. It enters into the very essence of every other corruption, and is the life and soul of every other sin; and, till this is brought down and mortified, no work of God can be going on within, nor can any grace grow and thrive.[1] In every single thought, desire, or action, that is not agreeable to God's mind and will, we are setting ourselves in opposition to and above God, as being gods to ourselves.

To destroy this spirit, is eminently the work of Christ, who came to destroy the works of the devil. Till this spirit be pulled down, the strong man armed is in his stronghold; and we are in open rebellion against heaven. The destruction of this is the life and strength of submission and obedience to God, of dependence on him, and resignation to his will: and without its being destroyed,

---

[1] 'Humility feedeth, and pride starveth, every grace.' (RICHARD BAXTER)

there can be neither obedience to the Law, nor submission to the gospel; God can have no place in our hearts, nor will his ways meet with our approbation. To bring us to live on God, and to him, as his creatures, and to make us willing to be saved by him as sinners, are things that are indispensable: and we are no further living to God or saved, than we are thus truly humbled.

Accordingly every dispensation of God towards us, both of providence and grace, hath an immediate and direct tendency to bring man, in every view, out of himself, and to lay him in the dust. When we are froward and wilful, determined to have our own wills and our own ways, God has a thousand ways to make us know ourselves, and to convince us that he is God. He will cause troubles, crosses, and disappointments, to meet us everywhere and in everything. If one light cross will not teach us to deny ourselves, he will double it in number and quantity, and will continue to chastise us, till we submit and acknowledge that he is God. And if the dispensations of providence have not this beneficial influence over us, that is, to bring us out of ourselves to God, they are worse than unprofitable and useless, they are a curse and not a blessing. God's gracious dealings with us, by his Spirit, have also the same effectual tendency and influence, to bring us down, to convert us, and to make us as little children. 'The weapons of our warfare,' saith the apostle, 'are not carnal, but mighty through God to the pulling down of strongholds, casting down imaginations and every high thought that exalteth itself against the knowledge of God, and bringing into captivity every thought to the obedience of Christ.'

God by his providential dealings, brings us as creatures to live on his fullness and all-sufficiency as our Creator; and by the influence of his Spirit, by the way of grace, he brings us as sinners to accept of and live on the Saviour and the salvation he hath provided. There is not one single blessing of the gospel that can be received, but by a humble spirit: nor can we be partakers of the consolations of Christ, but in proportion as this spirit prevails. That we may receive strong consolation, and that Christ may be to us all in all, 'every high' thing must be cast down, and every thought must be brought into captivity to the obedience of Christ. And when the gospel is made to us the power of God unto salvation, herein does its power most eminently show itself, to the everlasting glory of the Saviour, and to our own growth in true holiness, peace, and joy.

2

Humility

Who maketh thee to differ from another? 1 Cor. 4:7.

In all the works of God, order, beauty, and proportion, are evidently to be seen; and every particular part contributes to the beauty of the whole. This is remarkable in the human frame, as well as in every object which we behold. The different parts are beautifully ordered, connected, and proportioned. The new man in Christ is no less perfect and beautiful. A Christian is not a monster in form: but all his component parts have their being and growth together; they are beautifully connected and proportioned. Like the different members of the same body, all the graces of the spirit are connected with the head – that is, Christ – receive their supplies from him; grow together; and gain strength in an equal degree. It is true, one grace may be called forth into exercise more than another, and thereby gain more strength; yet all the other graces are influenced by it, and grow in some proportion to it. No one grace grows alone.

For instance, the grace of knowledge (not the *gift*), cannot but influence our faith and love, our humility and repentance, our patience and meekness, etc. If it be the grace and fruit of the Spirit, all the other graces will be influenced by it, and bear some proportion in their growth. In like manner, all those graces which more immediately act towards God in Christ will be accompanied with those corresponding graces which influence our conduct towards mankind. As our love to God is, so is our love to man. If we are humble before God, we are humble also in our outward conduct towards our fellow-creatures. If we are thoroughly sensible, that we have nothing but what we daily receive, our conduct towards those from whom God by superior gifts hath distinguished us, will be suitable to this sense of our poverty. It is in vain to pretend that we are duly humbled before God, and that we are sensible of our poverty, if our conduct towards man is proud and assuming.

This is the subject to be now particularly handled, that is, that true humility and a genuine sense of our poverty before God, will effectually influence our conduct towards all our fellow-creatures – and that the one, as it is the effect of the other, so it proves its truth and reality.

If we truly believe that we do receive everything good from God, we cannot glory, as if we did not receive it. In proportion as we believe this, we cannot glory in ourselves, in any respect, but in God only, the giver of every good and perfect gift. Have we grace? We have received it. Do we believe this? Then we cannot glory against those who have it not: but our conduct towards them will be full of modesty and humility, of pity and compassion. Are we eminently distinguished by gifts useful and ornamental? Are those gifts and our labours abundantly blessed? All these are from God: but do we believe this? If so, we shall not despise those who have them not; but we shall with all humility and industry employ them for the glory of God, and for the good of others. If we believe that we have received everything from God, we shall not find it possible to take anything to ourselves but shame; for there is nothing that we can call our own but sin. As to our understanding, all that is in it which is ours is its darkness; and in our hearts, all that belongs to us is their ungodliness and deceit; and if our hands and tongues have done any good, God has so employed them. All the light that is in our minds, whether it be the gift or the grace of knowledge, is from the Father of lights; and all that is good in our hearts, cometh down from above. There is nothing which is our own, but sin and shame: and if we glory in ourselves, we must glory in our shame.

That we may better know ourselves, and know the spirit we are of, I shall endeavour to throw some light on the subject, by *contrasting* the different workings of pride and humility, as they show themselves in divine things. These two principles influence the *mind* to think differently, the *tongue* to speak differently, and the *whole man* to act differently. They are exactly opposite to each other in all their workings.

I. They *think differently*.

Pride is apt to think ill of others; but humility leads a man to think ill of himself. While pride is observing the defects of others, their coldness and deadness, their ignorance and weakness, and is ready to condemn them without mercy; humility has work enough at home; is most jealous of itself, and most suspicious of the deceit of the heart which it occupies. The man who has it knoweth that in him dwelleth no good thing. He sees sin so prevalent, and has so much to do to watch against all its motions, that he cannot at the same time attend much to others. *His* complaints are against himself; and with sincere grief he laments his own coldness and deadness, his great unfruitfullness and slow progress in the divine life. He is ready to think others better than himself, and is willing to hope, that there is no one so barren and so devoid of love and gratitude as himself. Humility makes a man to see the good of others, and the evil that is in himself; and whilst he aggravates his own sins and his own deficiencies, he sets forth what is good in others to the best advantage.

If duty calls the truly humble man to mark and reprove sin in any of his brethren, he does it with humility, and restores him that is taken in a fault, in the spirit of meekness. With what humility and gentleness did our Saviour reprove his disciples, when they showed such coldness towards him in his hour of distress? 'What! Could ye not watch with me one hour? The spirit is willing, but the flesh is weak' – making an apology for them at the same time that he reproved them. In proportion as the mind which was in Christ is in us, our conduct will be the same. But the heart is best known by the fruits it produces, let us therefore:

II. Attend to the *different language* of pride and humility.

The language of pride is severe; but that of humility is compassionate. The one is bitter; the other is mild and gentle. The one is contemptuous; the other is loving. Pride speaks of the sins of others

– the enmity of some, the formality of others, and the delusions of the third; and speaks of them with bitterness and contempt, and it may be, with ridicule: but humility speaks, if it must speak at all, with compassion and godly sorrow, and with fervent prayer for them – well knowing, that if there be any difference between him and the vilest sinner on earth, it was grace that made it. The truly humble, in all he says and does, puts on 'the bowels of mercies, kindness, humbleness of mind, meekness, longsuffering.' As humility prevails, bitterness and wrath, anger and evil-speaking, with all malice, will be rooted out; and the opposite graces of love, kindness and pity to all mankind, will govern the mind and guide the tongue.

In speaking of the enmity, opposition, and persecution of the world, spiritual pride is apt to enlarge a little, to speak often and dwell much on the subject in a revengeful and contemptuous spirit, 'reviling again.' But true humility is the spirit of Christ, 'who, when he was reviled, reviled not again; when he suffered, threatened not, but committed himself to him who judgeth righteously.' He conquered enmity with love, pride with humility, persecution with prayer, and all contemptuous treatment with: 'Father, forgive them, for they know not what they do.' It was the meekness of the lamb, and not the rage of the lion, that triumphed over all the rage and malice of men and devils. The Apostles of the Lamb fought also with the same weapons. 'Being reviled we bless'; saith Paul, 'being defamed, we intreat; being persecuted, we suffer it.' Intent on their Master's business, they passed by unnoticed the injurious treatment they met with. By meekness and patient continuance in well-doing, their enemies were disarmed and vanquished; and the honour and interest of the gospel were greatly promoted. Indeed nothing so highly adorns the gospel, and so effectually brings down God from heaven in behalf of his people, as this spirit of meekness and patience under sufferings. 'God will cause judgement to be heard from heaven; the earth shall fear and be still: and God will arise to judgement, to save all the *meek* of the earth.' When Aaron and Miriam, stirred up by envy, opposed Moses the servant of God; it is particularly observed of him at the time, that 'he was meek above all men on the face of the earth'; doubtless because he then gave an eminent proof of his meekness; and God as eminently appeared in his vindication.

Christian fortitude does not consist in vehement passions and bitter invectives; but in steadily maintaining calmness, meekness, and benevolence of mind, in the midst of all the rage and tumult of the world: and it most eminently distinguishes itself in opposing and suppressing our spiritual and most dangerous enemies within, when occasions offer themselves from without, to stir up their natural fury, and give them some hopes of success. Many a self-confident professor, under the influence of pride, may, without any fear, expose himself to the enmity of the world: for by thus losing the favour of the world, he knows that he will be more powerfully recommended to those of his own party and persuasion. But Christian fortitude, guided by humility, operates universally against all difficulties – against the smiles of friends as well as against the frowns of enemies. A single eye to God guides him in all, regardless of consequences on the one hand and on the other. The contempt of friends is far more difficult to be borne, than the hatred of the bitterest enemies. And the duty which calls us to this trial of being neglected by our friends, of being despised and disregarded by our party, is a more convincing proof of our faithfullness to Christ, than our forwardness in exposing ourselves to the reproach of opposers.

When I have heard some talking of the persecutions they had met with, and the difficulties they had to pass through, with malignity of spirit and with contemptuous triumph, I have been often much grieved, and thought that such language ill suited the humble servants of a humble Master, and savoured too much of Jehu's spirit, when he said to Jehonadab, 'Come with me, and see my zeal for the Lord.' A true Christian zeal is the most humble, mild, and benevolent temper, that can influence the hearts of men or angels. It is the fervour of Divine love; and 'love is kind; vaunteth not itself; is not puffed up; is not easily provoked, but beareth all things.' Bitterness and wrath against any persons, even against avowed enemies, are as different from Christian zeal, as darkness is from light. Love and humility enter into the very essence of it; and the more anyone is influenced by it, the more loving, mild, and benevolent he is both towards the evil and the good. Its force is directed, not against persons but things, not against sinners, but against sin dwelling in them. It opposes sin principally in the heart where it exists, and, in the next place, sin universally, wherever it is found. The primitive Christians contended earnestly for the faith – but how? Not by the shedding of the blood of others, but by shedding their own blood. Those who bear all things with the greatest meekness and patience, contend most successfully for the faith, and make the noblest stand in time of persecution. Revenge is sweet and gratifying to the old man, and is the natural and immediate offspring of unmortified pride. But not to resist evil, not to avenge ourselves, but rather to give place to wrath, and to commit ourselves cheerfully to God, the sovereign ruler of all things – this is what nothing but grace can teach us; and is always the inseparable effect of true humility, according to the degree in which it prevails in the heart.

The truly humble, always suspicious of himself, improves even by the reproaches of his enemies. He seriously examines whether there is too much foundation for such accusations – whether in a careless and slothful frame of mind, he hath not been too remiss in watching against sin in all its motions. In everything, he who is poor in spirit and contrite in heart, trembling at God's word, seeks and finds ample cause for self-abasement, shame, and godly sorrow, well knowing, that he has all evil in himself to suspect and to be ashamed of, and that he has nothing good but what he daily receives. How can he then glory, as if he had not received it? But the spiritually proud learns wisdom by nothing. The reproofs of friends and the reproaches of enemies have no good effect upon him. He swells; grows more assuming and confident: and instead of suspecting himself of having done wrong, he is ever apt to run into greater lengths in those very things for which he is blamed. Being without a real conviction of the evil within him, he never suspects himself; and not practically believing that whatever good he possesses he has received, he glories, as if he had not received it.

III. In the whole of the *outward conduct* there is an evident difference between spiritual pride and true gospel humility.

This shall be instanced only in one particular. Pride shows itself by a certain irreverent, self-confident boldness in approaching God, and also in the outward demeanour towards man. Humility, on the contrary, shows godly fear and reverence towards the Almighty, and due deference and respect towards man. Though we 'have access with boldness to the throne of grace through the blood of sprinkling,' yet this free access ought to be, and always is, accompanied, in the truly humble, with holy reverence and godly fear. The ineffable glory of the Divine Majesty fills saints and angels in heaven with self-annihilation, profound awe and reverence. Though fully satisfied of his favour towards them, and of their love to him, yet the glory and majesty of his infinite and inconceivable perfections eternally fill them with such humility, adoration, and reverence, as bear some proportion to their infinite distance from him. If these be the dispositions, and if this be the conduct of the holy inhabitants of heaven, it is evident, that those, who are vessels of mercy in the Lord's hands, preparing for the same place, must have something of the same spirit in them. Though 'perfect love casteth out fear' – the fear of coming to God as a reconciled Father in Christ, and of walking in communion with him as such – yet this love rather augments than destroys the holy fear of God's divine majesty. Not only the submission of a creature, but also the becoming humility of a pardoned sinner, even in heaven, will bear proportion to all other graces in glorified saints. There will be in this respect an eternal difference between saints and angels. Saints in heaven never forget that they were once sinners, though the remembrance of this be entirely free from pain or fear; yea rather accompanied with deep humility, which sweetly enlivens all their praise and joy. But while on earth, our fear of God cannot be such as if we were already perfect, and fully delivered from all the effects of sin: but it is such an apprehension of God's

Humility

glorious majesty, as constrains us to be highly jealous of his glory, and humbly fearful of every indication of his displeasure, as in times past we have offended him – and lest in future we should offend him. It therefore becomes the holiest man on earth, 'to serve the Lord with fear, and to rejoice before him with trembling.'

By frequent free access to God in Christ, this holy reverence is in danger of wearing off and spiritual pride will creep in secretly, unless our hearts be, as it were, in our hands, and our eyes be continually upon them, watching all their motions. This may be, and is often the case with the true Christian himself; but this never fails to be the case with those who have the scheme of the gospel in their heads, unaccompanied with corresponding impressions on their hearts. This wicked generation,[1] having hearts unbroken, and spirits unhumbled, in general neither fear God nor honour man: to whom the caution of Solomon would at no time be unsuitable, 'Be not rash with thy mouth, and let not thy heart be hasty, to utter anything before God; for God is in heaven, and thou upon earth.' If they saw the vast distance between God and them, the very thought of irreverence would make them tremble with horror and confusion. When we are taught to pray to God as our Father, we are at the same time taught to address him as our Father who is *'in heaven'* – high above all, commanding reverence and humility, fear and obedience from the whole universe.

With this irreverence before God, is always connected a bold and an assuming carriage towards man. Such men in every respect

---

[1] 'There is in some a most unsuitable and unsufferable boldness in their addresses to the great Jehovah, in an affectation of holy boldness, and ostentation of eminent nearness and familiarity; the very thoughts of which would make them shrink into nothing with horror and confusion, if they saw the distance that is between God and them. They are like the Pharisee, that boldly came up near the temple, in confidence of his own eminence in holiness. Whereas if they saw their vileness, they would be more like the publican, who stood afar off, and durst not so much as lift up his eyes to heaven, but smote on his breast, saying, "God be merciful to me a sinner." It becomes such sinful creatures as we are, to approach a holy God, though with faith and without terror, yet with contrition, penitent shame, and confusion of face.' (JONATHAN EDWARDS)

'glory as if they had not received.' A spirit, truly humbled before God, will infallibly show itself in a conduct towards man that is humble and unassuming: and when it does not so, it is only pretended. If therefore our pretensions to humility before God be unaccompanied with a suitable behaviour towards one another, they are wholly vain. If we are still stubborn inferiors, haughty superiors, and self-willed equals, it is evident that our proud hearts have never been truly humbled, and that all our religion is of no value. True humility is known by its fruits. A servant of Christ, however highly distinguished by gifts and graces, thinks very humbly of himself, and deeply feels what he expresses, when he says, 'I am nothing.' And when a man truly says this, he will naturally esteem others better than himself, and consequently will not despise a weak brother. He is one who 'vaunteth not himself, doth not behave himself unseemly, but is apt to prefer others in honour.'

See how humble Abraham honoured the children of Heth, whom he yet knew to be far from God and accursed. 'Abraham stood up, and bowed to the people of the land.' See how humble Jacob, in a heavenly frame of mind, honoured profane Esau, a false and persecuting brother. 'Jacob bowed himself to the ground seven times, until he came near to his brother.' He called him Lord, and commanded his whole family to honour him in the same manner. 'Lord,' said David, 'my heart is not haughty, nor mine eyes lofty; neither do I exercise myself in matters too high for me.' Is not true humility still the same? Is not an high look, and a proud heart, as great a sin now as in former days? Did Christ humble himself to make us proud? Or are we not rather to learn of him, who was meek and lowly?

But see spiritual pride in its effects. Haughty and assuming, it little regards any honour, or deference, due to superiors in rank, fortune, natural gifts, or spiritual attainments. That amiable fear and modesty in inferiors towards superiors, is wholly laid aside. The Scripture rule is, 'that others should behold our chaste conversation, coupled with fear.' And there sobriety, sober and humble thoughts of ourselves, and shamefacedness, are particularly

Humility

recommended. In everything, and towards all, our deportment ought to be that of the humble disciples of a humble master. But the young in years, and younger in grace, influenced by spiritual pride, will be forward and busy; opening wide the mouth in every matter, without fear; and often giving ready decisions on points on which those who have three times their age, knowledge, and humility, perhaps very justly and modestly entertain doubts. Always forward and assuming, they speak with decisive authority, treat the sober judgement of others with contempt, and expect that their determinations should be implicitly received and acquiesced in. While the truly humble looks to everyone for assistance, the spiritually proud, instead of showing the humble deportment of a disciple who wants instruction, is swift to speak, and slow to hear, as if everybody wanted his teaching. Whatever deference is paid to him, he looks upon all as his undoubted right: and those who acknowledge not his merits, he treats as weak and ignorant fools. I cannot forbear inserting here an excellent passage on the matter in hand from the pious Baxter.

> Art thou a man of worth in thine own eyes, and very tender of thy esteem with others? Art thou one that much valuest the applause of the people, feelest thy heart tickled with delight when thou hearest of thy great esteem among them, and much dejected when thou hearest men slight thee? Dost thou love those best who most highly honour thee, and doth thy heart bear a grudge at those that thou thinkest to undervalue thee, and entertain mean thoughts of thee, though they be otherwise men of godliness and honesty? Art thou one that needs have thy humours fulfilled, and thy judgement must be a rule to the judgement of others, and thy word a law to all about thee? Art thou ready to quarrel with every man that lets fall a word in derogation from thy honour? Are thy passions kindled, if thy word or will be crossed? Art thou ready to judge humility to be sordid meanness or bareness, knowest not how to submit, and wilt not be brought to shame thyself by humble confession, when thou hast sinned against God, or injured thy brother? Art thou one that honourest the godly that are rich,

[29]

and thinkest thyself somebody, if they value and own thee, but lookest strangely at the godly poor, and art almost ashamed to be their companion? Art thou one that canst not serve God in a low, as well as in a high place, and thinkest thyself fittest for offices and honours, and lovest God's service when it stands with preferment? Hast thou thine eye and thy speech much on thy own deservings, and are thy boastings restrained more by wit than by humility? Dost thou delight in opportunities of setting forth thy parts, and lovest to have thy name made public to the world, and wouldest fain leave some monument of thy worth, that posterity may admire thee, when thou art dead and gone? Hast thou witty circumlocutions to commend thyself, while thou seemest to debase thyself, and deny thy worth? Dost thou desire to have all men's eyes upon thee, saying, 'This is he.' Is the end of thy studies and learning, of thy labours and duties, of seeking degrees, titles, and places, that thou mayest be taken for somebody abroad in the world? Art thou unacquainted with the deceitfullness and wickedness of thy heart, or knowest thyself to be vile only by reading and by hearsay, and not by experience and feeling of thy vileness? Art thou readier to defend thyself, and maintain thy own innocence, than to accuse thyself, and confess thy fault? Canst thou hardly bear a close reproof, and dost digest plain dealings with difficulty and distaste? Art thou readier in thy discourse to teach than to learn; to dictate to others than to hearken to their instructions? Art thou bold and confident of thine own opinions, and little suspicious of the weakness of thy understanding, and a slighter of the judgement of all that are against thee? Is thy spirit more disposed to command and govern, than to obey and be ruled by others? Art thou ready to censure the doctrines of teachers, the actions of thy rulers, and the persons of thy brethren, and to think, that if thou wert a judge, thou wouldest be more just, or if thou wert a minister, thou wouldest be more faithful in doctrine, and more faithful in overseeing, or if thou hadst had the management of other men's business, thou wouldest have carried it more wisely and honestly? If these symptoms be undeniably in thy heart, beyond doubt thou art a proud person; pride hath seized on thy heart, which is the principal fort. There is too much of hell abiding in thee, for thee to have any acquaintance with heaven: thy soul is too much like the devil, for thee to have any familiarity with God.[1]

I shall now conclude, with a *caution* to those whose situation lays them open more particularly to Satan's temptation, and the workings of corruption in this way: I mean, those who by their gifts and usefullness have the pre-eminence in the church of God.

It is not easy to have the pre-eminence, and at the same time not to be like Diotrephes, who *loved* to have it among his brethren. It is right and proper that they should have the pre-eminence, whose qualifications entitle them to it; but for them to *love* to have it, is sinful and abominable in the sight of a jealous God. However justly they may be exalted and highly esteemed, yet what they should *love*, is to be the servants of all, because they are better qualified to minister, than those who have not their gifts. Whatever qualifications, by gifts and endowments, God bestows on any, they are all those of servants; that is, they ought, as servants, to serve with him. But how difficult it is for those who carry within a proud and devilish nature to keep their place in this respect? The old man will be ever showing himself off with the ornaments of the Holy Spirit; he would willingly borrow plumes from heaven to gratify his pride. 'Dathan and Abiram were *famous* in the congregation,' they were men of eminence for their gifts and usefullness; but they loved to have the pre-eminence, strove against Moses and Aaron, yea, saith the word, 'strove against the Lord.' They gloried, as if they had not received; and their pride hurled them down into hell.

What shall we say of Moses himself? That eminent servant of God, meek above all men on the face of the earth, fell by this very sin at the waters of strife, and was excluded on account of it, from the promised land. He had zeal for God; but his own passions were mingled with his zeal, and he spoke unadvisedly with his lips. 'Hear now ye rebels,' said he. It is true, they were rebels; but his

---

[1] *The Saints' Everlasting Rest*, Chapter 12, sect. 1, 5.

words breathe strongly of bitterness and impatience. He assumed also to himself too much: 'Must *we* fetch water out of this rock?' *We!* What! Is the Lord laid aside? Is *he* not wanted? Was it *you*, or the Lord, that divided the sea, and opened the rock on a former occasion? It seems at least to me, that his eye was not so directly to the Lord, as in his former difficulties. He considered their rebellion before, as principally against the Lord; but here self seems to creep in, both in his reproof, and in performing the miracle. Let the punishment of Moses make us tremble, lest we fall into a similar provoking sin. Moses, so holy, so humble, so meek, fell by it. 'Let him therefore that thinketh he standeth, take heed lest he fall.' Should we not tremble, when we hear that God punished his faithful servant Moses, with whom he spoke face to face, and to whom he had in a peculiar manner revealed his glory? His temptations to this sin were in various ways strong; his provocation at the time was by no means small; and yet *all* did not excuse him. God is above all things jealous of his glory.

When all opposition and every other temptation fail, the devil is in this often successful against the servants of God. Satan never bid fairer for victory over Barnabas and Paul, than when, after their very successful preaching of the gospel, and confirming it by signs and wonders, he stirred up the people at Lystra to worship them as gods. It was perhaps the boldest attack that Satan ever made on the apostles. The temptation had everything in its favour. There was all the food to nourish pride which it could desire. Paul had but just before cured, by one word, a lame impotent man, and had for some time past been eminently successful in converting many, both Jews and Gentiles. Satan also might easily transform himself into an angel of light, and persuade them, that this good opinion, which the people entertained of them, if promoted, might be exceedingly useful in gaining converts to their doctrine. But the Lord signally kept them in the hour of temptation, and made them more than conquerors over this enemy. 'We are men of like passions with yourselves.' Thus is the triumph proclaimed.

To conclude: He who judgeth rightly of himself, measures every day his religion by his humility, and measures his humility by the degree of influence it has on the mind, in enduing it with those mild, benevolent, and heavenly tempers, which suit a miserable sinner, who lives by the patience and mercy of God, and in adorning the whole outward man with that amiable, humble, and courteous deportment, which becomes one, who can glory in no good thing, as if he had not received it. May the Lord make and keep us humble.

3

The Operations of the Holy Spirit

The salvation of fallen man is wholly, from beginning to end, the work of God. The Father, Son, and Spirit have jointly engaged in covenant and by promises, to accomplish this stupendous work. In this gracious engagement there could have been no other motive but divine love, ascribed peculiarly to the Father, though not to the exclusion of the Son and Spirit. The love of each person is the love of the divine nature common to each; it must therefore be the same in each. The Father 'so loved the world, that he gave his only-begotten Son.' The Son loved us, and gave himself for us. And the apostle beseeches the Romans, that 'for the love of the Spirit, they would strive together with him.' This free love engaged them in their respective undertakings: the Father to elect, the Son to redeem, and the Spirit to sanctify the redeemed. But this love is particularly ascribed to the Father, because as he is in all things the first mover, so also in redemption. The salvation of man, and all the blessings it includes, proceed *from* the love of the Father, *through* the grace of the Son, and *by* the operations of the Spirit. The Spirit graciously reveals and applies the love of the Father, and the grace of the Son, which otherwise would never have profited us, any more than light can profit a blind man, or food a dead man: we have no eyes to see the one, nor appetite to feed on the other.

The Spirit is promised as the gift of the Father and of the Son: he therefore voluntarily cometh in the name and by the authority of both. The same love which influenced the Son, when he 'took upon him the form of a servant, and became obedient even unto death,' influences the Spirit in his condescension and undertaking as a Comforter and Sanctifier. He is infinitely free in all his operations. 'Our unworthiness has no more influence on him in what he does, than it had on Christ's coming to redeem the world. Christ died for the ungodly: and the Holy Spirit comes to, abides with, and sanctifies the ungodly. He comes into the heart, when it is nothing but filth, a hellish scene of all abominations and iniquities, a horrid darkness, a miserable confusion, like the world in its chaotic state. He so loves his people committed to him, that he abides and dwells with them forever, acting with authority and power, according to his own pleasure, as their various circumstances may require. He prepares and strengthens them for every event, reveals to them what they must needs know, in the time and way most fit, inclines their hearts in the way and degree he pleases, and controls all their inward enemies.

As Christ is head over all things to the church in the outward world, ordering and directing all things, in the way most conducive to his own glory and to the real good of his people; so the Holy Spirit dwells in them, putting forth the exceeding greatness of his power in renewing, supporting, comforting, and restoring righteousness, joy, and peace. Every avenue of the soul, every one of its faculties is under his eye and over-ruling control. Every rebel within, every worldly and sensual lust, and every filthiness of the spirit, he observes, restrains, and gradually subdues. He brings these by various means out of their lurking places, strips them of their false appearances, and exposes them to view in all their guilt and deformity. The Spirit's work shall now be considered; the work of him who leads us into all truth, particularly respecting ourselves and God: of him who convinces of sin and of righteousness.

I. The Spirit *convinceth of sin.*

'When the Spirit is come,' saith our Saviour, 'he will reprove the world of sin.' Sin is already in the world, but the world sees it not. 'Every imagination of the thoughts of our hearts is only evil continually.' As every imagination and every thought is only evil, there is nothing within us, by which evil can be discovered and condemned; for it will neither discover nor condemn itself. It is light only that can discover the hidden things of darkness; but within us, in our natural state, there is no light. We are 'darkness' and we 'sit' in darkness, contented and satisfied with the state in which we are; we see not the evil of it, nor seek any deliverance out of it. There are indeed, as to most, some gleams of natural light remaining in the conscience, which may be strengthened and improved by education, instruction, and example; but at best they are but faint, and the knowledge they convey, is merely intellectual, floating in the head, vague, uncertain, and unaffecting; the heart continuing still as dark and unknown as ever. This light never did nor can discover sin to be sin – to be what it really is, 'exceeding sinful.' Both the discovery it makes of sin, and the sentence it passes on it, are unfruitful and useless: it neither truly humbles us on its account, nor causes us to flee from it. It may make us fearful and uneasy; but it will not make us repent and turn from it to the living God. But when the Spirit enters the heart, with the glass of the law, as it were, in his hand, and shows sin in this glass, then we see it to be sin; to be 'exceeding sinful'; far beyond all imagination sinful, so that the mind is overwhelmed with the vastness of its guilt.

Sin is in general within us without the law. So the apostle saith, 'I was alive without the law once'; that is, he was alive in sin and self-confidence, without any spiritual knowledge of or attention to the law, which condemns it. But the law may also be with us: in our hands and in our heads; and we yet, not knowing its extent and spirituality, continue ignorant of the true nature of sin. It is holding a glass before us in the dark, which cannot discover our wrinkles and deformities. We may fancy, because we see none, that we have none. The truth is, we have no light to see our true figure. But when we view ourselves in the glass of the law by the light of the Spirit, then we see what we are, how corrupt and deformed; we then see sin to be sin, that it is exceeding sinful. When the commandment thus comes, and sin is beheld by the light of the Spirit, then sin *revives*, appears in a far different light to our mind; and we feel it by its power working, and by the authority of the law condemning; for the strength of sin is the law. Not some gross outward sins only are discovered, but the Spirit enters the deepest recesses of the heart with the law, as it were, in his hand; he goes from chamber to chamber, searches every corner, discovers, tries and condemns secret lusts and spiritual filthiness, totally unknown and unthought of before. And as these secret lusts are discovered and condemned, the curse due to each is awfully pronounced, with divine authority, in the name of the eternal God. And as our sins are thus gradually discovered, and brought to light, as to their number, nature, and guilt, the soul sees condemnation still enlarging before it, the curses of the law sound louder and more terrible, and the scene becomes exceedingly dreadful: every sin appears far greater than was ever before thought of, and their number becomes infinitely increased. The individual would willingly turn his eyes from such wretchedness, would extinguish the light which discovers it, or would by some means take a brighter view of these dreadful objects: but all he can do is fruitless. He would forget his sins; but he cannot. He would excuse and palliate his offences, or seek some goodness to balance them; but this also is impossible. The law comes still more home; and light, clearer and brighter, shines upon the mind, discovering and condemning every evil thought, every sinful imagination. He may and will resist these convictions; 'for the flesh lusteth against the Spirit,' but it will be 'hard to kick against the pricks,' when the Spirit worketh effectually, making known the exceeding greatness of his power in enlightening the understanding to see the exceeding sinfullness of sin.

When the Spirit thus worketh, what discoveries does he make! What infinite guilt does he show to be in every spot and stain of sin! With what horror and amazement does the awakened sinner view his own pride, seeing it as comprehending all the atheism and enmity against God, which actuate the inhabitants of hell! Envy, malice, and revenge, the natural offspring of pride, he now sees to be the very tempers and dispositions of the devil himself. He now sees and feels the force of the command: 'Thou shalt not covet,' and by it lust is made known to him in all its greatness and guilt. His careless neglect and disregard of God, in what light does he view it! To live without thoughts of God, the Spirit within us condemns as practical atheism; and to think of him at all without the profoundest reverence and the deepest humility, without supreme love and submission, appears not much better. When the Spirit shows sin to be sin, every frame of mind unsuitable to the divine majesty and purity is exceedingly felt and lamented: shame, sorrow, and indignation, the deepest self-abasement and abhorrence, weigh down the soul, and humble it to the dust. Yes, there is a sort of infinity in the abasement of the soul, when the Spirit shows sin to be sin; he would still be more humble, and sink, were it possible, still deeper; he grieves, because he cannot grieve more; he abhors himself, because he cannot be still more detestable in his own sight. He sees an infinity of evil in sin, which he cannot fully comprehend, any more than he can the holiness of the law, or the greatness of God, against whom it is committed. He would therefore that his sorrow, humility, and self-abasement, should bear some proportion to it.

This is not a frame of mind which is only once known, when the sinner is first awakened; but is in an increasing degree his frame of mind, as he grows in holiness, joy, and peace in the Holy Ghost. So far is it from being inconsistent with his comforts, it heightens his joys, sweetens his consolations, and effectually promotes holiness. Without this, all fancied joy and peace is a delusion; and all imagined holiness has no existence but in the pride and darkness of our own deceived hearts. This is the only frame of mind that can fit us to receive blessings from Christ, and to walk humbly with him, who 'filleth the hungry with good things, but sendeth the rich empty away,' who 'giveth grace to the humble, but seeth the proud afar off.' This conviction of sin is, whilst in this world, forever deeper, clearer, and more abiding, as the believer enjoys nearer communion with God, and grows in faith, love, and peace. And without the continual communion of the Spirit, thus with us, walking humbly with God is impossible.

II. The Spirit *reveals Christ* in the fullness of his merits, and the sufficiency of his grace.

'He shall glorify me,' saith Christ, 'for he shall receive of mine, and show it unto you.' 'All things that the Father hath are mine;

therefore said I, that he shall take of mine, and show it unto you.' Those things which the Father's love hath prepared, and which Christ by his condescension and death hath procured, the Spirit receiveth, taketh and showeth unto us. He first shows unto us our own things, our sins: 'he bringeth to light the hidden things of darkness, and maketh manifest the counsels of the heart.' Then he taketh the things of God and of Christ, and shows them to us in all their glory and excellence, and enables us by faith to receive them. The Scriptures are express on the point, that without the Spirit we can neither know nor receive the things of God: no more know them than we can know each others' thoughts without communicating them. 'For no man,' saith the apostle, 'knoweth the things of a man, save the spirit of a man which is in him: even so the things of God knoweth no man, but the Spirit of God.' Even when they are proposed to us, and we have an intellectual knowledge of them, they cannot be received; but they will ever be foolishness to us, till the Spirit shows them in their own glory and true light, and opens the heart to receive them. 'The natural man,' as the apostle declares, 'receiveth not the things of the Spirit of God; for they are foolishness unto him; neither can he know them, because they are spiritually discerned.' The things of the Father and of the Son are here called the things of the Spirit, because he takes of them, shows them to us, and enables us in his light spiritually to discern them.

This points out to us the way and means by which the Spirit comforts and sanctifies his people: he leads them into a clearer knowledge and into a more steadfast belief of the eternal love of the Father, and of the fullness and ability of Christ to save: the things of the Father and of the Son he taketh and showeth unto us.

The Spirit searcheth all things, yea the deep things of God. The whole mind and will of the Father he thoroughly knoweth and fully comprehendeth. And when we have received the Spirit, which is of God, then we know the things that are freely given us of God, for the Spirit revealeth them. He revealeth them as originally the things of the Father; but he taketh them as they are the things of Christ also, and shows them as coming to us in no other way but through him. He leads us to the source of all spiritual blessings, divine love; and gives also a clear view of the channel through which they are conveyed to us: the atonement and righteousness of Christ. Thus he teacheth us all things, 'as the truth is in Jesus.' He showeth pardon, reconciliation, and grace, as they are in Jesus. These are the things of Christ which he takes; and he shows and teaches them as they are in him, in all their infinite fullness and glory. By his light we see the glory of the only-begotten of the Father; are enabled to believe that Jesus is the Son of God; and he shows grace and truth – the things of Jesus as they dwell in him, in fullness great and equal to the dignity of the person in whom they dwell. Hence it is, that 'no man can say that Jesus is the Lord, but by the Holy Ghost.' None can behold his glory as the only-begotten of the Father, but in this divine light; and without a spiritual apprehension of the dignity of his person, the fullness of grace and truth dwelling in him must be forever unknown.

Thus the believer has a regular and complete view of divine things, given him as they are revealed in Scripture. There is no deficiency in any material part, no disorder, no confusion, but a beautiful connexion and regularity. He sees them in their source, in the channel through which they are conveyed, in their dependence and influence. And when the Spirit thus shows them, they are sure to have the desired effect, and carry full conviction to the mind. It is the demonstration of the Spirit and of power; it is, as if the sun shone at midnight with meridian splendour. The objects before unseen become visible as they are, in all their glory. We clearly and distinctly see what before we could only feel after in darkness. And together with this divine light, life and power are communicated to revive, comfort, and fructify the dead and barren soul. There is 'the demonstration of the Spirit and power': so that what we see clearly, we feel effectually working with the power of the divinity. When the Spirit showeth the love of the Father, and sheds it abroad in the before unbelieving and disconsolate heart, it is with such clearness and power, that all the sense of sin, guilt, and unworthiness, and the clear view of the just vengeance due to sin, shall not be able to raise a doubt within us. By the clear evidence of the Father's love and good-will, he beareth witness with our spirit, that we are the children of God, so that we are able to cry out, 'Abba, Father.' In this case, sin and Satan, pleading against us, are overpowered, and conscience and the law are silenced, being satisfied.

Similar also is the view which the Spirit gives of the person, righteousness, and grace of Christ. The person of Christ, though before 'without form or comeliness' is now altogether lovely. The believer sees him to be such a Saviour as he wants, one of infinite dignity, majesty, and power. He sees the obedience unto death of such a dignified person, forming a divine righteousness, perfect and consummate, amply sufficient to justify the most guilty, and deliver from condemnation those obnoxious to ruin. On it he rests with confidence, being fully persuaded of the Saviour's ability to keep that which is committed to him, and to save to the uttermost. The fullness of grace also, that is in him to sanctify and support the soul, in opposition to every inward corruption and outward temptation, appears to partake of the infinity of Christ himself; a source that cannot be exhausted; an ocean that knows no bounds. These things of Jesus, when thus showed, and thus seen in the light of the Spirit, effectually comfort the soul. Though the burden of sin and guilt was before intolerable; though innumerable evils had compassed him about, and his iniquities had taken such hold of him, that he was not able to look up, and his heart failed him; the things of Jesus, thus seen, bring him effectual relief, so that he is surprised and astonished at so unexpected, so suitable, and so full a deliverance. The gloom of despair and the cloud of God's wrath, disappear: and he has 'beauty for ashes, the oil of joy for mourning, and the garment of praise for the spirit of heaviness.'

Thus the Spirit is with us as our comforter and advocate, pleading within us, with divine light and energy, our cause; answering every demand of the law, and every accusation of a guilty conscience, of sin, and of Satan; he takes of the things of Jesus, and shows them to us. Until this is the case, we have nothing but our own things to produce and oppose to these bold and forcible accusations. No marvel then if they are never silenced, and we can obtain no comfort: for our own things only strengthen and confirm still more the accusations laid against us, and effectually ruin our cause. Others also may try to comfort us with the things of Jesus; but alas! they cannot *show* them to us, they cannot cause them to shine in their glory in our hearts, any more than they can cause the sun to shine at midnight. But when the Spirit showeth them and beareth witness with our spirit, the dispute is at once at an end; peace is restored, and joy in the Holy Ghost abounds. And when the things of Christ are thus by the Spirit shown to us, and he by them pleads our cause against all accusers, to secure to believers their actual interest in them, and the sure accomplishment of all the promises, he seals them to the day of redemption. They are sealed *now*: 'Whereby,' says the Apostle, 'ye *are* sealed,' Eph. 4:30. The things of Christ, the blessings of pardon, reconciliation, and grace, are made sure and certain to them in particular, the free grant of them having the seal of heaven annexed to it. And they are sealed also 'to the day of redemption'; whereby the promises and blessings included in them are irrevocably confirmed, and the accomplishment of them is made certain and infallible, till they are in the full enjoyment of the purchase made for them by Christ, when he obtained for them eternal redemption.

By the same means by which the Spirit within us comforts our souls, he also *sanctifies* them. True spiritual comfort and holiness are inseparable. Neither of them can be alone: where one is, there the other is also. They are effects of the same cause, and produced by the same means.

This work of the Spirit in teaching, comforting, and sanctifying, is aptly and beautifully set forth by the expressive simile of anointing: 'ye have an unction from the Holy One, and ye know all things' – 'the anointing which ye have received of him abideth in you, and ye need not that any man teach you: but as the same anointing teacheth you of all things, and is truth, and is no lie' 1 John 2:20, 27. It is an allusion to the Judaical anointings, by which persons and things were set apart and consecrated to any office or service which the Lord appointed. Persons were thereby appointed and consecrated to offices; when at the same time they were endowed and qualified with the gifts requisite for the discharge of those offices. In allusion to this custom true believers are said to have an unction from the Holy One, and to know all things. Things dedicated to the service of the Lord were also by holy oil consecrated for this purpose, and were ever afterwards regarded sacred and holy. This sets forth the Spirit as the sanctifier, separating God's people from the unholy mass of the world, to be a peculiar people, zealous of good works. There was also the oil of joy and gladness, to give a cheerful countenance to the sorrowful. So does the Spirit fill us with joy in believing.

As the unction therefore from the holy One, he teaches, comforts and sanctifies his people: and those things which he teaches them are the means of their comfort and of their sanctification. The things of Jesus are still the materials with which he works, to produce every holy and desirable effect within the soul: for he is made to us of God, wisdom, righteousness, and also sanctification. This will at once appear abundantly evident, if we consider the different parts of holiness enumerated by the Apostle as the fruits of the Spirit. 'The fruit of the Spirit,' he says, 'is love, joy, peace, longsuffering, gentleness, goodness, faith, meekness, temperance.' Gal. 5:22, 23. 'The fruit of the Spirit,' he says in another place, 'is in all goodness, righteousness, and truth,' Eph. 5:9. All these are the different constituent parts of holiness, the different lineaments of the image of God restored on the soul. But they are nowhere to be found but where the Spirit dwells and abides. We may as well expect fruit without a tree to bear it, as look for these graces where the Spirit is not. Without the Spirit changing the inward man and abiding within us, no waterings, no skill or application, can ever produce these fruits. There is this which materially distinguishes these graces from all other gifts of the Spirit – these sanctifying graces are fruits produced by the Spirit, as from a root dwelling and abiding within them; while the gifts of the Spirit are only the works and effects of his operations *on* men, and not fruits of his producing *in* them. The one proves that the tree is made good, and has life and vigour in it to bring forth fruits; but the other only shows that it is formed and shaped for a particular use; and may, when the end is answered, become useless and unprofitable.

But how does the Spirit within us produce these fruits? Is it not by taking of the things of the Father and Son, and showing them to us? How is love to God produced, but by his love being shed abroad in our hearts? 'We love him, because he first loved us.' The brightness of his love shining, by the Spirit, upon our dark and barren hearts, can alone produce this heavenly fruit. And without the things of Christ being shown, what peace, what joy can there be for a guilty sinner? Without the righteousness, merits, and grace of Christ being revealed, we may as well expect to hear the voice of melody in the mansions of eternal misery, as to find spiritual peace and joy in the sinner's heart. But when the love of the Father and the grace of the Son are shown to us, then, and not till then, love, joy, and peace are produced. Unsound professors, who have no root in themselves, and therefore can produce no fruit of any sort, may and do receive the word sometimes with joy; like Herod, who 'did many things and heard John gladly.' But this empty and temporary joy differs as much from true joy as blossoms do from the fruit. Like blossoms, it is unsubstantial and short-lived; the least severity of weather puts an end to its gay appearance, and having no root, it soon vanishes. But true joy is a real fruit, solid, substantial, refreshing, and nourishing. It revives, strengthens, and establishes the soul. Whatever is a fruit of the Spirit, hath a flavour and relish in it, which nothing else, however similar, can ever have. This true spiritual joy Christ calls his joy; 'that my joy,' he said to his disciples, 'might remain in you, and that your joy might be full,' John 15:11. It is *his* joy materially as the cause of it. It is a joy in believing *in* the Lord *by* the Holy Ghost. 'The meek shall increase his joy in the Lord.'

So also, if there be longsuffering, gentleness, goodness, meekness, etc. in the world, they are all the fruits of the Spirit; and they are nowhere to be found but in the believer's heart. Without the appearance, indeed, of these, in good breeding and civility of manners, the world could not go on without utter confusion, dissensions, and misery: but the fruits themselves grow nowhere but where the Spirit of God dwells and abides. They are alone produced by his enabling us by faith to see the riches of God's goodness, forbearance, and longsuffering to us unworthy and offending sinners. The bowels of mercies, kindness, humbleness of mind, meekness, and longsuffering, are then only put on, when we perceive the greatness of Christ's mercies towards us. We forbear and forgive when and as Christ has forgiven us; it is when we see what debtors we are to him, and how freely and undeservedly we must obtain forgiveness, if at all, that we forbear: as he hath forgiven us, we forgive. And the more lively sense we have by the Spirit of his continual longsuffering and continual forgiveness to us, the more ready we shall be to forbear and forgive one another.

Thus all the graces of the Spirit essentially differ from any semblance that may be of them in the world. They have a different, even a divine root, and are produced in a very different manner. 'We all,' saith the Apostle, including all believers till the end of time, 'we all, with open face, beholding, as in a glass, the glory of the Lord, are changed into the same image, from glory to glory, even *by* the Spirit of the Lord.' The Spirit is the great agent who effects this change, by showing to us the glory of the Lord in the face of Christ: and we are changed into the same image, the same mercy, the same compassion, the same goodness and grace, which by faith we see in him exercised towards us: and they are produced in us *by* the Spirit, and exercised by us towards others.

We may vainly pride and please ourselves now with some appearances of these graces, but we may be well assured, that nothing will be found to be real fruits of the Spirit, that are not produced by these effectual means, and in this way of holiness. If we have seen by the light of the Spirit, the glory of the Lord, we must be proportionally changed into the same image, and by no other means can the change be produced.

The Spirit dwelling in our heart, as the implanter and former of every grace, is the *earnest* of our inheritance, which God hath given to assure us of the entire accomplishment of all his promises, and of the full possession of the inheritance itself. And as the fruits produced by this divine agent are a proof and pledge, so they are also a part, of the harvest which is to follow – as they are a part, so also they must precede the harvest. He who hath not the firstfruits, can have no ground to expect that a harvest will ensue. Where these firstfruits of the Spirit are not, there the Spirit himself cannot be, as an earnest of our heavenly inheritance: and if God hath not given us an earnest of future glory, our expectations are certainly groundless, and will in the end be disappointed. Those who have the firstfruits of the Spirit are feeding here in the wilderness on the grapes of yonder Canaan, the land of their inheritance: and by the taste they have here, they know the excellence of the country to which they are travelling. And they groan within themselves, waiting for the adoption, that is, the redemption of their body, and for the full enjoyment of that country, where they shall reap their full harvest in joy for evermore. While here, they still go on from strength to strength, feeding on these fruits; the Spirit daily helping their infirmities in the midst of their inward and outward troubles, giving them strength in weakness, light in darkness, wisdom to direct, and grace to support them, till they appear every one before God in Zion.

Thus we have seen what the work of the Spirit is: he convinceth of sin, making it to appear sin, even exceedingly sinful; and he also taketh of the things of Jesus, and shows them to us, by which means he effectually comforts and sanctifies our souls. He is thus with his people during the whole of their pilgrimage, still humbling them more in the dust, and still bringing the things of Jesus before their enlightened eyes with increasing glory. Those who have had the things of Jesus shown them by the light of the Spirit, still long to see them more clearly. They see greater glory, yea, riches of glory, after which they stretch, and to which they would attain: and when they obtain their desire, they rest not, but would still go on to greater glory. They dig deeper and deeper into the unsearchable riches of Christ, and would comprehend more fully what they find still passeth knowledge – the love of the Father and the grace of the Son, in their greatness and infinity. They find an excellence in the knowledge of Christ, in comparison with which all other things are but loss and dung: and this excellence is what they daily study to make progress in – to go on from glory to glory. This knowledge of Christ with them never grows old, or stale, but is still new, refreshing and more glorious.

From what has been said:

I. The *necessity* and *importance* of having the Spirit appear evident.

The Spirit is the life and soul of all true religion, the conveyor of all spiritual consolation, the implanter and nourisher of every grace and holy disposition. Without him, whatever we are, we have only a name to live, and are indeed dead whilst we live. We can no more live spiritually, in fellowship with God, without the Spirit, than we can live a natural life without breathing. His light, life, and energy, are every moment wanted to enable us to see and feel spiritual things, or to produce any holy fruits of righteousness. From him only can we receive light; and unless he continues to shine daily upon us, our light will be turned unto darkness, our comforts will cease, and the graces of the Spirit will wither and die away. We may have a natural or intellectual knowledge of the things of God, by the exercise of our reasoning faculties; but to discern spiritual things spiritually, we can no more do without his continual agency, than a blind man can see the light of the sun. The Scriptures, without the Spirit, are at best only a dead letter, unefficacious and unanimating; and we have, in our best frames, only the form of godliness without its power.

Are we sensible of this? Are we looking to the Father, and praying earnestly for the Spirit of his Son to dwell in us, and to work effectually all his good pleasure in our hearts? Are we renouncing our own wisdom, becoming fools, that we may be wise? Is it not evident that we must be converted and become like children in this respect, humbly submitting in everything to be taught of God? Is the Spirit daily within us, convincing us of sin, and taking of the things of Christ, and showing them to us in still clearer light, and with more transforming efficacy? Are we going on from strength to strength, and also from glory to glory, seeing new glories and excellences in Christ and him crucified? There is no other means of comfort and sanctification provided by the Father, nor any possible way of walking humbly with God.

O pray earnestly that God take not his Holy Spirit from us! Though he take away all your outward comforts, and make you as poor and as afflicted as Job, yet the Holy Spirit, being within you, can bring you effectual peace and comfort. Let him make the cross ever so heavy, empty you from vessel to vessel, cause you to be destitute, afflicted, and tormented, still the Holy Spirit, being within you, can fill your hearts with joy unspeakable and full of glory. 'Peace I leave with you,' saith Christ; 'my peace I give unto you; not as the world giveth, give I unto you.' The world cannot give peace and joy, without removing the cross and the affliction, the cause of our trouble: but not as the world giveth, give I unto you, saith Christ; he giveth peace in the midst of trouble, while it still continues; the Spirit within us causeth us to glory in tribulation, to rejoice *under* the cross, and to triumph even in death. This is a blessing, which, we are sure, God never did, nor ever will, deny to any one that asks it of him: 'If ye being evil,' saith Christ, 'know how to give good gifts to your children, how much more shall your heavenly Father give the Holy Spirit to them that ask him.' To them that ask him, be they who they will, he is surely given willingly and freely. 'Ask and ye shall have,' is his gracious declaration: and those who seek this blessing, he will never send empty away. O seek earnestly, and plead this promise, and you are sure to succeed. 'Although the fig tree should not blossom, neither fruit be on the vine; though the labour of the vineyard should fail, and the field should yield no meat; though the flock should be cut off from the fold, and there be no herd in the stalls,' yet ask, and ye shall have a blessing, that will amply supply the want of all these things, and your hearts shall rejoice, and your joy no man, no devil, can take from you.

II. From what has been said, we see how great is the *sin of grieving* the Spirit.

Next to the unpardonable sin, this doubtless is the most aggravated, and the most provoking to God. The unpardonable sin is a deliberate and final rejection of the Spirit in all his gracious operations as a comforter and sanctifier; which includes a virtual rejection of the whole economy of redemption – of the love of the Father and of the grace of the Son, which the Spirit comes to reveal and seal to us. The grieving of the Spirit partakes also, in some degree, of the same rebellion and guilt: and we grieve him, when we take little or no notice of his amazing condescension and love, in coming freely and willingly to be our comforter and sanctifier; when we study to make no returns of love by bringing forth, in a holy walk and conversation, the fruits of the Spirit; and when, it may be, by careless neglect and unwatchfullness, we fall into those habits and those courses which he abhors. He cannot pass by unnoticed the unkindness and ingratitude thereby shown; but he is grieved and greatly displeased: though in this, there is no wilful rejection of the Spirit, yet there is a great disregard, and an undervaluing of his consolations; especially if we fall into such courses after long and abundant experience of his comforts. He is grieved, because he loves us, and has our happiness much at heart: for to promote our holiness and happiness is the object of the office he exercises towards us. When we put obstructions in his way, as he discharges his office, and we still promote our own misery – how is the Spirit of love grieved! It is much, if bitter experience teach us not, how grievous this sin is.

Let us therefore, above all things, attend to his motions, and beware of a barren and unfruitful profession of religion, and of defiling by secret indulgences, the temple and habitation of the Spirit. 'If any man defile the temple of God, him will God destroy,' – what awful words! How should they make every believer tremble before God, and cause him to take more earnest heed to the frame of his heart, and to his outward conduct and conversation. Defile *his* temple, who dwells with us as our comforter – how unworthy, how base a conduct! Shall we, who have tasted that the Lord is gracious, by our negligence, sin and folly, grieve him who is come on purpose to comfort us? How deservedly then do we walk in darkness and have no light. Shall we grieve him, without whom we cannot live, cannot think one good thought, nor breathe one good desire! Grieve him, whose presence in the soul is heaven, and whose absence is a hell of corruption, darkness, and misery! Is it possible that we should make such base returns for such love, and be such enemies to our own happiness! Alas! What is man! In what dust and ashes ought even the best of us to lie down before him!

Shall we not rather take notice of his love and his kindness, and thankfully receive all our comforts from his hands, and observe his love and grace in every refreshing thought put into our minds? Yea, shall we not carefully watch and promote all his strivings and motions within us, and cheerfully comply with them, however self-denying and contrary to flesh and blood? When he convinces of sin, let us set our hearts mightily against it. When he speaks comfort, let us hear him as the Lord our Comforter, making known the riches of love and grace in the Father and the Son, to our souls. And when we have no comfort, 'walking in darkness and having no light,' let us honour him by looking to and waiting for him only, for our light in darkness, our joy in sorrow, and our peace in trouble.

4

Sanctification

Sanctification is aimed at by many, if not by most who are religiously inclined. Even the heathens talked much about a virtuous life and a conduct conformable to right reason. But it is understood only by a few. That holiness, which adorns God's people, greatly surpasses all the painted virtues of the heathens, and all the scrupulous morals of the Scribes and Pharisees. The boasted virtue of the heathens and Pharisees had its rise in self and terminated in self: they meant no more than to exalt themselves and to quiet their consciences. But the Christian's holiness has its origin from God, and terminates in him: his glory animates the believer, and leads him to the performance of every action by which it can be displayed.

The nature of sanctification and the means of attaining it are expressed in 2 Cor. 3:18.

It consists in possessing the mind that was in Christ, and a conformity to his image. He is the pattern which we are to copy, and the perfect example which we are to imitate. He has in his own person marked the path to glory; and we are to follow his steps. He teaches us not only by his word, but also by the example of his life. He says both by his words and by his actions – 'learn of me.' His word points out the way; and he having trod the road himself, we have the prints of his feet in which we may step. It is a very great blessing to have the holiness of God exactly delineated, and painted in natural colours in his written law: but it is there like a picture, without life and motion. It is a much greater blessing to have his holiness, which is portrayed in the law, living and animated, as it is in Christ. He, as man in our own nature, pure, uncontaminated with vice, holy, blameless and undefiled, is a living law to his people. Christ is to be considered in a threefold respect; as

Man, Mediator, and God. What he did here on earth, as mediator and God, is not proposed to us for our imitation. As a mediator he was circumcised, fasted forty days, was tempted in the wilderness, offered himself a sacrifice for sins, performed the offices of prophet, priest and king – in these respects he is not to be imitated by us. Nor is he to be imitated in what he performed as God – in his miracles, in all those actions which manifested a supernatural power. But as the Son of Man he is a bright example to us, and a perfect pattern of every virtue. Of *humility*: he who thought it not robbery to be equal with God, emptied himself, and was found in fashion as a man, and took upon him the form of a servant. He placed himself in the lowest station in life, had not where to lay his head, nor had even money to pay the tribute required. His parents were poor; his friends and companions were the poor of this world; the afflicted, and those that were distressed and despised by the world, found a friend in him. Of *meekness*: he was meek and lowly in spirit. When tribute was unjustly required of him, that he might not 'give offence,' he commanded Peter to discharge it. He was the meek and harmless lamb of God, and guile was not found in his mouth. Of *patience*: he endured willingly the contradiction of sinners. Though he was led as a sheep to the slaughter, yet like a lamb, dumb before his shearers, he opened not his mouth, but was obedient even unto the death of the cross. Though he was loaded with reproaches, yet he bore them all patiently. Of *unwearied perseverance* in well doing: he was continually going about doing good. Persecutions and ingratitude from the objects of his kindness did not deter or dishearten him in his friendly purpose. Of *disinterestedness*: he sought not his own advantage or profit, but the good of others. Of *zeal* for God's glory, which was so great that it had eaten him up. These and many other virtues, blazed forth with the most perfect splendour and glory in the person of Christ. He represented in his human nature the image of God, in which the first man was created. He possessed and practised all the virtues of a rational creature, without any defect:[1] so that he is in the fullest

---

[1] The character of Christ, as given by the evangelists, is such as could never have

manner proposed for our imitation, and is the standard by which we are to form a judgement of our attainments in holiness and the divine life.

But let us next consider the *means* by which we may attain this most desirable of all blessings. It would afford but a very small consolation to a person cast on a desert coast, where he could find nothing to subsist on, to hear that an island, a few leagues off, was well stored with all sorts of provisions, suitable to the necessities of man, unless he was able by some means or other to cross over to that island. The poor man at the pool of Bethesda found no benefit from the angel troubling the water at a certain season, for he was unable to step in; for while he 'was going, another stepped in before him.' Nor will it avail us anything, to have received a perfect pattern, unless we be enabled to copy it: and it will be no advantage to us to hear of such a happy state, unless it be one to which we can attain. Various have been the means proposed by man's fertile imagination to accomplish this, but all equally wide of the point.

The Mystic will gravely tell us that there is no avoiding the contagion of sin, or refusing the poisonous cup daily offered to us, but by shaking off human nature and running into solitary deserts, and associating with the wild beasts of the forest. The Brahmin and the monk will advise us to afflict and excruciate the body with the severest chastisements. But all these things have been found inefficient. Let us, therefore, hearken to what an inspired apostle teaches us on this subject: 'We all, with open' or unveiled 'face, beholding as in a glass the glory of the Lord, are changed into the same image from glory to glory, even as by the Spirit of the Lord.' It is by looking unto Jesus and beholding his glory, that the blessed change is produced in us. Nowhere else does virtue and holiness charm us

---

been invented by the wisest of men, much less by poor illiterate fishermen; being totally different from anything that ever has been heard of, or conceived by any before or since. The glorious perfections of the Godhead shine forth in everything he did. Such being his character, it is, and will be, an irrefragable proof of the divinity of the Scriptures, as long as the world stands.

with so pleasing an aspect as in Christ: and the more frequently it is viewed with the eyes of the mind, the more the beholder is transformed into the same image. When Moses had been admitted into a familiar converse with God on the mount, where he spent forty days, the skin of his face shone with such effulgence, that the eyes of the Israelites could not bear it. Thus it is with those who on Mount Zion view Jesus, the king of glory in his beauty, with unveiled face, by the Spirit of God. The rays of heavenly glory, issuing from Christ, pervade the inmost parts of the soul, and convey new vigour to the spiritual life. The oftener the believer beholds Christ by the Spirit, the more clearly he knows his perfections, of which his holiness is the ornament: and the more clearly he knows them, the more ardently he loves them; and the more ardently he loves them, the more like them he desires to be. Nay, love is in itself of a transforming nature. You insensibly catch the habits and manners of a person you love, and you are sweetly and imperceptibly cast into his mould: and love itself, when reciprocal, produces a great similitude. Again, the more ardently a believer loves God, the more frequently and attentively he will seek to behold him; as the more you love one of your fellow-mortals, the more pleasure and delight you find in his company, and the more you regret his absence. So, the soul by beholding and loving, by loving and beholding, gains something by every act, and acquires a new feature of this most glorious image.

Nothing less than the supreme being himself can satisfy an awakened immortal soul. Could we conceive any being above God, God would not content the soul; for it aspires after the supreme. But the perfections of the supreme cannot be fully known or clearly seen but in the face of Jesus Christ. Therefore the soul flees to him as Moses did to the rock, that it may behold his glory, and bask in his bright beams till his piercing rays pervade its inmost parts, and change it by degrees to his own glorious nature. By this means a dead and dark soul is enlivened, and becomes exceedingly transparent, bright, glorious and beautiful. As looking on the brazen serpent expelled the deadly poison and healed the

Israelites, and as the bright beams of the sun disperse the thickest darkness, so do glorious views of the lovely Jesus dislodge sin from its mansion, and heal the wounded soul. As our growth in holiness here depends on the views we have of Christ, so our perfection in the state of bliss will be in consequence of the brighter and clearer discoveries we shall have of him there. We shall be like him, 'because we shall see him as he is.' Like him! Whom? God. O glorious state! O happy condition! Who, considering this, would not cry: 'Come, Lord Jesus, come quickly!'

These views of Christ are necessarily attended with *proper views of God*. In Christ, as in a glass, we shall see all the perfections of the Godhead – his unsearchable wisdom, superabundant goodness, and infinite holiness, his justice and mercy, his truth and righteousness, and especially his incredible love to mortals; which is calculated to melt down the most stubborn hearts, and kindle them into brightest flames of mutual returns of love. 'The love of Christ constraineth us.' All these perfections meet harmoniously in Christ. Connected also with these views of Christ, is a sense of the *detestable nature of sin*. It was sin that made it necessary for the Lord of glory to come down from heaven and take on him the form of a servant. Sin was the cause of his deep humiliation, abasement, and sufferings. So oppressed was he with its ponderous load, that the blood was forced to quit its usual channel, and at last he groaned and died under its weight. Viewing sin through this medium, the believer abhors it, and regards it with perfect hatred. He therefore diligently strives against it, and strenuously resists Satan, from whose iron chains he believes he could never have been delivered, had it not been for the death of the Son of God. Meditation on his sufferings produces a deadness towards sin, and a life unto righteousness. For, while the believer seriously considers the sufferings and death of Christ, he undergoes in his own soul some of the bitterness, pain and torture, (though mingled with sweetness) which Christ suffered in a greater degree: he views the melancholy scene, and utters groan for groan, and sigh for sigh, till his soul is overwhelmed with sorrow and grief;

and this produces a kind of death within. And again, when he sees the mighty conqueror rising triumphant from the tomb, his soul is transported with joy, and ascends with him to the mansions of bliss. Thus we die and live, with and through Christ; and thus we are enabled to mortify sin: (see Rom. 6 throughout). Sin will never appear in its own deformity and horrid nature, till we see it in its effects in the Son of God: till we 'behold the Lamb of God' taking it away. Christ crucified, like a magnifying glass, exhibits to view every feature of this hideous monster. But when we consider the many and great difficulties that are in the way of the believer, while pursuing after holiness, it seems necessary that he should be animated with many and powerful motives, to overpower all opposition. Of these we will allude to some:

1. *Love* is a very strong motive.

It is the leading passion of the soul. Like a general in an army, wherever it presses, all the rest will follow. It is strong as death, overcomes all opposition, and surmounts all difficulties. It makes all things easy. It is said of Jacob, that when he served a hard master seven years for Rachel, they seemed to him but a few days, for the love which he bare her, Gen. 29: 20. And many find it easy to do much for parents, children, and friends, because they love them. But there is no love like that which a redeemed sinner bears to him who has loved him and washed him from his sins in his own blood. Further, love produces the greatest effects when it is mutual. We are willing to do and suffer much to gain the affection of a person we regard, though we are not sure of success; but when the affection is reciprocal, it adds strength to every motive. Now the believer does not love at an uncertainty; he knows that Jesus loved him first; loved him when he was in a state of enmity; and that nothing but the manifestation and power of this love could have taught his hard and unfeeling heart to love him whom he never saw, 1 Peter 1:8. This love therefore affords two sweet and powerful encouragements in his service:

First, *A cordial desire to please.* Love does what it can, and is sorry that it can do no more. We seldom think much either of time, pains, or expense, when the heart is warmly engaged. The world, who understand not this heartfelt spring of true religion, think it strange that the believer will not run into the same excess of riot with them, 1 Peter 4:4. They wonder what pleasure he can find in secret prayer, or in reading and hearing the word of God, and they pity the poor mortal who has such a melancholy turn, and gravely advise him not to carry things so far. But the believer can give them a short answer in the Apostle's words: 'the love of Christ constraineth me,' 2 Cor. 5:14. His ruling passion is as powerful as theirs, which makes his pursuits no less uniform and abiding, though the objects are as different as light from darkness. They love the perishing pleasures of sin, the mammon of unrighteousness, and the praises of men; but he loves God and the Saviour and the things of another world.

Secondly, *A pleasing assurance of being accepted.* If we know not whether what we do will be favourably received or not, we become remiss and indifferent . But it is not so with the Lord's people; for they are assured, that he will not overlook the smallest services they may be engaged in, or the slightest sufferings they may undergo, for his name's sake; and this greatly animates them. He has told them in his word, that if they give but a cup of cold water in his name, and for his sake, he will accept and acknowledge it, as if it were done immediately to himself, Mark 9:41.

2. Another very powerful motive which animates the believer, is *confidence and assurance of success.*

The Lord considers the Christian's cause as his own, and has engaged to finish the good work that is begun. When the children of Israel were marching to the land of Canaan to attack the strongholds of the well-fortified inhabitants, the assurance of success which the Almighty had given them, the assurance of his being with them, and delivering the nations into their hands, made them overlook all difficulties, and encouraged them to attack nations, united together by compacts and interests, each of whom were much more powerful than themselves. So it is with the believer. Though his enemies are many and powerful, the difficulties on the road great, and he himself but a feeble and weak creature; yet the Lord has promised to be his strength and shield, and however great his danger may be, his strength shall be equal to it. 'This consideration makes every difficulty vanish. Should the one increase tenfold, yet if the other be increased in equal proportion, it amounts to the same thing. What is hard and difficult for a child is easy for a man. What is hard for flesh and blood is easy to faith and grace. The power on which the believer depends is not his own, nor in his own keeping, but is treasured up in the covenant of grace, or in the Lord Jesus, in whom all fullness dwells, and it is always to be obtained by prayer.' Tempestuous indeed is the believer's passage through this world, yet his life is secured; and he is confident of reaching the happy shore to which he sails, and of entering the desired haven safe, by and by: and this comforts him in all dangers and difficulties, be the storm ever so alarming.

We shall now consider some of the chief branches of sanctification:

1. *Love to the Saviour.*

When the understanding is enlightened to see the amiableness and loveliness of Jesus, and the glorious perfections of the Godhead beaming forth in him, the soul becomes inflamed with ardent love to him. Nothing then is so delightful, so charming, so desirable, as to dwell on the contemplation of his glories: the soul sees him altogether lovely, the chief among ten thousand. It is therefore enraptured with his excellences, and feels an inexpressible longing after him. In this respect the soul greatly resembles the Deity himself. God's own infinite excellences render him lovely in his own sight. He being the chief good and possessing all conceivable perfections, he cannot but love himself; nay, it would be contrary to right and justice for him not to be filled with complacency on a view of his own infinite excellences. The more, therefore, a creature loves God, the more he acts in unison with him, and the more conformable he becomes to the Divine image.

The believer also *acts* from a principle of love. He has no will of his own; but 'Christ lives in him.' Love to Christ makes the soul embrace willingly what he bids: and being enabled to run the way of his commandments, the believer avoids everything that may displease him. The glory of God is the mark he holds in view, and the end he aims at in everything. He considers God as the centre of his happiness; and nothing wounds him so much as when he hears his name blasphemed, or sees his precepts transgressed. He can say with David, 'Rivers of waters flow down mine eyes, because men keep not thy law.'

2. *Deep humiliation of heart.*

This is an inseparable concomitant of the Love of God. When the Highest manifests his own perfections, as they shine forth in Jesus Christ, in such a degree as to fill the heart with ardent love, then we abhor ourselves in dust and ashes, because we have sinned against such a good and holy God. Every bright view we have of God's perfections reflects back on ourselves, and shows to us more than ever the exceeding heinousness of our sins. The angels are said to prostrate themselves before the throne of heaven, covering their faces, to signify their inability to bear the lustre of his majesty; and hiding their feet, to express their sense of vileness in comparison with God's holiness. But the believer's humility differs much from theirs. He is blinded with tears of grief and sorrow; with contrition of heart and abhorrence of himself. They and he live in the valley of humiliation; but the believer waters his with the tears of repentance, Luke 7:38. O what self-annihilation is there in a good man, when he has a lively sense of the Divine purity! Yea, how detestable is he in his own sight! He abhors himself as the vilest sinner, and repents in dust and ashes, Job 42:6; Gen. 18:27. When Isaiah saw God's glory, he was ready to faint away, and cried out, 'I am a man of unclean lips.' This spirit of an undeserving beggar, with which the Christian is *clothed*, can never be assumed by hypocrites and pretenders to religion, it being so exceedingly contrary to our nature. But it is the believer's brightest ornament, and serves as a coat of mail to keep off many a fiery dart shot at him by his hellish foes, which would have wounded his inmost soul. When the sinner falls down at God's feet, he spreads his mantle over him and keeps him under the shadow of his wings as in a strong tower. This spirit is highly valued by God himself; for he delights in and dwells with the humble and contrite in heart.

Whoever possesses this spirit within him, will manifest it in his life and conversation. He will no more show pride, passion, and resentment towards his fellow-creatures. Having learned of Jesus, he is meek and lowly both before God and towards man. Conscious of the manifold transgressions and numerous sins he has to be pardoned, every day and every hour of the day, he can easily forgive his fellow-sinners when they offend him. Sensible of his own frailty, he is tender and merciful to others. And we may safely say, that whatever views and feelings we have, which do not tend to humble us before God, which do not lead us to abhor ourselves, and make us compassionate and tender towards our fellow-creatures, they cannot be from God, but from Satan transformed into an angel of light. 'God sees the proud afar off, but giveth grace to the humble and meek,' not to make him proud of his attainments, but to make him still more humble, and still more vile in his own eyes. The believer needs not to proclaim to the world what blessed and glorious views he has, and what happy feelings he enjoys; for these will manifest themselves in his poverty and humility of spirit, if they be from God. Hence we see that to grow in grace, and to grow in humility, mean the same thing, and should convey the same idea to our minds.

This humble state may appear to the superficial and religiously vain, who think themselves never free from legality until they be brought to the confines of sensuality, gloomy, legal, and comfortless. But if we advert to what the Scriptures say of it, we shall find it to be quite the reverse. Though it be a valley, yet it is a valley well watered with the salubrious streams of salvation; and through it the still waters of comfort flow; and here are the rich green pastures in which the shepherd of Israel feeds his flock, and restores their souls to the image of God. What is said of Satan may, with equal propriety, be said of his subjects: 'They walk in dry places.' But God's sheep have a portion well watered with the upper and lower fountains. In this valley is the well of living waters and through it the streams of Lebanon flow, Song of Sol. 4:15. Here is the garden of the Lord, enriched with many sweet-smelling flowers. Here is his vineyard, stored with all manner of pleasant fruits, yea, 'the fruits of the valley,' Song of Sol. 6:11. Here the generous vines flourish, and the fragrant pomegranates bud; and it is a land flowing with milk and honey. Here let sinners come from their dry and lofty places, and drink wine and milk without money and without price. Though the inhabitants sometimes, with David, water their couches with their tears, yet God bottles their tears, and these shall be turned into wine at the marriage-supper of the Lamb. The woman mentioned in Luke 7 was an eminent inhabitant of this valley. So full was she of the waters of life, that she poured them down in streams on the Saviour; she washed him with tears who washed her in his blood. 'She loved much' – this expression shows her happiness and the excess of joy which filled her heart. Her comfort was proportioned to her grief, and her joy to her sorrow. These go hand in hand in the Christian. If rivers of tears flow from their eyes, they drink also of that river which makes glad the city of God.

Hence it appears, that they and they only, who live in this humble and penitent state, 'find pasture' and thrive. It is barren and dry everywhere else; and God's sheep go astray when they quit this valley. If it is good to walk humbly with God, notwithstanding all our eminent graces and high attainments, the contrary must be hurtful to ourselves, and dishonourable to God. If Enoch found heaven by walking humbly with his God, those who are encompassed about with pride as with a chain, walk in slippery places, and shall be cast into destruction. The Lord looketh upon him that is 'poor and of a contrite heart,' but his 'face is against the proud.'

5

Affliction

How utterly unable are all things below to bring us any comfort or any relief, when God's finger even slightly touches us! They are at all times equally impotent, though our thoughts of them may be very different. Time and recovery should not give them any more power or influence over our hearts. Such a season will return soon again. Sickness, and death itself, are not very far, but just at the door. And neither of them will come in a pleasing manner; but the one will be painful, and the other will be awful, if not terrible. May we be better prepared to meet them both, by a blessed improvement of past afflictions.

The sad remembrance of former sicknesses unimproved, and of the views they have had in them, haunt the dying curtains of many, and speak such home-convictions, as they are at the season ill able to endure. After recovering, most of us live as if we had made a covenant with death, and seem to think that we shall neither die, nor be sick any more. But though we are reprieved, we should remember, that we are not released. Death hath power over us, and at the appointed time will exercise it. 'It is *appointed* for all men once to die,' and this appointment or decree cannot be altered. The appointed hour may be very near, and slight indispositions may be sent on purpose to warn us of his coming. In the mean season we should improve all these kind visitations for the furtherance of our growth in grace and in the divine life.

'Affliction cometh not forth out of the dust, neither doth trouble spring out of the ground,' but they are all sent in wisdom and love; and every circumstance, as to time and manner, is exactly ordered for the best. Were every circumstance more narrowly examined, it would doubtless give us a great insight into the wisdom and love of God in all his afflictive dispensations. God doth not willingly afflict any of his children: but they always stand in absolute need,

Affliction

at the very time, of the very affliction which he sends. It could not be laid aside, nor delayed, nor altered for another, without great hurt and injury to the soul.

God's *designs* in afflictions are various; but all gracious, and for our good. He may intend to bring us to repentance for some past sins, as the three days' pestilence was sent to humble David for numbering the people; or, it may be to prevent our being taken in some dangerous snare, into which we may be in great danger of falling: and it is better to endure the heaviest affliction, than to carry about with us a guilty conscience. 'Anything rather than sin,' is the language of the Christian's heart. Or it may be to exercise some grace, that it may thereby gain strength, and the soul be prepared for some trying circumstances into which it is soon to be brought; as was the case with Joseph. The trials with which he had been exercised, prepared him for his future exaltation, and some of them contributed to bring it about.

These designs may for a long season be *concealed* from the believer himself, as was the case with Joseph. Yet, inasmuch as God hath assured us, that all things shall work together for good, patience and resignation to the divine will in all things is our duty. In his good time he may give us to see such wisdom and goodness in all, as to fill our hearts with transports of joy. To follow him is our part, without murmuring, without complaining. How gracious is the design to bring us to repentance for sin, or to stop us from falling into temptation, or to prepare us by previous discipline for some humbling service! Is not all this good? Away then with all impatience and all murmurings. Nothing befalls us without a cause: and no trouble comes upon us sooner, or presses more heavily, or continues longer, than our case requires. What our short-sighted ignorance calls adversities or evils, are in reality and truth, well-designed and gracious blessings, and form a part of the means employed by God's goodness and grace to prepare us for the exceeding and eternal weight of glory.

All our desire in this world should be to live holily and live usefully: and affliction, by the blessing of God, hath great influence in promoting both. It greatly promotes holiness, and is also no small preparative for usefullness. It is working out at the same time a far more exceeding and eternal weight of glory in the other world. God always chastens us for our profit. Though we may thereby lose earthly comforts, ease, and enjoyments; yet it is a profitable loss. What we lose in these things, we gain in holiness. It is for our profit, to become partakers of his holiness. It is for our profit, to be brought to repentance for every sin, to be delivered from ensnaring temptations, or to be prepared for any service to which our master may call us. If we cannot see the end the Lord hath in view, still let us believe, that it is for our profit in some way or other, yes, and in the way of all others, by which we can profit the most, and be the greatest gainers.

What profit *have we* experienced? Have we become more watchful against such sins as have at any time brought correction upon us, that we might repent of them? Are we contending earnestly and strenuously against them? Are we aware of any such corruptions as might necessitate our heavenly Father to prevent us from entering into such circumstances of life, as would foster the temptation to them? Are we now more strictly on our guard against such dangerous circumstances? How have we conducted ourselves in such circumstances, places, and stations, as God has prepared us for by corrections? Have we been earnestly diligent in such duties, having in all things a single eye to his glory?

6

The Tares and the Wheat

We are taught by the parable of the tares and wheat, that there will always be a mixture, in this world, of good and bad men, which no care or diligence can prevent. In every place, in every society there will be a mixture. Whatever discouragements may be given to evil, and whatever care and diligence may be taken to purge and keep out the wicked, the enemy, still more vigilant, will find an opportunity to sow his tares. And though we would often think and act otherwise, yet the Lord, for the wisest reasons, permits the tares and the wheat to grow together until the harvest. The tares and the wheat are sown in the same soil, and fenced by the same mounds; the same rain and the same sun cause both to grow and to ripen.

It is the nature of grace to *grow*, and therefore it is compared to seed, to trees, to a child: things which have but small beginnings, but which, if healthy and properly taken care of, will infallibly grow. The tares also grow; the wicked are also in a progressive state, and are continually ripening, yea, ripening for destruction. They may enjoy the same means of grace and be partakers of the same outward privileges, with the righteous; and yet it is only for destruction that they are ripening. The same soil, the same sun, and the same rain, may nourish an unfruitful prickly thorn, as the most fruitful tree.

We are also taught how *vigilant*, how zealous, how industrious, the *enemy* is, to do mischief. For it is not said that he sowed the tares while men played or were careless, as if there had been any negligence laid to their charge: but 'while they slept,' without which they could not live. Sleep they must, nature requires it; but then it was that the enemy did the mischief. Watch him as narrowly as you will, yet still he will do his work in spite of all care and diligence. If you will but step aside, to do what must be done – to eat, to drink, or to sleep – he is ready to take his opportunity of sowing his tares.

And the *ground*, which will not answer the husbandman's hope without toil, labour, and cost, will produce the bad seed of its own accord, and yield but too plentiful a crop. This is an exact picture of the human heart. What toil, what labour, what care and diligence will it cost to produce anything good in it! And when it is sown there by the heavenly husbandman, what watchfullness is required to prevent its being injured! Our eye must be continually upon it, and the most diligent care must be exercised. But the tares will grow without any care; the soil exactly suits them. May this teach us to be more watchful, to prevent, if possible, the enemy from sowing his evil seed. If that is not possible, let us endeavour to distinguish between the wheat and the tares, that we may not be mistaken, and think that we have a good crop of wheat, when more than half of it is only tares, which are unprofitable, and will in the end be burned.

The tares and the wheat, it appears, are to *grow together*. They are not to grow in a different, but in the same field, and intermix together. Where there is a stalk of wheat, there you may find at least one tare, or it may be, many tares. This is doubtless permitted, and ordered for the wisest purposes. We are apt to complain, that the world is so sinful and so wicked, thinking, that were it otherwise, we should live more holily, and be rid of many temptations, which now give corrupt nature an advantage over us. Were there none but godly people in the world, and the field free from all tares, O what a happy thing would it be! We are apt to think how much benefit would we then derive to our souls! But the Lord's thoughts are not our thoughts, nor are our ways his ways. 'Let both grow together,' is his appointment. And no doubt, this is one of the 'all things,' which work together for good to those who love God.

Let us then patiently bear the evil, and diligently seek from it some profit and spiritual improvement.

1. This is one great means of increasing *grace* in those who love God.

Living among those who are enemies to true godliness, keeps patience, forbearance, and self-denial in constant exercise. Were all humble, loving, and condescending, how should patience and meekness be exercised, and thereby gain strength? We should be apt to deceive ourselves; and while we enjoyed our own wills and ways, we should be ready to think that there is no such thing as gall within us. But an evil world, the tares continually among us, show us what spirit we are naturally of, bring us in one way or another perpetually to the test, and prove to us what desire there is still lurking within us, of having things in our own way. The obstinate stubbornness of the people of Israel was one great means, in the course of providence, of promoting meekness in Moses of making him more watchful over his own heart, and thereby, of gaining greater victory over himself.

2. This state of things promotes *faith*, which alone can daily give victory over the world.

If we live a sober, righteous and godly life in this present evil world, faith will be continually exercised and tried, and tried by all the force which customs, practices, and long habits can bring against it. The fewness of real Christians leaves us often to walk, as it were, almost singly in the narrow way. The number also and prosperity of the wicked, may cause us at times to search and examine the grounds of our faith: and shaking it to its very foundation, may make it more steadfast, and render us immoveable in the midst of all storms, raised by an evil world. We are forced continually to the most vigorous exercise of this grace, and thereby it is more strengthened and confirmed. Without being strong in faith, it is impossible to 'endure as seeing him who is invisible,' to esteem the reproach of Christ greater riches than the treasures of the world, and to choose rather to suffer affliction with the people of God, than to enjoy the pleasures of sin for a season.

The world, lying in wickedness, calls forth faith, in one way or other, into perpetual exercise. While we live differently from the world, not swayed by its customs, not led by its maxims, not influenced by its favours, not awed by its frowns, we must 'live by faith.' 'This is the victory that overcometh the world, even our faith. Who is he that overcometh the world, but he that *believeth* that Jesus is the son of God.' It is a perpetual warfare between the world of sinners on one side, and faith on the other: and victory must every day be gained, or we are enslaved. The world gives faith no rest; and faith puts forth its strength, which is Christ, continually to oppose it. The world, with its glory, pomp, wealth, and care, on the one hand, and shame and suffering on the other, is an enemy that cannot be easily vanquished: nothing but the continual exercise of vigorous faith can make any stand against it. The Psalmist felt the power of this enemy: 'My feet,' said he, 'were almost gone, my steps had well nigh slipped' – and why? – 'I was envious at the foolish; I do also see the ungodly in such prosperity.' But when he saw them thus easy, secure, and prosperous, to what did this lead him? 'I thought,' said he, 'to understand this; but it was too hard for me, till I went into the sanctuary of God.' He betook himself to the ordinances of God; and thereby his faith was called forth into exercise, and gained strength, and he was helped over a great stumbling-block to a clearer insight into the secret mysteries of God's providence, and to a more steadfast belief of his promises.

3. The intermixture of tares and wheat, of sinners and the godly, is, by the blessing of God, one great means of *mortifying our love* to this present evil world, and of *engaging our affections* to the world above.

How strong is the love of present things in our hearts! Though we see nothing but sin in the world, yet how unwilling we are to leave it! If, when full of sin, as it is, we are in general too fond of it, what would be the case, were it exactly according to our wishes, and were everything about us just what we would desire? What can be more suited to mortify this love, and to engage us to the pursuit of higher things, than the very sight of the world itself, and a little feeling of the prickly thorns with which it abounds? The sinfullness of the world, and a continual abode among the enemies of God and of godliness, hath the desirable effect upon the gracious soul, of weaning it from such a scene of sin and misery. When the Christian reflects on the evil that is daily done under the sun, and when by peculiar circumstances it is brought home to him, he finds an edge set on his desires after God, and after the new world, wherein dwelleth righteousness. His soul grows sick of this dungeon and sink of iniquity where he is confined, and he loathes himself for having set any value on the things of earth.

Thus we see how the intermixture of good and bad in this world, tends to our spiritual improvement. Corruptions are hereby weakened, and grace improved and strengthened. We have sinners daily around us, as thorns in our eyes and scourges in our sides; and the best of men are full of daily infirmities, which call forth patience, forbearance, and forgiveness. The present state of things should not be left unnoticed but made to minister to our edification and improvement. Let us not be impatient and complain of our particular situations: but be our situation what it may, let us look up to that God, who can cause *all* things to work for our good – who can make even the sins of others to turn out to the spiritual and eternal good account of his servants. O what wisdom does God display in all his proceedings! With what submission therefore should we acquiesce in his disposal of us! And what grounds have we in all things to depend on him, and to wait, with full assurance, for a blessing in everything. He can make poison to be flourishing food, and what proves fatal to others, beneficial to his people.

Well then, since this is the will of heaven, that the tares and wheat should grow together until harvest, let us never expect it to be otherwise: but let us look for something to exercise grace in everything, in every situation, and in every individual. God will have it so. What cause then for contentedness, and also for continual thanksgiving! Let us become more dead daily to the world, have our affections more steadily fixed on things above, and more diligently seek a better country.

7

Divine Guidance

WELL might Moses say, 'if thy presence go not with us, carry us not up hence.' He would not move one step without him; and with him he cared not whither he went. By the pillar they were directed in their way; and also protected and defended from their enemies, whilst they followed it, Exod. 14:19, 20, 24. The cloud that was as smoke by day, and as fire by night, was also a shadow, a place of refuge, a covert, a protection and defence, Isa. 4:5, 6. It was as their guide and director, for 'when the cloud was taken up from over the tabernacle, then the children of Israel went onward in all their journeys. But if the cloud were not taken up, then they journeyed not till the day it was taken up,' Exod. 40:36, 37. This pledge of God's presence was the beginning of all their movements and rest, the guide and director of all their undertakings. So that they moved and rested, proceeded and stood still, according to his will and counsel in every instance. Thus he guided them by his eye, and led them by his counsel, Psa. 32:8. Sometimes, perhaps, they were full of ardent desires, forward, active, and impatient of delay: but if that were not according to his mind, he would cause a cloud to abide on their tabernacle, which would darken their way, distract their consultations, and prevent their moving one step forward. Though their desires were great and their intentions good, yet this cloud would be upon them, and they could not know their way. At other times they might be heavy and cold, fearful and slothful, imagining that there was a lion in the way at every step, that giants were in possession of the land, that difficulties and perplexities lie in the way before them in such and such undertakings, that the way was so long and perilous, and that it was better to return than to go forward. But now, it may be, they must decamp, pass on, and engage. The cloud shall break up and go before them; they shall see *so* far on their way, as to go forth with cheerfullness. But when the cloud was taken up, they knew they were to go forward, and journeyed accordingly, following the cloud; yet they *knew not whither* they went, nor *what* and *where* would be the end of their journey; only they were going forward, still nearer and nearer towards the land of promise. And therefore it is said, 'that when they journeyed, the ark went before them to seek out a resting place for them,' Num. 10:33. It was carried on, to see where the pillar or cloud of direction would stay; and there they rested, wherever it was.

When God gives us so much direction and so much intimation of his will, as that we see that it is our duty to go forward, and trust him as to the issue, though we at present see not the end, nor know what and where our resting place will be; still by this we may conclude that God hath given us a sure pledge of his further direction in every time of *necessity*, and of his *continual* presence with us.

Thus God leads his people now through the wilderness of this world. They have the cloud and pillar of divine presence to go before them, and lead them in the right way. Without this they can neither move nor take any rest; and they follow it, not knowing whither they are going, only they are assured they are going towards the promised land, believing that all things work together for good. And on great emergencies and on extraordinary occasions, God relieves them by some especial appearance of his glory. The cloud shall not merely rest on their tabernacle, but *fill* it also with a more eminent token of the divine presence and favour. In the 'mount will the Lord be seen.' This will relieve them, when in all things they are at a loss. Glorious appearances in great straits and difficulties are eminent testimonies of God's regard. What these tokens are, ordinary and extraordinary, of the divine presence, which God's people now enjoy, and by which they are led and directed, no believer can be entirely ignorant. Often have they found him inclining their hearts insensibly yet powerfully – fixing the bent of their spirits effectually, (their hearts being in his hands as the rivers of water which he turns as he pleases) – supplying them with reasonings and considerations far beyond their own wisdom: proposing occasions, invitations and provocations; enlarging them in prayer, or shutting them up, making walls on one hand, and opening paths on the other. With innumerable such ways as these, infinite wisdom is pleased effectually to guide and direct them in the way in which they should go. In the use of means through patience and waiting upon him, they shall doubtless be directed to that which is pleasing to him. He is with them in every instance, and will never leave them nor forsake them, till he brings them safe in the *right* way, to be *ever* with the Lord.

However, they shall not in general see *far* before them, but must be contented to follow the cloud daily by faith, not knowing where it will rest. Thus have *I* found it in former times, and thus do I now, in a particular manner, find it to be. For the just shall no otherwise live here than *by faith*, every step of his journey. And is it not the happiest, as well as the safest life? For what is the life of faith, but choosing rather to follow the wisdom of God than my own wisdom, and resigning myself to his guidance and disposal? O for faith thus to live, and then I cannot but be happy and safe! Happy in the care of infinite goodness and love, and safe under the guidance and protection of infinite wisdom and power. 'The Lord only maketh us to dwell in safety,' Psalm 4:8.

What we are in continual danger of, in following the cloud of divine presence moving before us, is *impatience*, the bitter fruit of unbelief. We are impatient often of delay, and in haste to take possession of the land of promise: and this often is the cause of grievous sins, as well as of great perplexity to the soul. This hurried the Israelites into the great sin of idolatry at Mount Sinai. They were weary of waiting for Moses' return, and for the cloud moving before them. They had a God that stayed with them and manifested his presence to them by the cloud on the mount; but *that* did not suit their impatient and discontented spirit. They must have a God to 'go before them.' Rather than wait longer, they would themselves devise signs of God's presence with them, and leave Moses and the cloud behind on the mount. But this impatience proved the utter *ruin of many*, and the *plague of all*; 'And the Lord *plagued* the *people* because they made the calf.' But he that believeth doth not make *haste*. Patient waiting is always the language of faith. 'Though the vision tarry, wait for it.' 'Behold his soul which is lifted up, is not upright in him.' This weariness of waiting betrays us unto many and sore *temptations*. Here began Saul's ruin; he stayed for Samuel *to* the last hour of the time appointed, but had no patience to stay that hour, 1 Sam. 13: 11, 14. So Israel here, had they stayed one day longer, they would have seen what was become of Moses. 'The Lord is a God of judgement,' and must be waited for, until he comes.

We shall not lose our labour, for he that shall come, will come, and will not tarry beyond his own appointed time, though he may tarry beyond our time of expecting him. God is not to be limited, nor are his times prescribed unto him. We know our *way*, and the end of our journey. But as to our stations of special rest, we must wait for him to determine, when, where, and how long, we are to rest, as the people did in the wilderness. 'Our times are,' and will be 'in his hands'; and he will order them according to his own will and wisdom. Owing to the sins of the Israelites Moses spent another forty days on the mount; so their haste did not tend to their good speed.

8

Spiritual Appetite

May 24, 1782.

There is no image in the whole Bible, more frequently made use of to express the workings, affections, and desires of the new man after spiritual things, than the craving of our bodily appetites after food and nourishment, namely, hunger and thirst. And, what proper food is to a hungry man, that, spiritual things, Christ and the blessings of the gospel, are to the renewed soul. 'Blessed are they, which hunger and thirst after righteousness.' Hunger and thirst are the strongest of all our bodily appetites. They are also unceasing and continually more and more craving and importunate till we either eat and drink, or die. And nothing will satisfy them but meat and drink. Offer an hungry man the world and all things in it, he will despise and reject them, and say, 'These are not the things I want, give me food or else I die.' So are the desires of the new man in Christ, after spiritual things: the grace of Christ, the favour of God, and conformity to his image. They are strong and unceasing, craving after spiritual food with more and more importunity; and nothing but this will satisfy. Riches, honours and pleasures, are all lightly esteemed. 'Give me grace, give me peace and reconciliation with God, give me holiness, or else I die,' is his unceasing language.

A hungry man finds in food a suitableness, a taste, a relish, and refreshment. And so do they in divine things, who have *tasted* that the Lord is gracious. There is a suitableness in them to the soul's wants, and satisfaction and refreshment in the enjoyment of them which is great and inexpressible. 'They are sweeter to his taste than honey or the honeycomb.' Till he feeds upon them, the soul is miserable and refuseth comfort, like a person ready to perish with hunger: but when he has a sense of the goodness, power and efficacy of them on his soul, he is filled with joy unspeakable and full of glory. He feeds upon them with *joy*, however any of them may be in their own nature, or in their dispensation, bitter to flesh and blood. The cross is sweet and refreshing, if under it he can taste how gracious the Lord is. Everything that is wholesome food, and good nourishment, though it be bitter herbs, is sweet and refreshing to him that is hungry.

For this reason divine things are compared not only to bread and water, but to 'wine and milk, to fat things full of marrow'; things that are not only *nourishing*, as bread and water, but also *relishing*, *refreshing*, and *reviving*. If the soul is in health and hath strength to digest its food; if its appetite is not lost by spiritual sickness, vitiated and corrupted by any prevalent sin, and heavenly things thus become unsavoury and tasteless, 'like the white of an egg'; if this be not the case with the renewed soul, spiritual things are always relishing, refreshing, and full of nourishment; and by them it grows and gains spiritual strength.

These two things are inseparably connected with the things of the Spirit of God to a renewed soul that is in spiritual health: he finds in them *savour*, and *nourishment*; he is *refreshed* and *strengthened* by them. A vitiated taste and a false appetite may relish things that are not proper food – that have little or no *nourishment* in them. But a man in health and vigour of body, can live on no such things. So a soul sickly and weak, may have a taste and a pleasing relish given to the fancy by the dispensation of the word, and in the use of the means of grace, when at the same time it is in no degree nourished and strengthened by grace itself in the use of the means; but the soul is as weak and sickly as ever, and still finds an emptiness, a craving, painful and uneasy, and a feebleness, which unfits him for every undertaking that is spiritual and difficult. But a soul in health must have the *sincere* milk of the word; it will be satisfied with nothing else, and it *groweth* thereby – gains renewed strength, fresh vigour, increasing alacrity and delight in the things of God and the ways of God. The gospel and its heavenly doctrines are never stale, tasteless, or unsavoury to him, but daily more refreshing and more nourishing. He feeds upon them more heartily and more frequently, and his stomach is not overloaded, because he can *digest* his food; so that his appetite is keen and his soul more and more nourished. He hath increasing discernment also to know more exactly what is proper food for him, and rejects those things, which he knows, have more tendency to fill the soul with wind and humours, than to minister nourishment and strength. 'Being of full age, by means of use he hath his senses exercised to discern both good and evil.'

No sign can be worse than a cold indifference towards the things of God, when they become as it were stale, without any relish, or nourishment, like a tale that has been told a hundred times over. In this case the soul can have no experience of the life and workings of spiritual things, nor any comfort or refreshment from them. He, who is in this state, *honours* not the gospel by any fruits of love, zeal, or delight; nor is he *useful* in any way to others. 'He is a tree, whose fruit withereth, without fruit, twice dead, plucked up by the root.' This is a state, which of all others Christ is most displeased with. In temptations, the Lord, who is compassionate and gracious, pities those who are tempted. In persecutions, he suffers with the afflicted. He intercedes for his people in their sudden and unexpected surprises. But he severely threatens those who are in spiritual decays, who are in a cold, formal and lifeless state, Rev. 2:4, 5. This he cannot bear with, because it reflects so much dishonour upon him, and on the provision he hath made in the gospel. It will, if not quickly prevented by a speedy recovery, prove the certain ruin of the soul. Yes, Christ will bear longer even with those who are utterly dead, and make no pretensions to religion, 'I would,' he says, 'thou wert cold or hot: because thou art neither, I will spue thee out of my mouth,' Rev. 3:16.

We cannot be too jealous and watchful over ourselves on this point. Everything hath a tendency to deaden our souls, quench the Spirit, and blunt the edge of our desires and affections after spiritual things. Our own corruptions always resist grace; and the world around us would by every way bring us unto some little compliance with it. And here the company of dead and formal professors also cannot but greatly damage the soul. Their company, if much frequented, will, like ice when handled, strike a chill and damp into the soul that was before alive, fervent, and active. This is the last effort of the devil; if he cannot by his temptations turn us back, or draw us aside from the ways of God, he will by all his art, craft and malice, endeavour to enfeeble our strength, cool our zeal, and diminish our ardour in the good way, into which the grace of God hath brought us.

We should beware of these decays in our souls, in their very *first beginnings*; or else recovery will be more difficult and more doubtful. But here is the cause of the utter ruin of many. At first they listen to the carnal reasonings of their *own* minds, strengthened it may be, by the suggestions of formal professors and lifeless Christians, till they are gone so far in decay and consumption, that their recovery becomes doubly more difficult. Some would confine all warmth and fervency of affections about spiritual things to *first* convictions, to youthful days, when the heat of the animal spirits is greater. A dangerous insinuation! For does not this highly dishonour the things of God? What! Are we *more* affected by them, the *less* we know of them? Is it their *novelty* only that gives them their efficacy? Is food more refreshing to a *child*, than to a hungry man in *full strength*, after the labour and toil of the day? Far from it. The objects of creation, the more we contemplate, minutely examine, and thoroughly know them, the more we are amazed with the exquisite wisdom and power displayed in them, and the more they command our admiration. Are the wonders of grace and salvation more easily comprehended? Or are we less interested in them? Surely not. The reason why the works of God in creation, providence and grace are unnoticed by us, and we are unaffected by them, is because we know them so *little*, and our *minds* are turned to different objects.

But the decay of the animal spirits, it may be said by some, diminishes the efficacy and lessens the effect of divine things. It ill suits any to make this excuse, who, whilst they are dead and lifeless about spiritual things, are alive, active and intent upon other things; for instance, the lawful enjoyments and comforts of life. If a man in his old age, *grows* more in love with the things of the world, and less in love with the things of God, surely this must proceed not from the decay of *nature*, but from the decay of *grace*, and the growing strength of sin. The decays of nature, will not, cannot, effect decays in holiness of life, and in diligence in religious duties; it will never diminish the vigorous and firm adherence of the judgement and will, at least, to spiritual things. And where the heat and warmth of the affections are not so lively as they were in former times, whatever the decays of nature may be, the soul, if alive to God, cannot be satisfied in this state; it is his grief and burden; and he preserves a godly jealousy over himself, lest his decays should not be *outward*, but *inward*; not in the *natural*, but in the *spiritual* man.

The life, comfort, and honour of religion, is to find the things of God always new and refreshing, and our appetites keen for them. Without this there can be no real consolation of the gospel, no growth in grace, no adorning of religion, no recommending of it to others. But the soul will become barren and unfruitful, a 'mere *walking, talking skeleton* in religion.' Good Lord, deliver me from this cursed state of soul! Rather empty me from vessel to vessel, put me in the furnace, let me rather die than live thus to dishonour thee and thy cause.

9

God Affording Seasonable Help

July 5, 1782.

Relying upon God's power and faithfullness to keep us in the midst of temptations, is the only way to obtain strength against them. All my best resolutions and determinations as to watchfullness, have often proved ineffectual, weak, and feeble in the hour of trial; but relying upon God's faithfullness, 'that according to thy day, so shall thy strength be,' and that 'his grace is,' and shall be, 'sufficient for me,' this never disappointed me. In one way or other I have always found a way of escape, but often in a way unexpected and unthought of. There is no peace, till we can see ourselves safe from the workings of inward corruption, and outward temptations, in the hands of God, exclusive of everything *we are or can do*. The Lord *thinketh* on those who are poor and needy, and is their help and deliverer, Psa. 40:17. And though his 'enemies may be *lively and strong*,' yet the Lord will make more haste to help them, is stronger, and must prevail, Psa. 38:19-22. Faith in the living God opposes *lively* enemies; and to 'the Lord strong and mighty,' it looks for help against strong enemies.

As God is faithful and true, this faith must always prevail, for the Lord is a very *present* help in trouble to those that trust in him: not help at a distance, which we may have cause to fear will come too late, but a *present* help. 'When I would do good, evil is present with me,' saith the Apostle; but the Lord is a 'very *present* help,' against present evil, Psa. 46:1. This is the life of faith, and the Christian's warfare; he hath present help every day, against present daily evil. Help will never come too late to those who by faith look and wait for it. David speaking of the Church's safety says, 'God is in the midst of her; she shall not be moved; God shall help her and that right early.' Help may seem to us to be delayed, but it will surely come, 'right early,' in sufficient time to bring us effectual deliverance. It will be when it comes, a *morning* help also. The Lord will act vigorously, as a man goes to his work in the morning with alacrity, with fresh spirits and renewed strength; and having the day before him, we may well expect something from him before night. So the Lord works for his people; he appears for their relief in good time, and carries on his work with effectual vigour, till the whole is finished.

With future evils we have nothing to do; we have no more to do with the evils of *tomorrow*, than with the evils that will be a thousand years hence. Our danger always is from *present* evil. Against this the Lord is a present help, bringing us deliverance 'right early.' May my trust be only in him! It will be a help manifest and evident to all, 'right early,' or in the face of the morning, as in Hebrew, clear and evident to all, that God may be glorified thereby. Our safety and his glory always go together, and he will bring help and deliverance in due time to secure our safety, and in that moment also which will show forth his glory most conspicuously – 'in the face of the morning' – or of the sun. So was the deliverance of the Israelites at the Red Sea; timely help was administered to deliver them from their pursuing enemies, and at that moment of time, which served mostly to show forth the glory of God's power, faithfullness, and goodness towards his people: in the *face* of the morning, he caused the sea to return to his strength.

Let us have a regard to God's glory as well as our own safety, and be contented to wait patiently for deliverance, till 'his hour is come, when the Father shall be glorified.' Christ's mother was in *haste* to have a speedy supply of wine; but she fixed the time too soon; 'mine hour is not yet come,' saith Christ. He meant to grant her request, and give them a supply; but much depended upon the time *when* this supply was granted, and the miracle was wrought, to carry full conviction into the hearts of all present, of his divine mission, authority, and power. For their good therefore he would reprove his mother, and wait till the hour was come, which would at the same time bring them *timely* supply, and show forth his glory more illustriously. Thus the Lord often deals with his people. They must wait patiently and quietly for his salvation, till his hour is come to glorify himself; but he will never forget their *safety*, though he principally respects his own glory. His hour will never come too late, but always in *due* time, Four thousand years passed before the long expected hour came, when the seed of the woman was to bruise the serpent's head; but in the fullness of time God sent forth his son, made of a woman, in full time to save his people, to bruise the serpent's head, and to glorify himself. He came right early, in the face of the morning; his salvation was prepared or effected before the face of all people; he came forth in the morning, strong and vigorous for work, he travelled in the greatness of his strength, till the work, great and arduous, was all finished. Let us wait for him he will come and will not tarry.

10

The Gift and Objects of God's Love

Nov. 1, 1782.

A DISCOVERY and a belief of God's love to us, when sinners, rebels and traitors, only can produce love in our hearts to him. But the belief in this love of God to us in all its freeness, fullness, immensity, and eternity, worketh by love to him with invincible strength, and with unwearied diligence in God's service. And as the effect is always proportioned to its cause, so the clearer our comprehension of, and the more firm our belief is in God's love towards us, the more ardent will be our love to him, and the more active our diligence in his service. Here is the mystery as well as the difficulty of the faith that worketh by love; for mysterious indeed it is to all but those who thus live, and even they know but little of it.

Nothing can conduce more to strengthen our faith in the free love of God, than an enlarged knowledge of the dignity and the glory of the person of Christ: for by this we know the love of God, in that he gave his Son to die for us. The greatness of the gift which love hath bestowed, proves the greatness of the love itself; and as we increase in the knowledge of the gift, so also shall we grow in the knowledge of the love that bestowed it, 'So God loved the world that he gave his only-begotten Son.' If you would know his love, consider his gift; for his love is as great as his gift. And it will heighten both, if we consider the objects of this love, on whom this gift was bestowed: a world of sinners, yet in their sins, and in the very height of their enmity against God.

Let us then 'behold what manner of love the Father hath bestowed upon us,' by viewing attentively the objects and the gift of his love. O! the height and depth of that love that comprehends two such extremes! What can be conceived more distant from, or more unsuitable to, each other! But behold, divine love brings them both together, and gives the Son of God to man in the extreme of his guilt and misery. Here is love, free and great indeed! The Son of God – who can conceive his dignity and glory! Yet so great is God's love. Man – who can comprehend the guilt, baseness, and deformity he hath brought upon himself, and also the dishonour he hath brought upon God by sinning! Yet so deep is God's love. What shall we say to these things, but believe and adore them, and in dust and ashes, with overwhelming gratitude confess, 'so would God have it.'

And what effect will the belief of this love of God as manifested in Christ, have upon our souls? The Apostle in the following words tells us, 'we all beholding as in a glass the glory of the Lord, are changed into the same image from glory to glory!' What this glass is, he tells us a little afterwards: 'God who commanded light to shine out of darkness, hath shined into our hearts, to give the knowledge of the glory of God in the face of Jesus Christ.' Christ in his person and office is the glass which represents with such transforming efficacy the glory of God to us; and when we see his glory in this glass, we are transformed into the same image. In this glass the scattered rays of divine goodness and love are, as it were, brought into a focus; they shine, they burn, and inflame the heart held before it. Conviction overpowers unbelief, goodness overcomes unworthiness, and love subdues enmity. When in this glass we behold the divine glory, we are efficaciously changed into the *same* image. That love, that goodness, that mercy and condescension which we see so gloriously manifested in Christ, produce, when viewed in him by faith, corresponding effects upon the believer. He loves God and man, does good, shows mercy, and walks humbly. He is cast into the mould of these divine truths and is formed and fashioned according to them. The freeness and greatness of God's love to him when an enemy, sweetly constrains him to love his enemies, to do good to the unworthy, to be in his own eyes less than the least, and to be in reality the servant of all. As Christ is the only glass which thus efficaciously represents to us the glory of God's love, mercy, and condescension, so also in proportion as we view them in this glass, is their transforming efficacy on the soul.

Hence then we see the necessity of making *Christ* our '*all* in *all.*' Would we then be holy, be changed into the divine image; would we love God, love man, show mercy, do good, forgive enemies, we must turn our eyes to this glass, and therein view the divine image, and the effect will be infallibly produced. And in proportion to the clearness and steadiness with which we view and believe God's free love, grace and mercy in Christ, so also will be the degree of that change into the divine image produced upon the soul. And consequently a defect here as to the cause, will also produce a proportional defect as to the consequence. Divine truths must be seen in *the light of God's Spirit,* as they are revealed in holy Scriptures, without anything added to them, to cloud their lustre and glory, or taken from them, to diminish their excellence. But our souls must view them by faith, just as they are in the divine light, or they will lose greatly their efficacy, and have little or no effect upon the soul. If a believer looks within and examines narrowly, he cannot but find daily this truth abundantly proved to him, that is, that as he believes in God's love, grace and mercy to him a guilty and depraved sinner, so do all the graces of the Spirit grow and thrive, or decay and wither. May the Lord keep the eye of faith strong, and give us divine light, to look, with more open face, and with more steadiness on the face of Christ: the glass in which the divine image is to be seen and viewed by us sinners.

11

The Sin of Grieving the Spirit

Nov. 23, 1782.

Lesser sins, habitually indulged in the heart and mind by believers, are doubtless much more grievous and provoking in the sight of God, than any great fall through the strength of some sudden temptation, as there is more deliberate wilfullness in the one, than in the other; and also more of the Spirit's convictions, against which it must be committed. The Spirit's office is to convince of sin, as well as to comfort our souls by taking of the things of Jesus and showing them unto us. Repeated indulgence, though it be only in the heart, of the same sin, after repeated convictions by the Spirit, of its sinfullness and guilt, and of our danger through it, exceedingly grieves the Spirit and provokes God to wrath. This will effectually cause God to withdraw himself from us. He may not do it all at once. He will first *hide* himself, and give less manifest and less frequent tokens of his presence. He will convince the soul of its sin and show its danger; and it may be, at intervals, give it some token also of his love and favour. But if all will not prevail with us to reclaim us and bring us to forsake and abhor the cursed thing, if we still keep it and indulge it, the Spirit will not always strive. It is much if bitter experience will not teach us how great is the sin of grieving him, who is the Comforter, sent by the united love of the Father and the Son, to sanctify and gladden the hearts of his people. He who at first is only grieved, may by our continuance and obstinacy in those ways by which he is grieved, at last be *vexed*, as he was by the Israelites of old, by their repeated rebellion against him, Isa. 63:10. The same love which influences the Father in sending his Son to die for sinners, for enemies and traitors, influences him to send the Holy Spirit to dwell in hearts so polluted and depraved. And the same love which inclined the

Son to come to die for us, when we were yet sinners, and ungodly enemies, inclines the Spirit also to come to those who are froward, perverse and unthankful, whom he knows will grieve, vex, and provoke him. In his love and tenderness doth he continue to do us good, bearing with our continual provocations.

As Christ loved us and gave himself for us; so also the Spirit influenced by love equally great, free, and eternal, comes to accomplish the necessary work of grace and holiness *in us*. Christ had his great undertaking much at heart, and how was he straitened until it was finished! From eternity his delight was with the sons of men, and in time it was his meat and drink to do the will of him that sent him. For the joy that was set before him in the salvation of his people, he endured the cross and despised the shame he had to pass through. In the same manner hath the Spirit also the work assigned to him, and willingly undertaken by him, infinitely at heart. To promote comfort, holiness, and joy, in the hearts of God's people, is his great business and delight. And with what infinite patience, condescension and love doth he carry it on! We know but little of his condescension and grace because we are so ignorant of the various workings of inward corruptions, by which his great work is continually opposed and obstructed. But when every secret thing is laid open to full view, and we see with divine light how we have resisted the Spirit in his gracious dealings with us, the love of the Spirit will no less overwhelm our souls with astonishment than the love of the Father and of the Son.

The Spirit hath our comfort and happiness, our complete holiness and glory, so much at heart, that anything that is a signal obstruction to the progress of this work at any time, is said to *grieve* him. We are not grieved by anything that befalls a person for whom we have no concern or regard; but in proportion to our love, is our grief for any one in misery. Others may provoke us to indignation; but there is no grief where there is no love. So it is with the Spirit of God. He is so concerned for those to whom he is engaged by his love as a comforter, that he is said to be *grieved* with *their* sins, when he is not so with the sins of others.

Nothing grieves us more in any one whom we love than unkindness and ungrateful returns for our love, especially after repeated forgiveness and forbearance. So it is also with respect to the Spirit of God. He is a Spirit of love, and all his actings towards us and in us, are the fruits of his love; all the joys and consolations we are partakers of in this world, arise from a sense of the love of God, given to us by the Spirit. 'He sheds abroad the love of God in our hearts.' He expects and requires returns of love and delight in obedience from us; and when he is disappointed, when we take little or no notice of his kindness and love, and care not to make suitable returns by showing forth in holy walk and conversation the fruits of the Spirit, and it may be by careless neglect, fall into those things and those courses which he abhors – he cannot pass by unnoticed the unkindness and ingratitude therein expressed, but it grieves and vexes him to the heart.

We are therefore to beware, above all things, of a barren, unfruitful profession of religion, and of defiling by secret indulgences the habitation of the Holy Ghost. 'If any one defiles the temple of God, him will God destroy,' 1 Cor. 3:17. How should the thought of defiling his temple and grieving the Comforter, fill our hearts with deep humility and godly sorrow! How unworthy a conduct, to grieve him, who comes for the very end and purpose of giving us consolation and joy! In infinite love and kindness he hath condescended to be our Comforter. This comfort he bestoweth willingly, freely, and powerfully. Nor is there the least hope, peace or joy to be obtained, but what he works and bestows; nor any relief in trouble, nor refreshment in perplexities, but what he gives freely. And shall we, who have tasted that the Lord is gracious, by our negligence, sin, and folly, grieve *him* who is thus graciously engaged to give *us* joy? Grieve him, without whom we cannot live – cannot think a good thought, nor breathe one good desire! Grieve him whose presence is heaven in the soul, and whose absence brings a hell of corruptions, darkness, and misery! Is it possible that we should make such base returns for such love, and be such enemies to ourselves! Ah! Alas; what a creature is man! In what dust and ashes ought the best of us to lie down! Shall we not take notice of his love and kindness? Shall we not thankfully receive all our comforts from his hands, and see his love and grace in every refreshing thought put into our minds? Yea, shall we not carefully watch and promote all his motions within, and cheerfully comply with them, however self-denying and contrary to flesh and blood?

When he convinces of sin, let us set our hearts mightily against sin. And when he speaks comfort, let us hear him as the Lord our Comforter, making known the infinite love of the Father and the grace of the Son to us. When we have no comfort, but walk in darkness and have no light, let us honour him by looking to and waiting upon him only for our light in darkness, and joy in trouble. And what and when he gives, let us readily receive. Above all things we have need to pray to God that he 'take not his Holy Spirit from us.'

12

THE INFINITE GREATNESS OF THE SON OF GOD

Nov. 30, 1782.

No words perhaps in the whole Scripture set forth the dignity and glory of the person of Christ more emphatically and expressively than the following: 'No man knoweth the Son but the Father.' Or as it is in the original, 'no *one*,' 'οὐδείς,' 'knoweth the Son but the Father.' It is not sufficient to say that he is far above all principalities and powers, infinitely above all created beings, but he is so great, and so infinite in his nature, and in the glory of his person, that none but the Father, who is an infinite Being, can know him. The imagination of a creature cannot even reach him. The distance is so great, and the glory so far beyond all comprehension, that the mind of the highest angelic being is overwhelmed with the vastness of the idea. Saints in heaven, and believers on earth, know him to be a sufficient Saviour for them: and this is a great deal; but what they know of him falls infinitely short of what he is. The Apostle saith, 'He is able to do for them exceeding abundantly above all they are able to ask or think.'

The divine mind only can comprehend the divine nature. A creature is known by a creature of the same order and the same nature with himself. Man knows human nature; for 'as in water face answereth to face, so does the heart of man to man.' An angel knows angelic nature; and so on to the highest orders of beings in the universe. But none except the Father knoweth the Son; therefore he must be far above all others excepting the Father. And in the same manner as the Father knoweth the Son, the Son also knoweth the Father. Therefore their minds and their natures must be equal and the same.

This gives us the largest possible idea of divine knowledge. It takes in and comprehends the divine nature in all its infinity of perfections and glory. So also nothing greater can be said of the divine nature, than that an infinite mind can know or comprehend it. Nothing greater can ever be said or conceived of the Father's knowledge, than that he knoweth the Son, nor anything more extensive and unbounded of the Son's knowledge, than that he perfectly knows the Father.

'The Father knoweth the Son.' When he entrusted him with the salvation of his people and sent him into the world to accomplish the arduous work, he knew into whose hands he had committed it, and was under no apprehension about the issue. He saw him with infinite delight entering the list with Satan; and he was not fearful of his veracity being sullied, when he said, 'The seed of the woman *shall* bruise the serpent's head.' He foresaw him travelling in the greatness of his strength; spoiling principalities and powers, and triumphing over them openly. He laid our help upon one whom he knew was mighty to save. He laid on him the iniquities of us all, well knowing that the Lamb of God would be able to take away the sins of the world. He knew his capacity to govern the universe, and to protect and save his people: therefore he hath committed all power and authority into his hands, yea, he hath committed also all judgement unto the Son. He knows thoroughly the infinite greatness of his love to his people, and that what his power is sufficient for, *that* his love will forever engage him to do for them. He knows that this love is as eternal, free, and unchangeable, as it is intensely great, and therefore will with infinite delight love those given him of the Father unto the end, however many their provocations, and however great their unworthiness – and that he will never leave them nor forsake them.

We know a little of this love from the fruits and effects of it towards us: but *our* minds are infinitely too narrow to take in its vastness, but are at once overwhelmed with its greatness. It is like looking on the midday sun in a clear summer's day. Our weak eyes are dazzled with its splendour, and unable to look on any longer. But the Father who possesses the same love, both in degree and duration, comprehends the love of the Son in all its immeasurable height and depth, length and breadth. O! With what infinite delight and complacency do the divine persons contemplate the workings of each other's heart and mind towards redeemed sinners here on earth! As the persons are distinct, so also are the workings of their minds distinct; but as their essence is the same, so also is their love, grace, and mercy, one and the same. We can only stand on the shore of the vast ocean of love, which inclined the Son to do so much for us, who are so unworthy: but the Father knows it, and comprehends it perfectly.

The Father knows also the infinite merit of his sufferings, and comprehends the full sufficiency of his satisfaction. All we know of his merits is, that they made a full and sufficient satisfaction for sin, and that more could not be required than what he was able to pay. Being an infinite person, he was able to answer infinite demands. But when we talk of infinite demands and infinite satisfaction, we understand but imperfectly the meaning of the words we use. Faith rests more upon the testimony of the Father as to the sufficiency of Christ's sufferings to make full atonement for sin, than upon any knowledge we have of it. But 'the Father knoweth the Son' – he fully comprehends the value of his merits, and therefore he is infinitely well pleased with him with respect to his people. 'Behold my servant whom I uphold, mine elect in whom my soul delighteth.'

The justice of God delighteth infinitely more in the satisfaction which Christ hath made for sin, than in the obedience of men and angels united. We distrust him and are afraid to rely upon his merits only for our salvation, because of our ignorance of the value of the satisfaction he hath made. But the Father knoweth it fully, is well pleased, and delighteth in it. From heaven he beareth witness that life eternal is to be obtained in his Son, by those who are most guilty and unworthy, 1 John 5:7. He is not fearful of resting the whole of the salvation of his people upon his Son's merits. All the attributes of God harmoniously agree in him, and unitedly advance the salvation of those who believe on him, and rejoice with infinite satisfaction on the glory brought to God in the highest, and on the peace shed at the same time on earth, by the merits of his all-sufficient atonement.

To comprehend the infinite value of his merits, neither men nor angels shall be able, to all eternity; but let us endeavour to believe what we cannot comprehend. The Father knows it fully; and the testimony of the Father in its behalf should outweigh everything else, and be a stronger recommendation to us, than the united voices of all creation. By believing the Father's testimony, our joy may be as full and our comfort as great, as if we were able to comprehend its whole wondrous extent. For in believing we rely on the testimony of one who cannot lie, and who cannot be mistaken, because of his perfect knowledge of the Son. With what joy then should we read the testimony of the Father from heaven: 'This is my beloved Son in whom I am well pleased.'

In short, such a Saviour hath the love of God provided for us – a Saviour so infinitely great and all-sufficient, whose merits are of such inestimable value, whose faithfullness is so inviolable, whose love, grace, and mercy are so great, so unsearchable and eternal, and his power so immense, that none but the Father fully knows him.

And as the Father knows the Son, the Son also knows the Father. This, if possible, adds to his dignity and glory, and shows forth the infinite comprehension of his divine mind. It would be blasphemy to say so of any creature whatsoever. No creatures know anything of the divine nature, but as it has pleased God to make himself known to them by some manifestation or revelation. But the Son is intimately acquainted with the Father, comprehends all the adorable excellences of the divine nature, and understands fully his love and good-will towards sinners. He knows the Father with the same perfect knowledge with which he knows himself. Each of the Divine persons is an express image of the other. They possess all the same perfections in an equal degree; the same Divine nature being common to them all; its properties are the same, and its workings are the same. Their knowledge, wisdom, and their power are the same, and always exerted at the same time. Their love, mercy, and patience are the same, equally great and astonishing in them all, and manifested to the same objects. In every view they are each one the image of the other, though the *Son only is expressly* so called in Scripture, because he only is the image of the Father to *us*, and in and through him we know all we can know of the divine nature. We see the glory of God only in the face of Jesus Christ. Were he not a divine person, of equal nature, dignity, and glory, with the Father, he could in no sense be his express image, nor could he be so called. He could not represent *him* unto us. For though a creature were as exalted as can be imagined or God could create, yet he must fall infinitely short of the divine excellences, and could not possibly give a just representation of them to us. But Christ is the '*express image* of his person.' He possesses the same identical nature and properties; and therefore is in every respect qualified to represent him to us. Consequently we are said to 'see the glory of God in the face of Jesus Christ.'

What a wonderful mystery of wisdom and contrivance is expressed in the constitution of Christ's person! He knows the Father in the same manner as he knows himself; his mind being infinitely large, takes in an infinite object in all its perfections. But the wonder is, the manner how he is become the image of the Father to us, giving us a full and exact representation of the divine nature, bringing it down, as it were, level to our capacities, without diminishing anything of its excellence and glory. He is become 'God *with us*,' at the same time that he continues what he was from all eternity; yet he is the image of God *to us*, and God *with us*. He reveals the *Father to us*. Others have given the world a revelation *from* God, but none revealeth the Father but the Son. In him we see the Father's excellence and glory fully expressed. 'He that hath seen *me*,' saith Christ, 'hath seen the Father.' The attributes and properties of the divine nature are made fully known to us in the Son; and in seeing his glory we see the glory of the whole Trinity.

13

ON WALKING WITH GOD

Dec. 21, 1782.

THERE may be *life*, where there is little or no strength. However, in that case, there can be no *walking*. To walk, especially to walk *usefully*, so as to answer some end or purpose, there must be health and vigour of body; the different parts of the body must be perfect and sound. A person that has strength, yet if he be lame or maimed, if his head be giddy, or his lungs unsound, or if he be altogether too corpulent in either of these cases he is altogether unfit for walking. And so it is in a spiritual sense.

But oftentimes there is a great deal more strength than is exercised. However, this inactivity is the most effectual way to lose what strength we have, to fill the body with humours, and is the certain parent of innumerable disorders. From some professors' conduct one would be induced to imagine, that they think to grow in grace and to go to heaven, merely by hearing, reading, and talking, without any endeavour to live to God in any sense. But such miserably deceive themselves; 'we are created unto good works, that we should *walk* in them.' The slothful and unprofitable will be cast into outward darkness, as well as the unbelievers. But a faithful servant, with a ready mind, waits upon God to know his will and execute his commands – and his obedience is like that of a dutiful child to an indulgent father, whose heart rejoices and exults in *his* service whom he *fondly loves*.

A traveller hath a *way* to walk in. He doth not walk at a random, without knowing where he is, and whether the path he is in leads to the place he is going to. A person may exert himself much and walk hard, yet if he takes no care to be in the *right way*, he may, after all his labour and pain, be as far from the end of his journey as the first moment he set out from home. So also spiritually, there is a way, in which if we are not found, it is impossible to walk with God, or to arrive at the rest that remaineth for the people of God. This way is Christ. 'I am the way,' saith he, 'the truth and the life.' The way that God appointed the children of men to walk in at the beginning, was the path of innocence and perfect holiness, according to the covenant of works. But by sin we have erred and strayed from this way, so that no one can find it any more. But God out of infinite love hath found out another, a new and a living way, *through* which we may have access *to* him, and *in* which we may walk *with* him. The other is old and out of date, but Christ hath consecrated a *new* way which can never wax old, never can be rendered impassable, and out of which we cannot err. Isa. 35:8. The other is now *dead*, and those who attempt to find it and walk in it, are going down into the chambers of death. But this is a *living* way, is not within the dominion of the king of terrors; it *gives life* to those who walk in it, defends them on the right hand and on the left, keeps them in peace and safety, and fills them with comfort and joy: so that they 'walk without being weary, and run without being faint.'

Christ is the mediator of all communication between us and God: all influences of grace, love, and mercy from God to us, are through him only; and all returns of faith, love, and obedience, from us to him, must be made the same way. God is in Christ reconciling the world unto himself; and when *we* are *in* him also, then, and not till then, are we reconciled *to* him, and walk *with* him, in communion and love. But when we are *in* him, then are we *with* God, 'who will bring the blind by a way that they know not, and lead them in paths that they have not known; who will make darkness light before them, and crooked things straight.' Isa. 42:16. Till we are brought this way, there will be forever an impassable gulf fixed between us and God, we being on one side, and he on the other. But the moment we are *in* Christ, the new and living way, we are *with* God; and in proportion as we *abide in* Christ, and walk confidently *in* him, we are also enjoying communion and fellowship with the Father.

But where there is life, strength and activity for walking, and a way to walk in, before we can walk comfortably with another in this way, there must yet be *agreement*, acquaintance, and confidence; there must be the same end in view and the same design in hand. 'Can two walk together, except they be agreed?' If they walk the same road, yet they will not, they cannot, walk *together*, except they be agreed, and on peaceable and friendly terms. So God and man must be agreed, before they can have communion and walk together. Since sin hath taken place, God and man are at the greatest possible distance. God declares wrath against us, and we are full of enmity against him. God reveals himself as infinitely provoked by our sins, and therefore preparing wrath against the day of wrath, when we and he are to meet in judgement. Our carnal minds also are enmity against him, and we manifest by our continual and universal rebellion, that we neither are, nor will, nor can be subject to him. We are darkness, and he is light. We are dead, and he is life. We are sinful, defiled, and abominable, but he is glorious in holiness. And what communion or agreement can there be between beings so opposite and contrary? None. God and we must be at an infinite distance, till he is reconciled, and we are changed. By Christ the new and living way, both these things are effected. He is our peace, making reconciliation for our sins by the sacrifice of himself, and also slaying the enmity in his own body on the cross. Eph. 2:14-16.

He removes the cause of God's wrath against us, and plucks up the root of our enmity against him, which is *sin*. So that now God is in Christ, reconciling the world unto himself: he is himself reconciled, and by the ministry of the Spirit he is slaying the enmity in us, that we may be reconciled too. In Christ, therefore, heaven and earth, sinner and God meet together and are reconciled. God declares, 'Fury is not in me,' and we are brought with delight and love inexpressible, to call him, 'Abba Father!' There is now harmony and agreement, love and delight; from heaven is proclaimed, 'peace on earth and good will towards men; and on earth glory to God in the highest,' is sounded with the voice of gratitude and love!

God is now perfectly reconciled to his people, and in proportion as the enmity is gradually destroyed *in them*, is their communion in walking *with* him. There are no means more effectual to destroy this enmity in us and bring us to him in love, than a firm belief of his reconciliation to us in Christ. This persuasion sweetly disarms the soul, softens the heart, brings down its pride with deep contrition of heart to 'walk humbly with God.' In the face of Jesus Christ alone can we see God reconciled to us. Therefore in him only can we walk in peace and communion with him.

There may be no enmity, and at the same time no communion between two persons. They may be strangers, without any intimacy or *acquaintance*, and therefore can have no fellowship together. And so in a spiritual sense, the natural enmity may be in some degree destroyed, and yet we may be without sufficient knowledge of God, and experimental acquaintance with him, to walk with him daily in communion and love. As a belief in him as reconciled to us in Christ is the most effectual means to destroy the natural enmity of our hearts against him; so also an increasing knowledge of his love, grace, and mercy, in all their freeness, eternity, and immensity, only can engage our hearts to him, and make his company above all things desirable and his presence delightful. Without this spiritual acquaintance with him, a sense of sin and guilt will drive us from him as from an infinite enemy, almighty to revenge. We cannot walk with him in love and confidence, till we know how *his heart* is disposed towards us, till we are convinced that it contains grace and mercy more immense than our sin and guilt, and love infinitely surpassing our unworthiness.

Walking with God implies a great degree of *confidence* in him as well as love towards him: confidence in him from an intimate acquaintance with the disposition of his heart and mind towards us. This knowledge of himself, God gives in us Christ, 'in whom we have boldness and access with confidence by the faith of him,' Eph. 3:12. In giving his Son he hath given such a demonstration of his love and goodwill, as far exceeds our faculties to comprehend. But we cannot take in this light, for darkness comprehendeth it not, till he has given us 'an understanding to know him that is true,' 1 John 5:20. Our understanding must be enlightened, and our minds enlarged to comprehend with all saints the height, and depth, the length and breadth of his love. A superficial, notional or mere head-knowledge will not answer the purpose; but 'he who commanded light to shine out of darkness, must shine *in our hearts* to give us the knowledge of the glory of God in the face of Jesus Christ.'

In proportion as the knowledge of the glory of God in the face of Jesus Christ shines *in our hearts*, so will our confidence and delight in him increase; and we shall cleave to him with full purpose of heart: cleave to him as our only refuge and solace, as our wisdom to direct us, and our strength to help us in every time of need. Thus those who walk *with* him, also lean upon him, as their only strength and support, their very present help in trouble; follow him as their guide every step of the road: so that without him they have neither strength nor knowledge to proceed one step forward. He is *their* God, *on* whom and *to* whom they live. They have his glory in view in all their motions, and they look to him as their *all in all*. They do not walk in the same way at a distance from him; one time running before him, and at another time lingering behind, but they walk *with* him, in closeness of union and nearness of communion. 'They ascend out of the wilderness, *leaning* upon their beloved.' Many may and do observe great strictness and severity of manners, who are at the same time far from God. They may make a great show of humility, but at the same time never walk humbly *with* God.

It is to be observed also that those who are *with* God, are *walking* with him – not sitting still, and continuing in the same place and station, but proceeding forward, growing and thriving in the divine life. When we make no progress, we may be well assured that God and we have not much intercourse with each other; for we are never *with* him, without receiving something from him. Those who are with him he daily feeds with the bread of life, renewing their strength with new communications of grace. He draws them after him with the cords of love, and never leaves nor forsakes them. He bears them up in his arms, and carries them in his bosom, as a nursing father, when they are faint and feeble. Thus those who are *with* him, are still proceeding forward, with patience and perseverance, running the race that is set before them.

14

God Our Light

March 8, 1783.

We are commanded 'to let our light so shine before men that they may see our good works and glorify our Father which is in heaven.' But how can we who are darkness, let our light shine? Darkness may as well and as soon shine with the light of the sun, as we shine by any light in ourselves. But it must be *our* light: 'let *your* light so shine before men.' Doubtless, therefore, as we have it not, we must receive it from God, and be made light in the Lord, before our light can shine. Can the moon shine when the sun shines not upon it? No more can we, except the sun of righteousness shines upon our souls. Why does not the earth shine at midnight? Is it not because the face of the earth is turned away from the sun? So also when our eyes are turned away from divine light, we can no longer shine. It is a beautiful image to set forth evangelical obedience as distinguished from everything else. All besides is darkness, however fair its appearance, but what comes directly from Christ. And so long as we receive from him, so long our light shines, and no longer. All the good works of a believer are the effects of an enlightened understanding, and of his seeing the glory of the Lord in the face of Jesus Christ. He must first be made light in the Lord; and as divine light shines upon our minds, showing us the things of the Father and the Son, and revealing to us those things which eye hath not seen, nor ear heard, neither have entered into the heart of man to conceive. In proportion to the revelation we have of these things by the light of the Spirit, so will our light shine before men, and our good works will be seen. Others may show the appearance of good works, but there will be no *light* in them, nor will our Father, who is in heaven, be glorified by them. The light which seems to be in all others, is in reality darkness itself: and their aim and intention is generally not to glorify God but themselves. But when we live in the light of God's countenance, and walk in the light, and in inward communion with God, then we are desirous that our light may shine, and that our Father, not ourselves, may be glorified.

God is light: God the Father is the original fountain and source of light. He is altogether light, and in him is no darkness at all. God the Son is also light; that light which shineth in darkness; that true light, which lighteth every man that cometh into the world. He, as a mediator, is to *us* as the sun in the firmament, giving us light. God is light, but this light cannot shine in darkness, but through the Redeemer, who is the Sun of Righteousness, the centre in which all divine light meets, and where only our weak and dark sight can behold it. If we turn not our eyes to Christ the light of the world, we can see nothing but darkness, and we shall still continue to be darkness. God himself is darkness and terror to our souls, till we see him in Christ reconciling the world unto himself. When in Christ we see him, then we know him, and not till then. And every true believer has this light *in* himself. He shines in his own light, not originally his own but derived to him continually from Christ. Others may have knowledge of divine things, when at the same time they have no light *in* them, but their foolish hearts are still darkened. But in a believer, who walks with God, *universal* light prevails: 'the *whole* body is *full* of light, having no part dark.'

The shining of our light wholly depends upon this; for if the whole body be not full of light, it cannot radiate from us, but in proportion to the darkness within, so will the darkness be without. When we have a clear view of divine things, and daily walk in the light, our light will shine and our Father will be glorified. There will be a life and savour in our conversation which nothing else can give. Others may be as regular, moral, and decent, may know and be able to converse about divine things, but if the whole inward man is not full of light, and we see not the glory of God in the face of Jesus Christ, all life and savour will be wholly wanting. Whatever is a fruit of the Spirit, hath a flavour and relish in it, which nothing else, however similar to it, can ever have. A little of this divine light in the heart, will shine brighter, and glorify God more, than all conceivable natural and acquired abilities. We may have a light, and this light may also shine; yet if it doth not *so* shine that our Father may be glorified, it is not a *true* light, but a false light, which glorifies ourselves and leads to outward darkness, where no gleam of light comes through eternal ages.

O blessed Father, shine thou in thy Son upon my soul, and then shall my light shine before men! I will not be ashamed of it; but it shall shine before those who hate it, and who hate me on account of it. There is a difficulty: the devil and our own deceitful hearts would persuade us to hide this light, because it maketh us so singular in a world of darkness, and stirs up the enmity and hatred of those who love darkness rather than light. But the Lord giveth us light that it might shine before men: all men, good and bad. O Lord! Brighten it, and cause me to own it freely, boldly, and thankfully. Are we not arrayed in thy livery, when we shine with light? And shall I be ashamed of what is thy glory? Nay, Lord, sooner reduce me into nothing, or strike me ten thousand fathoms under the earth! O help me to shine to thy glory; it is the very summit of my wishes, my highest glory and ambition! Cause my light to shine, though I be but a star, a very small star. But O! How wilt thou be glorified, when such a dark clod of earth shall shine forever, as the sun in the firmament! One poor believer thus shining, will reflect thy glories more than all the visible luminaries in this visible creation. O what eternal monuments of grace to thy glory, will each of them be! May nothing besides thy glory attract my heart anymore.

15

Natural and Renewed Conscience

Jan. 20, 1784.

THERE is a great difference between the workings of the natural conscience of an unconverted person, in the opposition it makes to sin, and the resistance which the renewed principle in a believer, makes to sin. The former may be, and *is* consistent with, the prevailing love of sin; but the latter is not, nor can possibly be. A man may *delight* in sin, at the same time his conscience every day accuses him of it. But where a principle of grace is implanted, *there* the inward man delights in the law of God, Rom. 7. Conscience only bears witness against it and condemns it as being wrong; but grace *hates* it, as being filthy and abominable. One malefactor may accuse another and condemn evil in him, and at the same time be very far from hating evil itself, Rom. 2:1. But none but a good man can hate evil itself. Conscience accuses the evil doer, and its accusations, strengthened by the law and its curses, the justice of God and its threatenings, may be dreadful and intolerable; but after all it will do no more. But the spirit *lusteth* against the flesh, draws effectually the soul and its faculties in opposition to it, wars, resists, opposes with unwearied, steadiness and perseverance, in every faculty, in all the workings of the soul, in all its thoughts and desires, in every imagination of the thought of the heart. The spirit *lusteth* against the flesh, meets it with courage, and entrenches (ἀντίκειται) itself against it.

Conscience acts as a judge, but grace acts as an irreconcilable adversary, that with implacable hatred pursues his enemy to death. Conscience *condemns*, but grace *slays* sin. Conscience bears witness against the dominion of sin; but grace dethrones it, crucifies and mortifies it, and will, in spite of all opposition, reign and rule alone. Conscience teaches us that sin *is there*, and that it is evil; but grace 'teaches us to *deny* ungodliness, and worldly lusts, and to live soberly, righteously, and godly.'

Grace will not suffer the soul to 'mind the things of the flesh,' but 'the things of the Spirit'; it carries the affections upward, and 'fixes them on things above'; it leads the soul in direct opposition to the flesh, and enables it, strengthened by Christ, 'to walk not after the flesh but after the spirit.' Grace acts universally in all the faculties of the soul, at all times and in everything, opposing evil where ever it is found. 'When I would do good,' saith the Apostle, 'evil is present with me'; – not when I would do this or that thing; no, but when I would do *good*: anything that is agreeable to the mind and will of God – evil is present to oppose and resist me. So is it also with grace, when a true Christian would do evil, grace is *present* with him. The flesh lusteth against the Spirit in every faculty and every part, and so doth the spirit against the flesh. They are two opposite principles in the same part, constantly acting in perfect contrariety to each other, like heat and cold in the same water. In the same mind there is the wisdom of the flesh and the wisdom of the spirit; in the same will, delight in the law of God, and lusting after sin; in the same affections, love of God and love of the world, fear of God and fear of man; each everywhere opposing the other and lusting against it.

Sin and grace in the same faculty, resemble Esau and Jacob in the same womb, dwelling and struggling together. It is not so in unrenewed persons. They are different faculties, and not different *principles* which work in them, as when the will and the affections are bent on sin on the one hand, and the understanding and conscience on the other condemning it. Between these faculties there is no enmity: for the same principle rules in all. But grace and sin in the same faculty, are as opposite as light and darkness. Grace has a respect to, and loves all God's commandments; it acts universally, continually, uniformly, and perseveringly in conformity to the will of God: and by it the soul 'bent towards God, lusteth after spiritual things, and is universally inclined to all duties of holiness.' 'It is a well of water springing up unto everlasting life.' Exactly in the same manner sin acts in opposition to it. But the power of godliness will in the end prevail; it will not cease in its operation till every thought is brought into captivity to the obedience of Christ.

But this will not be the case where natural conscience only operates, though strengthened by the law of God to condemn sin. Sin will prevail there in the end. The water may be dammed, but it is not *dried* up; and it will break forth with more force than ever, bearing down all resistance before it, at one time or other. Sin is not awed by its accusations against it. Conscience may condemn it, yet sin will do as it listeth. In hell, where conscience will be most faithful and clamorous, sin will rage more furiously than ever. But it is not sufficient for grace to accuse and condemn sin, it will have its death. And however weak it may be in itself, God's love, power, and faithfullness, are engaged to give it the victory. 'God is faithful, who has promised,' is its continual strength. Little David, relying upon his promises, will face a great Goliath. What reason have I to praise the Lord, that his strength hath hitherto been made perfect in my weakness, and that grace is still alive! Those blessed truths, which gave it being, still feed and nourish it. The gospel is the power of God unto salvation to everyone that believeth. It is so daily in an increasing degree, till they are saved from all enemies, and safe in glory.

I have good reason to hope that it is not conscience unrenewed, nor the law, that has carried me on hitherto in opposition to sin – no; but grace that feeds on the glorious truths of the gospel, and derives from them continual strength. This conscience does not. It has in itself strength enough to condemn, and it can do no more. But grace is continually looking to Christ for strength to continue the warfare; feeds on the gospel of Christ, lives upon it, and finds it to be bread that endureth to *everlasting* life, feeding, comforting, and strengthening the soul; that is, till he enters the joy of his Lord. This bread fed him in times past, it still endures; he finds it still the same, as nourishing as ever; and feeding upon it, he goes on from strength to strength. For ten years I have, I hope, lived upon it. And blessed be the Lord, it still endures and still nourishes. May the Lord help me to labour more after it, and feed more upon it. How infinite the mercy that I ever tasted that the Lord is gracious! O that I could feed more upon his grace, and live more to his glory.

16

Conformity to the Image of God

Feb. 7, 1784.

Do I find Christ indeed precious to me? Do I long to know more of him, and be filled more with his fullness? The Apostle says to the Galatians, that 'he travailed for them in birth again until Christ was formed in them,' Gal. 4:19. This was the end he had in view in all his labours and prayers. He was not willing they should continue all their days babes, but grow into manhood by having Christ formed in them, and living in them. He says of himself that 'Christ lived in him.' He lived, though in a lesser degree, as Christ would have lived, had he been then on earth, being influenced and strengthened in all his actions by the same Spirit, which dwelt above measure in Christ. If Christ 'lived in him,' Christ was also *formed* in him, both as to his knowledge of him, and conformity to him.

The image of God in which man was at first created, consisted, as the Apostle says, 'in knowledge, righteousness, and true holiness.' The *mind* of man took the *exact* form of God, according to its capacity; it had a just and true knowledge and comprehension of him, according to the discovery which he had made to him of himself. His love of God, trust in him, and obedience to him, were also proportioned to his clear and just knowledge of him. His moral character bore some distant resemblance to that of God himself. The law of God, which is a transcript of the divine mind, was in all its purity and extent written on his heart. Thus the true *form* or image of God was on his *mind* and on his *heart*. By the fall he lost from his mind the true knowledge of God; and from his heart, the inward conformity to God's moral character. The image of Satan succeeded in its stead, and he became 'earthly, sensual, and devilish.' 'Ungodliness and worldly lusts' now constitute the very essence of his character. He is conformed to the world in *heart* and *mind*, Rom. 12:2. He is 'fashioned' according to the lusts in the *heart*, which he follows through the darkness of his *mind*, 1 Peter 1:14. His mind sees no glory in God, and consequently *loves* him not. Satan shows to his mind, as he did to Christ, 'the kingdoms of the world and the *glory* of them.' Earthly things appear as the great image did to Nebuchadnezzar, full of glory, 'a great image whose brightness was excellent.' When things appear thus glorious to the mind the heart runs after them, and the heart cleaves and is conformed to them. But to destroy the work of the devil, was the purpose of Christ's manifestation. And by the preaching of the gospel the work of the devil within us is destroyed, the heart is changed, and Christ is formed in us.

Christ is the *express image* of the Father. He is so originally, as the Son of God. His person is exactly the same in all the divine perfections, common to each of the divine persons. He is ἐν μορφῇ Θεοῦ, in the form of God, essentially considered, from all eternity. And he is as God-man and Mediator, εἰκὼν τοῦ Θεοῦ, his image or exact representation to us. In the face or person of Christ alone, can we see the glory of God and of all the divine perfections. When we see his glory as held forth in the gospel, we see the glory and image of God. And by this believing sight, we are changed into the same image, we are 'renewed *after* the *image of him* that created us'; and thus it is that Christ is formed in us. He is first formed in our minds, and we have a just and exact knowledge of him, before we are transformed in our hearts. The gospel is the glass that exactly represents him, and holds him forth to a guilty and ruined world. Those who have their understandings *renewed* and *enlightened* by the Holy Spirit, see his glory in this glass, Eph. 1:18. And those who thus see him, are changed in heart, into the *same* image. In the law we see the glory of God, but it is a dead letter, and will not change a sinful heart. As a *covenant*, though not as a rule, the law is even now formed in us. But thus formed, it exceedingly hinders, instead of promoting, this change. As a covenant it must be destroyed before Christ can be formed in us.

But the gospel *represents* the glory of God *in Christ*, not absolute; and this representation is 'spirit and life,' – the power of God unto salvation to everyone that believeth. Here we see the glory of Christ's person, 'as the only-begotten of the Father,' equal with the Father in glory, eternity, and in all the divine perfections. The gospel sets him forth in ineffable majesty, and with all possible, and more than all conceivable glory. In the constitution of his person as God-man, we have the fullest manifestation of divine wisdom and power that ever was, or, it may be, ever will be given. Those in whom Christ is formed, have a glorious and just view by faith of his person as thus constituted, and in him they see the *Father* also. They have a just and exact knowledge also of the offices which he, as a Saviour, has taken upon him, in order to redeem and deliver his people. They see him 'made of God unto them, wisdom, righteousness, sanctification, and redemption,' 1 Cor. 1:30. And they see his *person* in each of his offices, adding worth, dignity, and efficacy, to all he has undertaken for sinners. When as a Priest he atones for sin, they see him making such satisfaction as is worthy the infinite God to give, and worthy to be accepted by the injured majesty of heaven. It is with unspeakable satisfaction they see God glorified, and man saved, in a way which in its contrivance and execution will forever be the astonishment of the whole universe. As a Prophet and a King, also, they see him acting suitably to the dignity of his person; teaching and ruling his people in a manner becoming himself, and in such a manner as none but himself could do. This believing view of his glorious person in all his offices, adding efficacy to all his undertakings, is the very joy, and comfort, and support of their souls! In his amazing condescension, in undertaking these offices, they see the fullest manifestation of divine love and mercy that their hearts can desire, or God can give.

When Christ is thus in the glory of his person and offices, *formed* in their minds, their hearts cannot be uninfluenced. No; but the glorious sight is most powerful and efficacious in proportion to its clearness, distinctness, and extensiveness. 'We are changed into the same image.' The gospel thus believed is the power of God unto salvation to everyone that believeth. The glory of Christ as seen in the gospel only can produce this effect. Consideration of other truths, separately viewed, may restrain sin and keep it under; but this only mortifies sin, renews the soul, and continually strengthens and enlivens all the graces of the Spirit within. The same means which produce the change at first, must carry it on. It is impossible to grow in grace, without growing in the true knowledge of Jesus Christ. Christ in the glory of his person, must be kept in the enlightened mind, and all divine truths must be seen *in* and *through* him; otherwise they will lose all their efficacy and power. Blessed are those who keep their eyes fixed on the sun of righteousness! They cannot but feel its enlivening warmth and quickening power. It is not sufficient that we have seen his glory formerly, a month or a year ago; no, but he must be, in the glory of his person and offices, always immediately present with us. He is the only *food* of the new man, the only object faith deals with, and is conversant about. We must still continually behold his glory *dwelling* among us, full of grace and truth, that we may *receive* out of his fullness.

If he is *formed* in us, he continually abides with us wherever we are. He is in us as a Spirit of divine consolation, under the continual sense of sin in its guilt and power. He is in us and with us, as full of grace and truth. Blessed commodities! Most needed! He is come from heaven *full* of them, that by distributing he might fill his people with them! When they are thus filled with his fullness, he is formed in their minds and dwells there; and he will and must be formed in the heart also: the heart will be changed into the same image. His character is stamped upon them; his spirit dwells in them; and those graces which so eminently adorned his whole life, appear in a smaller degree in all his believing people. The *same mind* is produced in them, which was also in Christ Jesus, Phil. 2:5. They are *humble* as he was, seeking not glory to themselves, but to God; seeking not their own but the good of others. They who come to Christ aright and to the saving of their souls, 'learn of him who is meek and lowly.' And though to the flesh it is a hard lesson, yet that grace which bringeth salvation, effectually and daily teaches them. Though perhaps they may have made no great advancement, yet are they willing, yea, desirous, of still continuing in this school, under the teaching of grace. They love and admire his conduct, and endeavour faithfully to tread in his steps. Under all their sufferings they keep him in view, and consider him daily, who endured such contradiction of sinners against himself, that their patience may be strengthened, that they faint not in their minds. Heb. 12:2, 3.

He is formed in them also as to his *love to God and man*. His love to God and his glory, to man and his salvation, which brought him down from heaven, carried him through all he did and suffered here on earth. What an amazing instance of both do we see here! How perfectly was the divine law written on his heart! Nothing could destroy, nothing could abate his love! He loved God and his glory, not only when he smiled upon him, but also under his frowns, under his greatest wrath and displeasure. He loved man when an enemy, when yet wallowing in sin and every abomination; yea, when hated and persecuted by him even to death. Whilst his bowels were melted with the wrath of God, his heart was still burning with unabating fervour of love; whilst sinners revile, he prays for them. O what a pattern is here! Lord, help me to contemplate by faith the glory of his person and character, till I am changed into the same image! What glory did his divine conduct reflect upon the holy and righteous God! With what conviction did he prove God's right to punish sin in the face of the whole universe! And what an idea must it give to all created beings, of God's amiableness and loveliness, to see Christ love him, even while he feels his wrath! Were we to contrast this conduct with that of the devils and the followers of antichrist, all of whom justly suffer for their own sins, how amazing the difference! Rev. 16:21. The one gives glory to God by loving him still with the whole heart, because he always in everything deserves it – deserves to be loved, when he punishes, as well as when he pardons sin. The other, under the just judgement of God, blasphemes the divine Majesty, and is filled with the bitterest enmity against him. Here is as much difference as there is between heaven and hell, between God and the devil. In this respect Christ is also formed in every one of his people: grace is the same in them as in him, though in a lower degree. Their love to God and man is of the *same nature* according to its degree. They cannot but love him, because in the face of Christ, they have seen his glory, even under his rod, when he chastises them, yea, when he hides his face from them. As *he* did, so do *they* also love their enemies, and pray for them who despitefully use them. It is only in proportion as they do so, that Christ is *formed* in them, and that the law of God is written on their hearts. What the law requires we see in the life exemplified in Christ. He yielded perfectly all that love to God and man which it demanded: and in what he paid, we see what the law in its spirituality demanded: universal, perfect love, on all occasions, in all circumstances whatever. It admits of no excuse for the breach of it. Under the wrath of God, and the enmity and hatred of man, it still, with equal force, demands love, because God at all times and in everything, *equally* deserves it.

O how comfortable to ourselves, how honourable to God, to have Christ thus formed in us, and the law thus written in our hearts! How much have I still to learn here! How far am I from the perfect pattern before me! But through mercy I can say, I *desire* to be as he is. I see such glory in God, in *all* he does, as infinitely deserves to be thus loved. He is glorious in punishing sin, as well as in pardoning it; glorious and amiable when he afflicts, as well as when he comforts. Never did God appear more glorious than when he was taking vengeance on the Son of his love for our sins. Justice and mercy, holiness and love shone with united and transcendent splendour. The same glory shines in punishing sin in hell, which appeared in punishing it on the cross, though not in the same degree. And does not God deserve to be loved for the one as well as for the other? Does he not *deserve* to be loved wherever and in whatever manner he causes his glory to appear? I believe we may safely conclude that that man never had true grace, who does not love God for punishing sin, as well as for pardoning it: for chastening as well as for comforting. Nor doth he in truth, and in a gospel sense, ever love his brother, who does not also love his enemy. Thus love showed itself in Christ, and if Christ is formed in us, the same love must operate in the same manner, according to its degree, in us. May this truth sink deep into my heart, and deeply humble me before God for my want of conformity to Christ! And let me always remember to cast away all excuses for want of conformity to God's law, however plausible they may appear, and artfully dressed by the devil or the flesh. How necessary to look unto Jesus by faith, that Christ may be formed in my heart!

17

Realizing Faith

Feb. 12, 1784.

We are told that 'this is the victory which overcometh the world, even our faith.' What is this faith that so powerfully operates? It is 'believing that Jesus is the Son of God': believing God's record or testimony, 'that he hath given to us eternal life, and that this life is in his Son.' If we believe that Jesus is the Son of God, we have the knowledge of the glory of God in the face of his Son; we see his glory as the only-begotten of the Father, and see the glory of the Father in the Son. A sight more divine and glorious cannot be conceived! Believing Jesus, the *Saviour*, to be the Son of God, we see a salvation accomplished by him worthy of the Son of God: a work worthy of such a glorious person to perform, and to own as his own work, in which he and the Father are to be forever glorified; and as such worthy to be offered to ruined sinners, and worthy of all acceptation by them.

In this case the soul, who believes the Saviour to be the Son of God, and that his salvation is worthy of him, cannot but rest all its hopes, in the face of all possible misery, on this wonderful salvation, believing the testimony of God that there is life for the chief of sinners. In his Son, the soul cannot but seek life on the testimony of God; and in seeking it he finds it. This life is *eternal*, is hid with Christ in God, derived continually from the Son of God to the soul. Faith thus acting on Christ, becomes to the soul, 'the substance of things hoped for, and the evidence of things not seen.' A new world opens to the view, a world infinitely glorious, eternal, permanent. There the believer sees glory, riches, honour, joy, pleasure, of far different nature from everything here on earth; surpassing them in glory as much as the sun does the glow-worm. 'Life and immortality are brought to light by the gospel,' and faith is the substance and evidence of them to the soul. Believing Jesus to be the Son of God, he sees eternal life in him for the guilty and undeserving. In proportion as he sees the glory of Christ as the Son of God, he sees eternal life in him; he has the evidence, clear demonstration, and a glorious view of unseen things in him. Believing Jesus to be the Son of God, he has an evidence of God's good will to sinners, he sees a just and sufficient title to all he hopes for, and he sees power sufficient to put him in possession of what he is thus entitled to.

When faith in Jesus as the Son of God, is thus to the soul the substance and the evidence of eternal things, the soul is at once disengaged from earthly things. They have no glory in them by reason of the glory that excelleth; no comfort, no joy, by reason of those things that are infinitely better. It is in vain the devil showeth the kingdoms of the world and the glory of them; for here are things showed by the Spirit of God, the glory of which it never entered into the heart of man to conceive. And now they are revealed, they are so glorious and so great, that the soul in its present state, cannot fully comprehend them. In this view the soul disdains to make any comparisons between them. Even the reproach of Christ is esteemed greater and richer than the treasures of this world, Heb. 11:26. To suffer shame for the sake of Christ is reckoned the greatest honour, Acts 5:41. When life and eternal life in Christ and immortality are brought to light, and the eye of faith gives 'the evidence' of them to the soul, as these are the most glorious and desirable things in the soul's view, so also the way of the cross, reproach, shame, and contempt, the loss of character and goods, surpass in glory and comfort all the ways of the children of this world in all their pomp and grandeur. The glory of the one is divine, holy, and eternal; the glory of the other, earthly, sensual, and perishing. While we look thus through 'Jesus the Son of God,' 'at the things which are not seen,' 'we overcome the world,' that is, we practically prefer the things which are not seen and eternal, to the things which are seen and temporal.

But that the soul may be thus continually influenced, unseen things must be kept in their glory habitually in view, and also our title to them founded on Jesus the Son of God. As our faith is weak or strong, in the same proportion is our deadness to and victory over the world. Faith, giving the evidence of things not seen, works by love to them, draws out the soul after them, rejoices in hope of the glory of God, and glories in tribulation on the way to possess them. But what adds strength to our faith in these things is, believing Jesus, the Saviour, to be the Son of God, and that eternal life is in this Son of God for us. Till we see eternal life in this Son, we can never see our title to it: in every other view the way to obtain it is forever closed against us. Sin and guilt, wrath and vengeance, face us everywhere, but as we look to Jesus the Son of God. *In him* are all things treasured up for us; pardon, grace, and glory, are all *in him* for sinners. No one spiritual blessing will or can be obtained, but in and *through him*. It is not an easy thing for a convinced sinner, to whom sin appears sin, to believe his title to these blessings, even to the smallest of them: nor can he ever believe his title to them, till he believes Jesus to be the Son of God, and sees eternal life in him for sinners.

Thus Jesus is the centre on whom the soul should rest; and he is, and must be, the life and strength of every grace. But if we believe not in him, we are slaves to the world, to our lusts, to the fear and praise of men, and seek our happiness in earthly things. If we believe not in Jesus, we look only, like the beasts that perish, on the things which are seen, and are 'strangers from the covenant of promise, having no hope, and without God in the world.' How amazing the difference between a believer and an unbeliever! How far different their views, their hopes, joys, and fears. He that believeth on the Son *hath everlasting life*, and he that believeth not the Son, *shall not see life.*

18

The Ground of Faith – The Testimony of God

March 4, 1784.

Faith in its very nature, and also in all its operations, is amazingly mysterious and glorious. But what is faith? To believe, is to give credit to a thing as true upon the *testimony of another*. And divine faith is to believe divine testimony respecting spiritual and divine things. Thus we believe truths which we could not discover, and cannot comprehend, only because God, who we are assured perfectly knows them and cannot lie, testifies that they are so. And this is, in some respect, the *same* as if we did know them; for God is the most competent judge of what he bears testimony to, and we may, with perfect safety, depend upon his veracity. When we believe the record he has given of his Son, we believe him to be infinitely more glorious than we can comprehend, because the Father, who knows him to perfection, says so. The Father, who knows him, and will not deceive us, commands us to believe in him, for our whole eternal salvation, in the face of all our misery; and therefore we *may* as confidently do it, and rest our guilty souls upon him, as if we had the same knowledge of him which the Father hath. 'God gave his Son, that whosoever believeth on him, should not perish, but have everlasting life.' We are afraid to believe in him; but the Father is not afraid to entrust the salvation of his people into his hands, nor afraid that by the perishing of any who believe in him, his testimony respecting him should be ever called in question. No, the Father knows the Son, and knows what he says, when he declares 'that whosoever *believeth* in him *shall not perish*.'

In proportion as we believe this his testimony, is our confidence in relying on Christ, and our assurance of salvation from all our misery. And, by believing the testimony of the Father respecting the Son, and acting accordingly towards the Son, we honour both the Father and the Son, and 'he that honoureth not thus the Son, honoureth not the Father which has sent him,' John 5:23. The Father hath honoured the Son, by giving him a divine commission, and qualifying him amply for the great work of saving sinners. We honour both the Father who sent, and the Son who is sent, when we receive him as thus commissioned and qualified. The Father testified in various ways, that he was well pleased with the undertaking when he came into the world; and by receiving him at last into glory, and sending the Holy Ghost, he has sufficiently testified that he is well pleased with the work as accomplished. We, on our part, honour the Father and the Son, when *we approve* of the wonderful plan of salvation, and glory in it as accomplished by the Son.

The Father has testified twice from heaven publicly, that Jesus was his beloved Son, and that he was well pleased in him; and he commands us to hear him as one divinely commissioned to reveal his whole mind and purpose. We cannot but approve of the whole plan, and also the glorious execution of it, when we believe God's testimony respecting both: for he only is competent to judge of them. The Father has testified, that Jesus is his only-begotten Son, and that in him he is well pleased, and that he hath glorified his name, and will glorify it again, in his Son. Believing this testimony, we believe that the honour taken from the divine majesty by sin, is again restored by Christ. We are not competent to judge of Jesus or of his work; but the Father is fully competent; therefore his testimony is more to us respecting both, than if we had without it the comprehension and the knowledge of the highest angel in heaven.

There is something divine in faith, which takes its flight far beyond the comprehension of all creatures, and is familiarly conversant with objects incomprehensible and infinitely great, with heights and depths of mysteries, which leave the capacities of creatures far behind. What, though the mind cannot see them, cannot comprehend them, and cannot fathom them, yet God can, and *we* have *his* testimony, which is more than all to give the soul satisfaction. Faith fathoms not with its own, but with *God's* plummet, which can reach the greatest depths; it measures infinite objects with infinite comprehension, and removes infinite obstacles with infinite power. 'God hath said,' is to faith, more than if it saw all that the angels in heaven see. And, perhaps, the record which God hath given to his church here on earth, respecting divine things, makes known to the inhabitants of heaven things which otherwise they could not know.

Faith will support itself on divine testimony, as on an eternal foundation, against sin, death, and hell. Divine testimony concerning the unknown merits of Christ's sufferings, will support the soul under all possible guilt. God knows both, and has testified that the latter is surpassed and removed eternally by the former. God knows, and has testified to us, of all the evil that is in sin; it is far beyond our comprehension. But he who knew what sin was, and also the ability of Christ to bear it, laid upon him the iniquity of us all, and made him sin for us, that we might be made the righteousness of God in him. 'So that where sin hath abounded, *grace* did much more *abound*.' He who knew the law in all its divine extent, testifies that Christ hath magnified the law and made it honourable. By his obedience unto death, he hath showed to the whole universe that it is eternally unchangeable, because it is holy, just, and good. In short, faith in contemplating all these divine objects, leaves our own understanding and our own reason behind here on earth, and takes God's understanding and reason as manifested in the word for its guide in their stead. The carnal mind will forever cavil at this, and say, 'How can these things be?' It may cavil, but no satisfaction can ever be given to the carnal mind; blind it is, and blind it will continue. But they who have the spiritual mind, understand and practically know what it is to take God's wisdom and knowledge instead of their own. There is no possibility of making a blind man see, but by giving him eyes; no more can a man discern spiritual things spiritually without a *spiritual mind*: without it we can as soon see without eyes,

But 'he that believeth the record which God hath given of his Son, hath the witness in himself.' Such amazing effects accompany this belief as nothing else could produce. He *finds* that eternal life which God hath testified to be in his Son. He hath this life in him as a witness in himself, corresponding to the record of God in his word. He hath within himself the substance of things hoped for, and the evidence of things not seen. The testimony of God is the *only foundation* of faith; but this witness within himself, proves that he indeed believes this record, and that his faith is genuine. If he find that life in Christ which God testifies to be in him, then hath he come to Christ indeed upon the belief of the record. To pretend to believe the record of God, and at the same time not to find that life in Christ which he testifies of, is in the highest degree to dishonour both the Father and the Son: it is making God a liar, and supposing that Christ died in vain. No, there is life eternal in Christ, and whoever in believing God's testimony respecting it, comes to Christ, is sure to find it. And in proportion to the strength of our faith in God's testimony, are our applications to Christ, and our consequent experience of life from him.

We must carefully observe that God's testimony is to be believed, *because* it is *his* testimony, and for no other reason. The bare testimony of God, faith sets in opposition to all reasonings to the contrary from sin and its guilt, the power of unbelief, and the accusations of Satan. If we endeavour to support it by anything else, we weaken its power and destroy its effects. And this record must be delivered just as it is, namely, 'that God hath given us eternal life, and that this life is in his Son.' The gift is great and the objects are unworthy; but great as it is, it is *freely given*; God will have it so, and we must not dispute. But 'this gift is in his Son.' To him we must apply for it, and from him we must receive it. All communication between God and sinners, is through him, and those who are not willing to receive all from and through Christ, will never receive one spiritual blessing. 'This life is in his Son,' that is, all the blessings of the covenant of grace, pardon, grace and glory, joy, peace, strength, wisdom, and comfort, all are treasured up in Christ, 'who dwells among us full of grace and truth,' for 'it pleased the Father,' in consequence of his obedience unto death, 'that in him should all fullness dwell.'

The Spirit of God only can enable us to believe God's testimony, and make us willing to receive life in the way which God hath appointed to bestow it. He who hath found no difficulty in this, is hitherto an utter stranger to that living faith which worketh by love and overcometh the world. The whole body of sin, the life of which is unbelief and pride, will forever oppose it. By nature we are as devoid of belief in God as we are full of enmity against him; nor do we seek for that life which he gives in his Son. How then can we believe his testimony without a supernatural change? How can we apply for this life till we see our need of and are in love with it? The carnal mind is enmity against God. It neither loves God, nor anything of a spiritual nature which he has to give, nor does it believe *anything* that *he says*. The carnal mind will have nothing to do with God in *any sense*. It believes the devil, and loves the world more than God. The spiritual mind on the contrary deals with God only. Its essence is belief in God, love, and submission to him. God's word is sufficient to rest eternal concerns upon: nay, it will have nothing else. The spiritual mind is exactly the opposite of the carnal mind in everything. But to enable it to act with efficacy in opposition to the whole body of sin, he who gave faith, or this believing nature, must enable it to believe in every particular case against all opposition.

In *all its operations* faith is mysterious and glorious. It acts something like God himself. It acts in opposition to difficulties with the same ease as when there are none. God's word removes everything. It is delightfully and familiarly conversant with things above reason, infinities and incomprehensibilities. It wants nothing but God and his word: passes by everything else, and deals with them only. And being of such a nature, so divine and supernatural, it cannot but overcome all things in the end. With infinite ease, the Lord at the beginning by his mere word, produced everything from nothing. But faith engages the same God and the same word in all its operations, and therefore it must prevail and overcome: yea, be more than a conqueror. Amen.

19

The Object of Faith – The Promises of God

March 19, 1784

FAITH hath for its ground and foundation the word of God, the record, or testimony of God, the word of truth – words implying the same thing. The testimony of God is about Christ, his person, and undertaking; the promises of God are made to us *in* him: they are all, *in* him, yea and amen. The promises are made to us in Christ on condition that he would fulfil all righteousness, 'finish transgression, make an end of sin, make reconciliation for iniquity, and bring in everlasting righteousness!' God's record or testimony respects the accomplishment of this work by Christ: that he hath by his obedience unto death finished transgression, and made an end of sin, and that consequently the Father is well pleased, hath given us eternal life in his Son, and that all the promises, however great, are '*in* him yea and amen' to us who believe, though ever so guilty and undeserving.

The promises of God in Christ, are therefore the object of faith. And the record or testimony of God *respecting* Christ and his work is the ground and foundation of it. The faith of the Old Testament saints had nothing but the promises only, both for its foundation and object: promises of Christ and all good things in him. But now Christ is come we have the testimony of the Father that Jesus is the Christ, the Son of God; that the Father is well pleased, and that eternal life is given us in his Son. In believing this record of God, we believe also on that ground in the person and work of Christ; and believe all the promises in him, in consequence of his work and sufferings, to be 'yea and amen.' In Christ all the promises were made, and in him, as our surety, they have all been already accomplished. The promises suppose man in a state of sin and misery, and they come to his relief while in that state. When taken collectively they are a sure revelation of that mysterious scheme

The Object of Faith – The Promises of God

planned in eternity for man's recovery; and the testimony of God respects the sufficiency of Christ and of that salvation which is in him in every point according to our necessities. Now if the promises come to the relief of man in a state of misery, it is evident:

1. That none but convinced and humbled sinners will or can believe them. None of us can truly believe any one promise, but when we are actually humbled by the Holy Ghost. And in proportion as our conviction of our sin and misery is carried on in the soul, do we see the necessity of the promises; value them as exceedingly great and precious; and believe them to the saving of our souls.

2. That as the promises are all made to us in Christ, if we truly believe them, we must believe them all to be, 'yea and amen' to us in him. Faith sees all the promises centring in Christ, just as God has made them to us in him. And as we grow in the knowledge of Christ, his person, and work, shall we grow also in the belief of the promises made to us in him.

3. That the promises made in Christ for the relief of man in misery, when believed, bring him that relief which is promised. They are 'yea and amen' to us, and are actually fulfilled in some degree, *when* we believe. 'He that believeth, hath the witness (record), in himself' – the thing promised is possessed. They are already fulfilled in Christ our surety. He hath removed the curse, vanquished all our enemies, is risen from the dead, and ascended into glory. When we believe, they are also, in more or less degree, fulfilled to us *in him*; we are made partakers of his conquests.

As the promises respect man's deliverance from sin and all its consequences, when the promises are believed, we experience at least, the first fruits of that deliverance from sin and all its consequences. And the enjoyment of the blessing promised, is the best and only sure proof that our faith is of the right sort.

On the testimony of God, therefore, we believe all the promises in Christ, in the face of all our misery, to be to us 'yea and amen.' No one knows the difficulty of thus believing, but those who actually believe; but *they* do know how hard it is to believe that a holy God could make any promises to sinners of so much guilt. And as it was impossible for God to make any promises to a rebellious world, consistently with the glory of his holiness, justice, and truth in the government of the universe, but in Christ: so is it also impossible for them to believe the promises, but in Christ. *Christ is the centre in which God's promises and their faith meet.*

When we have obtained this faith, having fast hold of it, there will always be the same difficulty 'to hold *fast* the profession of our faith without wavering.' It *is*, or *ought* to be, our daily care and work. Satan will seek to sift us as wheat; and it is our duty to pray, as well as our comfort to think that Christ hath prayed and still doth pray, 'that our *faith fail not.*' The Apostle brings God's faithfullness to his promises as a strong motive to hold fast our faith in his promises: 'He is faithful that hath promised,' Heb. 10:23. He is faithful: he is still of the same mind as when he made the promises; and he is abundantly able to fulfil them all in their utmost extent. 'He is of *one* mind, and who can turn him? And what his soul desireth that he doeth.' He is of one mind: there is not in him as in us, succession of ideas, purposes and designs. He is of one mind from eternity to eternity. His love, and the motive which influenced him in making the promises, is always one and the same: 'known unto God are *all* his works from the beginning.' His vast mind takes in the end from the beginning. No unforeseen subsequent event can happen to induce him to alter his purpose: for all things which *to us*, are past, present, and future, are in one view present to him, naked and open to his infinite understanding. Wherefore he having weighed all things relating to his promises in the covenant of grace, and adjusted every circumstance with the exactest wisdom, the covenant itself cannot but be everlasting, and all the promises of it unchangeable. To suspect his faithfullness, and to waver in our faith in his promises, would be to call his infinite knowledge and wisdom in question, and to suppose him such a one as ourselves.

The promises are the issue and dictates of his love. Divine love is the main spring in the whole scheme of redemption. This suggested the mysterious plan, and works with equal ardour in every transaction towards its final accomplishment. The covenant of grace is

The Object of Faith – The Promises of God

a dispensation of mere grace, wholly founded in love. *Divine love speaks every promise, and every promise is an express manifestation of it.* But divine love is not a sudden, unsteady passion, but a fixed determination, issuing out of his divine and unchangeable goodness. The same love which suggested the plan of redemption and spake all the promises, still operates as powerfully as ever in the divine mind; it is neither abated, nor changed. 'I am the Lord,' saith he, 'I change not; therefore ye sons of Jacob are not consumed.' David encourages his soul in this view of the unchangeableness of God's love, and pleads against the unbelief of his heart in God's promises: 'Will the Lord cast off forever, and will he be favourable no more? Is his mercy clean gone forever? Doth his *promise* fail for evermore? Hath he forgotten to be gracious, hath he in anger shut up his tender mercies?' All these things were inconsistent with God's nature, and therefore impossible. And he said, 'this is my infirmity.' I do not judge rightly of God, his nature, love, and faithfullness. The very mention of God's love and mercy confirms his faith in his promises, in his faithfullness in fulfilling them all. As we see that God's knowledge and love are unchangeable, his purpose of course must be unalterable; of which the promises are declarations by which it is made known. 'His purpose *shall* stand.' It will stand because it is his purpose who is unchangeable: the purpose of infinite wisdom, determined in every respect in that very manner, which is most suitable and conducive to his own glory. As what is purposed and determined is the best that could be, God cannot want righteousness and holiness to persevere without wavering in what he hath thus determined. 'There are many devices in man's heart, but the counsel of the Lord *shall stand*' – and it shall stand, because it is the product of the highest wisdom and holiness.

The promises of God are therefore unchangeable, because God is not deficient in wisdom, that he should determine amiss; or in righteousness, that he should repent of what he had determined aright; or in power, that he could not put it into execution. Nay, 'God, willing more abundantly to show unto the heirs of promise the immutability of his counsel, confirmed it by an *oath*.' What more could be done? May not we therefore safely conclude, 'that he is faithful that hath promised?' There is not one promise but hath the wisdom, love, purpose and oath of God for its security. The promises indeed are great, and we are equally unworthy. These two considerations taken together are enough to stagger the strongest faith. But great as the promises are and made to unworthiness in the highest degree: yet still, 'faithful is he that promised.' He stands to all his engagements made to us in Christ, and everlasting love and power are carrying them into execution.

Let us therefore hold fast what is so firm, without wavering. The foundation is good; it cannot fail, but will assuredly support us. May the Lord help me to see the foundation on which the promises stand! And then, though of *little* faith, there will be no cause to fear. The weakest degree of faith hath the fulfilment of all the promises annexed to it as well as the strongest. It is not said, 'He that believeth' with a *strong* faith, but he that believeth, whether his faith be weak or strong, if it be *true* – 'shall be saved.' Every branch in a tree is not equally strong, yet the least twig is united to and supported by the tree, and as really partaker of the sap as the largest branch. If the smallest twig is enabled to hold fast to the tree in the midst of storms, it will grow and thrive as well as the largest. It is believing the faithfullness of God to his promises, that will enable us to hold fast in the midst of tempests without wavering. To hold fast our faith in the promises, without wavering, we have need to be well acquainted with the nature of the promises, not as made to Adam in innocence, but to us sinners, being all 'yea and amen' to us as such, if we believe in Christ, and also with the solid foundation on which they stand, God's faithfullness, which cannot fail or in the least alter. We have need thus to be strong *in* the Lord, that we may be courageous and faithful servants of God. If we live to God, we must live by faith: our life must be continually derived to us by believing the promises. They contain the life of the believer, and all its supports in this world. And as we live on the promises, so are we weak or strong, dead or lively, barren or fruitful, spiritual or sensual, earthly or heavenly.

20

ENMITY AGAINST GOD

March 24, 1784.

THE essence of our nature as corrupted is 'enmity against God.' This carnal mind is enmity against everything in God, and every manifestation which God hath made or ever will make of himself. We *ought* to love God, love everything in God; for everything in him is infinitely *lovely*. We ought to love everything he does or says; and our love towards him should bear some proportion to the glory, clearness, and brightness of the discovery which God, in any way or at any time, makes of himself. But the carnal mind is not subject to the law of God, but acts directly opposite to everything which the law commands. And this enmity shows itself in proportion to the brightness of the manifestation which God makes of himself, the hatred of the light still increasing with its brightness. This explains those passages in Rom. 7 which speak of 'sin being revived by the law,' 'sin, taking occasion by the commandment, working in us all manner of concupiscence.' 'When the law is seen by the light of God's Spirit in its spirituality, as holy, just and good; in its extent, as preaching to the whole man, to his thoughts, words, and actions, and as extending to every sin, and condemning sin universally, and also the person in whom in any degree it is found; this spiritual view, in proportion to its clearness and extent, will set the dormant enmity at work, and cause it to rage. Thus 'working death by that which is good, sin by the commandment will become exceeding sinful.'

This enmity hates everything in the law of God: God's *holiness* in it, forbidding sin; God's justice in it, condemning every sin, and the person also in whom sin is found; God's goodness in it, giving happiness to his creatures in such a way of holiness. God's authority in it, and his government over all his rational creatures, are also resisted and hated by this principle of sin. The law is holy, just, and good, and represents God to us as such, and in the name and with the authority of God it demands love and obedience from us to him, who is infinitely deserving of it, being in the highest degree, 'holy, just and good.' It manifests God to us, and shows what is our consequent duty to him. God is unchangeably what the law represents him; the law, therefore, is unalterable, and our obligations to it are also eternally the same. As God himself, the original, cannot change, the law, the transcript or copy, cannot alter: and whilst God and the law remain the same, our necessary obligations to obedience must remain unalterable. When by the light of God's Spirit we look into the glass of God's law, we must see in it God's holy nature and perfections, our necessary obligation to obedience, our sin, and our doom. It cannot but command that which is holy, just and good, and with equal authority condemn what is *not* holy, just, and good, in all rational creatures. But can corrupt nature which loves what the law condemns and hates what the law commands, bear the sight of these things unmoved, which are so contrary to it? No, sin revives, collects all its strength, works all manner of concupiscence, πᾶσαν ἐριθυμίαν; every lust is called forth to action, all the forces are collected to oppose the threatening enemy, which it so thoroughly hates. Enmity and self-preservation actuate this principle against that which is contrary to it, with such force and power, that this is called *law* also – 'the law of sin in our members'; and with all the enmity, pride, and ungodliness of Satan, it commands and threatens. This is that law which has entered the sinner's heart, and has been *written* there ever since the moral law was obliterated by the fall. As a law it has universal sway and dominion in the sinner's heart, in all its motions and workings. It is said to 'reign unto death,' Rom. 5:21. It acts with authority, though not lawful; with power and efficacy. It hath, as a law, rewards and punishments. The pleasures of sin for a season are its rewards; and the deprivation of all sensual enjoyments with much inconvenience, are its punishments, threatened to all that disobey it.

But 'till the commandment comes,' 'we being without the law,' either in our minds or hearts, '*sin is dead.*' It dwells in the heart, but it is comparatively dead; it does not 'work *all manner of concupiscence,*' it does not 'war against the law of the mind,' because there is no law in the mind to war against; it doth not lust against the spirit, for there is no spirit to oppose it. But when the commandment comes in the demonstration of the Spirit and with power, sin revives; it puts forth enmity, and manifests lusts and concupiscence, before wholly unknown, aiming at the destruction of the law, and the giver of it, which is holy, just, and good; it commands with more authority, works with more energy, and its rewards and punishments are brought forth to view, the one in all its glory to allure, and the other in all its dreadful and black colours to terrify, Matt. 4:8. The law itself which is holy, just and good, cannot be the cause of sin, but sin takes occasion by the law to work all manner of concupiscence. Thus the law revives sin, but slays the sinner; sin revives and he dies. The gospel on the contrary slays sin and revives the sinner; the sinner lives and sin dies. St Paul says, 'the commandment which was ordained unto life, I found to be unto death,' for by it sin is revived, and all his hopes of life by the commandment which was ordained unto life, died forever. In this the sinfullness of sin evidently shows itself; when it 'works *death* by that which is good, it becomes exceeding sinful.' To live in sin whilst ignorant of that which is good, is not so exceedingly sinful: but when that which is good is made known and revealed, and sin still working death even *by* that which is good, by hating it with the most deadly and irreconcilable hatred, lusting against it, warring against it, and working all manner of concupiscence in opposition to it, in this case sin becomes exceedingly sinful.

We see from hence, also, wherein consists the great guilt of the sin of unbelief. The gospel contains the clearest, fullest, and most glorious manifestations God ever made of himself, and of *all* his adorable perfections. Unbelief comprehends in it a thorough hatred to God in the face of all this glorious light. It is the last and final opposition of the sinner's heart to God, in the face of all the divine light which has shed from heaven by the works of creation and providence, by that law which is holy, just, and good, but more especially by the glorious gospel of his Son. It is enmity in the fullest degree against God in all the glory of his awfully lovely perfections, and must bring down vengeance proportioned to the greatness of the guilt. This sin 'works death,' not only by the *law*, but also by the *gospel*, which thus becomes the savour of death unto death.

This natural enmity in the heart does not show itself much, but where there is some knowledge of divine things. We see in the whole conduct of mankind, their sensuality and worldly lusts, the lust of the flesh, the lust of the eye, and the pride of life: the one or the other, or all of them, appear in everything they do. But this enmity shows itself where there is some light from the law or gospel, or both, darting into the mind, and stirring up the whole serpent within. Those who have ever lived in darkness, cannot be said to hate the light, because they never saw it: but where the light shines, and it serves only to make people shut their eyes against it, or flee from it, or act in direct opposition to it, then it may be said that they hate the light, and 'love darkness rather than light.' And where this hatred and enmity increases with the degree of the glory that shines, it not only shows the desperate state of the person, but also, 'the exceeding sinfullness of sin.' The nature of sin is the same in all, but its workings may be more violent in some than in others, from stronger temptations, less preventing grace, or from more opposition to it by a fuller knowledge of those things which are contrary to it, and condemn it, and thereby revive its malignity.

This enmity to that which is good, is that evil in sin, which those who are truly enlightened take most notice of, and which shows them the true nature of sin, and fills them with the greatest grief and sorrow on its account. This is that which St Paul complains of in such expressive terms in Romans 7. It is the opposition which sin makes to the law, which is holy, just, and good, both as outwardly revealed, and inwardly written upon the heart, which is the same; and this it makes from its inconceivable enmity against God. It is this enmity to that which is good, which is the Christian's continual plague. Everywhere and in everything, it lusteth and warreth against all good. In prayer, hearing, reading, and meditating, this enmity is the grief of his heart. In believing, loving, hoping, and obeying, it sets itself, full of enmity, against that which is good, and the practice of it universally. This enmity is, as it were, the active principle in every sin, setting it to work with vigilance, activity, and perseverance. And this is it which the believer principally sets himself against; he hates this enmity, is deeply humbled, grieved, and distressed on its account; and he cannot but groan, being burdened, whilst he carries about him this body of death. When sin, being in any degree mortified by grace, has ceased to act in other ways, that is, in the lust of the flesh, the lust of the eye, and the pride of life, it will still be unceasing in its enmity and operations against all good, cooling or deadening the heart in God's service, indisposing his people for spiritual duties, and intimate communion with him. Whilst it has a being in the soul, it will have this enmity in 'its lusting against the spirit,' and 'warring against the law of the mind,' so that the most lively Christian is in a continual danger of being entangled by it, and becoming dead and formal in religion. It acts universally in the soul in every faculty, and in opposition to every good act of that faculty. Though conquered ever so often, yet whilst it lives, it is restlessly 'warring' with all its remaining power, be it ever so little, against the law of the mind. It is enmity also against everything in God, every attribute and perfection, every promise and every command, law and gospel, mercy as well as justice; in short it is an *universal* opposition in man to *everything* in God, which nothing but divine power can slay and abolish.

Hence we see the necessity of watching, of praying without ceasing; of looking up to God for wisdom and strength to resist, mortify, and crucify the flesh, principally in its enmity against God. From hence also we see the danger of having much and frequent communications with those who are outwardly civil and decent, or have only the *form* of godliness. However free they may be from gross sins and outrageous breach of God's law, yet their whole heart is under the dominion of this enmity; and they think and act, even in their best actions, agreeably to it. Their company is as dangerous, if not much more so, to the life and power of godliness, as the company of those who are openly profane. We find, or may find ourselves in a short time, infected with the same cursed leaven, gradually losing our spiritual mindedness, and a worldly spirit taking possession of us. They think and speak of everything in a carnal worldly spirit; and by conversing much with them we shall soon lose our ground, learn of them, and join with them. Enmity in us savours enmity in them, is encouraged, fed, and strengthened by it. They are to each other as iron sharpening iron. The old latent enmity in us begins to recover its edge and force; and the soul, as to its spirituality and heavenly-mindedness, will be infallibly sorely wounded and hurt by it.

He that is not watchful against the remainder of this enmity, avoiding all occasions of strengthening it, knows not what watchfullness means, experimentally and spiritually; and he who is not deeply humbled under a sense of it, knows not what true repentance means. He who hath seen this enemy as he is, knows how desperate and how dangerous he is, spends much time in searching him out, that he may not be murdered in the dark, is well assured he cannot be too watchful against so watchful and active an enemy, that all means of strengthening cannot be too much avoided, and all means for mortifying him too diligently used. The sense of this enmity fills him with godly sorrow, and keeps him in the dust all his days. He cannot live at large, as many do, in boldness and security, well knowing what a deadly watchful enemy he always carries about him. He cannot indulge, as others do, in carnal joys and pleasures, and in what are called innocent amusements, nor pursue his earthly concerns with too much greediness, knowing that by all these things the old enmity will be fed and nourished, and will gain more strength to war against the soul. If our eyes are not steadily fixed upon this point, if we are not diligently searching into our own hearts to know the enmity and deceit of sin, in all its various ways of working and deceiving, we are in great danger of being found hypocrites in the end, however well pleased we may appear to be with the doctrines of grace.

21

The Leadings of Mercy

June 2, 1784.

MAN truly humbled, is thankful for everything, seeing himself less than the least of God's mercies. In this frame of mind the Psalmist was; he saw everything in general providence, and in God's particular dispensations towards his people, as the effect of that 'mercy which endureth for ever,' Psa. 136. He saw himself wholly unworthy of every blessing: of the heavens above him, of the earth to support him, of the light of the sun by day, or of the moon by night. But that mercy which endureth forever, gave him all these blessings to enjoy. A man of a humble heart is still the same, and sees things in the same light. The Psalmist excites all to praise God; and among other things, for leading his people through the *wilderness*; for his mercy endureth forever; not only for bringing Israel out of Egypt with a strong hand and with a stretched-out arm, and for overthrowing Pharaoh and his host; not only for giving the land of promise in possession, and driving out their enemies before them; but also for leading them *through the wilderness* to this land of promise. The same eternal mercy was evident in the one as well as in the other. Infinite goodness and mercy brought them through the Red Sea to the wilderness, as well as through Jordan to Canaan. The same mercy which will at last give the crown, now lays the rod upon us; and the heavier the cross, the greater the expressions of mercy. This mercy appeared in bringing them *to* the wilderness, supporting, comforting, and leading them *in* it, and in bringing them *out* of it. God knew what was in their hearts, how deeply tainted they were with the idolatries and manners of Egypt, and what relish they had for sensual pleasures. Had God brought them thus into Canaan with their hearts so full of ungodliness and worldly lusts, the new inhabitants of Canaan would have been no better than the old ones. They would have been miserable in their sins, and God would have been forgotten, neglected and dishonoured in the face of the whole universe, by his own peculiar people. It would have been dishonourable to his glorious holiness to bestow such a blessing upon them, except in a way calculated to bring them acquainted with themselves, to make sin bitter and loathsome, and to humble them under a sense of their sins, under the mighty hand of God.

God gives every blessing to his people in a way that manifests his own glory, and effectually promotes holiness in their hearts, Deut. 6. The Israelites having lived in Egypt two hundred and fifteen years, had almost forgotten the true God and the true religion, and were sunk into the same spirit of ungodliness and worldly lusts with the Egyptians. Thus in every way distempered, they needed having all their old notions, tastes and tempers eradicated, and their minds wholly framed anew in order to be fit inhabitants of the holy land. God knew the work that was to be done, that they must, before they entered Canaan, be thoroughly weaned from Egypt: brought to 'cast away the abominations of their eyes, and to forsake the idols of Egypt'; and that they must be brought to know the true God, be made sensible of his infinite abhorrence of their tempers and ways, and have their hearts sensibly broken under a sense of their vileness, and be prepared to understand and to practise whatever he should reveal or command, that they might be an holy people to the Lord, a kingdom of priests and a holy nation, to his praise and glory in the midst of an idolatrous and benighted world. The wilderness was the means which infinite wisdom fixed upon as the best to accomplish this work. Mercy therefore leads them to the wilderness as well as to Canaan, that by the one they might be fitted for the other. It was necessary for *their* good, and for *God's* glory; it was necessary also for the use and instruction of the Church of God in every age. When we view the divine conduct in Egypt, and in the wilderness, we see as it were a most lively picture of the divine nature; and in viewing the conduct of the Israelites from first to last, we see a most lively picture of human nature, acted to the life. God's hatred of sin, and their love of it,

God's patience, and their impatience; God's wisdom, and their folly; God's power, and their weakness; God's right to command, and their obligation to obey; and the great evil of sin: all these are set in the strongest light.

The same mercy which brought them to the wilderness, supported, comforted and led them in it. Divine wisdom and goodness ordered every step, all their goings, and directed and influenced every event and occurrence. They were not brought to the wilderness, and afterwards left to themselves to fight their way through as well as they could; no, *mercy* led them through; it was their companion and guide, their strength and shield. Every particular event was under her influence, was ordered for good to make them more acquainted with God and with themselves, having a tendency to excite their love to one and their hatred to the other. At the Red Sea, they were to appearance full of love to God, and singing his praise; but mercy knew the vile hypocrisy of their hearts, brought them three days afterwards to Marah, where their religious affections being gone, he took occasion to show them the corruptions that lay concealed within their hearts. In short, every subsequent event was so graciously and wisely ordered as to teach them the knowledge of themselves and of God's majesty, holiness and glory, and thus to bring them to hate themselves, and to bring them out of themselves to live by faith on God only. God cannot show mercy but in a way consistent with his own holy nature. Every new trial, therefore, was absolutely necessary; for it was as necessary that they should be made holy, as that they should move forward in order to possess the land of promise. But God does not sanctify his people in a blind way, they know not how; no, but he first of all shows them what is in them; he so orders their circumstances, that they may be means of bringing out one lust after another: and thus he shows them in their true light as exceeding sinful. This sight humbles them; their repentance grows deeper and deeper: they sue for mercy and look for help against their sins. This end is obtained, and they are conquerors. Thus God leads them on in the knowledge of themselves: and as they grow in the knowledge of themselves, they must also grow in the practical knowledge of God, of his patience, mercy and love, of his wisdom and power, of his holiness and goodness.

Mercy thus *leads* them every step, and divine wisdom and power overrule all for good. In every removal, therefore, we ought to look for some signal trial and some signal blessing. Mercy led them to the Red Sea, where they were in great strait; to Marah and Rephidim, where there was no water; to the wilderness of Sin, where they were afraid of perishing with hunger; and to Sinai, where God's awful appearance made them exceedingly quake and tremble. Every step was ordered by the councils of divine mercy; it was necessary and profitable to them. At one time their ungodly and murmuring spirit was discovered; at another, their detestable idolatry; and at another, their inexcusable unbelief. At each time God effectually showed his holy hatred of these abominations, humbled them, and brought them to repentance. Again he went on to try them still more. Seeing more dross in them, he cast them again into the furnace of fiery trials. Every trial brought forth still more dross to view. This increased their repentance, and holy hatred of sin. Holiness is thus effectually promoted, and 'the trial of their faith is much more precious than that of gold that perisheth.'

Mercy also supported and *comforted* them. Their rebellious conduct rendered them in the last degree unworthy of the divine favour, but the mercy, which is as large and free as it is long in duration, bore with them, pardoned abundantly, fed them with manna from heaven and water out of the rock. They lived on mercy all the way. Though by their sins they were continually forfeiting every favour, yet mercy endured, continued still abundant towards them in a way of holiness, correcting and chastising them. Every fresh provocation was a fresh occasion of showing mercy. In the midst of judgement mercy was not forgotten, but powerfully operated in all.

In due time, when they had been sufficiently tried and purified for forty years, he at last brought them out of the wilderness, a holy people, to possess the holy land. The time and manner of their being brought out of it were exactly ordered by divine mercy. Even mercy itself would not bring them out earlier. Though they had been long in the furnace, yet were they not sufficiently purged to be taken out sooner. But now they being a holy people, freed from their Egyptian spirit, zealous for God and his cause, cleaving to him with a steadfast heart, they shall stay no longer in the wilderness. Though there were great obstacles in their way: many great and mighty kings at enmity with them, which must be overcome; a Jordan to be crossed; and their own unbelief, worse than all, to be conquered; yet, in the face and through the midst of all enemies, and innumerable obstacles and perils, and notwithstanding their own inexcusable unbelief, mercy led them through the wilderness, and brought them to the promised land. 'In the world ye shall have tribulation,' saith Christ; be it so; yet he that overcame the world, will keep them in it and bring them out of it at last. 'These are they that *came out* of great tribulation,' will be said of them all at last. They were in it, and they continued long, it may be, in it; but in due time they came *out* of it, like gold purified in the fire. Mercy followed them, mercy supported them, and never left them till they were brought out of great tribulation.

22

The Means of Mortifying Sin

June 15, 1784.

Both the old and the new man are strengthened by having their proper food administered to them; and their strength is impaired when this provision is withheld from them. For this reason we are exhorted by the apostle, not to make provision for the flesh, to fulfil the lusts thereof, that is, not to provide food for its support and gratification, Rom. 13:14. Every lust is strengthened by gratifying it, and weakened by denying it. Hence arises the absolute necessity of self-denial, of denying ourselves in what we naturally long after, or what the Apostle calls 'ungodliness and worldly lusts.' This is what we are, as sinners, composed of: ungodliness and worldly lusts; and in denying these, we deny ourselves. The word, 'denying,' implies that our flesh in its lusts, is forever craving, longing, and soliciting for its gratifications; but we are to make no *provision* for it, but to mortify it by starving it. Whilst the flesh is in us, it will lust, it will seek its own, and either by force or by stratagem, will be endeavouring to obtain what is suitable to its nature; but, saith the Apostle, however it may lust, whatever violence it may use, and however miserable it may make you; yet still, make no provision for it, but go on in mortifying and crucifying it. Earthly things are exactly suited to its taste; it relishes and feeds upon them, forces its way through all difficulties to obtain them. Therefore its lusts are called 'worldly lusts.' Hence arises the danger of enjoying abundance of earthly things. Without great grace and watchfullness they will become provision for the flesh; they will feed, gratify and strengthen it. The cares, riches, and pleasures of this life, whilst they choke the word, feed and pamper the flesh, and are suitable provisions for it.

In order effectually to cut off this provision, the Lord often brings his own people into straits and difficulties in their outward circumstances. He reduces them in the world, it may be; or if they possess the things of the world, he makes them find bitterness in everything they possess, by crosses, trials, and disappointments, that he may keep their hearts single to himself. When at one stroke, it may be, he deprives them suddenly of that, which of all other things is the most useful and valuable thing they have, he is only graciously cutting off what either is or would be provision for the flesh to fulfil the lusts thereof. God has his eye continually upon his people, carefully watches over them, sees the motion of every lust, and knows how effectually to mortify it. And in all his providential dealings, 'the end of the Lord, is very pitiful and of tender mercy'; and when this end is seen, wisdom and goodness will most evidently appear in everything. When this beast within is thus deprived of his prey, is in a starving condition, and yet still denied provision, we may suppose he will rage and miserably torment the soul. There is nothing that makes a creature more fierce and violent than hunger. But here that grace of God which bringeth salvation comes in with present help; and it appears glorious, when notwithstanding the misery of the soul tormented by his lusts, it yet effectually teaches to deny ungodliness and worldly lusts. But we must carefully remember that nothing but the grace of God can thus teach us: 'we mortify the deeds of the body *by the Spirit*.'

There are two sorts of lusts in fallen sinners: fleshly lusts and spiritual lusts, or what the Apostle calls filthiness of the flesh and spirit, and in another place, 'the desires of the flesh and of the mind'; which are the same with ungodliness and worldly lusts. The one is outward, the other inward; the one feeds upon worldly things, the other feeds upon the man himself. Of these spiritual lusts, pride is the foremost, and is the root on which all the rest grow: such as malice, envy, and hatred. This pride inwardly feeds upon something either real or imaginary in ourselves: our parts, our wisdom, our strength, or our goodness. These spiritual lusts are also mortified by making no provision for them. And self-knowledge will at once cut off all provision for feeding these lusts. When once we see our wisdom to be perfect folly, our strength perfect weakness, our own goodness to be perfect evil, and that we are in ourselves at best, earthly, sensual, and devilish, and the children of wrath – when we have this right view of ourselves, pride will be entirely deprived of all his provision; his throne will be demolished, and he will soon lose all his sway.

Man, fallen and estranged from God, lives upon himself and worldly things, independently of the Almighty. He seeks all his comfort and support from this quarter, living to himself and not to God. His whole employment in the world is making provision for the flesh, in one way or another, to fulfil the lusts thereof. But grace, by bringing divine light into the soul, teaches him to deny those things with which he was before gratified, shows ungodliness and worldly lusts in their true light, fills the soul with abhorrence of them and of the provision which supports them, and brings it to gratify different desires, the desires of the Spirit, and to feed upon different food, that is, Christ. Christ is the 'bread of life' on which the new man feeds. He is the provision which God hath made to feed and gratify the appetites of the new man. And there is something in Christ, which, at the same time that it feeds the new man, mortifies the old man of sin. He is poison to sin, whilst he is food to grace. A sight of him by faith bruises the serpent's head and gives the death-wound to sin.

What provision can pride have any more, when we see our own characters in the sufferings of Christ? There we see ourselves to be sinners and rebels against God, helpless and condemned, divine justice having demands upon us which we could not answer, though we should live forever in the bottomless pit. How can we make provision for the flesh any longer, when we see in Christ's sufferings what sin is, how detestable to God, how ruinous to ourselves! 'Our old man is crucified with him, that the body of sin might be destroyed, that henceforth we should not serve sin,' Rom. 6:6, Sin is there set forth to open shame; and the death-blow, as it were, hath been given to the whole of it. When by faith we see Christ dying for sin in our stead, the divine sight weakens every member of the old man; death effectually works in every part of the body of sin. There, in the wonderful transaction of the cross, we behold sin in every respect, and in all its workings, most shameful; and we behold everything contrary to it, shining forth most gloriously. God in his law, government, and all his divine perfections, appears most lovely and most glorious, and sin appears sinful in the very degree that God appears eminent in glory. What means, therefore, can more effectually mortify sin, and more effectually prevent us from making any provision for it? In this amazing scene of humility what can pride have any more to feed upon? In this wonderful instance of love to God and his holy law, to his just government and divine honour, and also of love to man, to sinners, to enemies, what can enmity to God and his law, or hatred to man, have to feed upon? By this astonishing instance of obedience, every nerve of the spirit of disobedience is weakened. In this unexampled instance of poverty, shame and reproach, the love of the world can find nothing to keep life in it. In short, when by faith we see Jesus crucified for sin and in our stead, the whole body of sin in us is crucified with him.

Here also is the food of every grace. The cross is the solid foundation on which divine *faith* stands in the face of sin, death and hell. Here it feeds, here it lives: Christ's satisfaction is everything to grace, and the more it feeds upon that, the more it is continually strengthened. It is the provision which God hath made for it, and the only provision suitable to it, and on which it can feed. Here also *humility, godly sorrow, love to God and man, patience* and *resignation* in the very worst condition, find support: in short, every grace has all its provision here. And the more Christ crucified is in view, the more they *grow and thrive*. Christ is the bread of life, and if he is not fed upon, life cannot be preserved; the *power* of godliness will decay, and our glory will depart from us. By making this provision for the spirit, or rather by feeding on the provision already made, the life of our soul is preserved, God is glorified, and we are comforted. Christ's humility is food for our humility; Christ's love is fuel for ours; Christ's meekness, patience, and perseverance, when he endured such contradiction of sinners against himself, animates, strengthens and supports ours; and his infinite atonement for sin is the constant life and food of faith. To faith 'his flesh is meat indeed, and his blood is drink indeed.' Every step of the way in walking with God we live by faith, and this faith lives upon the Son of God, and upon his flesh and blood. Faith rejects and despises everything else; *it will have none but Christ, and will have nothing with Christ*. It has enough in him; with him it is perfectly satisfied, having in him a foundation to support and proper food to nourish it.

If this be really true, those who are not making daily use of Christ, cannot in truth be mortifying sin, or growing in grace. This object must be kept steadily in view, if we would at all grow and thrive. We may be conversant daily about divine things, we may talk and reason much about them, yet if they are not seen directly in and through Christ, sin will, notwithstanding all, be able to keep up its head. Divine things may not indeed be considered wholly unconnected with Christ; yet if he be not immediate and present in view, and divine things not seen in and through him, the consequence will be, that the form instead of the power of godliness will be attained; sin will thrive within, and every grace will wither and decay, its proper food being withholden from it.

23

The Divine Witnesses

June 26, 1784.

St John mentions, in his first epistle, six witnesses; three in heaven and three on earth, that bear testimony to this truth, that is, 'that God hath given to us eternal life, and this life is in his Son,' 1 John 5:11. These have testified and do still testify, that eternal life is given of God to sinners who believe in his Son. The three first, I apprehend, are not considered as giving testimony by their works, but as with authority pronouncing and publishing from heaven, that there is eternal life for sinners in Christ, so that 'he that hath the Son hath life.' However dead in himself, guilty and accursed, yet if 'he hath the Son he hath life.' To the truth and certainty of this, each of the Divine persons has given an open and public testimony. What foundation is here for faith? Who then dares deny this truth? If God be for us, giving his testimony on our side, who can be against us? Let God be true, and every man and every devil a liar. This truth is recorded in heaven, and solemnly published here on earth by the united voice of the Father, of the Word, and of the Spirit. God would have it known, and would have it believed; and those who believe not God, make him a liar, because they believe not the record that God hath given of his Son, 'He received from God honour and glory, when there came such a voice to him from the excellent glory, This is my beloved Son, in whom I am well pleased.' But when we disbelieve this testimony, we signally dishonour both the Father and the Son. 'Verily, verily, I say unto you,' saith Christ, 'he that believeth on me hath everlasting life,' John 6:47. This is the record of the 'Word,' and he will be answerable for the truth of it.

There are three witnesses mentioned by our Saviour, in John 5:36, 37, the Father, the Son, and the works which the Son did by the Spirit. If they are the same which the Apostle means in both places, the Spirit must be taken in his descent upon Christ, remaining upon him, and working in him and by him. But in whatever manner they have given their testimony, it is certain they have testified to this truth, that there is life for sinners in Christ.

There are three on earth also; not were, but are; and they are to continue to the end of time. The Spirit is promised 'to abide with us forever'; that is, with the Church of God in every age of the world, and with every member of it whilst he is in the world. These witnesses give their testimony to the same most important and precious truth, that there is eternal life for sinners who believe in Christ. Christ is said to come by water and blood, 1 John 5:6, that he might be a perfect and complete Saviour; 'for it became him for whom are all things, and by whom are all things, in bringing many sons unto glory, to make the captain of their salvation perfect through sufferings,' Heb. 2:10. He came through water and blood to bring many sons unto glory. Afflictions and sufferings in the way, however terrible and full in his view, did not deter him from the undertaking; but he came by the water of great afflictions, and the blood of intense sufferings, and thereby was made a perfect Saviour for those many sons who will be brought to glory, and obtain the victory over the world by faith in him. The water and blood by which he came, bear witness that he is the true Messiah, and that the Captain of our salvation is perfect. Sin is abolished, and the world is vanquished; the blood and the water loudly proclaim it. To justify and to sanctify his Church, water and blood issued out of his side on the cross. That blood is shed, without the shedding of which there could have been no remission; and there is water also to wash away all our defilements. The Spirit bears witness by taking of these things of Jesus, and showing them unto us; he bears witness by the water and the blood, applying efficaciously both the one and the other. And the Spirit is truth, and what he shows us and leads us to for salvation, is truth: true satisfaction for sin; true, effectual and abundant grace. He beareth witness with the water and blood, that Christ is in every respect a perfect Saviour, and that his salvation is finished and complete. Without the witness of the Spirit, the water and the blood speak in vain; none will regard them: but when the Spirit shows them to the soul, shows blood to expiate, and grace to sanctify, then the soul will earnestly seek the one and rely upon the other, and really find eternal life in him who came by water and blood. And the consequence is, that he that believes this testimony hath the witness in himself, that is, hath in himself the eternal life which is in Christ.

But what will be the consequence of our receiving this life from Christ? As it is a life which we have in him and receive from him, it must be a life very different from the life we have in and of ourselves, and which all others have who have not Christ. It is a life wholly opposite to that of the world. By it we become enemies to the spirit of the world, and obtain the victory over it, 1 John 5:4. Will not the world therefore oppose it, and hate and persecute us on account of it? May not we be also called to go through water and blood in consequence of our receiving it? If so, is it worth having on *such* terms? Shall we have no cause to *repent* of our choice and portion? Are there any whose testimony we can rely upon for satisfaction on this point? That there is life eternal to be obtained freely, we cannot doubt; but is it worth having with all the consequences that may follow? St Paul says that we are compassed about with a great cloud of witnesses, each ready to give his testimony on this point, Heb. 12. They were all in the trial themselves, and what they say, they all speak from experience. Abel, first, will bear witness that this life is worth having: though the consequence should be the bitter enmity of a brother, which might end in death. Were we to ask Enoch and Noah, who walked with God, whilst the world in general were estranged from the life of God, what they think of this divine life: Is it worth being singular, being ridiculed and hated for by all the world? Were we to ask Abraham, who on the call of God left his own country, not knowing whither he went, and wandered as a pilgrim and a stranger in a strange country, what he thinks of this life: Is it worth having, though all earthly happiness should thereby be taken away? Ask what will Isaac and Jacob say of it? Joseph, what wilt thou say of it, who didst face the enmity of brethren, the prisons and dungeons and enemies on account of it? They all with one voice proclaim their sentiments, and by their conduct evidently show, that they chose it in the face of all consequences, however dreadful. Moses esteemed the reproach of Christ, much more the life of Christ, greater riches than the treasures of Egypt. Why! We see some tortured; others having trials of cruel mockings and scourgings, of bonds and imprisonments; others stoned, sawn asunder, tempted, slain with the sword; others wandering about in sheepskins and goatskins, destitute, afflicted, tormented: Why is all this? Why! Was it not because they preferred that life given us in Christ Jesus before all other comforts and in the face of all earthly misery? Was it not because they highly esteemed the reproach of Christ, and for the excellence of his knowledge, counted all other things but loss and dung? Being dead they yet speak, and testify the same things still to us. They call on us to tread in the same path; and, landed safe the other side, they encourage us to launch out into the ocean, however boisterous. Gone out of great tribulation, they encourage us with one voice to enter into it, assuring us that whosoever believeth in the Son, shall not perish but have everlasting life. In the midst of all their sufferings, their life in Christ enabled them to rejoice and to be exceeding glad; they marched forward in the face of all opposition. Though all comforts failed, yea, and life itself was taken from them; yet they were not of the number of those who drew back into perdition, but still lived the life of faith on the Son of God, clave to him steadfastly; and though the *body* perished, yet they believed to the saving of the soul.

But what is this great cloud of witnesses with which we are compassed, compared with Christ himself? His testimony on this point is more than that of all others. He 'for the joy that was set before him' in the salvation of his people, 'endured the cross, despising the shame.' That his people might enjoy this life, he thought light of, and despised all that he was to endure to obtain it for them. He thus testified how highly he valued this life; life for sinners was a joy set before him as that which he most of all valued, which he went through all difficulties to obtain. This was the main point he was aiming at; he neglected all joys and despised all fears, that he might obtain this joy set before him. He knew the value of it, and showed the value he set on it in such a manner as must eternally recommend it. Our cross, our shame and the contradiction of sinners against us, are only few drops compared with what he endured; but he cheerfully went through all for the joy set before him.

In him we see to perfection what grace is, the value of it, and the treatment it must expect to meet with from the spirit of the world. And we learn from him also, how we are to act under all storms, that is, 'not to faint in our minds.' He has proved that the joy set before us, is worth having at all events, that the faith is worth contending for, and that it is worth striving against sin even unto blood. Therefore the Apostle exhorts us, whilst we are listening to the cloud of witnesses, 'to *look* unto Jesus, and to *consider* him, lest we be *wearied* and faint in our minds.' He was neither weary nor faint in purchasing life for sinners, but went cheerfully through water and blood; look unto him, saith the Apostle, and consider him; have your eyes fixed immovably on the cross he bore, the shame he despised, and the contradiction of sinners he endured; and this astonishing sight will powerfully strengthen, refresh, and animate you to strive against sin with new vigour, resolution and patience, It is thus acting faith on Jesus that makes us conquerors. Listening to the cloud of witnesses is useful and encouraging; but looking unto Jesus invigorates the soul to act in some degree like Jesus. A sight of him by faith enduring the cross and despising the shame makes us partakers of his victories; the soul bears down before him the powers of earth and hell; and every enemy, filled with dread, flies before him. Looking unto Jesus and considering him, is the very life of the soul every step of the way. Whilst the eye is there, faith and patience cannot fail, the soul will be neither weary nor faint. Whilst we are looking unto him and considering him, we cannot but take up the cross, and follow him under the cross, shame, and contradiction. The reproach of Christ will become glorious and precious; to endure it, will become the very joy of the soul. In everything, this is the main point: 'to look unto and consider Jesus.'

Another thing they bear witness unto, is this, that faith alone is sufficient to support the poor believer under every trial, and in the face of every enemy. By faith alone they were able to go through so many difficulties, to perform such wonders, as far surpass all human power. They were 'destitute' of everything but this; yet though 'afflicted and tormented,' they were made more than conquerors. This alone was 'the victory that overcame the world in them, even their faith.' They were by this, out of weakness made strong, in the midst of poverty made rich, in the midst of sorrow made joyful, in the midst of misery made abundantly happy. They believed under all difficulties, and in the face of all enemies, to the saving of their souls, and often of their bodies also. Being strong in faith, when all other helps failed, they gave glory to God, and subdued kingdoms, wrought righteousness, obtained promises, stopped the mouths of lions. In short, to faith they found that nothing was impossible. Faith is still the same, its nature and efficacy are still the same, and its success in the end will be the same also. They, as a great cloud of witnesses, surround us, and testify to us, that in the face of everything we may safely venture by faith on a covenant-God in Christ, and patiently and confidently wait for a comfortable and glorious issue.

24

The Two Witnesses

Nov. 1, 1784.

St John mentions six witnesses – three in heaven and three on earth – that bear testimony to this truth, that God has given us eternal life, and that this life is in his Son. And besides these, he that believeth hath the witness *in himself*. The life which is in the Son of God, being, on believing, *in himself*, is to him an additional and very strong proof that there is life for sinners in Christ. The Apostle Paul mentions two witnesses giving in their evidences to prove that we have this life, and that we are in consequence of it the children of God: 'The Spirit itself beareth witness with our spirit that we are the children of God,' Rom. 8:16. To be assured that we are children enables us to enjoy the comforts and privileges of children, to honour, love, and glorify God as a Father. But how shall we be on good ground assured of this? For if we deceive ourselves here, we lay the foundation for false joys and eternal ruin. A false belief will of course have its effects, as baseless visions often exceedingly affect us. A false groundless belief will bring joys indeed, but they will be joys like the cause which produces them, wholly false; and they will all perish with the foundation which supports them. And our joys arising from such a persuasion, let them be ever so great, do not prove that we are children, for they ought to be the effect of that point already proved fully and satisfactorily to the mind. But who are the true witnesses that really prove this, who will be heard by God, and ought to be assented to by us in this important matter?

First, we have our *own spirit*.

The second witness never gives nor can give evidence without the first. But what are we to understand by our *own spirit*? The Apostle in this chapter speaks of two principles, by which all mankind are influenced: the flesh and the spirit. Of those who are influenced by the flesh, he says, 1. That there is a condemnation belonging to them, (verse 1). 2. That they are enemies to God and of consequence cannot please him, (verses 7, 8). 3. That they shall die, (verse 13). These therefore cannot be the children of God. And this principle cannot be meant here by 'our spirit.' But by 'our spirit' must be understood what the Apostle calls νόμῳ τοῦ νοός μου (chap. 7:23); τo Πνεῦμα (chap. 8:1); φρόνημα τοῦ Πνεύματος (verse 6); Πνεῦμα υἱοθεσίας (verse 15). The law of his mind – the spirit – the wisdom of the spirit – the spirit of children: that spirit in us which constitutes us really the children of God. God not only freely adopts his people for his children and heirs in Christ, but makes them truly and really his children, by sending the Spirit of his Son into their hearts. By this Spirit they are conformed to God as their Father, to Christ as their elder brother. And because they really are the children of God, he could not, without denying himself, but own them as such, and Christ will not be ashamed to call them brethren.

This spirit bears witness to all and to themselves, that they who possess it are truly the children of God. 'Love your enemies,' saith Christ, 'and do good and lend, hoping for nothing; and your reward shall be great, and ye shall be the children of the Highest: for he is kind unto the unthankful and the evil,' Luke 6:35. That is, it will be evidently proved, that ye are the children of the Highest, by your having the same Spirit which is in him. 'I say unto you, love your enemies, bless them that curse you, do good to them that hate you, and pray for them which despitefully use you and persecute you; that ye may be the children of your Father which is in heaven,' Matt. 5: 44, 45. That is, ye will then appear to be, and prove to yourselves and to others, that ye really are, 'the children of your Father which is in heaven.' 'In this the children of God are *manifest*,' 1 John 3:10, in this or by this, that is, by the Spirit which they possess, and by which they are actuated. Again, 'God is love, every one that loveth is born of God,' 1 John 4:7. It is evident that he is born of God, because he has the spirit of his father. This spirit of children gives evidence whose we are, to what family we belong, and where our inheritance is. This is '*our spirit*,' or the spirit by which we are influenced or actuated in the inward man, the very law of our minds, which rules with authority our inward parts – this beareth witness that we are the children of God.

Secondly, we have 'the Spirit itself,' that is God's, bearing witness.

The testimony from our own spirit *alone* and by itself is insufficient to prove to *ourselves* this great point There must be another witness, for there is evidence *against* us also. We have the old man within, a principle which belongs to, and characterizes, the children of Satan. This principle is within us, dwells there, works there; yes, it is enmity itself against God and everything that bears his image, wars against the law of the mind with irreconcilable hatred. This principle is an old inhabitant, has been highly honoured, has been ruling with authority on the throne. This enemy is still the same as to his nature, in no degree changed, as full of venom and enmity as ever, and it may be, has still great strength and vigour in his actings. Here, then, in the same person there are two contrary principles, witnessing one against the other, with great force and evidence, in a matter of the last importance. The soul is distressed and perplexed, unable to determine what or whose it is. Thus the matter may remain contested and in suspense for a considerable time. Our own spirit may have just strength enough to stand its ground, and not give over the point in despair; but still be too weak to carry the point in dispute. In this dilemma the Spirit cometh and beareth witness *with our spirit*, and the point is at once determined.

But *how* does he bear witness? Much depends upon rightly understanding this point. The Apostle says, 'He bears witness with our spirit.' It cannot therefore be in any immediate or unaccountable manner, *without our spirit*. It may be sudden and unexpected, yet it is still *with* our spirit. It is not a *revelation* that we are the children of God, or a strong persuasion in our minds that we are so; but he *proves* by clear evidence, that the matter is so. If he bears witness with our spirit, one would think, that the evidence of the divine Spirit is not different in nature from that of our own spirit, but the same evidence advanced with more strength and clearness. He by the belief of some word of promise, or by some clear discovery of divine things to our spirit in their glory and excellence, enables our spirit to put forth stronger acts of filial confidence in our heavenly Father, gives new life and vigour to every grace, and by making us more like our heavenly Father, proves incontestably that we are born of God, and that we are his.

I say again, that he does not *reveal* that we are the children of God, but as a true witness evidences it by undoubted proofs – by proofs which heaven will own, and which the devil cannot deny. Thus Christ at the day of judgement, proves those on his right hand to be his brethren, and the children of his Father, and consequently heirs of the kingdom, prepared from the foundation of the world, by their spirit of love, compassion and mercy to those who bore the image of God, however despised and distressed, Matt. 25. How does the Spirit prove that we have faith, love, and mercy? Is it not by increasing and strengthening these very graces? What can prove that I love God, but this very love and its effects? What can prove that I am merciful as my Father, who is in heaven, is merciful, but my being enabled to put forth this very act of mercy in the way and manner he does? It is contrary to both Scripture and reason to think of any other way. Can there be any other evidence that we are the children of God and the brethren of Christ, but by the same mind being in us which was also in Christ Jesus? Surely not.

Whatever discovery the Holy Spirit may give to our minds, the discovery itself does not prove us to be children, but as it works on our spirit; the new principle of holiness within us, drawing that forth into action, and enabling the soul to cleave to God more steadfastly in faith and love. This is the only true evidence that can be given, that the nature of things can admit of, that will do us any good, or that is honourable to and becoming the Lord to give. They that seek any other evidence, are already in the way of error, and should take care lest the devil should delude them to eternal ruin. The devil can work strong persuasions, but neither can nor will strengthen any grace. This he cannot do without demolishing his own kingdom within us. This is the work of the Holy Spirit alone, and thus he acts as a comforter; in comforting he feeds the soul with the bread of life; grace grows, and is strengthened, by his taking of the things of Jesus, and showing them unto us. *Nothing but the image of God, can prove us to be the children of God; and nothing but grace can give evidence that we have grace; grace will show and prove itself by its own workings; and the way to make it evident, is to have it increased.*

25

The Case of Judas

Dec. 6, 1784.

We see in the instance of Judas, how dangerous it is to give place to any lust, to feed and nourish it in the soul. We know not what may be the issue even in this world. Who could have suspected that Judas would ever betray his Master, had they seen him following Jesus, performing miracles, going to preach, without gold, silver or brass, without scrip or staves, that 'The kingdom of heaven was at hand?' Who could have thought that the love of the world could grow in any heart that had heard our Saviour's sermon on the mount, and many other discourses so severely condemning it? His conduct was in every respect irreproachable; there was no difference perceivable, but by him who knoweth the heart, between him and the other disciples. He preached, performed miracles, followed Christ, sat at his feet: yet all this while he was a devil. Why? Had he any intention all this time of betraying Jesus? We know not of the least intention of that sort; but on the contrary, it is said that after the sop, Satan entered into him, and put that purpose into his heart. But though he had no such purpose as this, yet the root of all the bitter fruits that followed always remained in his heart. He had religion on the surface; but the love of this world was all the while at the bottom of the heart. Notwithstanding Christ's repeated warnings, yet he took no care to root the thorns out of the ground. The thorns grew with the good seed; and they, instead of the good seed, brought forth fruit to perfection. He was unwilling to part with the evil root, and the fruit, of consequence, followed. Sermons were in vain, even from the mouth of Christ himself; warnings and reproofs were all useless; and at last one devil brought in another worse than himself, and hurried him to eternal ruin. The other disciples had their failings; they were in a great degree ignorant of divine things; they were at times rash, envious, and ambitious; yet notwithstanding all their infirmities, they 'had good and honest hearts': there was no bitter root growing within; no thorns with the good seed; they were entirely Christ's. Their whole heart clave unto him, and his interest was theirs in every view. They had no secret bags of their own to carry. If they were weak, rash, and ignorant, yet they were honest. They had no evil root within.

Judas on the contrary, had *a dishonest heart, loved the world more than Christ, was more for filling the bag than doing good; and in order to fill it, sold even Christ himself.* This I believe to be the main point in religion, to have *every* evil root eradicated. It is then that the doctrines of the gospel are duly apprehended and have their due effect, when they are effectual to this great work. If in everything we have not this in view, we cannot *profit*. My own experience tells me that there is more danger here than we can easily conceive. We cannot search ourselves too thoroughly. All our hearing, reading, and praying, all is to us unprofitable, if there be an evil root within. There is great deceit in sin, and in our hearts through sin. We may think there is no great harm in being attached to other things, and having a *little worldly* spirit. But what evil did this one secret root produce in Judas? He had no thought of such a dreadful issue of things; yet he stood against all Christ's close public discourses and private warnings – all were without effect: he saw no harm in loving and carrying the bag; as there was not indeed in carrying it, though it be difficult to carry it without loving it. It is for this reason that Christ speaks so much about a single eye, and the many good effects it produces: 'If the eye be single, the whole body is *full* of light,' that is, of holiness, comfort, and joy. St James says, that a double-minded man ought not to think he shall receive anything of the Lord. This doubtless is the cause why our prayers in general turn out so unprofitable to us; being double-minded, like Judas, we ask amiss: we do not ask for the right blessing which ought first to be obtained, a single eye. Before we can obtain the comforts and joys of the gospel, every evil root must first be eradicated. Whilst any one remains, we shall continue, as we surely ought to be, comfortless, unthriving, fruitless and unsavoury Christians, if we deserve the name. God will not bestow his grace and comforts (and it is a great mercy he will not), to cheer and nourish a carnal heart and a worldly spirit. Blessed is that man or that sermon, which helps us to discover evil roots within. It is the genuine gospel way of obtaining comfort and peace, of growing in grace. And these effects will infallibly follow, and will prove, when we have them this way, solid, substantial, and lasting. Comforts when they thus come are not empty dreams and fancies, but *strong* consolations to support the soul under trials and in the face of all misery.

26

The Saviour's Unchangeableness

July 8, 1785.

CHRIST is 'the same yesterday, today, and forever,' Heb. 13:8, – the same as to his person, the same as to his purpose of love towards his church; the same as to his offices being forever Prophet, Priest, and King to his church; the same as to his acceptance with God, and as to his relation to his people. His righteousness, his merits, and his grace are the same; his promises are the same and equally full at all times. 'Yesterday,' when he was here in the world, how meek and lowly, how full of compassion and mercy, how determined in his purpose of accomplishing the work in hand, notwithstanding the malice of men and devils! With what strength did he travel, with what patience did he endure the contradiction of sinners against himself! Isa. 62:1. With what fortitude did he conquer enemies! With what willingness and ability did he endure, and satisfy divine justice for sin! He is '*today*' the *same*, has the same work in hand, and still travels in the greatness of his strength. He is still as willing to engage for his people, and as able to conquer as then. He went then cheerfully between us and the wrath of God, and was made a curse for us; he is still the *same*. He then slew the enmity, and nailed the handwriting against us to the cross; he is 'today' the same, he can slay the remaining enmity in our hearts, and nail the old man to the cross, and destroy the work of the devil within us.

He 'yesterday' saw us in our blood, robbed, and wounded by thieves, and totally helpless. He had compassion upon us, took us on his own shoulders, and brought us to a comfortable lodging, healed all our diseases, and pardoned all our sins. He is 'today' the same in love, compassion and power, and is still able to save to the uttermost. Notwithstanding our backslidings, our ingratitude, and our barrenness, and our awful forgetfullness of him; yet as he loved us at first freely, so does he now, even 'today.' 'He heals our backslidings and loves us freely.' 'Yesterday' we were straitened on every side, like the Israelites at the Red Sea, and no way of deliverance appeared, and nothing but ruin had we to look to. In this hour of difficulty, the salvation of Jesus appeared unexpectedly, powerfully and gloriously, and the Red Sea, as it were, was opened before us, and our powerful enemies were seen weak and helpless, as they were dead. He is 'today' the *same*, and can work unhoped-for deliverance for us with the same glory as before. 'Yesterday' he enabled us to kill the lion and the bear. He is the same 'today' to go with us against Goliath. He was 'yesterday' a Prophet to his church, teaching them the will, and the things of God, and opening the understandings of his people to comprehend them. 'Today' he is the same, receiving blind ignorant sinners under his efficacious teaching. He is like the sun, 'today' as powerful as ever to disperse the thickest darkness before him.

He was 'yesterday' a high *Priest* offering a sacrifice of infinite value upon the cross. He is 'today' – with the same sacrifice before the throne in heaven interceding for his people; he is a priest forever after the order of Melchisedek, who, as to his *office*, 'had neither beginning of days nor end of life.' Christ was a lamb slain from the beginning of the world, that is, in promises and types; but he was fore-ordained before the foundation of the world to the office of Priesthood. And though the acts and administration of his Priesthood shall cease, when he shall have delivered up the kingdom to his Father, and have brought the whole church to God's presence; yet the virtue and fruits of those acts shall be absolutely eternal. For so long as the saints shall be in heaven, so long shall they enjoy the benefit of that sacrifice which did purchase, not a lease on expiring terms, but ζώην ἀκατάλυτον, an endless life, an everlasting glory, an incorruptible inheritance. As a *King* also he is the same. God laughs at all the rage and malice, plots and contrivances, of men and devils, against his king, 'whom he has set on his holy hill of Zion,' Psa. 2. He is king in heaven, he is king on earth; and even hell trembles under the greatness of his power and wrath. He is, and will be king in the heart of his people, 'the same yesterday, today, and forever.'

His *gospel* is the same 'yesterday,' under the Old Testament, 'today' to us, and will be the same 'forever.' It is an eternal gospel; and there will be no other way of access to God, no other doctrine owned and blessed by him to the salvation of souls. God is forever well pleased and satisfied with the one mediator, and would have no change. Every true believer is in some degree of the same mind with the Father. He is married to him and delights in him just as he is. And an unchangeable and glorious Saviour requires immutability of purpose in us, and of reliance upon him. He would have us cleave to him in the face of all difficulties, and to follow him under the cross, whithersoever he goeth.

LETTERS

To Mr David Charles, of Carmarthen

1. How the Convinced of Sin May Obtain Peace

Milborne Port, Aug. 21, 1782.

WHEN on your late visit to me, I recollect you asked me, 'When a soul is by sin brought into spiritual depths and distress of mind, *where* is it to look for support; *how* is it to be delivered from this darkness, and what are the *means* most likely to restore it to peace, and to a sense of the love of God?' As this question is of no small importance to every Christian, it may not be improper, and I hope by the blessing of God, it will be useful to enlarge a little more on the answer I then gave you. All I shall say on the subject is the result of my own experience; and without due attention to this, I daily find it utterly impossible to keep above water, and to walk forward with any degree of comfort.

What saith the Scripture? 'Let him,' saith Isaiah, 'trust in the name of the Lord, and stay upon his God,' and again, 'If any man sin,' – and thereby be brought to darkness and distress, (which is a sure consequence) – 'we have an advocate with the Father, Jesus Christ the righteous; and he is the propitiation for our sins.' This is the refuge which the Scriptures set before us; and is it not a sufficient refuge? Heaven cannot provide you with a safer refuge or a better support. God manifest in the flesh is set before us in the all-sufficiency of his merits and grace, to support us against sin, both in its guilt and in its power. But if we would obtain strong consolation and permanent peace, we must not be contented with vague and uncertain notions, with obscure views of him;

but we must earnestly seek after enlarged views of his fullness and sufficiency, and a firm belief in both. We must get ourselves well informed as to the dignity of his person, the value of his merits, and the fullness of his grace; and we must also be more fully acquainted with his condescensions, virtues and triumphs.

Here, I apprehend, lies the secret cause of most of our doubts and distresses on account of sin, that is, in our want of a clear knowledge of, and of a firm belief in, the fullness, sufficiency and ability of Christ to save. We have not examined narrowly the firmness and the everlasting stability of the foundation on which the salvation of God's people is built. We rest in, and are satisfied with general ideas of Christ and his salvation, without diligently seeking more enlarged conceptions of the dignity of the one, and of the sufficiency of the other. When sin appears sin, to be καθ' ὑπερβολὴν ἁμαρτωλός, exceedingly great, and beyond imagination sinful, even equal to the holiness of the law and the majesty of that God against whom it is committed. When this affecting and humbling view of sin is had, we have need of something more than human to keep the soul from downright despair. And where can this be found but in the infinitely meritorious death of the Son of God? In proportion to the evil which the soul sees to be in sin, must be the greatness of the atonement and satisfaction which it requires in order to gain solid peace. General hopes about mercy and pardon will not suffice, when sin appears sin; the soul must then have something that is satisfactory, something that is equal to the guilt of sin, the demands of the divine law, the majesty and the justice of God. And where can this be found but in Christ? And in him, the Son of God, *all* is to be found; yes, all that the soul can desire abounds infinitely in him. By his perfect obedience to the law, he hath put all possible, and more than all conceivable honour upon it; and by his death on the cross he hath made such an atonement for sin, and such satisfaction to God's justice, as ten thousand times ten thousand hells could never equal. *Were we oppressed with the united guilt of all the accursed rebels of earth and hell, the inconceivable merits of this infinite sacrifice are sufficient alone to remove it all*. Clothed with divine righteousness of such a dignified person, in the sight of all our guilt, in the prospect of death, and in the view of the judgement to come, we may joyfully say, 'Who is he that condemneth? It is *Christ* that died.' The salvation effected by this God-man is full and complete; it answers all the demands of God, and all the wants of sinners. It is all that despair can wish, the sinner can covet, or the saint can desire. It gives glory to God in the highest, brings peace on earth, and good will infinite to man.

This salvation, discovered to the soul in its vastness, and embraced by faith in all its fullness, will quiet the soul effectually in the face of everything that is discouraging, will stop the mouth of unbelief, and still the voice of conscience.

Labour therefore that sin may appear sin, may appear to you attended with all possible evil and guilt; and, at the same time, labour that Christ and his salvation may appear to be what they indeed are: sufficient to remove all guilt. Consider what God is in all his divine majesty and glory; to attempt to describe him is to debase him exceedingly: well, but the righteousness and salvation provided for sinners, is in every way equal to the infinity of God himself. His righteousness is equal to himself; but *his* righteousness is also *ours*, if we are his people; for he is 'Jehovah *our* righteousness.' Hide not your sins, but bring them forth and view them in all their guilt and aggravation. At the same time set this divine righteousness in opposition to them all; and accept of no peace but what proceeds from a discovery of it to your soul in the midst of darkness and misery. And will not this sight bring you peace? Yes, it will bring you peace which no sin, no guilt can ever disturb – a peace that passeth all understanding! If this righteousness is ours, all is safe. God, whom we have so offended, is perfectly reconciled; and we are as much at peace with him as Christ himself is.

Until we have this view of Christ's sufficiency, we cannot cheerfully and without suspicion of consequences, commit our souls, so guilty and so depraved, to his custody; and till we are made willing to live contentedly every day, as guilty and helpless to the last degree, upon his merits and grace only for life and salvation, we shall not be able to obtain peace, much less joy in the Holy Ghost; but we shall continually find, if attentive to the workings of our own hearts, causes more than sufficient to distress our minds and cast our souls into the lowest depths.

To believe Christ's ability to save us may appear a very easy thing to those to whom sin hath not appeared sin. The reason is, they being strangers to sin, are strangers also to the cost of redemption from it. But those who are truly convinced of sin find it a very difficult matter: and they experimentally know how hard, of all things hard, it is to believe that Christ is able to deliver them from it. The Spirit only can assist them on this point; and it costs them much searching of Scripture, much prayer for the Spirit's enlightening influences, before they gain any settled, confirmed and abiding belief of this truth. The reason is, because the remonstrances of conscience, the accusations of Satan, the natural unbelief of the heart, a secret leaning to self-righteousness, together with the whole body of sin, variously and forever oppose it.

We often find within us a doubting of Christ's *willingness*, when there seems to be a persuasion of his *power* and ability. But I am apt to think that we shall find, by attending more to, and knowing more of, the workings of our hearts, that we doubt the former, because we do not sufficiently believe the latter. Let us therefore above all other things study the *person* of Christ, and endeavour to get a deeper insight into the mystery of godliness; and we shall find that our peace and comfort will increase with our knowledge, and that true godliness will be effectually promoted. All peace that proceeds not from this source is carnal security; and all appearance of godliness is only the form without any life and power.

So far as we live by faith, we live upon Christ only, without respect to anything else in us, in heaven or in earth. He is our all in all – our all in everything, in every consideration, and in every circumstance. He is our all to support us under every difficulty, and to comfort us under every discouragement that meets us from guilt, from sin and every enemy. And in proportion as we make him our all, is our comfort in the face of guilt, our strength against corruption, and our victory daily over all our enemies. But we shall never be brought to make him our all, until we have a discovery made to our minds of the dignity, glory and majesty of his person, as the only-begotten Son of God, 'full of grace and truth.' This adds greatness and infinity to grace and truth; it is the grace and truth of the Son of God, and he is *full* of both; so that his grace and truth are equal to himself. Infinity is filled with grace and truth; therefore this grace and truth must be infinite too. When the soul sees Christ by faith in all the dignity of his person and the fullness of his grace, then and then only will the believer live upon him as his all in all. And when he is brought to this state, and continues in it; he may cheerfully bid defiance to all his enemies. But alas! With what difficulty is he brought to this state! How hardly is he brought as a lost sinner to rejoice daily in the Lord his righteousness.

The life of faith is so strange and mysterious, a life wholly unknown to every other creature in heaven and earth, but the true believer. It is so opposite to our reason, and so contrary to every notion of our natural hearts, that his progress in it is very slow and almost imperceptible. When he can no longer depend upon his own doings for righteousness, yet still he wishes to possess something in himself, on which to build his hopes and confidence, and will look to the work of the Spirit in the heart, making that the foundation which is only the superstructure. But we must well remember that there neither is, nor ever will be, any other foundation but the obedience and death of Christ only, for a sinner – in himself always guilty – to stand upon for his acceptance with God. Other foundation can no man lay. The holiest saint in heaven stands in equal need of it as the most profligate sinner. The building on this foundation is true, vital holiness. But great care must be taken, that the superstructure is not placed in the room of the foundation, and that we mix not with the foundation any part of those materials fit only for the construction of the building. Our mistake here is, I believe, *frequent*; and very imperceptible it may also be, but always distressing to the soul in its effects. It is more dangerous, because it wears the appearance of sanctity, comes under the pretence of high esteem for holiness: but it is only Satan transformed into an angel of light; and it is sure to weaken and distress the soul, if not quite ruin it. Holiness in all its parts neither is, nor ever can be, in any degree, the matter of our justification before God. For our acceptance with him we must forever stand, in time and eternity, on the only sufficient righteousness of the Son of God. But to this our natural hearts are most of all averse; and the soul, to whom sin appears sin, finds no small difficulty in relying simply upon Christ's righteousness, without respect to anything else whatsoever. It would gladly have something to mix with it. It knows not how to lay the foundation without some cement of its own, something *within* or *without* itself, something it hath done or intends doing. But the attempt is utterly fruitless. These things are wholly distinct in themselves, and must be distinctly considered by the soul. The confounding of them will only dishonour the grace of Christ, disturb our peace, and weaken our strength for obedience.

It is comparatively easy to see with the understanding that these things are altogether different: but to bring the heart to the point, is quite another thing. To act in the face of guilt and sin, as those who practically believe this truth – *here* is the difficulty. And the reason of this difficulty, I am convinced, greatly proceeds from our deficiency in the knowledge of the person of Christ, and from the weakness of our faith in his ability and sufficiency. For were we once convinced of this, what should hinder our being fully satisfied? Why should we look for anything besides? Had you a rich friend, with whose ability and willingness to supply all your wants, you were fully satisfied, would you not wholly cleave to him, and would you not live comfortable without any fear of poverty and distress? Doubtless you would. Such would be your conduct towards Christ also, as to your spiritual wants, did you entertain honourable and suitable thoughts of him. For the point is not, what your wants are, but whether he is able to supply them. Be your wants what they may, yet if he is able to supply them, the case is not desperate, there is no room for despair. Be convinced of Christ's sufficiency, and smile in the face of your complicated misery, being fully satisfied with *him only*. God is satisfied, and why should we be dissatisfied? Did we but know the worthiness and excellence of his Son as well as he does, we should be as well satisfied and delighted with him as he is. He wants, he requires nothing else. And his language respecting him on the behalf of his people, is, 'In whom I am well pleased.' Is he well-pleased? And why are we not so too! Alas! It is because we know him not. Did we but know his person, and, believe in him as the only-begotten of the Father, we should be able to say with Paul, 'I know in whom I have believed, and I am persuaded that he is able to keep that which I have committed unto him.'

But you will say, 'How shall I attain to this knowledge of and belief in Christ?' Why make frequent trials of him. When your case is most desperate, then go directly to him, and put his skill and ability to the trial. When you have nothing in view but ruin and misery, then call upon him, 'Lord, save me, or I perish.' In this case, you will not be disappointed. How often had Paul experienced his ability in working strange and unexpected deliverances for him? he had tried his skill and trusted in his power a thousand times before; therefore he could say, 'I know in whom I have believed,' and, 'I am *persuaded* he is *able.*' We may have a sort of belief in Christ, and yet not sufficiently know him in whom we have believed, so as to gain a firm persuasion of his *ability* to keep us, when sin, guilt, and wrath are in view. Grace and peace are no otherwise multiplied, but through the knowledge of Jesus Christ our Lord, 2 Peter 1:2. 'Who is he that overcometh the world, but he that believeth that Jesus is the Son of God' – that is, he who from the heart believeth in Christ's dignity, ability, and sufficiency as the Son of God: he it is that overcometh sin, guilt, the world and the devil. It cannot be otherwise, because he layeth his help upon one that is *mighty*. May you and I grow more and more in this knowledge of and practical belief in Christ Jesus.

2. The Means to be Used for Obtaining Peace

Milborne Port, Oct. 4, 1782.

HAVING in a former letter showed to you what can only prove a firm support to a soul in spiritual depths and distresses on account of sin, that is, a clear and enlarged knowledge, and a firm persuasion of Christ's sufficiency and ability to save sinners, the chief of sinners; without which I can see nothing to stand between him and despair and hell; I shall now enlarge a little further on what the duty of every believer is in such a state in order to obtain relief and enlargement to his soul. It is possible that something I may say may be useful, by the blessing of God, not only now, but on many future occasions.

When a person is in distress of any sort, what doth the nature of his condition require? Is it not *industry and diligence* in the use of all lawful means for deliverance? Not despondence, but vigorous exertions; not fruitless complaints, but activity, are the most likely means to bring us out of distress of every kind. It is in vain to complain that things are so bad, without earnest endeavours to give them a different and a more favourable aspect. And many instances daily occur which forcibly convince us how much care, frugality, and diligence, can do in the most desperate condition as to worldly things. What difficulties they will in the end remove, and what great ends they will eventually attain to! Their efficacy is no less powerful in spiritual things. 'The kingdom of heaven suffereth violence; and the violent take it by force.' Grace is not an inactive thing. There is nothing in the whole world of a more active nature. It is fire and life itself, even a *divine* flame and *spiritual* life. It cannot rest; it must be active according to its degree and strength. Difficulties and discouragements vanish before it. True godliness hath a life and power, and what our Saviour calls violence in it, that takes the kingdom of heaven – the blessings of righteousness, peace and joy – by force. The devil flees before it; the flesh and the world are vanquished by it; it lays hold on God himself, and wrestles for the blessings of pardon, grace and peace, till in the end it surely prevails. It is the noblest spirit in the universe, the admiration of angels, and the delight of heaven! And in proportion as it is put forth, always remember, is our progress in the divine life.

Are we then in doubt and distress, at a miserable uncertainty about our spiritual state? The language of Scripture to us in such a condition, is, 'Get ye up; why lie ye upon your faces?' as the Lord addressed Joshua when in despondency after his defeat before Ai. We must watch, pray, meditate and offer violence to our sloth and corruptions, press boldly to the throne of grace by prayers, supplications, and restless importunities; and thus our 'light shall break forth as the morning, and our health shall spring forth speedily.' This is the way to take the kingdom of heaven by force; these are the means appointed for the obtaining of peace, joy, and assurance. Without due attention to these means, I am fully convinced, that neither the one nor the other, will ordinarily be obtained. Those who obtain their comforts at an easier rate, have the greatest reason to suspect their being delusive and fallacious; and those who fondly imagine that they are going on in the narrow way, without these vigorous exertions, have as yet, I fear, never trod one step in it.

In what continual danger are we everywhere of running into extremes! While some, blinded and hardened by sin, never bestow one serious thought about their souls – insensible of the malady within, they despise the physician and disregard the means of recovery – there are others who think or at least *talk* of nothing else but of their disorder, saying how bad they are. Fruitless complaints, complaints of themselves and of their condition, is the sum and substance of their religion. If they can conjure up doubts respecting themselves, and form desponding complaints of their uncomfortable condition, they fancy that they have done their duty. I have myself known several who have spent a good part of their time in such spiritual gossiping – I know not what else to call it – in going up and down from one to another with their melancholy complaints and objections. But such conduct is utterly contrary to the life of faith. Had they spent half this time in pouring out their complaints before the Lord, or employed it in doing good to others, they would have been long ago fat and well-liking, thriving daily in holiness, and comfort, life and joy. I say not but that it is good, in our soul's concerns and spiritual difficulties, to apply to them who are furnished with the tongue of the learned, and who know how to speak a word in season to the weary: but what I say is, that for persons to fill their minds with their own complaints and objections, without endeavouring to mix with faith and practice what is spoken for their relief, and to go on still in their own slothful and obstinate way – that this is of no sort of use or advantage, but I fear of much real hurt to the soul. And yet some, I am apt to think, may even please themselves in such a course, as if it had somewhat in it of eminence in religion. But can they think to mend their condition by *wishing* it were better, or by complaining that it is so bad? If they do, they will most assuredly be disappointed. None of us will think so absurdly about worldly things. In such things we readily take an industrious course. The husbandman well knows, that if he be idle and slothful in seed-time, it will be in vain to form any expectations as to the time of harvest. 'The sluggard will not plow by reason of cold'; and what return hath he in harvest? he must 'beg in harvest and have nothing,' Prov. 20:4. So it is in spiritual things. The hand of the diligent alone maketh rich. Tell me how a man employs his time, whether he is slothful or industrious, and I will tell you what progress he makes in grace; for you may as soon gather grapes of thorns or figs of thistles, as enjoy those fruits of the Spirit, love, joy, and peace, whilst you live after the flesh, in self-indulgence, ease, and sloth.

Nothing requires more spiritual wisdom and prudence than administering comfort to complaining souls. A promiscuous application of gospel promises and comforts, without a previous thorough knowledge of his soul to whom they are applied, is very seldom useful, and oftentimes very pernicious. It therefore becomes all who love their own souls, and are fearful of being deceived with false hopes and delusive comforts, to take particular care how they trust their souls' concerns to those who have a good word in readiness for all complaints. The Lord hath denounced a most dreadful woe on all such lying deceivers, who 'put pillows under the armholes' of slothful sinners, who 'with lies have made the heart of the righteous sad, and strengthened the hand of the wicked, that he should not turn from his wickedness, by *promising him life.*' If consolation is administered, distinct and separate from watchfullness, diligence and spiritual violence in the way of duty, it is exceedingly dangerous, and will prove, if not worse, yet most assuredly useless. How doth the Holy Ghost counsel and advise those who would make their calling and election sure? 'Giving all diligence, add to your faith virtue, etc.,' that is, carefully attend to the exercise of all the graces of the Spirit, and to such a conversation in all things as becometh the gospel; 'for if ye do these things,' – if you are habitually found in the actual practice of them – 'an entrance shall be administered abundantly into the everlasting kingdom of our Lord and Saviour Jesus Christ.' You who are now on the borders of it, and are uncertain whether you belong to it or not, shall by these means have an entrance into the kingdom of Christ, and all the joys, triumphs, and glory of it shall be richly administered unto you. This is the advice the Holy Ghost gives in this case; and as we love our souls, let us adhere to it and not arrogantly pretend to be wiser than the Holy Spirit, by following our own inventions in a matter of so much consequence. Let us seek earnestly, wait patiently and persevere without fainting in striving and wrestling; and we shall in the end succeed. The vision will come and will not tarry. 'Faithful is he that hath promised'; he will eternally stand to all his engagements, and will abundantly perform them. Thus engaged in wrestling and waiting patiently upon God, we shall have all the promises in the Scriptures on our side. Let us not be slothful then, but followers of them, who by faith and patience have inherited the promises.

I should not marvel if sloth should reply to all this: 'Alas! we are so dull and are so dead! You can well talk, but we cannot do all this. Corruptions are so strong, temptations so violent, our hearts so hard, and our spirits so backward!' If this be in truth the case, the more reason you have to stir up yourselves and to strive earnestly.

But do you use *all diligence* – diligence at all times, in all ways of God's appointment – all manner of diligence within against corruptions, and without against temptations? Weak endeavours and ineffectual attempts are in this case far from being adequate means of relief. They will leave us just where we were before. If lying down at the foot of the hill, looking up towards the top and wishing we were there, would bring us thither, we should have very numerous travellers, and the road towards heaven would be much frequented. But it is not so. The kingdom of heaven must suffer violence by everyone that ever enters into it – killing words to sloth! Good wishes and good resolutions, I believe, ruin thousands of souls. They wish and resolve, and then they think the work is finished, and they are very good Christians. And when conscience stings them with remorse, they wish and resolve again; and there the work always ends, and not the smallest progress is ever made. 'As the door turneth upon its hinges,' saith Solomon, 'so doth the slothful man in his bed.' In the turning of a door on its hinges there is some *motion*, but no progress; it is still in the same place. So it will also be with us, whilst spiritual sloth prevails, and we rest in vain wishes and resolutions. We shall make no progress; but where we are one day, there we shall be the next; and where we are one year, there we shall be the succeeding.

The life of faith consists in earnest and diligent activity and enjoyment. We seek earnestly: we obtain the blessing; and this whets our appetite, and gives fresh strength to seek and enjoy still more. It is like the life of the labouring man, who daily works and toils hard for food and nourishment; and his labour procures him both food, and an appetite for it; and his present food gives him again fresh strength to work for more: and so it is a continual round of working and enjoying. Only there is this difference: the labour of the Christian doth not *purchase* food for him, but it is the way in which he must enjoy it.

Slothfullness in the service of God is as damning a sin as open rebellion against him; for the slothful and the wicked servants shall share in the same condemnation, Matt. 25:30. If we are not determined therefore to part with our ease, sloth, self-indulgence, and our unprofitable method of spending our time, and to mortify and crucify our lusts, we must be contented to spend our days without any real peace, and in the end to lie down in sorrow. How many are there, alas! who bewail the sins of their nature, the corruptions of their hearts, and the folly of their ways, in the morning and in the evening, and at the same time scarce stand on their watch against these sins and corruptions during any part of the day! But is this giving diligence, *all* diligence? It is grievous, it is lamentable, to see in the Christian world, professors who are daily indulging themselves in all and every species of vanity, pride, wrath, envy, sloth, and the like, and yet complain how uncertain they are about the state of their souls! I had almost said, 'God forbid that it should be otherwise with any who thus walk.' I *will* say, 'God forbid that we should speak peace to them, when God speaketh none.' To offer them peace and comfort, without due admonition of their duty to use diligence in attending to all the means of mortifying lust and crucifying the flesh, is to offer them the deadliest poison. Grace never seeks peace and comfort, but in the way of holiness, and never thinks it costs too much, if it can by any means be obtained. Comfort, unconnected with holiness and not influential to promote it in the heart, is a comfort which grace never desires, and which never proceeds from the Spirit of God the Comforter.

To this diligence then the soul in doubts and distresses must come, if it at all intends being delivered in a lawful way. Desponding complaints, and frivolous excuses for neglecting spiritual diligence, must be laid aside: if not, ordinarily neither rest, stability, or peace, can be obtained. Patient waiting, and diligent, vigorous activity, are in the Christian inseparably connected together, and are duties which he is daily called upon to exercise. His constant duty is patiently to wait, in the diligent use of all means, for God's blessing; neither prescribing the time *when*, nor the manner *how*, but being in this respect submissive to *his* sovereign will and pleasure, who causeth the wind to blow where and when he listeth.

Both these duties are very elegantly expressed by a very beautiful simile in Psalm 123:2. 'Behold, as the eyes of servants look unto the hands of their masters, and as the eyes of a maiden unto the hand of her mistress; so our eyes wait upon the Lord our God, until that he have mercy upon us.' Servants wait upon their masters and look unto their hands to receive intimations of their minds and wills, that they may readily comply with the same: 'So,' saith he, 'do we wait for mercy – not in a slothful neglect of enjoined duties, but in constant readiness to observe the will of God in all commands. Neither do we fix our own time, and if mercy be not showed soon, give over waiting through weariness and impatience; no, but we wait until he in his own best time have mercy upon us.'

A great example of all I have advanced in this long letter we have in the spouse in the Song of Solomon, chapters 3 and 5. Sleep is upon her, and she is indisposed for communion with Christ, to which she is invited. 'I sleep, but my heart waketh: it is the voice of my beloved that knocketh, saying, Open to me, my sister, etc.' This call of Christ puts her on framing excuses from the unfitness of the time, her present indisposition, and also her unpreparedness for the duty to which she is called; 'I have put off my coat; how shall I put it on?' Upon this Christ withdraws his presence from her, and leaves her at a loss as to her former comforts: 'I opened to my beloved; but my beloved had withdrawn himself, and was gone.' At first she seeks him on her bed: 'by night on my bed I sought him whom my soul loveth: I sought him, but I found him not.' Here she seems to have gone no farther than to entertain cold desires and ineffectual wishes, for she was on her *bed*, where no more could be done: but the issue was, as it always will be: 'she found him not.' Well, but what course doth she now take? Doth she still continue to make her former excuses and pretences? Doth she still remain in her indolent and slothful condition? No, no; but with all earnest diligence she engages with her whole soul in *all* manner of duties, by which she might recover her former comforts. She went 'about the city in the streets,' and 'sought him whom her soul loved.' When thus diligently and actively engaged,

'It was but a little,' until she 'found him whom her soul loved,' she 'held him and would not let him go.' The same also, I am fully convinced, must be the course which others must take, who would meet with the same success. They must shake off sloth, lay aside fruitless complaints, seeming excuses, and vain pretences for slothful inactivity; and they must abound in all diligence, and continue to show the same diligence to the end, if they would arrive at full assurance of hope, and enjoy permanent peace and comfort in their souls. They should always remember, that in the same soul and conscience, spiritual peace and sloth never did, nor ever will, dwell together; light and darkness, heat and cold, are not more contrary to one another.

Would we then enjoy the comforts of the gospel – would we grow in grace? We must give all diligence. Do you not find every day the necessity of this? If you be going forward, I am sure you do. For the world, the flesh, and the devil, always watchful and always active, will dispute every step of the way; and you may safely judge of your progress in the divine life by the constant exertion you are enabled by the grace of God to make against them.

But in everything and at all times, remember to keep your eye steady on Christ's ability and all-sufficiency, continually engaged to give you strength for every work. Without continual dependence upon him, your strength for everything is perfect weakness; and the world, the flesh, and the devil will laugh at the puny arm lifted up against them. Be first strong in the Lord; then resist the devil, and he will flee from you. All I have been saying will be totally useless to those whose religion lies only in their heads: but when it becomes a *heart*-work, I am certain the necessity of it will be daily seen and felt. A religion that costs us nothing is not worth having: it is the certain ruin of the soul, detested by God, and is the very derision of devils.

To Miss Sarah Jones, of Bala, afterwards Mrs Thomas Charles

1. Remedy for All Complaints

Milborne Port, June 5, 1780.

As to your complaints, I shall be always glad to hear them with attention, and esteem myself very happy to bear a part of your burden. I could likewise repeat numberless complaints in return: but instead of that, permit me to mention my 'cordial,' which, amidst all my complaints, helps me to many a quiet thought and many a sound sleep, which is: 'If God has given me Christ, *what* can I have to complain of?' But then you must know, that I take him as a free gift and attempt to cast myself wholly upon him; and according to Luther's advice, throw all *I am and do* into one heap, and lay it down at the foot of his cross. O! he has a world of merit in his hands for *you*, for *me*, and a gracious heart to bestow it. Nothing in this world troubles me so much as my ingratitude to such a friend. How are the armies of heaven astonished at our base conduct, when they view us as the most unworthy objects of such grace and love! Were there but this one sin of ingratitude laid to my charge, it would be enough to sink me to the nethermost hell.

But, O my friend, you and I have to do with a kind friend, the Father of *mercies*, who knows *all* and pardons all our sins. Hear the blessed language which proceeds out of his gracious lips. '*I will turn* again, *I will* have compassion upon you; I will subdue your iniquities, and cast *all* your sins into the depths of the sea.' 'Because *he delighteth* in mercy': this is the only reason, why we have not been given up to hardness of heart and a reprobate mind; and for the same reason I trust we shall be preserved to the end.

To Miss Sarah Jones

2. Christ Dying for the Ungodly

Milborne Port, Nov. 18, 1780.

WHAT returns can *we* ever make for Christ, the gift of the Father! The very thought confounds and oppresses my mind. What returns can we make the Son of God 'for his agony and bloody sweat, his cross and passion!' Poor creatures! We can do nothing but with amazement forever stand, and gaze and wonder at the height and depth of his love, and confess that none but God could show such love.

When I awoke this morning, the following passage came to my mind with no small degree of efficacy, 'When we were yet *without strength*, in due time Christ died for the *ungodly*.' Words cannot be conceived more expressive of our misery, wretchedness, and helplessness, and also of the freeness of Christ's love in coming to our relief. What can more strongly set forth our utter depravity than this expression 'ungodly'! It manifestly implies all that pride and constant hatred of God and enmity against him, which constitute the very character and disposition of the devil himself. As *ungodly* we are fallen under God's wrath, the most tremendous ruin! In this most deplorable state we are also 'without strength.' We are utterly helpless; we cannot rise up to make satisfaction to God for turning away his wrath from us. We are weak too in respect of any sufficiency in us to lay aside our ungodliness; for ungodliness constitutes the very essence of our fallen nature; and no creature can change his own nature. We hate God as perfectly as the very devils; nor can we love him by any strength of our own any more than they can. Will not God punish such daring and impious rebels? Will not his indignation burn forever against us like fire? We could expect nothing else: but unexpectedly we experience the reverse: 'Christ died for the ungodly.' O comfortable words! This is a sufficient ground of *rejoicing*, even for guilty, unworthy sinners. We shall no longer fear the strict demands nor the tremendous curses of the divine Law; nor be alarmed by the severity of God's inflexible justice. Let conscience accuse, let devils accuse, yet still will we rejoice, for 'Christ died for the ungodly.' We say not that we are not ungodly, we know that we are so; yea, and we know that but for Christ and that grace by Christ wherein we stand, we should have been more so. But what we say, and all we say, is, 'Christ died for the ungodly.' And herein we rejoice, yea, and will rejoice.

Let us believe this glorious truth, and not be afraid to look our enemies in the face. Under all the trials of life, accusations of conscience, and approaches of death itself, let us reflect with 'mirth in heaviness, and with joy in mourning,' on this truth: 'When we were yet without strength, Christ died for the ungodly.' In all things we *may* rejoice; for in all things we overcome by the blood of the Lamb. O happy moment that we were born into the world, to experience the efficacy and contemplate the glory of this precious truth: 'Christ died for the ungodly.' I love to repeat the words, because all my hopes, and comforts in time and eternity are grounded upon them. I am not afraid to depend on this foundation. I am sure it will never fail. This is the children's bread, and why should you think that you 'have no right to meddle with it?' Are you not ungodly? You cannot deny it. Well then, 'Christ died for the ungodly.' Is not this enough? O let us no longer doubt, but believe in him, love him, delight in him; and set forth his praises, not *only* with our lips but in our lives. It comforts my soul that you remember me at the throne of grace. Continue to pray for me. I cannot forget you whilst able to remember myself. May the Lord of all consolation fill you with all joy in believing.

3. The Fears and Doubts of a Gracious Soul

Milborne Port, April 16, 1781.

BUT why art thou so heavy, my dearest friend? Why art thou so disquieted within thee? Is it, because you do not *love* God? Surely this cannot be. For 'who are those with thee?' What are those ceaseless desires, and ardent longings after God and Christ? 'Are they not children which God hath graciously given his servant?' Are they not the offspring of the divine nature implanted in the heart? Are they of an earthly birth, or are they not of a celestial origin? Why is it that you are so uneasy, while Christ is absent from you; why so uncomfortable when he *seems* to frown upon you? Is it because you hate him? Surely not. Look upon the careless and the ungodly around you, who openly avow themselves the enemies of God. Do *they* feel any such sensations within them? Or are they not equally indifferent about his smiles and his frowns? The sensations you feel then evidently prove the love of God in the heart. Be thankful for them, and firmly believe that God will *satisfy* the longing mind.

But you are unhappy, because you think that Christ does not *love* you; and you dare even to say to him who intercedes for you in heaven: 'Thou dost not love me.' O say not so. First take a turn to Bethlehem, and view the stable and the manger; retire to Gethsemane, and see the bloody drops; ascend the top of Calvary, and behold the cursed and bloody cross. What can you see but scenes of astonishing love? What do you hear from the expiring Saviour but the cries of love! 'Father, forgive them, etc.' Are these the expressions of hatred? Does the Son love the Father? We cannot doubt it. But he left the Father's bosom for our sakes. Astonishing thought! It is almost too wonderful to be believed. Sometimes, when contemplating myself, I have thought it impossible that God should ever be merciful to me – *such* a sinner: but when I have considered the sufferings of the Son of God, endured for such as I am, I have been ready to doubt, on the other side, through the very vastness of the mercy. Can it be so? Is it possible that God should so regard sinners? That condescending love, which one while seemed incapable of reaching a case so wretched as mine, appeared at another time too great to be believed. I was amazed; I was satisfied. I could not deny the unspeakable gift – I saw and wondered. I said: 'What is God! How unsearchable are his ways! Who can find them out?'

He hath surely put his love beyond all suspicion of doubt. Who but the devil could have sophistry enough to persuade us that Christ, after all the proofs he has given, doth not love us? We have reason, often at least I have, to suspect *our* love to him, and to bewail sorely the weakness and coldness of our warmest affections.

Let us condemn *ourselves*, and repent in dust and ashes: but let us always endeavour to entertain honourable, enlarged, and suitable thoughts of Christ and of his love. I know from experience that nothing so sensibly pains and so deeply wounds, as a suspicion, in the object of our affection, of the sincerity of our love and regard. And may we not suppose that our suspicions of Christ's love towards us, do not a little grieve and pain him, especially when he has given us such amazing proofs? I am grieved and ashamed to think, that I should ever so dishonour him. O, may the Lord teach us to know more clearly this love which passeth knowledge. It is our life, our eternal life, to know and enjoy it. I think I hear you say, 'O, yes, this is all my desire, and all I long after, in time and eternity.'

4. The Difference between Unbelief and Holy Jealousy

Milborne Port, April 26, 1781.

THE apostle describes the character of those who are of full age, to whom strong meat belongeth, that 'by reason of use they have their senses exercised to discern both good and evil.' That is, by long experience and continual exercise, they are enabled better and more clearly, to distinguish between the actings of the *old* and the *new* man; which is often no easy matter, and they are not seldom mistaken, the one for the other. Not but that they are different, at all times, as light from darkness: but a person whose eyes are dim, or who is in darkness, cannot distinguish one thing from another. So light and eyes are necessary to distinguish things that are spiritual.

You condemn yourself without mercy for *unbelief*. But is it *really* unbelief that is the cause of your distress? For there is a spiritual *jealousy* in the renewed heart, which has the love of Christ for its foundation; and which is often mistaken for unbelief, to the no small perplexity and distress of the soul. Unbelief is a limb, I almost said, the whole body of the old man: but this spiritual jealousy is the gracious acting of the renewed part of the Christian, and proceeds from a deep sense of our unworthiness, and also of the excellence of Christ. How can the believer, who sincerely loves Christ, but be solicitous about Christ's goodwill towards him, being conscious of his own utter unworthiness to be beloved of him, or accepted by him? All groundless jealousies arise from a secret sense and conviction of the unworthiness of the person in whom they are, and from high esteem for him concerning whose love and affection anyone is jealous. So it is with this spiritual jealousy: the root of it is love, sincere love, which 'many waters cannot quench, nor the floods drown,' which nothing can utterly prevail against and totally overcome. This gives the soul high thoughts of the glorious excellences of Christ, fills it with ecstatic admiration of him, and with longing desires after nearer communion with him; which also are mixed with a due sense of its own baseness, vileness, and unworthiness.

Now it is an easy matter to see that these thoughts may proceed too far, unless faith showeth the soul, that the glory of Christ consisteth *principally* in that he is graciously pleased to *love us*, who are to the last degree vile and sinful, with love inexpressible, invincible, and everlasting; that his love knows no cause out of itself, but that he loved us *because* he *would* love us, when we were sinners, ungodly and abominable. Now this state of jealousy about Christ's love to us, we being so unworthy of it, may be mistaken for the questioning of the promises of God, and, may be supposed to be a defect of faith, when it is an excess of love. For there is no questioning of the promises here; but rather a strong belief of them. The soul firmly believes the promises to be infallibly true; but the deep sense it has of its own extreme unworthiness, renders it difficult for it to apply them to itself in particular. He believes Christ to be the only Saviour of sinners, approves of him as such with his whole heart, longs after him, ardently loves him, is 'sick of love,' and almost dies for want of some tokens of Christ's love towards him in particular. 'Jealousy is cruel as the grave': nothing affects, torments, and distresses so much. The soul would willingly give the world for an assurance, that the object whom it so passionately loves, does not despise nor disregard it.

That this state of mind is very different from unbelief, is evident. As faith is the root and spring of all other graces; and according as that thriveth or decayeth, so they grow and flourish, or wither and die away: so unbelief, the opposite of faith, is the cause of all deadness; it is a spiritless, deadening, disheartening thing; it renders the soul weak, stupid and lifeless. See it exemplified in Psalm 78:19, 20. But this spiritual jealousy is quite a different thing, and produces very different effects. It strengthens, quickens, and enlarges the soul, and stimulates it to activity, earnestness and industry in its inquiries after Christ. The spouse in the Song of Solomon prays to be set as a seal upon Christ's heart, and as a seal upon his arm; because 'love is strong as death, and jealousy is cruel as the grave.' The soul that is restless and earnestly pants after nearer and more sensible communion with Christ, is stirred up to activity and vigour in all duties. Like the spouse in chap. 5, he seeks after Christ, calls him, and never ceases till he has found him whom his soul loveth. Every doubt and fear that takes place about the love of Christ, stirs up the soul to more earnestness in seeking him, and to a more careful watching against everything that may keep him at a distance, or cause him to hide, withdraw, or absent himself from the soul.

But I do not doubt but that you understand this state of mind much better than I can describe it to you. I have but a very confused notion of it, through want of experience and the blindness of my understanding. But it may be, these few hints may be of some assistance to you in your inquiries after the state of your soul. May you find him whom your soul loveth, and be continually happy in the manifestation and enjoyment of his love. To know him is life eternal; to feel his love shed abroad in the heart, is heaven; it exalts above misery in this world, and makes infinitely happy in the other. O let us love him, live to him, and be eternally his.

To Miss Sarah Jones

5. The Christian's Treasure – 'It Is Well'

Milborne Port, July 30, 1781.

It is an observation often made, that wherever any person's heart and affections are, there *he himself* may be said to be. For this, among other reasons, it is, that real Christians are said to be 'pilgrims and strangers here on earth,' and 'fellow-citizens with the saints,' in glory. Whilst on earth, *their* hearts are in heaven, and their affections 'are set on things above.' The true believer's heart and affections cannot but be in heaven; for his treasure – Christ, 'the pearl of great price,' – is there: and in proportion as Christ is precious to him, his heart is departing and receding from the earth, and more immovably fixed on the unsearchable treasure laid up for him in heaven. It is therefore by no means to be wondered at, that his conversation and general deportment should so widely differ from that of the children of this world; for he is a citizen of, and lives in, another and far different country:

> The most of him to heaven is fled;
> His thoughts and joys
> Are all pack'd up and gone,
> And for the dear Redeemer plead.

Of all other things I find it the most difficult to say, at all times and in every situation, with the Shunamite, 'It is well.' When all things go according to our wishes; when there is nothing in providence that crosses our desires, or thwarts our designs, then it is an easy thing to say, 'It is well.' But when our finely fabricated schemes are unravelled, and our desires denied, then to say, 'It is well,' – here is 'the patience and faith of the saints.' But everything convinces me that it is what is most reasonable and proper: it is what God as a Sovereign cannot but require, and what it is for our present as well as our future happiness to yield. But there is a stubborn principle of corruption within, which nothing but the effectual power of God can subdue. I sometimes think that I find the influence of this diabolical spirit (for diabolical it certainly is) considerably lessened; at other times it seems to rise from the dead, gain renewed strength, and act with more outrageous violence and fury than ever. There is a world of work to keep the heart in any tolerable frame towards God for one day. Well is it for us, that 'God is greater than our hearts' and can form and fashion them with infinite facility, after the counsel of his own will: and this is the will of God, 'even our sanctification'; of which a proper, humble, and submissive spirit to the Sovereign will of God, is no small part.

6. Safety in God – Hopeful and Hopeless Death

Milborne Port, Nov. 13, 1781.

AT this unhappy distance, I can only pray for you, and commit you to his safe custody, who doeth all things well, because guided by infinite wisdom and influenced by infinite goodness. Viewing you and myself as under the shadow of his wings, I can rejoice in the face of perils and in the sight of difficulties numberless. What fiery dart of the enemy can penetrate the wings that cover us? And who can pluck us out of his hands who supports us: in life, in death, here is support, here is safety! When God appears in the majesty of his glory to the eye of faith, enemies, difficulties, dangers and temptations – all vanish at once, and we are more than conquerors before we encounter our enemies. Well might David say, having God for his strength and portion, 'On earth I desire none beside him.' He is *strength* to keep us from evil, and a *portion* to fill us with real, substantial happiness. This is the *good part* which can never be taken from us. Having this, we may willingly part with earthly goods and earthly pleasures. And having this we shall fear no evil in the valley of the shadow of death.

I have been much of late in the house of mourning. Dear Mr Lucas has been so ill that we more than once despaired of his recovery. But through mercy he is now better. In the whole of his illness he was in a very comfortable frame of mind – not experiencing any great joy in believing, but full of humble confidence, and entire submission to the divine will, rather longing to be gone and to be present with the Lord than otherwise. When the things of the world fail us, and withdraw from us their usual comfort and support, then to have the root of the matter within is precious indeed! When the world recedes, and eternity is advancing on our view, with all its awful and eternal realities, then the glory of Solomon and the wealth of Croesus appear in their real insignificance. Weighed then, they are trifles light as air. Nothing then but Christ and his all-sufficient salvation can administer any comfort, and support firmly our hope in the sight of things so tremendous and so important. I know of no sight more pitiable and distressing, than that of an ungodly sinner on the confines of another world; his earthly comforts, his gods, which he all his lifetime worshipped, singly or all at once leaving him, and the soul in that hour of difficulty left naked, friendless, hopeless, starting with horror, and looking wild with despair; eternity before him, and all his sins like so many harpies following close at his heels? Good God, what a condition!

7. Indwelling Sin – Growth in Grace

Milborne Port, Dec. 11, 1781.

A GREAT deal of our uneasiness often arises from some wrong apprehensions we form to ourselves of the Christian's state in this world. We are apt to imagine that some experience a peaceable exercise of the graces of the Spirit without any opposition from the contrary corruptions. But 'the flesh lusteth against the Spirit,' saith the Apostle. In all the actings and operations of the Spirit, the flesh thwarts and opposes him; not in some particular things, but universally. Unbelief opposes faith; the natural enmity of our hearts lusteth against the love of God; despair against hope, and presumption against humility. Sin as well as grace is inherent in every faculty of the soul; and they struggle, one against the other, in every faculty, like Jacob and Esau in Rebekah's womb. Sin is at all times in *every* faculty, and hath amazing life, power, and ceaseless activity; it lusteth against the spirit in every part. So that there are two opposite principles in the regenerate soul, in every and the self-same part, constantly acting in perfect contrariety to each other, like the opposition between heat and cold in the same water. In the same *mind* there is the wisdom of the flesh, and the wisdom which is from above; in the same *will*, a delight in the law of God, and also a lusting after sin; and in the same *affections*, the love of God, and the love of other things, the fear of God, and the fear of man.

But it must be observed, that the Spirit of grace sits in the throne, rules and governs the soul in every faculty. Yet sin is sure always to oppose this divine power and authority; so that we must not expect to do anything whatever without finding 'evil present' with us. When we would believe, it will be present with us in unbelief; when we would love, it will be present with us in enmity and apathy towards God. This it is which renders our danger so great, and our close walking with God so exceedingly difficult; and which calls loudly for continual watchfullness and prayer, and for earnest and resolute striving against sin in all its motions. Without this constant and earnest striving against it, in the strength of divine grace, sin is sure to make a terrible havoc of us.

This inward spiritual war is utterly different from that opposition of the *different* faculties of the soul, which natural men experience, when their wills and affections are bent on sin on the one hand, and the light remaining in the understanding, and the judgement in the conscience, prohibit and condemn on the other. For these contrary principles in the Christian are in the *same* faculties, continually resisting each other; though grace has invincible power, being continually supported by the Almighty, and will infallibly prevail in the end.

We have also often misapprehensions of God's method of causing grace to grow. When we pray for growth in grace, we are too apt to expect, that at some favoured hour, God will put forth the greatness of his power, and at once destroy sin, and put grace in the entire and quiet possession of our souls. But instead of this, it often happens, that corruptions are let loose and permitted to rage more terribly than ever; and these very eruptions of our corrupt nature are overruled for good; and grace gains strength by that very means which we have thought would have ruined it. The power of corruption being shown in a more fearful light than ever, God strengthens weak grace to oppose it. See this particularly described by the Apostle, Romans 5:3-5.

> I asked the Lord that I might grow
>   In faith and love and every grace,
> Might more of His salvation know,
>   And seek more earnestly His face.
>
> 'Twas He who taught me thus to pray,
>   And He, I trust, has answer'd prayer;
> But it has been in such a way,
>   As almost drove me to despair.

8. The Best Friend – Recovery from Illness

Milborne Port, Jan. 24, 1782.

WHEN I reflect on the goodness which God has lately showed me, both of a temporal and of a spiritual nature, I feel myself humbled to the dust; and my heart is filled with gratitude too big to be uttered but by tears. I had nothing wanting either from God above, or from man beneath: the one filled my heart with spiritual comforts and joys; and the other, in the most feeling manner, expressed a *willingness*, and at the same time an inability, to relieve my body. It is but very little that the kindest friend can do for us, when God puts his little finger to touch us. One would say to me: 'Well, how do you do now?' 'Very indifferent.' A second would add: 'What, no better?' 'No.' 'Well, I am very sorry for you indeed.' A third would observe: 'I wish I knew how to do you good.' But here it all ended. They could not diminish the motion of one drop of blood, nor remove in any degree my pain, nor add at all to my strength. But Jesus Christ is a friend, as you observe, in *need* and *indeed*. He hath power to make his love and his kindness effectual. To will, and to do, are the same things with him. He hath infinite power to put in execution what infinite love dictates; and in all he is directed by infinite wisdom. O happy hour when we meet with such a friend! I hope to cultivate this friendship, and improve my intercourse with him more than ever.

Through mercy I am now very much recovered, being easy in my body and comfortable in my mind. When I think of being useful in any small degree in promoting the Redeemer's interest and kingdom in the world, I feel strong desires after life; otherwise, the language of my heart in general is, 'To depart and to be with Christ, is far better.' O my dear friend, we know not the value of a Saviour, till eternity draws near. Then to be able to call him mine: What comfort! What joy does it bring! Nothing wounds me deeper, or humbles me more, than to reflect on the little value I have put upon him, on the insensibility and coldness with which I have often thought of him, and above all, on the unwearied kindness which he shows after such a treatment.

I never found myself so indifferent to the world. May the Spirit of God ever keep me crucified to it. But whilst I am in it, I desire ardently to be wholly engaged in peopling heaven, that blessed but much neglected region. This is the sum of my wishes and desires whilst in this wilderness. I sometimes feel some fears when I look at my own weakness, and at the many dangers and enemies I am continually surrounded with, inwardly and outwardly: but 'greater,' saith the Apostle, 'is he that is in us, than he that is in the world,' greater in every way, in wisdom strength, etc., etc. And though we may not, at times, feel it so, yet we have God's word for it, therefore we need not fear.

9. All Events under God's Direction

Milborne Port, March 1, 1782.

NEVER was a truer saying than this: 'Fod y Duw da, yn gwneuthur pob peth yn dda, er da i'w bobl' ('that the good God makes all things good, for good to his people'). Everything, the smallest as well as the greatest event, is ordered and directed by divine goodness and wisdom for their good. He is as much present with, and takes as much care of, every one of his children, as if he had no other creature to watch over and take care of, in the whole universe. A mother may forget her sucking child, or if she remembers him, she may be unable to help him, to ward off any impending danger and secure his safety. But the Lord is always equally as mindful of his people, as he is able to protect them. Nothing can happen without his notice, and everything will be directed by him to answer some good and important purpose. It is our duty, as well as our comfort, to see him in everything, both in small and great events, in an inflamed leg as well as in a burning fever.

Everything has importance in it, when we are taught by grace to improve it. What to appearance was but the carcase of a dead lion, afforded Samson honey and sweetness. Everything is great in proportion to its use effects, and consequences; and a great blessing may make that, which is in itself but trifling and insignificant, very great, beneficial and important. We ought therefore in everything to look to the great God for a great blessing: and according to our faith and expectations shall it be to us. He will never disappoint his people, who wait upon him; for he is able to do more than they are able to ask or think. O how great is his goodness. We can never depend too much upon him, nor expect too much from him. Let us never treat him as if he were such an one as ourselves; but let us form expectations from him, suitable to his infinite greatness, goodness and liberality.

10. Spiritual Communion

Milborne Port, March 15, 1782.

THIS is not an improper representation of the little I know of spiritual communication between my soul and him who is not ashamed to call sinners his 'friends' and to own them as his 'brethren.' Without hearing from him, and without speaking to him, life indeed would be intolerable; this long absence would be horrid distraction, and this wilderness would be the most dismal dungeon. There is no small comfort to be enjoyed in emptying my heart into his bosom in all my perplexities, and in waiting upon him, though he gives me no immediate answer. But when he speaks, 'his lips drop as the honeycomb'; his words are music in the ear, and jubilee in the heart. He 'speaketh peace to his people,' speaketh it with energy and power into the very centre of the distracted heart. He speaketh, and it is done. He rebukes with efficacy the winds and the sea; and everything obeys him. I would at all times say unto him, 'Speak, Lord, for thy servant heareth.' I have every reason to be very thankful, for he is not at any time for a long season silent. He is either rebuking, reproving, exhorting, or comforting; either telling what I am in myself, or what he is: what is his power, sufficiency, dignity, and glory. He loves, but never flatters; he reproves, but never hates; he is rich, but never answers roughly; he is exalted, but condescends to those of low estate. He is ashamed of none, however unworthy and miserable, but of those who are ashamed of him. Though his people be the offscouring of all things, though the world reject, persecute, and hate them; yet Christ will not be ashamed of them. Were they loaded with reproaches and scorn, and covered all over with the filth and dust of false accusations; were they in rags, in dungeons, and put to the most shameful death; yet Christ will own them and say, 'surely these are my brethren, the children of my father.'

But you know him better than I can describe him to you. However, as you love him, you will not be sorry, nor tired, to hear a poor, ignorant creature tell what he hath found him to be, and what he hath experienced from him. 'This is my beloved, this is my friend.' I think I hear you say: 'and mine too.' I am ashamed that I can speak no better of him; but he is 'beyond all blessing and praise.' The blessed time is hastening, when we shall think and speak of him in a different manner, in a manner more suitable to his love, goodness, and dignity. In the meantime let us honour him, by continually maintaining an intercourse between him and our souls, and by being active in his service and in promoting his interest. This is the highest honour we are capable of in this world, and the greatest happiness we can enjoy.

11. Human Counsel Not Safe

Milborne Port, March 29, 1782.

IMPLICITLY to follow the counsel of the best and wisest of men is to depend on an arm of flesh. They only are in the right and safe way, who make the glory of God their end, the word of God their rule, the Spirit of God the guide of their affections, and the providence of God the guide of their affairs. They may be confident that the Lord goes before them. Though he may not lead them the *nearest* way, yet he will lead them the *best* way; as it will surely appear, when they shall come to their journey's end.

Sometimes, indeed, the Lord moves before his people in a cloud. Everything to their view is involved in impenetrable darkness. They see not before them; nor can they form any notion of 'the end of the Lord.' But when they walk in darkness, and have no light, they may safely trust in the Lord; for he is moving forward towards Canaan both in the cloud and in the pillar of fire, both when things are dark and obscure, and when they are clear but trying. In all, grace follows God, trusts in him in the cloud, and rejoices in him in the fire. May he be our guide till death; and may our hearts follow him implicitly.

12. The Happy Effects of Real Humility

Milborne Port, April 4, 1782.

WE have every moment cause for praise and humility, for thankfullness and self-abhorrence, for exalting God and debasing ourselves. There is no fear of excess in either. When God is exalted in our praises far above all heavens, he is still infinitely beyond all blessing and praise. And when we are debased in dust and ashes, we are still far, very far, from being where we ought to be; we are even there highly exalted. This is the view we always have of God and of ourselves, when we are in a spiritual and godly frame; we think we can never love God too much, nor exalt him too high, nor debase ourselves too low. When our hearts burn most fervently with divine love, we think we fall infinitely short of our duty, and feel a secret humbling dissatisfaction with ourselves, because we cannot love and exalt him enough. So also when we have the most humbling and abasing sense of our own vileness, we are dissatisfied, and are full of indignation against ourselves, because we are not still more vile in our own eyes; we would sink as it were into nothing. St Paul felt what he said when he called himself 'less than the least' – he could not go lower – 'of all saints,' and the 'chief' of sinners. Words easily spoken, but not so soon inwardly and sincerely felt. People may talk what they please about religion; yet I am sure that we possess not one grain more of it, than we have of this humble and self-abasing spirit. It is the only frame in which we can hold communion with God, enjoy the comforts of the gospel and adorn religion in our lives and conversation.

Did we all possess this spirit, how easy would it be to live in this world! We could then find no difficulty in thinking others better than ourselves; nor could we then find any resentment in our hearts when slighted and neglected, but should naturally be contented in whatever state we should be in, whether honoured or neglected, whether poor or rich, whether in prosperity or adversity. We would then thankfully receive the water we drink from a bountiful God, being inwardly sensible, that we are less than the least of God's mercies, more worthless than the meanest blessing we receive from God, not only undeserving of the water we drink and the air we breathe in, but less than the least of all his mercies, more base and vile, and less deserving of God's notice. There is nothing wanted but this blessed humility to make us thankful, contented, meek and happy in every situation. The pride of others would then pass over our heads without obstruction or hindrance; their favour would not exalt us, or their frowns distress us. This humility would at once put an end to all contentions in the world; nor would the church be any longer pestered with those who 'love to have the pre-eminence.' We should be all little children. We *should* – but, alas! we are not. Would to God we were. Well, I hope I shall look upon every providence, every slight, every neglect, every reproach and shame, that hath the smallest tendency to humble me, as a choice blessing from God, I hope he will go on with his work, whatever the means may be which he is pleased to make use of, and throw down 'every imagination and high thing, and bring into captivity every thought to the obedience of Christ.' O blessed humility! It is the proper soil and nourishment of every grace. Pride starves, humility nourishes and strengthens every grace.

13. The Infallible Physician

Milborne Port, April 19, 1782.

As to 'the disease of soul' of which you feelingly complain, I have no uneasy apprehensions about it. You are in the best hands, and under the care of an infallible Physician. I doubt not but that the cure will be complete and glorious in good time; for he has never as yet lost a patient. If we feel his hand upon us, well and good: that is all we have to care for. Let us stick to him without any hesitation: and though the disease may at times seem to us to be inveterate and almost incurable; yet the cure is going on with more favourable symptoms than we imagine, and by ways and means we little think of. He hath had long experience, and possesses admirable skill. He perfectly knows the nature of every disease, and the intrinsic quality of every means and of every restorative.

Could we but take a peep through the veil by faith, we might see in heaven monuments of his skill, care and love, that would overpower us with astonishment. There we might see the 'woman that was a sinner,' Saul that was a persecutor, the thief that was a blasphemer, and Adam the vilest of all, that was everything that was bad – *all* perfectly cured – all healthy and strong, without the smallest seed of any disease in them: all glorious, without blemish, without spot or wrinkle or any such thing. Oh! 'he will be glorified in his saints, and admired in all them that believe.' Assure yourself of this, that whatever aspect the disease may put on, and however gloomy the prospect may be to you, yet the work now is, and in future shall be, in a progressive state. It is a work which Christ hath had at heart from all eternity, and will he be disappointed? No, no; 'he worketh and none can let.'

14. The Goodness and Love of God

Milborne Port, May 15, 1782.

THE Lord is very good indeed. Shame be to us for ever thinking otherwise! Thinking otherwise, when everything we have within us and without us, excepting sin, is a proof of it! Nay, and does not sin, that 'evil always present' with us, display his goodness and show it forth illustriously? His goodness to angels and holy beings is infinite: but what shall we call that goodness and love which are freely extended to sinners, to rebels, to traitors, to the ungodly! Is not this, were it possible, more than infinite? O the depth! In the contemplation of it may you and I live and die, and spend a happy (for happy it must be), a happy eternity. When we lose sight of it, all must be darkness, confusion, and misery.

Nothing but the free, undeserved, and eternal love of God, without any motive exciting it but what is in himself, can give us one gleam of hope or one ray of comfort in the midst of the horrid gloom into which sin hath brought us. But the belief of this darts ineffable joy into the miserable soul, as if the sun in all its meridian splendour, was to burst forth upon us in midnight darkness. I must proceed no further, for enough for a sermon comes at once into my head on the delightful subject. But I cannot drop it without wishing that you and I may live in the belief of John 16:27: 'The Father himself loveth you, because ye have loved me.'

15. Fear and Love – The Love of Christ

Milborne Port, Oct. 11, 1782.

HAVE you not more fears of losing Christ than anything else in the whole world? And does not this prove that you love him supremely, far, far above all other things? Let your fears then add strength to your faith, and encouragement to your hope. You can never have a surer proof of one's love to you than his fear of losing you; and love and fear are always proportioned to each other without absolute enjoyment. Christ looks kindly upon our fears, sees sincere love at the bottom, and is not backward to confirm our hearts in his love to us, and in the full and certain belief as to the full enjoyment of him. My love to you is ineffectual; it can be impatient at delays, but it cannot remove difficulties: it often is *a will without the power*. But Christ's love is effectual; it can with infinite ease remove all difficulties, and give us at once the full enjoyment of him. It *can*, did I say, I should have rather said, it *has* removed them. Difficulties and obstructions infinite between us and him, have been removed by his love.

Oh, what hath love done, or rather what hath it not done! We had other suitors and other lovers; but Christ hath conquered and effectually destroyed them all. There was great unsuitableness between us; for we were to the last degree unfit for him, and incapable of enjoying his fellowship; but his love undertook to make us what he would have us to be, and what we *must* be, to enjoy fellowship with him. We were in debt also, and consequently under the absolute power of our creditors: but his love hath freely undertaken to pay *all*. He finds us poor, wretched, and miserable, entirely depraved and deformed in every part; but his love makes us comely with *his* comeliness, rich with *his* riches, glorious with *his* glory; and when he will bring his Bride home to his Father's house, she will be without spot or wrinkle, or any such thing. There will be seen in her no blemish, no deformity; but 'Zion will be the perfection of beauty'; no wrinkle will appear, no sign of decay; but her beauty will be eternal, and unfading bloom will rest upon her.

Oh, what wonders hath his love performed and continues to perform! It is in itself mysterious and wonderful, and in its effects astonishing. Angels will never admire it sufficiently when they see before them, in the case of every believer, the amazing effects it hath produced. 'The beauty of the Lord their God will be upon them,' Psa. 90:17. What a change! Those who were before entirely defaced with the deformity of devils, will now wear eternally the beauty of the Lord! What an idea doth this give of the future holiness and glory of those who are now groaning under the burden of sin, and crying out daily, 'O wretched man that I am!' All expressions are too short to set forth their glorious state but this: 'The beauty of the Lord their God shall be upon them.' Shall they be delivered from sin and misery? Yes. Shall they be happy? Yes. Shall they be perfectly holy, free from every spot and the least stain of sin? Yes. How desirable is all this! The very thought of this brings heaven to the soul. But all this is only a part of their glory and happiness. To crown all, 'the beauty of the Lord their God shall be upon them.' This carries them to such glory that we lose sight of them in its splendour and brightness. They are brought so near the sun, that our eyes are dazzled to behold them: they are lost in a blaze of glory.

But let us remember, Christ loves us *now* in our rags, in our poverty, when deformed and depraved. With what difficulty are we brought to believe this! Hence proceed our fears. We love Christ; but at the same time, being conscious of our deformity, we fear he will not love us. Indeed reason would so conclude; but the gospel reveals to us different things. May the Lord enable us to believe his testimony in his gospel against reason and everything else, and to hope against hope. Nothing pleases him more than our confidence in his love, when we have the meanest thoughts of ourselves: that he will still love us, notwithstanding all the accusations of Satan against us, whether true or false. Satan thought surely that he succeeded against Joshua: but he was mistaken. The Lord rebuked him, and showed to him that he did not love Joshua *for* his beauty, but *to make* him beautiful. Christ gave him a change of raiment, and at once silenced the adversary. Let us believe and rejoice evermore in his free love.

16. The Furnace and the Refiner

Milborne Port, Oct. 29, 1782.

I HAVE often thought and reflected with profit and comfort, on that passage in Malachi; it is exceedingly beautiful and expressive, 'he shall sit as a refiner and purifier of silver, etc.' It emphatically expresses his wonderful patience, his great care and attention, his admirable skill and unwearied diligence. At the same time that he sits at the right hand of God, he sits over the furnace, superintending and directing all the operations: he puts the ore in; he keeps it there, and takes it out whenever he pleases; and the heat of the furnace is increased or diminished exactly according to his order. His eye is always in the furnace, seeing at once the operations of the fire, taking care that the minutest particle of the precious ore may be carefully preserved, and that nothing but the dross should he consumed. Sometimes he takes it out, and with what pleasure, think you, does he see the progress made in the purification of the precious ore! But still he sees some dross cleaving to it, he therefore puts it in again, and perhaps increases gradually the heat of the furnace; but still takes care that the ore is not impaired. It must be melted indeed, and the fire must enter every part where any dross is: but it shall consume nothing but the dross. When these operations are going on, doubtless the devil is not far off. Many a load of fuel does he bring, and often attempts to contrive that the ore may be consumed with the dross. But, blessed be the Lord, Christ is never absent and never unwatchful. He checks the devil and puts on the fuel himself in exact weight and measure. He has, and ever will have, the management of the whole work till it is entirely finished. Whilst we ardently wish to part with the dross, let us joyfully welcome the furnace, and trust in the skill and care of the refiner. When we entrust ourselves to his care, his gracious promise is, 'When thou walkest through the fire, thou shalt not be burned.' But he will heat the furnace sevenfold before he will suffer any of the dross to remain; yet still the ore shall be preserved. Have you a mind to see the ore thoroughly purified? Read Rev. 7:13-15. It will glitter with such brightness that angels will be hardly able to look upon it.

True, 'it is not joyous now but grievous'; but is it not more grievous to have the dross still remaining? O yes! anything but the dross, any furnace, any fire; but no dross. And *so* says Christ. 'Take away all iniquity,' says grace: 'I will cleanse them from all their iniquity,' says Christ. When he seeth any unbelief, carnal security, false peace, or earthly-mindedness, mixed in an increasing degree with the opposite graces, he will not, he cannot, suffer this dross to remain. He kindles his fire, heats his furnace, and puts in the ore. Well, let him 'do all his pleasure,' and success to him in the name of the Lord. It is an infinite mercy to be under his hand, *in* the furnace or *out* of the furnace. Let the fire burn and rage ever so furiously; it is far better to be in *his* furnace, than to be in the devil's palace. Let us pray that the work may go on, whatever we may suffer and lose by it. It is a great thing to see our dross to be what it really is, not to overvalue it, but with St Paul, to count all things loss and dung, except the pure ore. Let us be willing to part with it, and suffer the Lord to take it away in his own way and manner. May the Lord make the present heating of the furnace profitable to your soul. Expect and wait for deliverance in the Lord's good time: but let me know when you are come out.

17. The Spiritual Contest

Milborne Port, November 13, 1782.

If I from others differ ought,
    Lord, 'twas Thy grace the diff'rence wrought:
If I one holy wish have known,
    That wish was giv'n by Thee alone.

To taste Thy love is sweeter far
    Than all earth's dainties, choice and rare:
'Tis heav'n to see Thy smiling face;
    'Tis heav'n, to feel Thy Spirit's rays.

I cannot pay the thanks I owe
    For tasting *once* Thy love below;
Yet cannot rest till I above
    Shall feast for ever on Thy love.

The smallest drop of precious grace
    Demands a ceaseless song of praise;
Yet largest draughts from mercy's store
    But make me long and pant for more.

For teaching this, Thy name I bless –
    That holiness is happiness:

To Miss Sarah Jones

> *Quite* happy I shall never be
>   Till I am *quite* conformed to Thee.
>
> O strengthen me Thy will to do,
>   And when Thou wilt, to suffer too:
> Imperfect here, I long to soar,
>   Where I shall disobey no more.
>
> Lord, be Thy pleasure always mine;
>   I wish to have no will but Thine:
> This, this, is heav'n enough for me,
>   Quite to be swallow'd up in Thee.

A friend of mine put these lines lately into my hands; and because they please me, I send them to you. It is not the beauty of the poetry, which is not great: but the piety of the sentiments, that pleases me, and would be as agreeable in animated prose, as in dull verse; yea, and more so. The law of my mind always says, 'This, this is heaven enough for me, quite to be swallowed up in thee'; but the law in my members speaks a very different language. It will be a thrice happy time indeed, when God shall be all in all. At times I fain would think he is so now, at least I ardently long for the time when he really will be so. But now alas! I often cannot do the thing I would. Enemies make inroads into my territories, and sometimes in so terrible a manner that I hardly know who is Lord over me; though I generally can say, whom I *desire* forever to rule and reign within. I endeavour in some poor way to call upon him, and remind him of his gracious promise, especially when I see but little progress made, and I am fearful of losing ground. This is the most effectual way I find of recovering lost ground, and of making some advances forward, that is, to remind a faithful God of his promise and call on him for help.

Through mercy I find, in the midst of my unworthiness, the truth of the following words, 'whosoever,' – let him be what or who he will – 'shall call upon the name of the Lord, shall be saved.' The Lord is 'a very *present* help in trouble,' not help at a distance that may come too late, but a *present* help; or as the Psalmist says of the Church, 'God shall help her and that right *early*'; in sufficient time to save us and glorify himself. He may not come as soon as *we* expect him, but he will surely come in a *seasonable* hour. Indeed I find it very difficult, when my strength fails me, and everything seems to be against me, to believe that he will come at all, conscience at the same time telling me that I am *deservedly* left and forsaken, if forever. Surely, I say within myself, he will no more be gracious to me, who hath made such base returns for former mercies, and so often grieved his holy Spirit. It may be perhaps in the midst of this unbelief and of these desponding and melancholy thoughts, that he will surprise and astonish me at once with the noise of his coming, and the glorious effulgence of his gracious presence. My soul is in amazement, and would fain cry out in the language of one of our Bala friends, O rhyfedd! rhyfedd! – O wonderful! wonderful!

The longer I live, the more I am puzzled with myself, and the more I am astonished at the Lord's conduct toward me. I have more than once found in experience the one and the same cause producing very different and opposite effects. Though men do not, yet I believe God can, and often does, 'gather grapes of thorns, and figs of thistles.' In everything he will show himself to be God, an absolute Sovereign, working *when* and *how* he pleases. Sometimes when I have found various corruptions, strong and turbulent within, I have been brought into great darkness, perplexity, and distress of mind, experiencing grace, weak and feeble and in its workings almost imperceptible, having no feeling view of God, Christ, or spiritual things, and tossed up and down between hopes and fears. At other times, to my great astonishment, though I found corruptions full as strong and restless, yet God hath graciously continued to shine upon me by the light of his countenance, given me a sense of his love, and enabled me to rejoice with joy unspeakable and full of glory.

O the depth of the riches both of the wisdom and the knowledge of God! His paths are past finding out! But in general, he who walks holily, walks comfortably: and there are no comforts that even come from God without immediate and direct tendency and influence to promote holiness in the soul. This is an infallible mark by which they may be known from all illusions and false conceits: for whatever promotes vital holiness cometh from God; and everything that comes from God effectually promotes holiness.

18. Zeal – Resignation – Heaven – Christ Our Rest

Milborne Port, Nov. 29, 1782.

I wish we had a little Welsh zeal in this country. But, alas! we have hardly any zeal here, except in the service of Satan. I am glad to hear that the Lord's work prospers anywhere. There is nothing worth living for, but to advance it. May the Lord engage my heart more thoroughly in it. I can sincerely say, that I would far sooner die than to serve myself. At the same time I find it no easy thing in all things to deny myself.

I shall be humble, I hope, and thankful, if the Lord grant me my request. My friends at times rail at me and say, that 'I make as much ado as if there were no other woman in the world but you, or that could not live without you.' My answer is, 'There is no one that suits me so well, nor can I live comfortably without her, till I can see clearly that Providence absolutely denies her to me.' Well, 'but I am so impatient.' My reply is, 'Not so: I love her, and shall be thankful for her, when Providence gives her to me.' I am very glad that you are calm and easy: this will greatly contribute to make me so. Through mercy I find my mind at once acquiescing in the Lord's disposal of M. D. When his determination and my wishes disagree, I can be at no loss to know who is in the right. However, it is one thing to know, and another to acquiesce. I doubt not, when I shall see 'the end of the Lord,' but that I shall be thankful. For all these waters that are now bitter, will one day be turned into wine; and the review and remembrance of all present perplexities will be humbling and pleasing. I shall in everything see enough of my own sinfullness to humble me, and of the Lord's goodness to make me comfortable and thankful.

Blessed be the Lord for the pleasing prospect of that happy time, when knowing and feeling will be the same thing. Here we know but little, and feel less: but there we shall know as we are known, and everything we shall know will have its due effect upon us. O happy world! Into which sin hath no admittance. It will be a heaven indeed. Angels will know but little of our joys, because unacquainted with our sorrows. To emerge out of misery so great, and find ourselves in bliss so consummate – this will be transporting indeed! We shall play on strings which angels never touched. But alas! Where are we now! In what sin! In what misery! At what distance, shall I say? Nay, may we not be near the banks of that river which divides both worlds! Will the crossing of it bring us to God? Shall we then be ever with the Lord? This is the important question, the solution of which is of more eternal consequence than ten thousand worlds. All I can say is, I shall be happy when delivered from *sin*, and *never* till then. I can truly say, 'I groan, being burdened.'

But what do I hear? Hear? Yes, I hear words sounding in my ears with heavenly melody; I hear the Lamb of God who taketh away the sin of the world, saying, 'Come to me!' And who? 'All ye that are weary and heavy laden.' And what for? 'And *I* will give you rest.' Oh! blessed Saviour, and wilt thou take our burden and give us thy rest? and are we all invited to partake of this rest? Am I called, one so unworthy, so sinful, and so unthankful? '*All* ye that are weary and heavy laden.' But, Lord, my burden is so heavy that I cannot move under it; I cannot come. 'The Father who hath sent me,' he adds, 'shall *draw* him.' Yes, Lord, when the Father draweth, I shall come to thee and find rest to my soul. There is deliverance to be had; we need not languish under our burden, however heavy it may press, and however unable we may be to bear it. O! ten thousand thanks for rest in Christ! O Father! *Draw* us to him.

19. Walking with God

Milborne Port, Jan. 8, 1783.

To know the mind and will of God is the peculiar privilege of his own people. 'The secret of the Lord is with them that fear him.' As all others are wholly devoid of any real desire to know or to follow

To Miss Sarah Jones

his will, so they are also, in a spiritual sense, totally ignorant of it. The light of the sun they are destitute of and despise, but follow a light of their own kindling, which, at every step leads them in the wrong way, deceives and ruins them. 'But,' saith the apostle, 'We have the mind of Christ' – we have it as our light and our guide, which we follow with comfort and safety. Partly with this view it is said of some of the saints of old, that 'they walked with God.' They had such a knowledge of God, how he was disposed towards them, and such an intimate acquaintance with his mind and will, as a friend has of his intimate associate, between whom there is the greatest freedom of intercourse. It expresses such a degree of confidence, intimacy, and familiarity, as must bring the greatest comfort, and afford the fullest direction in every perplexity, and the most abundant security in every difficulty. And this is not a privilege peculiar to some of the more eminent saints; but all are entitled to 'walk humbly with God.' Indeed some are enabled to cleave more fully and steadily to God than others, have more intimacy and confidence in him, enjoy more of his love, and know more of his mind and will: but it is a privilege, set before all believers, to walk with God as a Father; and they are *all* expected to 'cleave to him with full purpose of heart.'

There is something very expressive in the words, 'Walk with God.' They are *with* him. They do not walk in the same way, but at a distance from him, at one time running before him, and at another following afar off and lingering behind; but they walk *with* him, in closeness of union and nearness of communion. They 'come up out of the wilderness, leaning upon their beloved.' They are also walking *with* him, and never without him. They follow him, as the Israelites did the cloud in the wilderness. When he moves, they move; and when he rests, they rest. Can they at all walk without him? No, not in the right way. God is their life, their light, and their strength; and a man who has neither eyes, nor legs, nor life, may as soon move and walk as we can walk in the narrow way without God. But believers can, and do walk *with* him; with him who is their only strength and support, their present help in trouble; with him who is their guide, leading them on every step of the road. Without him they have neither strength nor knowledge to proceed one step forward; but with him darkness is light before them, the weak is strong, the faint courageous, and those who could do nothing can do all things. He is their God, on whom and to whom they live and walk: they have his glory in view in all their motions, and they look to him as their all in all. God also abundantly answers all their desires after him and confidence in him; he bears them up in his arms, and carries them in his bosom as a nursing Father, when they are faint and feeble. He feeds them with the bread of life, renewing their strength and refreshing their spirits with the abundant communications of grace daily. Thus Enoch walked with God three hundred years. Surely it was a long heaven on earth! And have we the same privilege? We have indeed. We have the privilege of walking *in* Christ and *with* God, Col. 2:6. If it be so, why should we be perplexed about the way. If we walk *with* God, doubtless he will lead us in the right way every step.

Unbelief and Satan would indeed suggest at times that 'the Lord hath forgotten,' that 'the Lord hath forsaken us.' But what saith God? 'Can a woman forget her sucking child? Behold I have graven them on the palms of my hands.' And do we walk with a Being so overflowingly full of love and tenderness; and will he not hear us? Will he not help and direct us 'in time of need?' We may as well think and believe there is no God, as that he would act thus. God forbid that we should ever thus dishonour him, by thoughts so unsuitable to his being, his love, his covenant, his oath, and his promise! Let God be love, let God be true, let him be what he is, and what he has revealed himself to be to us, though we should be on the dunghill with Job. Who ever saw the righteous forsaken? Not the devil himself. God gave Job indeed into his hands; he could not be in a worse place this side hell. But Job walked with God, and God was with him, and brought him out of the furnace like gold purified in the fire. God is the same still. Granting we have not Job's grace, still I trust we have Job's God, and that is enough. Well, then, I hope in every case we shall be enabled to cleave to God; and he will make rough things smooth, and crooked things straight before us. With what gratitude should we reflect on his amazing condescension in taking our poor concerns into his own hands and management! When by faith I can commit all to him, and see all in his hands, I look forward with confidence, with comfort, and with joy. Intricacies and perplexities vanish at once. I see him bringing order out of confusion, light out of darkness, and accomplishing his purposes by the most unlikely and unthought-of means. I see all in his wise and omnipotent hand: angels above and devils below, sinners in the world and believers in Zion; all, whether willing or unwilling, obeying his orders and accomplishing his purposes. O, blessed be the Lord for his goodness. When I reflect on my own unworthiness, I know not how to believe anything: but his goodness overcomes all.

20. An Overhasty Spirit – Worldly Cares

Milborne Port, Jan. 25, 1783.

IN everything we need to watch against ourselves; and in few things more than against an overhasty spirit. What brought that trouble and vexation upon Sarah, from her maid Hagar, but too much haste to have the promise of a son accomplished? She could not wait the Lord's time; but as she had no child, she would give her maid to her husband, and have the promise accomplished in her own time and in her own way, instead of leaving the Lord to work for himself. This was the case also with Rebekah. She knew that Jacob was to obtain the blessing, and that the elder was to serve the younger, but she thought that the Lord had forgotten his promise, when the day was come for Esau to receive the blessing; and therefore she would take the work out of the Lord's hand and manage it herself. This lost her the beloved son, and brought all the future trouble on poor Jacob for complying with the unjust means his mother had made use of.

Rebekah's temptation was no doubt very great. She believed the promise of God to Jacob; at the same time she saw everything going against the accomplishment of it. Isaac favoured Esau, and followed his own inclinations too much, with little regard to God's declaration, that the elder was to serve the younger; and he was on the point of bestowing the blessing upon him whom God had not loved. To prevent this, Rebekah steps in, as if nothing could preserve God's veracity but her officiousness. All this doubtless was written for our learning. There is as much difficulty in waiting the accomplishment of the promise as in believing it. Neither of which can we do till we are dead to ourselves and give up all to God. 'He that believeth shall not make haste.'

I would make one observation upon what you say about worldly cares, which lately occurred to me in reading the parable of the sower. It is this: It is not the passing through our rounds of worldly cares that injures the soul, but their *taking root* and *growing* there. The thorns were rooted in the same ground with the good seed, and grew with it. These thorns our Saviour explains to be the cares, the riches and the pleasures of this life. When all or either of these are *rooted* in the soul, and grow in it as in their own proper soil, they must damage it inexpressibly. Cares and riches often fall in the way of the true Christian. He is obliged at times to handle these thorns, however uncomfortable it may be to him; but they must be carefully kept *without* him; and he must see above all things that no such bitter roots grow in his heart. Where these are rooted and thriving, however promising the appearance of the good seed, yet no fruit can there be brought forth to perfection. It will only be an empty blade, without any real grain. The good seed will never bring forth fruit to perfection but in a single heart: a heart single to God, where there is no other root, nor anything else growing besides the good seed.

21. The Guidance of the Holy Spirit

Milborne Port, Feb. 28, 1783.

STRANGE are the effects of sin upon the heart! It is most amazingly stupified and rendered insensible often:

> Goodness and wrath in vain combine,
> To stir this stupid heart of mine.

To Miss Sarah Jones

Nothing but the Holy Ghost can give us any feeling of either, or enable us to retain it when we have it. We see nothing spiritually, and we feel nothing effectually, but as he is pleased daily to work in us and upon us. I am happy to think that I am wholly in his hands, that he observes every avenue to my soul, and can turn every spring that gives it motion; and therefore can turn and influence it in the way, degree, and time he pleases. This is my chief spring of consolation both as to temporal and spiritual things. The Spirit can in everything influence my heart, guide my thoughts, and direct my inclinations according to his own will. If his will be so, he can incline me to a place or thing, and effectually open a way through the thickest darkness and greatest difficulties for the accomplishment of his own wise purposes.

In walking with God – to take up a former and to me a very comfortable subject – we are *led* by the Spirit. He brings us through Christ to God, and leads and guides us in our walking with him. He also helpeth our infirmities. Our infirmities, alas! how great, and how numerous! They would forever be an insurmountable obstacle to our walking with God, were it not that the Spirit effectually overcometh them all, supports us under them, and enables us to prevail over them. Infirmities we must expect to carry about us, to groan and travail under, while in the world: but whilst the Spirit is with us to help them, we have no great cause to complain. Let us endeavour to look more to our helper than to our infirmities; and then we shall not be greatly discouraged.

In everything we have our infirmities: in prayer, in hearing, in meditation, in our conversation and daily walk. But in everything the Spirit helpeth our infirmities. Infirmities are all ours; but the help is all God's: and whatever help we have against them is entirely from his Spirit. When I attempt to believe, to love, or to obey, alas! how do I often feel my infirmities pressing me down! But often when I am just ready to sink, the Spirit helpeth, and all is at once easy, and my difficulties are over. Here is a comforter that will never fail, though all others should forsake, frown upon, and hate us. O happy despised believer, that hath the Spirit to help him! The following words have been in my mind all this evening: 'As many as are led by the Spirit of God, they are the sons of God.' May you and I be ever led in everything by this safe guide.

22. The Single Eye

Milborne Port, March 25, 1783.

I SHUDDER at the thought of living to the world and to self. Surely this would be the greatest curse that could in this world fall upon me. Last night and this morning I have thought a great deal on the following words of our Saviour, 'If thine eye be single, thy whole body is full of light.'[1] A single eye is that which hath but one object in view; and a double eye and a double heart is that which views and follows after more than one object at the same time. This one object is the one thing needful; and David tells us what it is when he says, 'Whom have I in heaven but thee; and on earth I desire none but thee.' God and his glory, then, is that single object which we ought to have in view: and when it is so, 'the whole body is full of light,' the whole soul is full of divine knowledge and clear apprehensions of divine things; doubts, fears, and perplexities are banished; and the path in which we should go, and the work which we are to do, are clear before us. 'The whole body,' all we are and all we do, 'shall be full of light' – full of holiness, peace and joy. If there be any consolation in Christ, if any comfort of love, if any peace that passeth all understanding, if any rejoicing in hope of the glory of God, surely he whose eye is single is a partaker of them, for his 'whole body is full of light.' Without this single eye, there is no such thing, I am fully persuaded, as walking with God, nor living usefully to him; but we must be ever overwhelmed with the cares and perplexities of this world. I have more than once observed respecting myself, that the want of the single eye hath been the cause of all my perplexities and fears. When I looked forward and

---

[1] Probably the exposition given here of this text is not quite correct; but the divinity of what follows is altogether correct and scriptural. The 'single' eye is properly the *sound* eye, an eye that can see clearly, being not diseased or injured by any spot or defect.

thought I saw clouds gathering, how hath my heart sunk within me! But why? Because I had my own ease, interest, and credit too much at heart, and knew not how to part with them. Had mine eye been taken off from these, and fixed upon God only, my fears would have at once subsided; and calmness and confidence would have possessed my soul. I have found it so. When God and his glory was the only object in view, I have been calm and joyful in the midst of thick clouds and storms; so true it is, that when 'the eye is single, the whole body is full of light.'

An expression of Mr Whitefield in one of his letters, has been often on my mind. After enumerating some difficulties he had to encounter with, he says, 'But a single eye will carry us through all.' It will indeed. I am never happy nor prosperous as to the soul, when I possess it not. I often judge of the frame of my mind by this one thing. If I find my eye single to God, it is no bad season, he is not far off. Acting and living daily in opposition to self in every way, and for God and his cause, is the best means in the world to make and keep the eye single. We must consider everything we are and have, as of no farther or other use, than that of devoting it in one way or another, to God and his service. Like the poor widow, we must cast daily into God's treasury all the living that we have, were it but two mites. Two mites we all have, that is, soul and body. Let us put them in God's treasury, if we have no more, and spend and be spent for him, who gave himself for us. The thought of living to God here, when my eye is single, is a sort of heaven to my soul. In every other view I am tired of the world, which is so full of vanity, sin, and folly.

23. Trusting the Lord – His Promise to Be with Us

Milborne Port, April 1, 1783.

How little do the best of us believe and trust the Lord! We know not how to content ourselves with a bare promise; except we can see some probability in the means made use of to accomplish his wise designs, and except we know the particular way by which he will bring his purposes to pass, we hardly know how to believe his promises at all. But in this case, do we not trust ourselves more than God! We think ourselves quite ruined, when we have nothing but God and his sure word of promise to depend on. Like Adam, we would be as gods, knowing good and evil, being not satisfied that God should know and choose for us: and like the prodigal son, we would have our portion in our own hands, else our comforts are gone. But is it thus? Are we left to our own care and finding? I hope not. I would not have it so for the world. No, O Lord, keep all in thine own hands, and enable us as beggars to live upon thee.

I cannot help thinking on Jacob's words: 'If God will be with me and keep me in the way that I go, and will give me bread to eat, and raiment to put on, then shall the Lord be my God.' I think I can repeat the same words with some degree of comfort. O what a mercy! What condescension! God to be with us! Not an angel, not a seraph, no; but the infinite God himself; not *for* us only, but *with* us, as an intimate companion and friend. With whom? With angelic beings? With the spirits of just men made perfect? This would be condescension indeed. What shall we say, then, when we hear that God is with us sinners, rebels and traitors; us worms who are nothing, yea, less and worse than nothing, being sinful, abominable and wretched. What a blessing! How great, how free and undeserved! Yea, how full of infinite and endless comforts! Let this suffice amidst all the cares and perplexities of life. Let this suffice us in every state; suffice us in life and in death.

24. Clouds and Storms Necessary

Milborne Port, May 13, 1783.

THE promise without some trial annexed to it, is not unlike rain without a cloud. Who expects any such thing? But when we see a cloud, then we naturally expect rain; and the blacker the cloud, the greater are our expectations. Clear sunshine is comfortable; and a black cloud also, we must remember, is highly profitable. Who regrets the loss of the sun, when a pregnant cloud in a summer drought, conceals it from us? What cheerfullness did every appearance of a cloud and of an approaching storm, spread lately among all ranks of people, when their fields and their gardens were dried up and withering? Clouds and storms are of no less use in the spiritual, than in the natural world. An alternate interchange of sunshine and of storms and fruitful showers, makes the most fruitful summer. The one without the other will not do. In winter we have clouds and storms without much sun; but vegetation is then stopped, and the earth is barren. In summer also, if we have sun without clouds, the earth will still be comparatively unfruitful, Let us therefore patiently expect and be also thankful for storms sometimes, as well as for sunshine.

I do not mention this as if I saw an approaching storm ready to fall on either of us. Quite the reverse. It is sunshine above me, though I cannot see far before me. And is it not so with you? But should an unexpected cloud gather, and darken the heavens above, let us joyfully expect a shower of rich blessings from it. And when the blessing is come, the clouds will again disperse, and the sun will shine brighter than ever.

25. Review of the Past – Christ the Only Refuge

Milborne Port, June 3, 1783.

IN reviewing the three years I have spent here, I cannot help being amazed and overwhelmed with the very great and undeserved goodness and mercy I have experienced during this short space of time. I was a stranger in a strange land; but the Lord graciously provided friends to take me in, and put it into their hearts to show me every kindness in their power. Though not without the cross, I can say also, through mercy, I have not been without the blessing. I can say without fear, that the Lord's hand has been with me and upon me for good; and the light of his countenance hath comforted, taught, and sanctified me.

I am now about removing my tent; yea, and blessed be the Lord, I can see the cloud moving before. Where it will rest I know not. I will follow it with comfort, being well persuaded in my mind, that it will lead me safe. O for help to follow it! But what do I see before me? What but greater comforts still in view? And what besides, but a prospect of living more usefully in the world for the advancement of God's glory? Which is all my desire this side the grave. But what if all these are only dreams and shadows; Death may put an end to them all. Be it so; methinks I see still a brighter prospect beyond the gloomy vale. Grant, I may be disappointed of all my pleasing hopes in this world; how pleasing, how profitable the disappointment, when the comforts of another, a better, an eternal world, succeed in their place! O blessed exchange! The comforts of another world, who can enumerate, who can describe! May the Lord fix my affections on them in every state and condition, and stir up my most earnest desires after them.

But in the midst of these precious blessings, what cause for humility and shame! Every part of my conduct should fill me with godly sorrow. How unthankful, how unprofitable in everything! In what dust and ashes shall I lie, and where shall I hide myself for shame! Where but in him who is a hiding-place for his people? O blessed refuge! How I can see safety and eternal security in the midst of my unworthiness? When I can see none in myself, it relieves my mind to see worthiness enough in the Lamb that was slain. When I can see in myself nothing but sin, how comfortable it is to see eternal safety from the curse, its due, in him who was made a curse for us! Nothing but this can bring relief and peace to my mind. But how full, how glorious, is the relief and comfort which a view of this brings! The burden of sin and unworthiness is removed, and the weary soul finds rest and peace. Well might the Apostle count all other things but 'loss and dung,' that he might be found in him. Loss and dung, alas! everything that I have is infinitely worse than that even in my best moments. All that is mine is execrable, is devilish. If there be in me any good in any degree, it is his, and proceeds from him in whom I desire to be found. O happy time, when all that is mine will be wholly taken away, and I shall be filled with all the fullness of God. How grand, how glorious is the thought!

O let us not forget him who for our sakes became poor, that we through his poverty might be made rich, yea! filled with all the fullness of God. Every step and every transaction is mysterious. We cannot think of any of the circumstances without being filled with amazement. The riches conveyed are such as none but God could bestow; the objects on whom they are bestowed are such as none but God could take notice of; but the way of their conveyance, through Christ's poverty, if possible, exceeds all. What shall we say to these things, but cry out, O the depth!

Behold his love! See him laying aside his riches, and taking our poverty, leaving his throne, and entering our dungeon! Behold him in *all* things made like unto his brethren, having become in everything the same with us! He came to the same poverty, wore the same garment, spoke the same language of misery, endured our curse, and will not leave us till we are taken to the same place and the same glory, till we are filled with all the fullness of God. He was not, he is not, ashamed of us. He was, he is, he ever will be, in everything like to his brethren. He will wear the same nature, when he cometh with his holy angels the last day. He will appear as, the 'firstborn among many brethren,' in the height of his glory in heaven. We cannot think too much, or too well of him. May it ever be your and my only ambition to be in everything like him, and in everything to live to him.

To Mrs Charles

1. The Gospel, the Power of God – Success Expected

Shawbury, Jan. 5, 1784.

I WAS received here with great joy indeed, both by pastor and people. I think I feel an earnest desire to do something for God. But I am full of unbelief, and have but little expectation that God will own his truth. I seem to be preaching to no purpose. I often, indeed, through mercy, have a blessing and comfort myself; and I have often gone to preach with more expectation of receiving good myself, than of doing good to others. This is a wrong frame, and I must endeavour to get out of it. Help me, my dear, with your fervent prayers.

The preaching of the gospel is the means of God, appointed for the pulling down of Satan's kingdom, and for the promoting of the interest of his own kingdom in the world, and it ought to be preached in faith with this view. David calls the gospel, 'The rod of God's strength.' St Paul calls it, 'the power of God unto salvation.' It was so then, and it continues still the same. However, faith only can see it in that light, and preach it as such. I am ready to cry in the language of Isaiah, 'Awake, awake, put on thy strength, O arm of the Lord; awake as in the ancient days, in the generations of old. I long to see past times of the outpouring of the Spirit returning again, when the voice of God by his ministers was terrible, powerful, and full of majesty, Psa. 29:4. He is still the same: 'Jesus Christ, the same yesterday, and today, and forever.' The belief of this truth not a little refreshed my soul yesterday. I could not help thinking that we shall still see his glory more, and more wonderfully displayed. 'His arm is not shortened that he cannot save.' It is as long as ever, and as strong as ever. It can reach our misery and lift us out of it. May the Lord help us to pray much, to believe much, and to expect much.

I am apt to think that according to our prayer, faith, and expectation, so it shall be to us. A proper view of God in the glory of his power and love will much enlarge our hearts and strengthen our faith. We then shall see that we cannot depend too much on him, nor expect too much from him. Infinite power, engaged by infinite love and compassion, and directed by infinite wisdom: what cannot it perform! It is God that works according to the glory and majesty of all his perfections in a way of grace; and have we not sufficient ground to expect great things! Yes, the kingdom of Satan shall be effectually pulled down in God's good time, and the Lord alone shall be exalted.

2. God Nigh – Communion with Him

Shawbury.[2]

My comfort is, and I doubt not but that it is your's also, that there is one all-sufficient friend, always and everywhere to be found. He is everywhere 'nigh to them that are of a broken heart'; yea, he is their God, and dwelleth in them, as the father of mercies and the God of all consolation. He hath all consolation to bestow, consolation answerable to every sorrow, from whatever quarter it may arise. I hope much of his presence comforts you. 'Call upon him, for he is near,' Isa. 55:6. He is within hearing, however weak the cry. A sigh, a groan, if sincere, pierces his ears; nor will he be inattentive to the silent tear, if it comes from a broken heart; he will bottle it and keep it in remembrance; yea, these bitter waters shall ere long be turned into wine, when the marriage of the Lamb is come. Through mercy I find that communion with God sweetens everything, makes our comforts more comfortable and every bitter thing sweet. Wherever we meet him, it is not in vain. If we meet him when under a cross or in tribulation, his presence is sure to make it a heaven to our souls. Though he brings us into the wilderness; yet, if he speaks comfortably to us, the wilderness will soon be turned into a paradise.

[2] There are no dates to the six following letters. They were probably written in the former part of the years 1784.

We should endeavour to enjoy God in everything, and be particularly careful that nothing interrupt our particular and immediate intercourse with him. In all our comforts of every sort, let us look for God and by faith see him in them. In all our crosses and trials let us look for God. What are our prayers when in trials but vain repetitions, if we are not immediately dealing with God, if our hearts be not going out after him in holy desires and fervent affections? In the word also we must endeavour to see his majesty, holiness, mercy and goodness, or it cannot be profitable to our souls. Christ tells Paul that he was to be a witness of those things '*in* the which he should appear to him.' When the eye of our understanding is enlightened by the Holy Spirit, we see, not only the world itself, but we see God in the truth which it expresseth. We see him in his law, infinitely holy, just and good: and we love him because he is what he is; and we love his law, which is a just representation of him in his holiness, justice and goodness. We see him in the gospel also – see him in Christ reconciling the world unto himself. The whole plan of the gospel appears to be a scheme worthy of himself; and every step in the accomplishment of the stupendous contrivance astonishes us with new discoveries of divine wisdom and goodness. And in every promise we must see him, and see him in all the infinity of his power, faithfullness and grace, capable of accomplishing it, if we intend being partakers of strong consolation. The life of faith implies that we have particular dealings with God in everything; for nothing can satisfy faith but God in Christ. But I find that this is not to be obtained without difficulty, without continual watchfullness, and aids from heaven to keep me from losing sight of him.

Alas! in how many prayers have I been contented with little more than the mere performance, without any particular dealings with God at all. I see more danger in this every day. How often also am I found reading and studying the divine word without seeing anything of the divine glory in it. Indeed, generally when this is the case, I feel earnest desires for divine illumination, without which nothing profits me. The light may shine; yet if it shines in darkness, darkness comprehendeth it not. Let us earnestly pray that the Lord would keep the power of godliness alive and vigorous in our souls. Then our light will shine before men, and our Father will be glorified. An obscure old woman, that deals much with heaven, may glorify God more than many a gifted and shining preacher, who is a stranger to God in his soul. It signifies not where we are, nor in what sphere we move: but if we receive light from heaven, we shall shine to the glory of God; if we have salt in ourselves, we shall season the earth in some degree.

3. Blessings Received through Trials

Shawbury.

BLESSED be the Lord for his goodness. O that I could praise him for his mercies! No one hath more reason to take shame to himself and give glory to God. At present I have two prevailing desires within me, namely, either to live *to* God, or live *with* him. The Lord knows I desire to live to him *only*. I wish I knew *how* to live more so than I do. My comfort is that he knows *how* to glorify himself by me.

Sometimes I find worldly lusts turbulent, vain imaginations wild and distressing: but I hope I can truly say that my soul centres in God only. I can find no peace till these usurpers are quieted, and God is in peaceful possession of my soul. What a mercy that on such occasions he graciously comes to my relief, and interposes the greatness of his power in my behalf. I seem to be as it were carried away sometimes by a torrent of vain and wild imaginations, as full of self and ungodliness as they can hold. I endeavour to stem the torrent, and save myself from impending ruin; but I may as well attempt quieting *Llyn Tegid*[3] when most violently agitated. I cry to the Lord, 'Save me or I perish.' O how comfortable is the needful relief when it comes! I must add, that I generally find the Lord has some particular design in view when he wisely suffers it to be thus with me: that he means to bring some corruption to light which

---

[3] Bala Lake

has too much power over me, with the view that it may be resisted and mortified. I found it evidently so in a particular instance lately. We cannot too firmly believe, that 'All things work together for good.' I have no doubt but that the Lord has some design in my present frequent indispositions. His hand is in them; and I think I have reason to expect a blessing from them. I hope to be in a humble and waiting frame, expecting what the Lord has to say to or bestow upon my soul. The blessing is worth having, by whatever means it may be conveyed: and we may be well assured also, that every blessing will be bestowed in the best manner on which infinite wisdom can fix, to promote his glory and our real good.

It is no small matter to have our hearts made willing to receive God's blessings in his own way of bestowing them. We are desirous of the blessings, it may be, at least we think so; but we love not the way and manner in which they are conveyed. It was not so with St Paul. He rejoiced not only in the hope of the glory of God; but moreover 'gloried in tribulation also' – the way to obtain that glory. It is here where all hypocrites and unsound professors fail. To talk about the glory of God, one would think, is very pleasing; and they hope to attain to it: but as to the way which God has pointed out as leading thither, it is, as you will soon perceive, unpleasing and forbidding; and they turn away from it. Mortification, self-denial, living godly in Christ Jesus, and much tribulation, are such sour things as flesh and blood cannot endure; the very mention or appearance of them is extremely troublesome. But what saith St Paul? The way, he saith, that leads to glory, we highly approve of, and we glory in it. Why? 'Tribulation worketh patience, etc.' In this way only do we gather the peaceable fruits of righteousness. Every step we take in it, however unpleasing to flesh and blood, brings to our souls the very fruits we long after, and the only fruits on which we can feed. They are the very grapes of Canaan, given to none but those who glory in tribulation, Rom. 5:3; Heb. 12:11.

There is a near similarity between that way in which God bestows eternal life upon his people, and that in which he bestows every lesser blessing. We have the peaceable fruits of righteousness in that way only which leads to glory. Not only must we not expect the crown without the cross, but we must not expect any spiritual blessing whatever without a proportionable cross: and true grace approves of the one, as well as of the other; nay, it sees wisdom, beauty, and goodness in the cross, as well as in the crown; it would not wish to inherit the crown but in the way of the cross. The peaceable fruits of righteousness on which he feeds under the cross, enable him to bear it with cheerfullness, yea, and to glory in it. There is no surer proof of our being in the way to glory, than our approving of the way that leads thither.

4. Faith, an Enemy to Sin

Shawbury.

I FIND a danger, through stoutness of heart, of 'despising the chastening of the Lord' and by that means, of losing all the benefit, and also of adding sin to sin. It is one thing for our *own spirits* to bear us up under a cross; but a very different thing to be supported by a living faith. 'The just lives by faith.' Faith is all his support; he rejects and casts away all other confidences. This faith is not a blind presumptuous grace: no, but it sees things rightly, sees them in their nature, causes and effects, weighs things deliberately between the soul and God, brings everything to the bar, tries it, justifies or condemns it according to evidence. For support in everything it deals only with God in Christ, abhors sin, trembles before the majesty of heaven, and at the same time cleaves to him only for all comfort and strength. And faith is not satisfied that it has support only, and that the soul is enabled to bustle through crosses and troubles: but it looks further; it would have the blessing: it cries out:

> Un ergyd eto ar ben y ddraig,
> Yn enw Duw Jehovah
>
> (One stroke still more on Satan's head,
> In God Jehovah's name.)

Faith is thankful that it sees the hand of God lifted up against sin in the soul, and is ready to say, whatever the means made use of may be, 'Down with it, down with it, even to the ground.' Everything is more tolerable to a true and living faith than sin. It views its utter destruction, looks to God's promise for the accomplishment of it, and in everything waits upon God in prayer, that his hand may be engaged in the work.

There is not one thing more certain than that grace loves holiness, admires it, delights in, and longs after its increase. If so, it cannot but approve of and rejoice in all the means made use of in promoting it. It would rather have the cross, than suffer sin, whatever it may be, to have the ascendency. In saying this, I cannot but think of you. Is it not so with you? Do you not love holiness; love it, I say, in your very worst frame? When you are most dull, when corruptions are most prevalent, and when you are in doubt whether sin or grace has the dominion over you – yet you still love holiness; you abhor yourself, because you are not more holy; you long above all things for the enjoyment of holiness, and there is no heaven that you desire separate from it. Is not this, I say, the case with you? Why then encourage doubts?

5. Doubts Injurious to the Progress of Piety

Shawbury.

I AM sorry you conjure up again your old doubts and fears respecting your state. They are frightful spectres. Be well assured they will never do you any good. Is there no such thing as bringing things to a clear and determinate issue? And is it not your duty to do so? If they are harboured long, I am certain they will eat out your vitals. They are directly opposite to that living faith which strengthens, nourishes, and feeds the soul. Condemn and abhor yourself as much as you please, yea, let us mourn over our barrenness, earthly-mindedness, want of spirituality and love to God, to the greatest degree. There is no danger of excess here. The more we know ourselves and God, the more this godly sorrow will abound. This will do us good. This is consistent with, yea, inseparable from that living faith by which we derive all our spiritual joy and peace. But as to doubts respecting our state, let us give them no quarter,

To Mrs Charles

but bring the matter as soon as possible to a determinate issue. We must give ourselves no rest till this matter be seriously, solemnly, and thoroughly determined between us and God. I do not say that it can be determined when you please, but I think that the anxiety and earnestness, which the importance of the matter demands, should influence us till it is so. Till this is the case, it is utterly impossible that we should walk with God, have confidence and trust in him on all occasions, or have our eye steadily fixed on him in Christ as our all in all. Nor do I think that we shall be equally watchful over our hearts and minds, equally observant of our internal frame, or equally progressive in holiness, till things are brought to an issue respecting our state. For whilst we ought to be pressing forward in the road, we are standing still, full of doubts, whether we are in the right road or not.

I need not tell you, I am persuaded, that I say nothing of all this to distress you, but to help you out of your distress as far as in me lies, that you may obtain peace and joy for evermore. I need not tell you what I think of your state; that is already sufficiently known to you. I see in this very letter such fruits as never grew 'in your natural soil.' But it is not sufficient that *I* see them; I would have *you* see them too. 'But will not this make me proud?' We may as well think that the sun will make us blind. I am sure doubts never did nor will promote humility in the smallest degree. True humility arises from a very different cause, and is most abundant in those who have the fullest assurance of faith respecting their state: but doubts harden and alienate the heart from God. It is one thing to doubt and quite a different thing to loath sin and abhor ourselves. The former may be, where there is not one spark of true grace; but the other is the effect of grace only.

I feel most anxiously concerned for your spiritual comfort and happiness. Were it not so, I should think I had a very poor regard for you. That love that is confined to the body and its welfare, and extends not to the soul and its happiness, is not worth having. But whilst I love you thus, I cannot love and encourage what John Bunyan calls, an 'army of doubters.' I hope you will believe that they are enemies to 'Mansoul,' and that as such you will oppose and resist them with all your might.

6. The Sabbath

Shawbury.

THE sabbath is approaching, and on the sabbath day night this will come to your hand. I hope we shall find it a precious day of rest to our souls. It commemorates the accomplishment of that stupendous work which brings deliverance to guilty sinners, by the resurrection of Christ from the dead. It is an emblem of that rest which sinners find in Christ for their weary souls, in consequence of his having finished the glorious work he had undertaken. This is also a pledge of that rest that yet remaineth for the people of God. As sure as we are now enjoying the one, we shall soon enjoy the other, if indeed we are pilgrims and sojourners here on earth.

The Jewish sabbath, being the seventh day, was to them a commemoration of their glorious deliverance from their Egyptian bondage, a sign between God and them, and a pledge of the promised inheritance. It looked backward and forward, it reminded them of their slavery and deliverance from it, whilst by faith they were looking forward to the land of promise, where they should rest from their wanderings in a barren and dangerous wilderness. *Our* Sabbath also speaks the same language: it reminds us of a bondage infinitely dreadful, and of a deliverance infinitely complete and glorious, and also of a rest eternal in the heavens. It directly looks to Christ as the glorious author of this deliverance, and in whom only we can find rest to our souls. This rest is his purchase and gift, 'I will give you rest.' When we consider what this rest cost him, can we help admiring his love and his kindness? 'The travail of his soul' is our rest. 'With his stripes we are healed... he hath borne our sorrows and carried our griefs.' What words are these. His sorrow is our joy, his travail is our rest, his stripes are our medicine, and his death is our life. How strange the mystery!

You see, my dear, where we are to go for rest, when weary and burdened: Jesus gives it. And if we have it not, the reason is, because we go not to him for it. The sabbath reminds us both of a duty and of a privilege in this view. It preaches to us, whilst our bodies rest from worldly toil, that we should seek rest also for our weary souls in Jesus. Christ hath 'ceased from his work,' having gloriously finished it. God the Father looks upon everything which Christ has done in our behalf, and says, 'Behold it is *very* good,' that is, comely, glorious, satisfactory and sufficient, bringing glory to God in the highest, and peace and happiness on earth. May the Lord open our eyes to behold also the glory of the stupendous work. In the light of the Spirit it will appear to us to be *very* good. We shall with astonishment admire and rejoice in it, as the means of our present and eternal rest.

There is rest now in Christ; but the apostle saith, 'There remaineth a rest to the people of God.' They have rest to their souls now by faith in Christ; but there remaineth a rest, both for body and soul, eternal in the heavens. Our rest now in Christ is the firstfruits; the harvest will soon follow. The sabbath is a sign of the one, and a pledge of the other. Let us not therefore be weary in well-doing, but be steadfast and unmoveable, *always* abounding in the work of the Lord. Let us with cheerfullness bear the cross. It is but for a little while. If the road is rough, let us not complain, for it leads to a glorious rest which nothing shall ever disturb. Let every returning sabbath revive our drooping spirits with this glorious hope, and assure our faith with increasing confidence, that whilst now we are by faith resting in Jesus, all our toils, crosses, and troubles will soon be forever at an end.

7. Humbling Views of One's Self

Shawbury.

BLESSED be the Lord, that his mercy is free. Guilt and unworthiness are obstacles which it easily surmounts. Nothing but free mercy could save my soul, or bring me this moment one drop of comfort. I have no comfort in myself; but I can see infinite consolations in God, and I long after a fuller enjoyment of them. I am a burden to myself; but I am happy in looking to that glorious deliverance from self, etc., which Christ hath procured for all his people. To live to ourselves and to the world is that hell into which we are fallen; but to live to God is that heaven with which Christ exalts all whom he delivers from hell. No words so exactly suits my experience at present as the following: 'O wretched man that I am, who shall deliver me from the body of this death! I thank God through Jesus Christ our Lord.' I groan, being burdened; but in Christ I see deliverance. Blessed be God that I sorrow not as one without hope. Deliverance will be precious when it comes. In the meantime I hope to be thankful for everything that is a mean of wakening and slaying my corruptions.

This is the greatest comfort and blessing we can enjoy in this world; to find the hand of God with us and upon us, for good, mortifying our corruptions and strengthening our graces. I am sure there is great need. The old enmity against God is still strong and vigorous; at least I find it so. 'When I would do good, evil is present with me.' Will you pray for me? What use the Lord will make of a creature so depraved and sinful I know not. He can do what none else can do; and into his hands I endeavour to commit myself. I should be glad to serve him, I believe, I can truly say. But my best services are so poor and unworthy of his notice, that it is a wonder that he has not spurned me from his presence for ever. Well, 'we have an advocate with the Father, Jesus Christ the righteous.' Ah! The thought of Christ is reviving. When he comes into my mind, it seems as if the day had already dawned, the birds had began to sing, and all nature looked gay. It will be heaven enough to see him as he is, to be like him, to love him with all the heart, and to be with him forever.

To Miss Wright of Tarvin, Chester

1. Consolations to the Afflicted

(*No Date*)

I was concerned to hear of your indisposition; and I shall be very glad to be informed by *yourself* how you are. I trust the Lord is near to your soul in all the supports and consolations of the Holy Ghost. We talk of submission, resignation and dependence upon the Lord; but it is the Lord the Holy Ghost only that can make us possess these things. He can give us a holy and comfortable frame of mind in an instant, and with infinite ease. When the Lord afflicts, it is with great tenderness and compassion. He afflicts but one part, when he might afflict us in every part; one thumb, or one knee, and not both at once. This is kindness. When he afflicts, it is not willingly, that is, not from any injustice or cruelty in his nature; no, infinitely far from it. Afflictions proceed from his *goodness*; and they are ordered by perfect wisdom and the greatest tenderness. 'Though he cause grief, yet will he have compassion, according to the multitude of his tender mercies' – kind thoughts! And they are *just* thoughts of the Lord, and our supports under those things which are grievous to nature.

Remember, my good friend, he spared not his own Son, but delivered him up for us all! Can we think unkindly of him? He is still the same God of love: and is it possible for us to think well enough of him? Should we not be humbled and ashamed, forever entertaining for a moment an unkind thought of him? Oh! he has much to forgive us; *that* he also will do with *delight*; for 'he delighteth in mercy.'

2. Forgiveness Connected with Penitence, etc.

Bala, April 9, 1802

It is proverbial among the Welsh, that 'a debt is never diminished by delay.' I acknowledge myself your debtor for a very friendly and judicious letter which you sent me in February last. If I have trespassed, you must freely forgive me, and then we are friends again. The doctrine of forgiveness, whether received or bestowed, is very suitable to us in this world, full of failings; and continual infirmities as we all are. It is my *only daily* remedy. Were it not for pardon, dearly bought, but freely bestowed upon me, a guilty wretch, *daily*, I should sink in a moment into all the gloom of eternal despair. But 'there is forgiveness,' and we 'have redemption through his blood, the forgiveness of sin,' and that 'according to the riches of his grace.' Charming words! Though utterly ruined, we are thus made up forever.

Our sinfullness and misery are great; but there are no bounds to the riches of the grace of an infinite God: and forgiveness is dealt out according to those riches to guilty sinners who believe in Jesus. O how suitable is the gospel to our wretched state! It is a joyful sound indeed! Forgiveness! Yes, and repentance too! We could not enjoy the comfort of pardon without a penitent frame of mind. It is impossible for an impenitent sinner to taste and relish divine consolations. A penitent frame of mind is the working of holiness in a peculiar way in the heart of a sinner. Holiness is the same, wherever it is; but it differs in its effects in different subjects. An angel hates sin; and so does God and Christ. Holiness in them manifests itself in the hatred of everything contrary to it. But holiness in the heart of a guilty sinner can never exist, not only without hatred, but without a penitential frame of mind, conscious of criminality, and inexcusable guilt. And the deeper our sense of God's immense goodness, love, and grace in Christ, the more penitent, and self-abhorrent we shall be. For in proportion as God's goodness, against whom we have sinned comes to view, we shall perceive the vile and abominable nature of sin, and our extreme and inexcusable criminality. May the

Giver of repentance and forgiveness cause them to abound towards us both, and the whole church of Christ.

Though I have met with sorrows and considerable discouragements in my labours in Chester, yet as the cause is the cause of Christ, I fear to offend him by withdrawing myself from it, or by being unconcerned about it. When I think that some good is or may be done to immortal souls in your parts, by spreading the knowledge of a Saviour, I feel very willing to bear everything, and to spend and be spent. But it cannot but grieve me, that those who have professed to be friends to the blessed cause, should prove themselves its greatest enemies, and do all they can to ruin it. What am I, that they should fight against me? If it had not been for my Master's cause I could never have been among them. But all is well. The Lord can bring good out of evil. Perhaps things unpleasant are often wanted for various reasons. Our great point is to walk in the way in which we should go, and to please him; and then he can make us friends. … I very sincerely thank you for your kind letter, and very friendly advice. Indeed I think it was blessed to me then, in the troubled state of mind I was in. I pray the Lord abundantly to bless you.

To Mr Richard Jones of Wrexham

Man's Nothingness – Need of Christ – Spiritual Blessing

Spa Fields, August 16, 1797.

To write anything about myself would be useless. I am a poor, unprofitable creature, a worm of the ground, that just lifts up its head above the surface of the earth, to look round for a moment, and then to recline on the same dust, and be no more. It is no small comfort to me to think that there is a *God*, and that he is *such* as he is revealed in the gospel. I cannot help looking up to him from my own nothingness and unworthiness, and crave being, life and rest in him. I would wish most earnestly to cultivate familiar intimacy with him, and to make in him, and with him my eternal home. Where else can I rest: with whom besides can I live? For all things are perishing around me. A life hid with Christ in God, seems to suit well a guilty, poor, weak, helpless worm. Here let me make my abode. I believe I am welcome.

I hope you go on with the nursing business with success, and that your little man thrives and grows. Let God often hear that you have such a *sinner*. He wants all that the gospel salvation comprehends. You have clothed his body; but he wants a garment for his soul; yes, and washing in the blood of Christ. Take him naked and polluted, to him who can clothe and wash him. You will never find the comfort of him till you have, like Hannah, lent him unto the Lord as long as he liveth. I hope Mrs Jones got home safe from Bala, and that some spiritual blessing bore the expenses of her journey. God can never pay us better, than when he rewards us in spiritual blessings, which revive and comfort our souls.

To Mrs Ann Jones of Wrexham

1. Living to God – Kind Thoughts of Him

London, November 26, 1805.

EVER since I left home, the Lord has been very kind to me as to my health; and I am under the greatest obligation, every day, of living not to myself anymore, but to him that died for me and rose again. I think I can say with truth, that it is my constant desire so to do. Every other end of living is mean and unimportant: yes, is sinful and highly criminal. It is not only honourable and comfortable to live with that noble design in view; but it is highly criminal not to have it in view in all things – it is practical atheism. And if the end and motive are criminal, all our actions must partake of the same criminality. Ah! My dear friend, we are sinners in a degree we are little aware of! It is well for us that there is forgiveness with God, yes, and grace also to heal all our diseases. His salvation exactly suits us; and no wonder, for it is the grand contrivance of infinite wisdom and goodness. It was designed by him, who never mistakes the means for accomplishing his own ends, as a remedy for our great sinfullness and misery. I feel sometimes, yes, daily, an earnest desire for the *full* participation of all the blessings treasured up in Christ Jesus. The *full* participation of them would prove my complete remedy forever. Instead of that I have to lament and mourn over a thousand infirmities daily. The little I know of Jesus is all my comfort, and the foundation of all my hopes.

I hope you are enabled continually to look to him, who is a friend that sticketh closer than a brother, who is touched with the feeling of our infirmities, and is able to succour those who are tempted. Cultivate kind thoughts of him. We never think *justly* of him, but when we think *kindly* of him; for he is altogether, and perfectly, a *kind* being. Every unkind thought of him, is an unjust thought of him; and therefore a very sinful thought. The sinfullness of our thoughts in this respect is very aggravating, for which it becometh us to be exceedingly humbled. O may he renew a right spirit within us!

Commit yourself, and your dear little ones, to him, whose you are, and who most assuredly careth for you. I am very sure you have abundant reason to think so of him. For has he not cared for you hitherto? I think I hear you say, yes, with humble acknowledgement, and tears of thankfullness. Honour him by trusting him for futurity.

2. The Necessity and Benefits of the Bible Society

Bala, Jan. 15, 1811.

I HAVE sent you three reports of the Bible Society; and more may be had if wanted. I have directed two to the reverend gentlemen whose names are upon them. I hope when they read the contents, they will feel a strong impulse on their minds to exert all their influence to form an Auxiliary Society at Wrexham. It is a most noble and important Institution. It has in view to promote the eternal felicity of all the inhabitants of the globe till the end of time, by the most unexceptionable and the most effectual means, that is, by the dissemination of Bibles among them.

It is a most melancholy and distressing truth, that two out of three, if not four out of five, of all the inhabitants of our globe, never had the Bible in their native tongues, and must therefore be totally ignorant of its divine contents. Here at last, near the close of all, there is an Institution formed that grasps the mighty object of supplying them *all* with the divine oracles. The energy of its exertions is already felt almost over the whole circumference of the globe. The furthest parts of the eastern and western worlds are already put in motion by its exertions: and every poor Briton in his hut feels the beneficial effects of it by the daily perusal of the Bible with which he has been supplied by it.

It would give me very high gratification to hear that an auxiliary Society is to be established at Wrexham, for the promotion of the same noble design, with Sir Watkin at the head as the President of it. Leave no stone unturned. Speak to Mr Lewis and Mr Brown, and all you can think of, about it. Not only pecuniary aids to the funds of the Society in London, will be a desirable object as the fruits of its formation; but the greatest benefit may also accrue to the public in a religious point of view, by having the attention drawn from meaner things, and concerns of a temporary nature, to those which are divine, sublime and of a religious nature. The mind is debased by meaner and less important objects.

The mind of man is immortal, is made for eternity; and it feels itself ennobled and highly gratified by being occupied on the sublime and most important concerns of the gospel. It feels supreme pleasure whilst viewing and grasping objects vast and eternal. Let none deprive themselves and others of the honour and high gratification of aiding such a noble institution. It appears to me to be the brightest jewel and the greatest glory pertaining to the nation where it was formed. It is exerting its mighty influence all over the world. I hope a letter from you will bring me good tidings.

To Robert Jones, Rhos-Lan,[4] Lleyn, Caernarvonshire.

Contributions to the Trysorfa – a Magazine, etc.

Bala, Jan. 4, 1799.

Disgwyliais yn fawr eich cyfarfod yn *association* Dinbych; a galarus oedd gennyf weled eich lle yn wag. Cyfarfu yr Arglwydd â'i bobl yn ôl ei arferedig ddaioni; a thrwy ei rad drugaredd bu'r cyfarfod yn adeiladol a chysurus i lawer. Eich mab Dan, a'ch merch

---

[4] This excellent man was a preacher. One of his letters to his son, Samuel, at Liverpool, which appears in his Memoir, lately published in Welsh, is so striking and characteristic, that a part of it shall be given translated here. The date of it is May 12, 1807:

'I would counsel you, my son, once more, before I go to the grave, to pray much and contend manfully against five fiends that are some of the worst in hell: 1. *Pride*, the eldest son of the devil. The proud is so high in his own esteem, that all others despise him. 2. *Lasciviousness*: this monster has dragged multitudes of fair youths into thousands of sorrows, such as shame, poverty, disease, death, the grave, and hell at last. 3. *Loose Company*, this is the highway to every unruly conduct, and the wide gate that leads to perdition. 4. *Drunkenness*, which makes a man like the swine and much more filthy. 5. *Theft*: if once the joint of honesty be put out of its place, all the physicians of the world cannot put it right. Leprosy in the forehead is this, to be seen of all; and on its account thousands have been brought to the gallows. The first four monsters mentioned above drag thousands into this, like pampered horses in a carriage. Very few who foster such monsters do not at last fall into the ditch of theft.

The protection against these monsters, is, to believe that there is a God, who is everywhere present, from whose sight we cannot go for a moment; to believe that there is to be strict judgement; to experience the love of Christ; to join in sincerity with the church of God; to watch continually; to pray without ceasing; to put on the whole armour of God; and to withstand in the evil day. Our course is but short, and our warfare temporary; but long is forever, and endless is eternity: intolerable is the wrath of God; but infinitely delightful is his peace and love: a continual feast is a conscience cleared from guilt, and cleansed from pollution. May this be yours and mine. Amen.'

Hannah, oeddent yn gweinyddu arnom ym Mharcytwll gyda llawer o garedigrwydd a sirioldeb. Llawen iawn oedd gennyf eu gweled ym moreuddydd eu bywyd yn nhŷ yr Arglwdd, yn ymglymu mor hollol i Dduw a'i bobl. Nis gallant gael gwell lle. Yno y bont byth, yn goedwig byw, yn blodeuo, yn dirfion ac yn iraidd. Nid yw fy enaid yn dymuno amgenach rhan ac etifeddiaeth i'r eiddo finnau. Nid wyf ddieithr i galon Abraham pan ddywedai, 'Oh, na byddai fyw Ismael ger dy fron di!' Ymbiliaf, disgwyliaf, gobeithiaf; y mae graslonrwydd ein Duw ni yn peri hyder.

Y mae yn rhaid i'r *Drysorfa*, mi debygwn, fyned ymlaen. Y mae arnaf chwant iddo i fod o **wir ddevnydd** i'r Corff a'r wlad yn gyffredinol. Ond nid wyf yn golygu y bydd felly heb ei fod yn un yspryd ac un galon â'r Corff. Y mae'r Corff wedi ei fabwysiadu. Ardolwyn, fy annwyl frawd, rhowch gymorth i'w fagu a'i feithrin, rhag iddo nychu dan ein dwylo, neu fagu rhyw afiechyd marwol yn ei gychwyniad o eisiau ymborth iachus ac ymgeledd addas. Meddyliais am yr hen dad, D. Rowlands. Adgofiwch ychydig amdano. Darluniwch â phin ac inc, oreu ag y medroch ei agwedd syml, dyfnderoedd ei faterion, helaethrwydd ei ddoniau, nerthoedd yr Yspryd Glan yn gweithredu trwyddo, a'i fawr lwyddiant yn y weinidogaeth. Dechreuwch ar y myfyrdod, a chanlynwch ef i'r lle ac yn y dull yr arweinio yr Yspryd chwi. Rhowch ychydig hanes o ddechreuad a chynnydd crefydd yn Môn ac Arfon; y rhwystrau oedd ar y ffordd, a'u symudiad; yr offerynnau a gyfodwyd, a'u llwyddiant yn ol eu hamrywiol ddoniau a'u hamrywiol sefyllfaoedd. Ar eich taith chwi a gyfarfyddwch ag ambell i wreigan wen, ffyddlon, lafurus, yr hon fel Mair 'a gymerodd lawer o boen' yn yr achos mawr, ac a lwyddodd. Gwna hon un gwrthddrych hardd yn y darluniad. Dro arall daw ambell i gynghorwr ar eich ffordd: bydd hwn a'i lafur, ei ffyddlondeb a'i lwyddiant, yn harddu yr ysgrifen mewn rhyw gongl arall. Dichon y gorchwyl fod yn ddifyrwch i chwi, ac yn adeiladol iawn i'r oes a ddel. Ysgrifennwch eich sylwadau a'ch myfyrdodau ar rhyw faterion defnyddiol, profiadol, athrawiaethol, neu ymarferol; esponiadau ar ysgrythyrau, etc.; yr olwg sydd gennych ar grefydd yn bresennol a'i phroffeswyr; pa bethau defnyddiol sydd yn cael eu hesgeuluso; i ba ochr yr ydym yn gwyro yn ormodol; pa bwnc o athrawiaeth sydd angen craffu arno, etc., etc.

Wele, meddwch, dyma ddigon o waith rhawg. Gwir; byddwch chwithau helaeth ynddo. Gweithiwch tra byddo hi yn ddydd, y mae'r nos yn dyfod. Mae ynof awyddfryd i adael drych i'r oes a ddel, ym mha un y gallant ganfod agwedd crefydd yn ein dyddiau, a choffadwriaeth o ddaioni Duw i feibion dynion yn ein hoes ni ac yn ein gwlad. Os bydd mwy gogoniant yr oes nesaf, goreu o gwbl. Os teimlant fwy o nerthoedd y byd a ddaw, os gwelant ddirgeledigaethau teyrnas Crist ym mhob ystyr yn fwy goleu, bydd hawdd ganddynt faddau'n tywyllwch ni, a diolch am i ni weled dim. Os daw yr awen arnoch i gyfansoddi pennill neu ddau o hymn, neu englyn, cewch *gyfnewid geiriau* yn rhydd heb ddim perygl o esgymyndod.

Os bydd dim elw oddiwrth y gwaith, wedi talu pob costiau, rhennir hynny rhwng y siroedd at gynnal ysgolion rhad. Gobeithio yr ydwyf y daw yr achos i orphwys ar eich meddwl oddiwrth yr Arglwydd. Os felly, ni rhaid i mi ychwanegu. Os na bydd hynny, nid gwaeth er tewi. Yr ydwyf yn ddigon boddlon iddo fyned i'r dim, os na wna Duw ddefnydd o hono er lles i'n cydbechaduriaid. Cofiwch fi a'm gwraig yn dra charedig at Modlen afiachus. Â llygad ffydd trwy ddrych y gair edryched tu draw i'r bedd ar gorff iachus, anllygredig, a gogoneddus, ar ddelw'r hwn a'i prynodd, yn myned i gyfarfod a'r hwn a'i carodd, ac y mae hithau yn ei garu fwyaf. Gwna'r olwg hon iddi waeddi, 'Byr ysgafn gystudd – tragwyddol bwys gogoniant.' Galarus oedd gennyf glywed heddiw gladdu John Thomas, Pwllheli ddoe, a gŵr Bodeuan hefyd. Beth yw dyn ond gwagedd yn ddiau! Gobeithio yr wyf y caiff eu gwragedd druain olwg eglur ar fawredd a graslonrwydd Duw, yr hwn a all wneud a fynno heb ofyn cennad neb, ac sydd anfeidrol ddigon iddynt hwy yn weddw, ac i'w plant yn amddifaid. Oh, ei fawredd! Oh, ei raslonrwydd! Dyma ddigon!

To Robert Jones

The Same Translated

Bala, Jan. 4, 1799.

I EXPECTED fully to meet you at the *Association* of Denbigh; and was grieved to see your place empty. The Lord met his people according to his accustomed goodness; and through his free mercy the meeting was edifying and comfortable to many. Your son Dan, and your daughter Hannah waited on us in Parcytwll with much kindness and cheerfullness. It rejoiced me much to see them, in the morning of their day, in the house of God, having joined so entirely to the Lord and to his people. They cannot have a better place: there may they be forever, as living trees, blooming, fresh, and luxuriant. My soul desires no better portion and inheritance for my own. I am not a stranger to what Abraham felt when he said, 'O! that Ishmael might live before thee.' I importune, I expect, I hope: the gracious bounty of our God encourages confidence.

The *Trysorfa*, (a Magazine) I think, must go on. I have a wish that it should be of *real usefullness* to our connection and to the country generally. But I do not consider that it will be so, except it be of the same spirit and temper with the connection. The connection has adopted it: and pray, my dear brother, give help to nurse and nourish it, lest it should languish under our hands, or breed some fatal disease at first from want of wholesome food and suitable protection.

I have been thinking of the venerable father, D. Rowlands. Try to recollect some things of him. Describe with pen and ink, in the best manner you can, his solemn appearance, the depths of his ideas, the extent of his gifts, the power of the Spirit working through him, and his great success in the ministry. Begin with the subject and follow it in any way the Spirit may lead you. Give some account of the beginning and increase of religion in Anglesey and Caernarvonshire, of the impediments in the way, and the removal of them, of the instruments which have been raised, and of their success according to their different gifts and their different situations. As you travel you may meet with some one of those lovely women, faithful and laborious, who like Mary has laboured much in the great cause, and have been successful. Some one of these would make a beautiful object in the picture. At another time some exhorter would come in your way; let him and his labours, his faithfullness, and his success, beautify another corner. The work might be amusing to yourself, and very edifying to the coming age. Write down your observations and thoughts on useful subjects: experimental, doctrinal or practical; comments on texts of Scripture; your view of religion and its professors in the present day; what useful things are neglected; which side we too much lean to; what subject of doctrine it is needful to dwell upon more fully, etc., etc.

Well, you may say, this is work enough for a long while. True; and may you abound in it. Work while it is day, the night cometh. I have a desire to leave to the coming age, a mirror in which they may see the form and aspect of religion in our days, and a memorial of God's wonderful works towards the children of men in our age and in our country. If the glory of the next age should be greater, the better it will be. If they shall feel more of the powers of the world to come, if they shall see in every way more clearly the mysteries of the kingdom of Christ, they will easily forgive our darkness, and be thankful that we have seen at all. If the muse will visit you and lead you to compose a stanza or two of a hymn, or an epigram, you may *change words* without being in any danger of excommunication.

If there should be any profits, after defraying all expenses, they will be divided between the counties to support free schools. The matter, I hope, will be impressed on your mind by the Lord. If so, I have no need of enlarging: but if not, I may as well be silent. I am quite willing that it should come to nothing, if the Lord will not employ it for the good of our fellow-sinners. Remember me and my wife very kindly to sickly Margaret. With the eye of faith, through the glass of the word, let her look, beyond the grave, on a sound body, incorruptible and glorious, in the image of him who has redeemed her, advancing to meet him who has loved her and whom she chiefly loves. This view will make her cry out, 'Short,

To Robert Jones

light affliction – eternal weight of glory.' It grieved me to hear today that John Thomas, Pwllheli, was buried yesterday, and also the occupier of Bodeuan. What is man but vanity indeed! I hope the poor women will have a clear view of the greatness and gracious goodness of God, who doeth what he wills without asking leave of any, and who is infinitely sufficient for them who are widows, and for their children who are orphans. Oh, his greatness! Oh, his gracious goodness! Here is enough!

To Mrs Thomas Colley, of Cefngwifed, Near Newtown, Montgomeryshire

1. Condolence on Her Husband's Death

Bala, May 4, 1812.

It was this morning that a friend brought me the 'Shrewsbury Chronicle,' in which was announced the melancholy tidings of the death of your good husband and of my valuable friend. I most affectionately condole with you in your bereavement, and lament much the great loss which the country in general has sustained. I am sure that hundreds, as well as myself, lament the loss of him. But in the midst of our lamentations we should not forget the thankfullness we owe to God for raising him up and continuing his valuable life so long. The loss, I am fully persuaded, is only confined to his weeping friends, and does not extend to him. His departure was his great and eternal gain. We ought surely to rejoice in his behalf, for he has entered into the joy of his Lord and Saviour.

I need not remind you of your duty and source of consolation on this season of trial and distress. The duty is *submission* and *confidence*: submission, absolute submission to the divine will, who has a sovereign right to dispose of us and ours at his pleasure. He was *your* husband; but when the Lord gave him to you to be united in that most endearing connection, he did not relinquish his own right to him, or his right to call him to himself whenever he pleased. Confidence in the Lord is also as much your duty as submission: confidence in his goodness and wisdom, that he doeth all things well; confidence in his sufficiency and faithfullness, that he will care for you and your young family, support, direct, and comfort you under every trial. He calls for our confidence in him as our Father and friend; and he is infinitely worthy of confidence. We are no losers ultimately by being bereaved of most dear relatives and friends, if it be the means of drawing us nearer to him, and leading us to exercise a more entire and simple dependence on him. It is a very important point gained, in going through this wilderness, to have CONFIDENCE in the Lord Jehovah. Without it we shall be always peevish, murmuring and miserable. The Lord did not inform the Israelites previously, nor even his servant Moses, which way they were to be brought to Canaan; but they were commanded to follow the cloud and pillar, with perfect confidence in their Leader. What is our duty is also our comfort.

The only source of strong consolations for us in every circumstance is the Scriptures: 'That we through patience, and comfort of the Scriptures might have hope.' The two immutable things which will give us strong consolation are God's promise confirmed by his oath. God, willing that we should enjoy, even here, in this miserable world, strong consolation, hath provided in his faithful and most suitable promises, a strong foundation to build upon. I pray the Lord, my dear madam, to cause to shine upon you, through this dark cloud, the light of his countenance.

2. The Education of Children, etc.

Bala. (No date, sometime in 1812.)

ON my return from Chester yesterday, I found your favour of the 16th inst. waiting for me. I rejoice much that you are in some degree supported under your heavy affliction, and that your thoughts are directed to the Lord, with some degree of submission to his sovereign will, and of confidence in his goodness, care, and faithfullness. I can say that the heaviest affliction I ever met with was one of my greatest blessings. I refer you to three Scriptures which were peculiarly blessed to me at that time and often afterwards, to wit, Rom. 8:32; Heb. 6:17, 18; Isa. 54:10. Supported by these strong, unshaken and immoveable pillars, it was easy for me to bear all.

I feel much for your anxious concern about the education of your dear little boy. It is a concern of the utmost importance to your comfort and to his future progress through this world, and also to his eternal happiness, in another. There are so few schools that can in any point of view be recommended, that I am in general at a great loss what to say to my enquiring friends on that subject. A good commercial school, I have no doubt, may be obtained either at Shrewsbury or Chester. But little attention in any of them is paid to their religious instruction, I fear. They may tolerably watch over their morals, but as to religious instruction, few have that of a proper kind to communicate, or suitable gifts for the communication of it in an engaging and edifying manner: at least I know of none. This is a defect in the education of children which I have for years deplored. By the Sunday Schools this deficiency is remedied in many parts of our country among the poorer sorts: but among the middle classes and the higher ranks, religious instruction should and might easily accompany every other instruction, if proper plans were laid down, and proper methods pursued. I think, dear madam, you might keep him well employed at home, without fatiguing yourself, by proper arrangements and suitable books, until an opening offered which would meet your views and wishes.

It is a great point gained in the education of children, to bring them to employ their thinking and reflecting powers. Until the mind is employed, learning never becomes a pleasure, and very little advancement is made in the acquisition of useful knowledge. Some are much slower in acquiring the habit of thinking and enquiry than others: but when they have once attained it, they will pursue it steadily, and make speedy progress. I remember, when I was a boy, Rollin's Ancient History fell in my way; and it was the first thing that gave me any taste for reading. 'Nature Displayed' by La Place, was another work which engaged my attention much. When I received serious impressions, I read everything in divinity I met with; but very injudiciously for want of a proper guide. A little work containing the first principles of Christianity in a plain, familiar, and practical manner, confirmed by Scripture references, might be a very useful employment for him one part of the day to learn out.

I think great familiarity, and meekness, and patience, ought to be exercised towards children to bring them on. I know a contrary conduct would have never succeeded with me. And above all there should be prayer to the Lord for divine influences on the mind. He can in a moment give, in a natural and spiritual point of view, a turn to their minds, which all human efforts can never produce. Of this I have had many very convincing proofs, during the five and twenty years that my attention has been particularly engaged about the instruction of children. God is everything; though that by no means supersedes the necessity of our utmost assiduous activity in pursuing the wisest, and the most likely means to gain our point. May the good Lord direct you and me in all things.

I think our friends in glory pity our over-anxiety about our little concerns here in the world, perceiving, without a cloud, how tenderly, how kindly, and with what unerring wisdom and efficacy, the great Lord of the universe orders all things to answer his designs, and the good of his people.

To Miss Eliza Colley, of Cefngwifed

Thoughts Respecting Schools, etc.

Bala, July 2, 1812.

IN answer to your letter, please to inform your mother, that I am not sufficiently acquainted with the seminary near M——, to give an opinion respecting it. From what I have known of dissenting seminaries, having been four years in one of them myself, I should give a decided preference to private tuition under the care of a pious clergyman, if such a situation could be obtained.

I am sorry to hear of your dear mother's indisposition. Under all infirmities, and in all our troubles, we may look up to the Lord for relief, support and comfort. He is everything we need in all our trials through life, and can bring us safe to a country where none of the inhabitants complain of sickness. Jesus, the lovely Jesus, is a physician for soul and body also; and he never fails to hear the prayer of those that call on him in their trouble. Do you *know* him, my dear young friend? Ask the important question to yourself often. If you really know him, you cannot but love him, for he is 'altogether lovely.' If you love him, you are blessed; for it was not flesh and blood that revealed him to you. You will have in him a heart most tender, who is touched with the feeling of our infirmities, an arm most powerful to assist, and a faithfullness that is inviolable and never failing. Let us read the blessed Bible, that we may know more of him, and in the growing knowledge of him, may grow in love to him, and in the growing love of him, may devote ourselves *more entirely* to him.

To Mr John Walker, of Chester

Christ Our Peace – The Hope of Glory

Spa Fields, January 11, 1805.

Nothing particularly interesting transpires in this great place. The rumour of a speedy peace prevailed yesterday. What foundation there was for it I know not, except it be the arrival of a messenger from France. I wish it may be true; and I pray that the time may speedily arrive, when they shall learn war no more. But after all no temporal blessings have any great importance attached to them, if devoid of spiritual.

Peace with God through our Lord Jesus Christ is to us sinners a blessing, which in value, and in its happy effects, passeth all understanding. Jesus is our peace: our peace-purchaser, our peacemaker, our peace-ratifier, and our peace-preserver forever. He himself is everything to us. After our peace is made, we forfeit it every moment in ourselves; but in him, our head and surety, it is still preserved; and we enjoy all the comforts of the blessings arising from it. A free traffic is stipulated, and in everything we are the gainers. We have nothing but groans and complaining sighs to send to heaven; but in lieu of these we have joy unspeakable and full of glory. The ports above would be soon closed against us, being such traitors and so unfaithful, did not Jesus keep them open. When we clearly see how much we are obliged to him in everything, we shall then most unfeignedly praise him, and adore him.

My present experience is a dependence upon him and a constant concern for his interest and glory. On Christmas day, I found comfort in preaching on John, 1:14. I saw a little of his glory 'as the only-begotten of the Father, *full* of grace and truth.' I long to see more, and shall never be satisfied till I see him as he is, and never lose sight of him. What a blessed hope! I dare not dwell too long on it at present, but hope to mind my work till I fully realize it. The world and its concerns have very nearly lost all their importance. What is not immediately, in one way or another, connected with salvation, is hardly worth a thought.

The death of my much esteemed friend, Lady Ann, has affected me much since my coming here. Her room is empty. The hours I conversed with her, being all past scenes, daily recur to my mind. It seems, somehow, strange that they can never be enjoyed here anymore. Thus musing one day after another, I have thought often with comfort on Eph. 4:13. We shall meet again – *all* meet, the whole family, in their Father's house – all well – all happy – all conquerors – all immortal and glorious, with our elder brother among us. What a thought! With all the mighty exertions of glorified minds, in one continued eternal act, they will all sing, without ceasing, the high praises of God and the Lamb. I must sincerely wish you, my dear friends, that felicity. I can wish you no more; and you can neither desire nor enjoy more. May the divine Spirit with his holy influences help us forward continually.

To Mr and Mrs John Walker, of Chester

1. Congratulations on Their Marriage, etc.

Bala, August 7, 1808.

Had I been at home, I should have congratulated you by a letter sooner on your *happy* union; such I sincerely hope it will prove, and I earnestly pray the Lord to make it so by his blessing upon you. I must not consider you to be two angels united together; and were you so, you could enjoy no real happiness without the Lord. But you are two sinful worms, much bruised and hurt by sin, and need daily help from the Lord, and have need to bear much with one another, and administer every comfort you can to each other. We should never expect from each other more than what may be reasonably expected from a creature. And when we consider ourselves as *sinful* creatures, with every joint at best *half* out of its place, if not totally so, instead of expecting great things from such a creature, we should by every means in our power soothe his pains, and apply often for him to the good Physician to administer his salutary restoratives.

In fellowship with the Lord, and by his blessing, we may prove in the conjugal state happy supporters of each other's infirmities and promoters of our mutual felicity and progress in the divine life. He is our salvation; yes, our all. But as the conjugal state is his ordinance, and when properly entered into, he generally crowns it with his blessing, we may with confidence look up to him for the needful aid, for mercy and grace to help in our time of need. Committing you in your new situation to the Lord, and imploring his blessing upon you, I shall add no more, but that when an excursion is agreeable and convenient, we shall be very glad to see you at Bala, to stay with us as long as you can.

2. Fellowship with God, etc.

(*No date.*)

I HOPE your souls thrive spiritually in the abundant enjoyment of the Lord's presence and divine aid. There can be no real solid comfort without fellowship with the Father and with his Son Jesus Christ. I think I feel daily in an increasing degree, the emptiness and vanity of all other enjoyments. This fellowship is heaven above, and it is heaven begun below in proportion to the degree in which it is enjoyed.

I am glad that it is my employment through life to speak of him to helpless sinners. I am glad that others can speak better of him than I can. But he is infinitely beyond what any of us can think or speak; and we ought to be ashamed of ourselves when we speak with the most light and warmth of him. The more we know of him, the less we shall think of our knowledge of him, and the more we shall long to grow in the knowledge of him. It is a very cheering consideration, that our darkness and ignorance shall *soon, very soon*, be forever done away, and we shall know as we are known. Then we shall be perfectly like him: and when we shall awake with his likeness, we shall be forever satisfied; but not till then. Towards this mark, this our high calling, may we be daily pressing forward.

I trust the Lord has a cause begun at Chester which will continue with increasing strength, whilst the sun endureth, to the Lord's glory, and to the eternal salvation of thousands yet unborn. As everywhere and in all ages, it must experience changes: winters as well as summers. There are so many weeds that grow in summer, that it seems to me that we could not go on so well without our winter, with all its short days and biting frosts. Carrying into the barn will not do without threshing and winnowing, May we thrive under all dispensations.

To Mr and Mrs William Astle, of London

1. The Difference between Conscience and Grace

Bala, June 25, 1789.

THE points you touch upon are of great importance, and deserve our most serious consideration. But l would have you in the first place to be fully convinced and satisfied, that nothing but the Spirit of God can teach us in the things of God to any useful purpose. He must lead us into all truth, and 'seal instruction on our minds,' otherwise our knowledge of divine things will be indistinct, confused, inefficacious and unprofitable. God has promised his Church this divine Teacher. The Church of Christ, and every member of it, has found this invaluable promise fulfilled in a degree more or less. We may expect the same; nor are we ever in a proper frame of mind, but when, and in proportion as, we are living in dependence on the promise, or experiencing it actually fulfilled. May this then be the daily subject of our prayers.

As to the very different and opposite feelings to which you are at different times subject, and the different frames which you experience, I do not in the least wonder at them. I apprehend that it cannot be otherwise with the best of Christians whilst they are in part corrupt, and the whole body of sin remains unexpired within them. Corrupt nature cannot but be active whilst it has existence; and if it works at all, its workings will be suitable to its nature, which is made up of everything that is devilish in the devil himself. Be well acquainted with the state of the Christian in this world. He is not all grace, nor is he all sin; blessed be God for that! But there is a body of sin and also a body of grace within him. They are both alive and both active; they are two different principles in every faculty of the soul, working, lusting, and warring in direct opposition to each other; and each aiming at the other's destruction. He that doth not find impure mixture in his best services, I will venture to say, hath all to learn of the spirituality of God's law, and of the corruption of his nature; that is, he is without genuine repentance.

Now, my friend, the question is not, whether you have any sin, or the whole body of sin within you; but, whether you have a principle of grace, lusting against it, and acting in opposition to it. I say, a principle of grace, for I believe that persons unrenewed may experience the strivings, and the powerful workings of the Spirit of God. But the real Christian has a holy principle implanted in every faculty of the soul, in opposition to the body of sin, called by the apostle, 'the law of the mind' – 'his mind' – 'the spirit' – 'the divine nature' – 'the new creature' – 'the new man.' Now this is the knot, I apprehend, you want to be untied, and the difficulty which perplexes you. You want to have solved, the difference between the workings of this principle against sin, and the workings of natural conscience enlightened, and of everything else which an unrenewed man may experience. Consider attentively the following observations:

1. Conscience unrenewed *condemns* sin and the sinner; but grace *mortifies* sin and *saves* the sinner.

2. Conscience is partial and blind, condemning only *some* sins; but grace is universal in its aim, at least, and *endeavours* in mortifying every sin and the whole body of sin.

3. Conscience acts only at intervals, and is temporary; but grace is permanent and lasting.

4. Conscience may condemn with real hatred any one sin as sin; but grace hates it altogether and irreconcilably; therefore nothing will satisfy it less than the total destruction of sin.

5. There is an impotence in the workings of the natural conscience, and it is soon discouraged; but grace deals much with Christ and his gospel, finds strength to help in time of need, and is unwearied as well as courageous, in its lusting and warring against sin. The language of grace is evermore, 'In the Lord have I righteousness and strength.' It will not therefore yield or give over until it has obtained a complete victory and deliverance.

6. There is nothing of true genuine humility in the workings of natural conscience; but it is peevish, and murmuring, and at variance with God, his law, and his providence: but grace is supple, rolls in the dust, and is sweetly humble, and falls in, as it were naturally, with God and his ways, with his law, gospel, and providence.

As grace is the divine nature implanted, so there is in all its workings something divine, holy, and heavenly. Had we more of it, we should be better acquainted with it, and be able to distinguish it easily from everything that bears any resemblance to it. It is specifically different from everything else; and I apprehend that nothing can make it evident but itself. Wherever it is, it will manifest itself. More particulars might be easily added; but consider the above.

You ask me again, 'what it is to trust in the Lord.' Trusting in God, I apprehend, implies:

1. A real, practical sense of our own weakness and insufficiency for anything that is good.

2. An apprehension of, and looking to, the help held forth in the promise to the sinner as such, that is, a real, practical belief of the promise.

3. A turning from, and a rejecting of, all other helps, and a resting upon the promise only for relief and support.

In proportion as you see the fullness and sufficiency of the promise, and rest upon it, so will be your peace and comfort. It is a belief of God's sufficiency only that influences our minds to trust in him: and this Almighty sufficiency is held forth for our relief, *through* Christ, *in* the promise, which testifies of him. You see therefore from the above hints, that there can be no trusting in God without a real, practical sense of our own utter weakness, and a practical belief of God's fullness and sufficiency in Christ, that is, without repentance and faith.

2. The Gospel Comforts

Bala, April 11, 1795.

I HOPE and trust you will not forget to pray for me. Though in general I am not left comfortless; I know what it is to experience divine supports and divine influences: yet I am at the same time practically taught to know what I am if left to myself. Therefore, my dear friends, do me the kindness of remembering a poor, weak, and sinful worm at the throne of grace often. In every case there is relief there – effectual relief and sovereign remedy for every disease. I hope you are enabled to go on, full of comforts of the gospel. Gospel comforts are supported by an immovable basis, and derived from an inexhaustible fountain: they will therefore continue and abound when all other comforts fail. 'Being justified by faith, we have peace with God' – 'We rejoice in hope of the glory of God' – 'yea, we even *now* joy in God through our Lord Jesus Christ, by whom we have *now* received the atonement.'

Here is comfort, supernatural and divine, and that joy in God, supported by no less a foundation than the all-sufficient atonement of Christ. We ought, my dear friends, eternally to bless God for evangelical ground to live upon, and evangelical pasture to feed in. It is there alone that sinners can find a firm footing and soul-refreshing food. I can wish you no greater happiness this side heaven, than an increasing experience of those comforts and supports which the gospel affords.

3. Children, God's Gifts, to be Devoted to God

Bala, Feb. 4, 1796.

I VERY sincerely congratulate you on the addition of a little son to your family. If, as you say, you wish him, like Samuel, to be called to serve the Lord in his youth, you may be well assured that your heart cannot entertain a wish respecting him, more pleasing and acceptable to the Lord. You have the same God to go to in his behalf, as Hannah had; and the way to him is as free to you as to her. I trust that, as she did, you will be also enabled to lend him

To Mr and Mrs William Astle

or return him, as long as he lives, to the Lord who gave him. It is the best thing you can do for him, poor dear little infant; and I am perfectly assured, that the Lord will take it kind of you and in good part. 'Children are an heritage of the Lord; and the fruit of the womb is his reward.' It is all he wants from the earth, all the fruit he expects as the reward of his wonderful humiliation and sufferings. 'he shall see of the travail of his soul and be satisfied' What shall he see? The fruit of the womb as his reward, justified, pardoned, sanctified and eternally glorified. He will people heaven with the fruit of the womb.

When I consider how salvation smiles with infinite grace upon the children of men, I feel, amidst many an anxious thought, unspeakable comfort in being a father, and that I have two little empty vessels to carry with me to the throne of grace, to be filled with the rich treasures of mercy. Grace is in the best hands in which it can be, treasured up in Christ, who is our Kinsman and Brother. He who now sits in infinite majesty on his high throne in heaven, wielding the sceptre of the universe, knows what it is to have been a little infant himself. Unto us a *child* is born, who can sympathize with, and save our little babes, when they have nothing but existence in a very weak and feeble manner in the world. But will he receive them? I must believe that he will, until it be made manifest to me, that he ever refused any. As a father I have my tender feelings, and all the care and anxious thoughts to which all but parents are strangers; yet I feel strong consolation bearing up my mind triumphantly in the midst of all, when I find liberty in their behalf at the door of our heavenly Father, though at present I see no signs of a change in them. To be enabled to ask is the next thing to receiving. 'Ask and ye shall have.' God will stand to his word, as sure as he is in heaven. Let us therefore mind our duty.

It is a great thing to *ask* of God. It is much easier and much more natural for a carnal mind, to fear, fret, vex, dispute, and contend, than as a poor unworthy sinner, on gospel ground, to *ask* of God. In asking, the intention of our minds must be upright and without guile. When we ask for our children, we must with full purpose of heart *intend* them for the Lord and his kingdom. Hannah *vowed* when she asked a child, and was enabled to perform the vow. And for the one she gave the Lord, the Lord gave her five, three sons and two daughters. The Lord, blessed be his name, is always willing that we should have the best bargain. To deal with him in sincerity, is to deal with one who will enrich us to eternity, and will bless and thank us for every favour we ask of him, and for every empty vessel we bring to receive out of his fullness. Were it not, I shall not say, for our unworthiness and guilt, for they are no hindrances in the way, but were it not for our legal spirit and unbelief, we should live as princes on earth, having a free access to the unbounded fullness of Christ and unsearchable riches of his grace. With hearts enlarged by the Spirit of the Lord, may our intercourse with Christ be daily improving, and our contempt of all besides be as evidently manifested.

I have but little to write respecting myself. Through mercy, myself and family are all well. I am now at home in winter-quarters, though much tempted by the mildness of the season speedily to begin my rounds. As to the state of religion in our country, we have much cause for thankfullness. The storms we were exposed to last summer are quieted; and we are going on peaceably and comfortably. In many parts of the country, the prospect is improving, and many souls are called. Our last quarterly meeting was a very glorious one. Much of the presence of the Lord, and of the power of his gospel, was evidently felt by the thousands who attended.

P. S. When you have half an hour to spare from prating and smiling in the face of your little one, I shall be glad to hear from you. If you mean to enjoy him long, don't make an idol of him. You know the fate of the golden calf.

To Mr and Mrs William Astle

4. An Unworthy Sinner and a Pardoning God

Bala, Sept. 11, 1796.

I FIND I must a little longer live on forgiveness. I find no standing on any other ground. Though often I am very unwilling to get on this ground for want of *true* repentance; yet I must say I bless God for it sometimes. No wonder the prophet should express himself full of astonishment on this subject: 'Who is a God like unto thee, that pardoneth iniquity!' 'he retaineth not his anger forever, because he *delighteth* in mercy.' I think you want to deal more familiarly with this *pardoning* God. He not only delights in holiness, in your love to him; but he delights also in *pardoning*. Do you believe this? If so, you will delight in asking pardon daily and hourly. You will weep over your sins, and rejoice in a pardoning God, at the same time. A guilty sinner and a pardoning God, are well met. God rejoices in the meeting. He cries aloud, 'I have a ransom,' – 'I shall be no loser, and you will be eternal gainers.'

It is good to be holy; but, remember it as long as you live, it is at the gate of mercy alone you shall be made holy. Let us there make our abode, there live, there die; there bewail our sins, abhor ourselves, and yet rejoice in a pardoning God. For my own part, I find that when I am on that ground, I am *with* God; every grace thrives, and every enemy falls before me. God, if he means to save us, will have us down in the dust, and will keep us there, that grace and mercy may be eternally exalted by us. I find access to God and communion with him in no other spirit. The more I am immersed in it, the more of God I enjoy.

You say, that 'you feel a strange backwardness in approaching the throne of mercy.' I am glad you *feel* it; but mind, the deeper you drink into the spirit of Job when he said, 'I abhor myself and repent in dust and ashes,' the more you will find that backwardness removed. Our aversion to close and frequent dealings with God proceeds, either from enmity, unbelief, or pride, or most likely, from the three together. Indeed, nothing less than the mighty energy of the Holy Spirit could ever bring a sinner, so full of enmity, unbelief, and pride, to God, in the low way of humility, self-abasement, and cordial repentance: but he can make this way of God to us a way of pleasantness. Salvation brings us to the dust, and in the dust saves us. Live there, and you will live with God; and though you do not deserve the crumbs, you shall yet enjoy a little of the children's food, and shall be permitted to 'drink abundantly.' It is here that I see the grand deficiency in the religion of modern times. We all have something, either gifts, graces, or experiences. It is well to have these things; but still in our dealings with God, let us be sinners. If we have them, we have still more cause to be humble, to be ashamed and confounded. O God, give me daily to enjoy the comfort and sweetness of a broken and a contrite heart!

You say, that you 'feel strange contrariety and contradiction in yourself.' So did Paul: 'When I would do good, evil is present with me.' 'What I hate, that I do.' 'I find a law in my members, warring against the law of my mind.' Here are two laws, two opposite principles, in the same faculties, warring against each other. Do you not see some of your own features there drawn by the apostle in relating his own experience? He groans, 'O wretched man that I am!' and with the next breath he cries out, 'I bless God through our Lord Jesus Christ.' He can complain, and bless, and praise with the same breath. What contradictions are these! But in these contradictions the Christian's experience is to be found. Where there is none of these contradictions, there true grace cannot be. But these contradictions, however, shall not continue forever. Mortality, or that which is dead or is to die in us, shall soon be swallowed up of life. There will be another birth at the resurrection; a birth to the perfection of glory. Then sin, and therefore sorrow and sighing, will be forever at an end. O blessed hope! My soul this moment reaches forward towards it.

In November I hope to have the pleasure of seeing; you all, and I trust, rejoicing in Christ's full and free salvation. I hope you often pray for me. When you are offering up yourselves and your little one to the Lord, breathe a petition for a poor worm, who wants daily help to be faithful. Please to present my kind respects to Lady Ann and all friends.

To Mr and Mrs William Astle

5. God in Christ Receiving Sinners

Bala, Jan. 6, 1798.

I HAVE at last arrived at a degree of certainty as to two points in religion; *First*, that I am altogether a sinner, loaded with unworthiness, a fit companion, every moment of my life, for the poor publican, (I love his name), or to the poor woman that was a sinner. I look upon the ground on which they stood often with no small degree of delight. With them I would wish to spend my days: and as they did, so should I upon that ground conquer all my guilt, sin, the world, and the devil. I am convinced that it is the only ground on which we can conquer and thrive. The *second* point of which I am certain, is, that God receiveth sinners, *as such*; and that therefore, as such, I may go to him and am welcome at all times to go to him. This last point is the very life of the little religion I have. Often blind, obdurate, unbelieving, sensual and devilish, yet I am no more or less than a sinner; and as such, God receives and relieves me. There is a new and living way consecrated for us. We have boldness or full liberty to enter; and we have a great High-Priest, not only *in* but *over* the house of God. Since all these things are so graciously ordered by infinite mercy on our behalf, let us draw near in full assurance of faith. I repeat it again, that all my life and comfort depend on this point; yes, the strength of every grace, and the defeat of every enemy, are continually derived from this one source. With this point in view, the moment I am a sinner, I am with God, and my relief comes: lusts and temptations are subdued, comfort is freely communicated, and holiness is transferred through all the powers of the soul. Gospel-holiness will never thrive, God will be never pleased, and Christ will be never glorified, on any other ground. What a stupid being I have been! Eight and twenty years I have made some sort of profession; yet after all these years, I have in a great degree to learn what it is to be a sinner, at least, to live in that spirit, and to commune with God in that frame of mind. I do most earnestly pray the Holy Spirit to teach me that lesson better. I think, with some degree of assurance, that he does and will hear me.

I hope if we live to meet each other again in this world, we shall greatly rejoice together in the free and full salvation of the gospel for sinners. It is the only remedy to heal all our diseases, to wash away all the filthy stains of sin. His people are sinners; and he saves them *from* their sins. As sinners, let us have much to do with him, and never rest till we are filled with all the fullness of Christ. Every new year must be a happy one, while we live thus as sinners with and upon Christ: and whether they be few or many, will be of no great consequence. May you and I begin and end every year with, and in dependence upon, the dear Redeemer, till at last we finish our course with joy.

6. The Fullness of Christ Is Our All

Bala, Feb. 16, 1799.

IF my poor ministry (poor as to the instrument, but not as to the subject) has been in any degree blessed to your spiritual edification and comfort, I desire to be thankful, and to give all the praise where it is justly due. I consider myself as nothing. Like a sponge, I have not a drop to give, though ever so much pressed, unless I first receive it. The Lord may well ask me, 'What hast thou which thou hast not received?' Nothing, nothing, must be forever my reply. However, on your account I rejoice and am thankful that the glorious ministry of reconciliation has been blessed to you. Live upon it, glory and triumph in it. I cannot desire, nor you enjoy, a richer blessing.

It is a truth that there is a fullness in Christ; and it is true, that God wills us to live entirely upon that fullness. Without living by faith upon that fullness, it is impossible for our souls to thrive and prosper. His 'fullness filleth all in all.' It is not a fullness for himself alone; but whatever he is in himself, he is that to us. *His* all filleth *our* all. His all of fullness filleth our all of wants. He is not something, but all, and that in our all, in all our emptiness and want. *His* all is triumphant. His all of merits triumphs over our all of guilt; his all of grace triumphs over our all of impurity; and his all of power is made perfect in our all of weakness. God does not give us half but a whole Christ. Let our faith be as large in receiving as his heart is in giving. And this whole Christ, when received by faith, filleth all in all. In him we have enough; we have no room for more. God is satisfied, and the mind of the believer is satisfied. Here God rests, and let this be our resting-place. He giveth rest to the soul of the sinner. Who besides can do this? None in heaven, and none on earth.

When I look on myself, my grace, enjoyments, performances, I see nakedness, I see some gap open still; but when I look to Christ, he filleth all. Between God and man, one Mediator filleth the breach; and he filleth all our wants and is able to satisfy them eternally. To live by the faith of Christ is the noblest life that ever was. We are thus what he is, for he is ours. We have all the dignity of his person, the merits of his cross, and the riches of his grace for our own. It is our great sin, our shame and misery that we look to any other object but to him alone.

To bring us out of ourselves unto Christ is the great work of the Spirit of God in the hearts of his people. Let us be contented and thankful for humbling dispensations. We must be beat down and brought to nothing, that he may be our all. We have our high things that exalt themselves against the knowledge of God in the gospel, which must be pulled down in order to captivate every thought into the obedience of Christ. It is easy to talk of Christ being our all; but nothing short of the mortifying dispensations of God's Holy Spirit will ever bring us to take him as such. There is an universal renunciation of self in this case, of all that we are and have as belonging to the first Adam, that we may be planted in the second. We are rooted out of the former soil, and planted in a new soil, where a *sinner*, dead, guilty, and unholy, may be made alive, righteous and faithful. No change, but a change as it were of soil, will ever produce these blessed effects. We must be eradicated and planted anew in Christ, where alone a sinner can thrive. But being in him and trusting in him, we shall be 'as a tree planted by the waters, and that spreadeth out her roots by the river,' Christ and his fullness. Then we shall 'not cease from yielding fruit,' Jer. 17:8.

The various and continued actings of faith on Christ are compared to the roots of a tree spreading out by the river, and thence drawing all its sap, nourishment and fructifying virtue. So doth faith from Christ; and it is impossible to live upon him, and not to bring forth fruit, rich and abundant. If we have been planted together with him in the likeness of his death, we shall be also in the likeness of his resurrection.

7. God's Mercies – His Promises to Sinners

Bala, Dec. 24, 1799.

I REJOICE at the restoration of Mrs Astle's health, and the continued mercies extended to your family. How great and undeserved are his mercies to us! What will he not give us, who spared not his only-begotten Son, but delivered him up for us all! Consider the force of that word, 'delivered him up,' and then say whether he is not infinitely good to us sinners. To spare *us*, he delivered *him* up; both could not be spared. But the guilty was spared, and the innocent, the just, the harmless Jesus suffered; yes, suffered as a sacrifice, suffered to make atonement, suffered, not under the hand of a Father correcting, but of a just God pouring forth his wrath and vengeance. What would you not suffer to spare a dear child? But God spared not the Son of his love to spare us. He laid upon him our iniquities: and for them he wounded and bruised him. How can we ever in this view call him a hard Master, or look upon him as merciless? None but a God of infinite mercy could have acted as he has done. Yes, there is forgiveness with him, and he keepeth mercies unto thousands.

I do not see, my dear friends, what you have to do with the point, whether your children are the vessels of mercy or not. You are sure that they are *empty* vessels. Take them as *such* to the fountain of grace and mercy. It is enough for me to plead with God whilst I live, that 'the promise is to us and to our children.' If we have a promise to plead, it is enough. A promise from the mouth of God is an immutable thing; and it is spoken by him with the express design that we should believe it and seek for the blessing

To Mr and Mrs William Astle

it contains. Plead it for yourselves, and plead it for your children also. Plead the promise of a new heart, till the heart is made new, etc., etc. The promise is a flagon which brings wine from the cellar of the gospel to cheer and strengthen us, We are apt to think that the promises are to the whole, the good, the righteous, and the godly, But remember, that were it not for the promise, there would not have been a godly man upon earth, nor a saint in heaven. If they are whole, it was the promise that brought the medicine that healed them; if they are renewed, it was the promise that brought them the new heart.

For my own part, when I can see a promise, all is well at once. The promises have virtue in them to conquer sin, to quicken the soul, and to make us fruitful in every good word and work. Let us as poor sinners live upon them, till we are fed as it were with marrow and fatness. But you will say, 'It does not belong to me.' I will answer as I have often done in my own heart, 'It belongs to a sinner, and I am a sinner; and therefore it belongs to me.' Most of the promises are quite useless to everyone but a sinner. Who wants a new heart but a sinner? Who wants cleansing and pardon but a sinner? Who wants the opening of his eyes but a blind sinner? Well, here are promises for sinners; let us live upon them till we are made saints by participating of the blessings contained in them. Here bring your empty vessels, your children and your all: and there is enough and you are welcome.

I am very glad that Mr Astle lays himself out so faithfully in the service of poor children. I have no doubt but that he will gather fruit sooner or later from this his labour. I firmly believe that 'no labour is in vain in the Lord.' What we do for him and in his strength and Spirit shall succeed in a degree more or less. As our day is far spent, I hope that he and I, during the few hours of our day that are still behind, shall *double* our diligence, and be instant in season and out of season.

8. God's Gifts – Christ Our All – Spirituality in Ministers

Bala, July 15, 1805.

LIFE and health are the Lord's; and he dispenses them according to his own will, and to answer his own designs. It is no small favour to be enabled to see everything in his hands, and to receive all as his free gifts whilst he bestows them, and to be submissive and satisfied when he withholds them. He must surely know what is best for us; and he cannot, from his goodness, but order all things accordingly. Amidst all the various infirmities of your weak frame, kind thoughts of God, and believing views of his love and grace in Christ Jesus, will prove your most effectual support. How kindly the Lord invites, yea, commands us to look unto him: 'Look unto me, and be ye saved.' This is actual salvation brought home to the mind. And what is this looking unto him, but believing the testimony of the word respecting him, and being daily influenced by that belief to act towards him accordingly. He really is what the unerring testimony of the divine word represents him to be. If we believe that testimony, he must appear to us infinitely lovely and amiable indeed, exactly such a one as we want; and in the enjoyment of whom we cannot but be eternally happy.

A poor woman in our country frequently on her deathbed repeated the following words: 'Jesus and I exactly suit one another; I have nothing, and he has everything.' I have nothing more to say in my best hours; and when I can say this, it is well with me, it is my best season, I triumph. This Jesus, with all his infinite fullness, was *designed* for us. He suits none else so well. We are invited to come unto him, to receive him and take him for our own forever. This is the real truth, however astonishing it may appear. Now, my good friend, what lack we? Nothing but the constant belief of this truth, and to act suitably towards him. Thus a great salvation appears at hand; it is near us; it is in our hearts by believing the truth. The Comforter is promised to take of the things of Christ and show them to us. So in every way we are provided for. Not unto us, but unto his own name be the glory.

To Mr and Mrs William Astle

I have not seen Mr James but he has written to me a kind letter since his arrival at Chester. They are both well, and seem pleased with their new situation; and the people, I believe, are pleased with him. He has a wide field before him, and I pray the Lord to bless him abundantly. I have wished for years past to have him there for trial. I have had my wishes so far. Now to see the Lord's work prosper in his hands would crown my wishes. I rejoice in hope it will be so. No solid, permanent work can be expected where the piety and spirituality of the instrument is low, whatever his gifts may be. Gifts create a great deal of bustle and noise and show; but little good, I will not say none, is done, where evangelical spirituality is wanting, or low in its degree. I trust Mr James is a tree planted by the rivers of waters; and when that is the case, some fruit may be expected.

Good Dr. Ford informed me lately that the Sunday School at the Spa Fields prospers; which gives me great joy indeed. Surely the Lord looks on the rising generation with an eye of kindness and mercy. He indeed smiles on every attempt to instruct them in divine things. I feel very unwilling that Satan should have any of their service. Could we but bring them all over to the kingdom of God's dear Son, what a thing it would be! Well, the attempt is glorious, and is sure to succeed in some degree.

To The Rev. Mr John Mayor, of Shawbury

1. Gratitude to God and Man

Queen Camel, March 18, 1779.

NOT to acknowledge the many obligations I am under to you for the friendly assistance you *gave*, as well as *procured*, to enable me to support myself in the University, would indicate a mind totally void of principle, and a heart unsusceptible of any grateful feelings. I can assure you, sir, that however unable I am to requite your undeserved kindness, the grateful sense of it can never be obliterated from my memory, whilst I am possessed of any sensibility, and not judicially given up to stoical apathy. If unable to express my obligations to earthly friends, what then shall I render to the Father of *all* mercies, to that faithful friend who sticketh closer than a brother, for the *inestimable favours* he is continually bestowing on an unworthy wretch! It relieves my anxious mind to think, that the time is hastening when I hope to love him better and praise him louder. May redeeming love constrain me to yield *myself* up, and all I have, to his service, and enable me to make it my continual study and delight to proclaim his infinite goodness and astonishing mercy to perishing sinners. When I consider the ardency of his eternal love, when my heart glows with the warmest zeal, I am ashamed to think that I am speaking upon such a grand and noble subject. Here the fervour of a burning seraph is cold like ice. Well might St Paul call it 'love that passeth knowledge.'

2. Dependence on God – Marriage – Trial

Bala, Sept. 5, 1783.

I WAS very glad I called at Shawbury in my way here. I spent my time there very agreeably, and found my heart more united to you than ever. I hope and pray that the Lord would be with you and bless you, and that is comfort and happiness enough. We cannot depend too simply, or too much, upon him. An arm of flesh, whatever promises it may make, is sure in the end to disappoint us: but the Lord has never disappointed any that depended upon him. He is 'abundant in truth,' performs more than he has promised or we can possibly expect from him. May God the holy Ghost enable you and me to put our dependence entirely upon him and have all our expectations from him. A single eye to the Lord will bring us more solid comfort than if men and angels were our friends.

I have the pleasure to inform you that I was married on the 20th of August. A change that has a material influence upon the whole of our future life, must be looked upon as an important one. I doubt not of an interest in your prayers, that I may in every state be enabled to live wholly to the Lord. This is our happiness and our glory both on earth and in heaven. May my eye be single to this point while I live. I have every reason to be thankful to the Lord for his goodness to me. Indeed his goodness is so great, that I sink under the burden. Where shall I begin to praise! How inadequate is every grateful return I can make for the blessings I receive! You will acknowledge with me, that a partner through life, that fears the Lord, to say nothing else, is a great blessing.

… The church I was engaged to serve in this country, I was dismissed from, after preaching there two Sundays. I now assist Mr Lloyd. One of his churches was the second Sunday shut against me by the parishioners; and I expect every Sunday to be my last in the other. What the Lord means to do with me, I do not know. I find myself easy and comfortable, not doubting but that the Lord will direct and lead me in the right way. It is an honour to be but a doorkeeper in his house, and to be employed by him, were it in the meanest service he can put us to. I pray the Lord always to give me an honest heart and a willing mind to serve him in the gospel of his Son while I live.

3. Watchfullness – God a Present Help

Bala, Oct. 6, 1783.

I FIND in every state the necessity of taking heed to our Saviour's admonitions to unceasing watchfullness and prayer. The first step towards our deliverance from danger is a proper sense of it. Till then we shall not look up for help to him who is mighty to save. Be assured, dear Sir, that I very sensibly feel with you under your present trials. I hope the Lord will be a 'present help' under present and pressing evils. 'God is our refuge and strength,' saith the Psalmist, 'a very *present* help in trouble.' He is everything for us that we can want in every state and under every trial. May the Lord help us to rely upon him as our *all* in *all*; and then I am sure that *all* will be well.

4. Afflictions Necessary

Bala, Feb. 26, 1784.

WE were all exceedingly glad to receive your letter, and equally sorry to hear of the affliction which has visited you and your family. By this time we may hope that things wear a different aspect, and that your sorrow is turned into joy. It shall be well at *last* with the righteous: and though for a season a dark cloud should hang over him, yet he may be well assured, that every cloud is big with blessings; and the darker it is, the more blessings it contains: and when it has emptied itself, the sun will shine comfortably. The cloud and its contents are as necessary as the sun. Without the cloud the heat of the sun would burn the earth, so that it would bring forth no fruit to perfection. The rain and the sun together make a fruitful season. Let us therefore bless God for the one as well as for the other. I can assure you, my dear friend, that I heartily sympathize with you. At the same time I cannot but believe that all is for good. I am sure you cannot expect too much from God. If he lays one hand heavy upon us to afflict us, let us look to the other; and there we may confidently expect to see a blessing proportioned to the affliction. We dishonour him much when we expect little things from him:

and I believe we often receive a small blessing, because our expectations are small – wholly unsuitable to him with whom we have to do. May the Holy Spirit enable us to think honourably of him, and act honourably towards him, in all our dealings with him. We sin more than we are apt to imagine by our narrow views and contracted thoughts of him, and by our unworthy expectations from him. Alas! 'How general is infidelity,' as you justly observe, 'among those who talk much of God and religion'; and how few are there who *practically* believe God to be what he is! We often, the best of us, act towards him, as if he were such an one as ourselves, having as little to bestow as we have, and giving what he has with as much difficulty as we do. In the *right* knowledge of him standeth our eternal life. Here true religion begins; in this it thrives; and here it ends. The more we grow in the true knowledge of God, the more we love him, fear him, believe him and obey him.

I thank you sincerely for an interest in your prayers. I think the prayers of the godly were never so much valued by me as at present. It comforts me exceedingly to think that any one puts up a petition for me and for the people committed to my care. They are, I may say without erring *much*, *all* of them in the gall of bitterness and the bond of iniquity. But he who sent St Paul to 'open the eyes of the blind and to turn them from darkness to light, and from the power of Satan unto God,' does still own his gospel to the same blessed purpose. Nothing in this world would rejoice me more, if I mistake not, than to see it made the power of God unto salvation to many souls. The Lord help us to be faithful. I am in *some degree* sensible of my utter insufficiency: but the residue of the Spirit is with God; and he can work with weak instruments as well as strong ones. I endeavour simply to look to him for ability to speak and for a blessing on what is spoken.

5. Divine Teaching – Support in Affliction, etc.

Bala, March 29, 1784.

I HAVE just received the books, and I am very much obliged to you for sending them. I mean to spend a little time in studying the pleasing and interesting subject of which they treat with all the application I can command. But he who gave us his word must also give us light to understand it, and power to make it profitable to our souls. It is he that must still 'open to us the Scriptures.' We cannot be too sensible of this: and the more we look up to God for the teaching of his Spirit, the more we shall be led to understand, and feed upon, the divine mysteries. The more we grow in grace, the more humble we are in this view, and the more practically convinced, that we know nothing as we ought to know, but as we are daily taught of God. We may know them indeed; but not as we *ought* to know them, that is, humbly, practically, and profitably to our souls.

We were all very sorry to hear your account of Mrs Mayor's poor state of health. My poor prayers, such as they are, shall attend you to Bristol for a blessing on the means made use of. I beg you would present our kindest love to her. I need not direct you and her where to find comfort. 'The everlasting covenant, ordered in all things and sure,' is an inexhaustible source, which hath supplied many a weary pilgrim with strong consolations under all the pressures, troubles and trials which he has had to pass through. This covenant is still the same. It is still 'ordered in all things and sure.' We can want nothing which it cannot supply. May the Lord keep us always drinking out of this fountain of living waters.

I very much wish to see you before you set out on your journey: but I cannot possibly come to you before Easter week, as we have service every Wednesday in Lent. And as my time is short, having only four Sundays more, I would not on any account miss one opportunity of delivering my message to the very many who willingly attend to hear, even on weekdays. I had an absolute promise of the curacy; but promises are nothing when there is an heretic in the case – 'No faith to be kept with heretics.' After my appointment three clergymen, in Dolgelley and its neighbourhood, gave themselves no rest till they got me dismissed. However I verily believe the Lord sent me there, and I hope not in vain. He can bless one sermon as well as ten thousand. I was apprehensive my continuance would not be long: therefore I endeavoured to make the best of the short time I might be there. What I am to do next is known only to him who orders all things after the counsel of his own will. I endeavour to look up to him and depend on him for direction. If I can but see the cloud moving before me, all will be well. Will you pray for me, my dear brother!

6. Reflections on Mr Lucas's Death.

Bala, March 11, 1785.

I HAVE the melancholy intelligence to send you of the death of poor dear Mr Lucas. Mr Newman sends me the account as follows: 'I came here last night, and heard Mr L. preach a most excellent discourse, and stayed with him till 9 o'clock. He was very cheerful and seemed quite well, and desired me to call upon him in the morning to take a walk with him in the garden, which I intended to do. About seven Mr Marsh went into his bed-chamber to call him; but having no answer, he concluded he was asleep. He spoke to him again; and then opened the window-shutter, and found him dead. I imagine he was taken off by an apoplectic fit, as he never moved. His hand was under his cheek, as was his usual way of sleeping. The whole town is in tears.

This is the account I have to send you of the dearest and most valuable friend I ever had. Never anything came nearer to me. But I rejoice in the fullest confidence of his happiness; nor would I wish him back again. It is a pleasing and melancholy reflection to look back on the precious and comfortable seasons I spent with him in conversing about spiritual subjects. Some of my happiest moments were spent in his company; and I received more instruction and benefit from him, than from all my other friends besides. Dearest man! His memory will be ever precious and fresh to my mind; and I rejoice at the thought of spending an eternity with him, dwelling on no other subjects but those which often warmed our hearts together below. The comfort I have *now* in reflecting on the time we spent together in spiritual conversation, will, I hope, make me more watchful in redeeming the time with the remaining few of my living friends. Nothing but this will afford us hereafter a pleasing reflection, that they and I have been acquainted. All my time with him seems to be entirely lost, but what we spent spiritually together.

7. The Religious State of North Wales

Bala, April 15, 1785.

I AM just this moment come home from three weeks' tour through Caernarvonshire and Anglesey, and embrace the first opportunity of answering your two kind letters, after they came to my hands. And first as to the curacy, I believe I must not entertain the thought of accepting it and leaving my present line of labouring in the Lord's vineyard. The fields here all over the country are white for the harvest. Fresh ground is daily gained. Whole neighbourhoods, where the word has been heretofore opposed, call aloud for the gospel. Thousands flock to hear: and many in different parts of the country, we have good reason to believe, are effectually called. Whilst the prospects here continue so promising, I cannot in conscience quit the field here and remove to another place. My dear friend, pray for me. I am often from the ground of my heart crying out, 'Who is sufficient for these things?' I endeavour to cast myself on the Lord, persuaded that he is all-sufficient; nor am I without experiencing that he perfects his strength in my weakness. I should have been very glad to have accompanied you to the meeting, were it possible. I beg you will give my Christian love to all the brethren there, Messrs. Riland, Scott, Griffin, Sanderson, etc., etc. and I hope the Divine Presence will be with you.

8. Welsh Bibles – Mrs Charles's Illness – Mr Scott's Writings

Bala, March 23, 1787.

YOUR last letter quite rejoiced my heart with the smallest prospect of having some Welsh Bibles. Mr Scott's friend could not think of anything that is more wanted, that would be more acceptable and useful to the country at large. I have often, in my journeys in different parts of the country, been questioned whether I knew where a Welsh Bible could be bought. And it has hurt my mind much to be obliged to answer in the negative: for there are not any to be bought for money except Mr Williams' Bibles with Notes, which are too high in price for the poor people to purchase. I mean to write to Mr Scott immediately in answer to the queries he has sent you. I could dispose of 1,000 or 2,000 to very good use.

What 'vague report' you have heard of dear Mrs Charles, I do not know; but the truth is this: she was taken extremely ill about three weeks before her time: but the Lord in mercy wonderfully interposed. I was obliged to live above a week (and a most trying week it was) tossed between hope and fear. She was extremely reduced and her strength was very nearly exhausted. The whole of her recovery is the Lord's doing, and I believe in answer to prayer in extremity. It is well to have an *all-sufficient* Friend to go to. When I gave her up to him, I received her back from him by a favourable turn being given to her illness. We cannot but see the Lord's hand in it from first to last. It was he that 'killed and made alive.' She recovers but slowly, and is still very weak; but she is recovering: and what comfort that affords me, your own feelings must tell you; for I cannot. I desire to be thankful to the Lord for his goodness, and to live whilst I live to his glory. Praise the Lord with me.

You ask me how I like Mr Scott's publication. You know thoroughly my sentiments: they are still the same. I have disapproved, in my own mind, for many years, of the manner in which the doctrines of the gospel are set forth by some of our English friends. But I think Mr Scott had better not set himself in full opposition to them, but to endeavour by degrees to introduce a different mode of preaching. I have great regard for Mr Scott, and wish him abundant success in his present important station. His sermon well answers the intention of its publication: but I do not think it would suit our people. They do not trouble their heads much about refined niceties of doctrines. Plain, practical, useful truths are the food they are nourished with. They care but little for how *many* Christ died, so they can believe there is salvation sufficient in him for the vilest of sinners. They rejoice, yea leap, and *jump* too if you will, for joy, at the glory and sufficiency of that salvation revealed in the gospel. You may hear hundreds of sermons preached in our connection, without one word about election. And yet they all believe the doctrine; yes, and experience the comfort of it. This I firmly believe: that it is not sufficient to make a minister of the gospel, to have a system of wholesome doctrines in the head, except he is led by the Holy Spirit to see and feel the glory of the person of Christ, and the excellence of the work accomplished by him for sinners. The truths which he preaches must be his own food and nourishment, and not food to be talked of to others only. What need have we to be humble, and fervent in prayer for divine illumination and teaching! If we ourselves live far from God in daily communion, we can do but little good to others with our refined notions. I doubt not but that those who raised the clamour against Mr Scott's practical preaching would have been better employed in practising those truths which he inculcated, instead of measuring the truths which he preached by the rule of their own refined notions.

9. On the Death of an Infant

Bala, Jan. 23, 1788.

I WRITE this to you from the house of mourning. My little girl died yesterday, after a twelve months existence in this our world, in almost continual affliction and sorrow. At last death prevailed and separated her soul from her afflicted body, to meet again, when both the one and the other will be fuller of holiness and felicity than they were here of sin and sorrow. How free was the grace which saved her and took her to glory! It came to her unthought of, unsought for, and undesired. Her sin was taken away without any sorrow for it, hatred towards it, or striving against it. Without any contest she got the victory forever over all the enemies of our souls! Without travelling one step of the wilderness-road, she got safe to Canaan. The grace implanted within her is got to its full growth without the nurture and discipline which others require and are exercised with. Here it was but as seed under-grown; but now it is full-grown and loaded with the richest fruits. Blessed be God for his full salvation! I think myself happy to be the parent of this little vessel of mercy to be filled with eternal glory. 'The Lord gave; the Lord hath taken away' – nothing but his own; 'blessed be the name of the Lord!' – My health has been but indifferent at intervals all this winter; but at present through mercy I am tolerably well. This poor house of clay will be soon in ruins. Blessed be God for a house not made with hands eternal in the heavens! Do not forget me and mine at the throne of mercy.

10. Strength for Duty – Sin and Self

Bala, Saturday Night. (No date.)

I HOPE the Lord will strengthen you both in the inner and the outward man for your duty. Remember, if your strength is not proportioned to the labour, it is your duty to proportion the labour to your strength, and to look by faith to God for a *great* blessing upon the *little* you are enabled faithfully to perform.

I sincerely wish much of the Divine Presence, great success and comfort in your ministerial labours. Let us walk humbly *with* God, live steadfastly by faith *upon* him, and act boldly and faithfully *for* him: and all will be well. The cross, which we must expect to meet daily in the way, will hurt nothing but sin and self: and surely we would not wish to spare them. I hope it is our happiness to think that God is against them, and has determined their destruction in his own way. Blessed be the Lord, there is a world where righteousness only dwelleth, and where sin and self shall no more trouble us forever! Till we arrive there, may we be enabled to set our faces against them as our determined and irreconcilable enemies.

11. Mr Charles's Experience during His Illness

Bala, March 25, 1801.

I THANK you for your very affectionate letter. Believe me, my dear friend, I felt sensations of a very pleasing nature in the perusal of it, both as it brought fresh to my memory past seasons of endearing friendship between us, and also as it rejoiced me much that our mutual affection continues undiminished to this day. Nor have I any doubt but that it will continue when time is no more. I am sensible that it is undeserved on my part; but I hope I shall not be backward in faithful returns of sincere regard and Christian affection.

As to my health, my hand is quite well and free from pain; but it is not yet, and perhaps never will be, recovered to its usual strength and pliability. My general health also is gradually improving, though a considerable degree of languor and imbecility still cleaves to me. I cannot bear cold and damp weather without being very sensibly affected. However, I am in all respects wonderfully recovered, considering the extremely weak state I was in. My all is in the Lord's hand, and I am fully satisfied. He will doubtless grant me that degree of health and strength, which, all things considered, is best for me.

During the whole of my indisposition I had daily proofs of the Lord's great faithfullness in fulfilling his promises graciously made to us in his word. As my day of trial or suffering was, so was my strength. Soon after the commencement of my complaint, when I understood the very serious consequences likely to follow, he graciously favoured me with such glorious views of HIMSELF as produced a comfortable, calm frame of mind and a *joyful* resignation to his will, I never had such views before, (I mean in the same degree of clearness and continuance) of his sovereignty, and justice, of his goodness and tenderness. It was impossible for me to believe, that he, who gave his life a ransom for me, would do me ultimately any harm, but the greatest good. It was the amazing sight, by faith, of a crucified Saviour, that conquered all the rebellions of my will, and banished all my fears. Under whatever character I viewed the Lord I could not help loving him, and having confidence in him, and rejoicing with joy unspeakable and full of glory.

The loveliness of his character as set forth in his word, the infinite dignity of the person of Jesus, the fullness of his salvation, the immutability of his councils, were brought before my view with such overpowering evidence and glory, that my feeble nature could hardly support itself under it. I found a nearness in my mind to the eternal world, which I never experienced before; and heaven was almost in view. To worship God with all the heart, and to adore his divine perfections, would, I thought, be a heaven of eternal joys enough to satisfy any soul forever. All things here on earth were at a distance from my mind. But I felt a continual care on my mind for his blessed cause and interest in the world, and I rejoiced that it could go on and prosper without my assistance. The government is on Jesus' shoulders, and that is enough. Because he lives, his cause shall live and flourish abundantly. Jesus and 'him crucified,' was my all for the eternal salvation of my poor and guilty soul. All other knowledge, but what I knew of him, was totally useless and of no value. But I felt inexpressible thankfullness for the little (Oh how little!) I knew of him. I was glad I had endeavoured to speak of him to poor perishing sinners; but I was sorry and ashamed that I spoke no better of a character so infinitely deserving of every commendation, and so necessary for sinners to be acquainted with. I rejoiced that he was exalted on earth, and would be exalted till time is no more. I felt great love to, and value for, all those who, as public ministers, were endeavouring faithfully to set forth his glories. After all the vain talk that is in the world, Jesus is everything to a lost sinner. He is *all* and in *all*. I could hardly bear bestowing a thought on any other subject.

Thus I have related a little of God's gracious dealings towards me: and as you have been induced to remember me (unworthy indeed) in your prayers, I hope you will bless and praise the Lord for me also.[5]

[5] A letter to Mr Charles, in the year 1791, from the Rev. W. Williams, Pantycelyn, Carmarthenshire, contains sentiments very similar to those of this letter. Being so very excellent, they shall be subjoined, translated from the *Trysorfa* for June 1799.

'I have been very ill, and beyond hope of living in my own opinion and in that of others: and yet for some secret purpose of the Lord, I still live. I found no lessening of my pain, until the Lord himself became my

Physician: and this came to pass through the Church having taken my case in hand, and crying for help; and he, according to his promise, heard them. I have now faith to believe that one earnest prayer is better than all the physicians in the world. I have had, I believe, the prayers of some hundreds in this affliction; and in answer to their prayers, a verse came to my mind with such power, that I believed I should be raised again for a short time; and that was Psalm 118:17. 'I shall not die, but live, and declare the works of the Lord.' My tender and beloved Father has given me ease, though I am not yet able to come out of my bedroom. I ask him nothing, but he gives it me: and I have never had such faith to pray to him, as I have at present. I know that the Lord hath put this affliction upon me; and I know that whether I live or die of it, it shall be for a blessing to me. I have learnt during these ten weeks more of myself, and of God's goodness, than during the last forty years that have passed. I was brought to read the Bible, which I before read in great measure for the edification of others, now wholly for myself, as the only book by which I shall be tried in the great day of judgement. Though I have hundreds of books, yet I had no such taste for any as for the Bible.'

He then mentions *three* things, into which he had a clearer insight in his illness than ever before, namely, the plan of salvation through Christ; the necessity of especial communion with God in all religious duties; and the importance of a conversation worthy of the gospel. Having somewhat enlarged on these points, he thus proceeds:

'These are the things which greatly engaged my thoughts in my illness. O my dear, dear brother, work while it is day: the night will come upon you as it has upon me, when you can no longer travel about and preach. I should like nothing so much, as to go again through North Wales as in former times. It would be my endeavour to spend no time but in speaking of the things of the Lord. May the Lord make you strong against the enemy and all his attacks and devices! He is trying unweariedly and incessantly to allure us from the path of truth by one thing or another: by unruly conduct, or by false opinions and heresies, by indifference and carelessness, or by hot-headed intemperate zeal for things of small importance. God has preserved our connection wonderfully from errors for nearly sixty years. It has not been without many dreadful onsets from without and from within: but hitherto it has been kept sound in the faith, notwithstanding all, to the benefit of thousands of our fellow countrymen. I doubt not but that God will yet take care of us, as a connexion, for ages and generations. Exhort one another to examine God's word particularly, that you may be strong in the Scriptures. Exhort the young preachers

To Miss Mary Ashwell, of Milborne Port, Somerset

1. Humility and Thankfullness

Bala, Dec. 18, 1783.

I SINCERELY thank you for your kind congratulations on the occasion of my marriage, and for your good wishes in our behalf. I am unable to express the pleasing sensations of gratitude I feel for the very sincere affection and kindness, however undeserved, which my dear friends at Milborne have on all occasions showed to me. I shall ever think of the time I spent with them, though I hope with humility and self-abhorrence for not living more holy and more useful, yet at the same time, with a great deal of pleasure and satisfaction. May the Lord make and keep me thankful and humble! There is never wanting an abundant cause for both: and I believe that the one cannot be without the other. We must first be made truly humble, before we can be truly thankful: and nothing but an unhumbled spirit prevents our being thankful for *everything* and in *every* condition this side hell. 'I am less than the least of all thy mercies,' and 'I abhor myself and repent in dust and ashes,' has been the invariable language of true humility from the time of Jacob and Job to this day. And where this is the genuine language of the heart, we may be well assured that thankfullness occupies no small part of it. When we are little in our own eyes, every mercy is great; and when we abhor ourselves, then God appears to us, as he is, infinitely good, holy and glorious; and when he appears so, we can neither murmur nor complain against him.

---

to attend especially, next to the Bible, to the doctrines of our venerable Reformers, as set forth in the Articles of the Church of England, and the three Creeds: the Apostles', Nicene, and Athanasian. Remember me to all the brethren in the Lord. The chief thing I now desire is, to love the great God, who clothed himself in flesh to redeem vile sinners such as I am.'

True humility, if I may judge by mine own heart, never murmureth against God nor man – is never impatient in any circumstance nor under any cross; but, like that divine love which St Paul describes and of which humility is the inseparable companion: 'beareth all things.' How hard, nay, how impossible is this to flesh and blood! This duty, which is the ornament and glory of the Christian, and which so appears to a truly humbled man, is, I believe, thought to be by every unhumbled heart the most unreasonable thing in the world. That it may be proper at some times and on some occasions to bear *some* things, and they must be little things, a proud heart may be brought to acknowledge; and whilst it does so, it is still feeding pride. But true humility 'beareth *all* things,' whether they come from God immediately or from man; it beareth all things, according to its degree, with cheerfullness and thankfullness. How beautiful and glorious is such a disposition and conduct! It is the divine nature and the very image of God on the soul. 'God beareth with much longsuffering': and we may be assured that true grace, wherever it is, according to its degree and strength, copies exactly after this divine pattern. Grace is a child of God, and partakes of the divine nature: and those things which the child sees, admires and loves in the Father, he cannot but earnestly desire growth in, nor be satisfied till he be filled with all the fullness of God. And as grace sees a beauty and glory in holiness that makes it infinitely desirable to the soul; so also it does not only *bear* all things, but approves of, delights and glories in everything which promotes true holiness in the heart, Rom. 5:3. It is willing, yea, it rejoices, that God should carry on his work in his own way. It sees wisdom, goodness, and beauty in the narrow way of the cross, which God hath appointed, as being the fittest and best to lead to the crown. It desires the crown in no other way, nor can it possibly conceive how sinners could be brought to a heaven of perfect holiness, but in the way of the cross. How can gold be purified but in the furnace?

Truly humbled, the believer is duly sensible of what he deserves; therefore he 'beareth all things'; and having under the cross that faith which is 'the substance of things hoped for and the evidence of things not seen,' and thereby seeing the end which God has in view, he 'hopeth all things.' And there is no danger of our desiring or hoping for too much from God in the way of holiness. Let us enlarge our desires and expectations, and be in no fear of disappointment. But when we seek for the blessing, we must be willing to have it in God's own way, that is, beneath the cross: for not only, 'no cross, no crown,' but also no cross, no one spiritual blessing can be received; yea, the cross will bear some proportion to the blessing. Shall we startle at this? No; but rather let us adore and be thankful that a blessing is to be obtained in *any* way. True humility will certainly do so. It cries with Rachel, 'give me holiness or else I die,' and presumes not to prescribe to God the way of bestowing it. Though pangs of labour and sorrow may be endured in obtaining it, yet still it desires it; and though flesh and blood should call it Benoni, (son of affliction,) yet grace will certainly call it a Benjamin, (son of my right hand). Oh for grace to follow after holiness, and to submit to God in all things!

… We are not as yet settled in a house of our own. As we live so very comfortably as we are, we do not hurry ourselves about settling. So excellent a wife would be a sufficient reward for ten thousand times more anxiety and labour in obtaining her than I have experienced. But however, I hope ever to see by faith that all my comforts of every sort proceed wholly from the Lord, and that the creature is only made use of, as the channel by which it is conveyed. Praise the Lord for me, my dear friend; and pray for a continuance of his undeserved blessings.

2. God's Care of His Children

Bala, Nov. 26, 1786.

I LONG to hear from you, and to know of your welfare, how you go on, and whether you mean to continue at Milborne. How mysterious are the ways of Providence! You came to Milborne to be with your friends; and behold they have all left you. I trust you are enabled to keep an eye of faith steadily fixed upon him, who has promised 'never to leave us nor forsake us.' And you know he is *all-sufficient*. We can never trust too little in man, nor too much in God. I am convinced of this by daily experience. Our main point and study should be to keep close to God in daily communion; and he will take care of us and of all that belong to us. Has he given his Son to die for us; and will he not take care of us the few days we are on our journey to our Father's house? The thought is unworthy of him. No, my dear friend, we have not such a Father. Let us honour him and testify our good opinion of him by trusting him with the care of our souls and bodies – with our temporal and eternal concerns. Though all should forsake us and prove unfaithful, yet faith will say, 'This God is our God forever and ever; and he will be our guide unto death.' Mark, he will be 'our guide unto death,' – what can we want more this side death? He is 'our God forever and ever,' – here is enough after death and to all eternity. Here is a portion! Here is a husband! Here is a friend! Oh may we rejoice in him more and more! Can he be poor and friendless who has God for his God? Can his condition be bad who has all-sufficiency in possession? True, we are poor, yet if God's children, we have a rich Father; and our elder Brother has all power and authority given him in heaven and earth. Whilst we are here without the veil, faith and hope enter into that which is within the veil, and look upon the riches, the glory, the peace, and the joy which are at the Lord's right hand. 'Lord! 'tis enough that thou art mine, etc.' I should be glad to know how religion goes on at Milborne. Are there many of those whom we looked upon as hopeful, that stand their ground? And are there any new ones added to their number?

3. The Hope of Meeting Above – Revivals

Spa Fields, August 15, 1793.

THOUGH I have reason to be deeply humbled at the remembrance of every part of my past life, yet I do reflect with a great deal of pleasure on the few years I spent with my dear and much valued friends at Milborne. And as you and Mrs Taprell are the only two remaining of them, to meet you both together once more this side eternity, I should esteem a high treat indeed. But if we never meet here, I have no doubt but we shall meet more holy and more happy than we ever met in this world. That will be a glorious meeting indeed, before the throne of God and the Lamb! All the company will be perfectly holy, forever freed from sin and all its dreadful consequences. They will be all *conquerors*, who shall have won battles, the most glorious that ever have been fought. They shall have obtained the victory by the same means: 'by the blood of the Lamb and the word of their testimony.' They will be all King's children, and joint-heirs of the same glorious inheritance. They will be all of full age to possess this inheritance. They shall all possess one heart and one spirit; all engaged in the same blessed work, singing songs of praises to the Lamb that was slain and redeemed them to God. Though there will be millions and millions of them together, not a jarring note shall ever be heard. It is but a little time, and we shall, through undeserved grace, be amongst them. This is my humble trust and expectation. In the meantime may we be 'steadfast and unmoveable, always abounding in the work of the Lord!'

Well, perhaps a little account of what is going on in this miserable world may not be unacceptable to you. Here in London a considerable deadness seems to overspread the religious world. The empty noise of politics has had its influence in promoting it. A fresh outpouring of the Spirit, another Pentecost, is wanted to revive his drooping cause. But, however, I hope some good is done, and I trust more will be done. In Wales, the prospect I think is as pleasing, if not more so, than ever. A very general awakening now prevails through the greatest part of the county of Caernarvon. Some hundreds have been effectually brought to the Lord, beside a mighty shaking of the whole country. In some parts of Anglesey and Denbighshire a great work is going on. At Bala awakenings are not so frequent, nor is the work so lively, as it was a year ago. But most of those who were then called, stand their ground and go on well: and a few are 'added to them daily.' Upon the whole we go on with much comfort; and the pleasure of the Lord prospers in our hands. Did you understand the Welsh language, I should not fail earnestly pressing you to come and see us; but as you do not, I am afraid you might feel yourself uncomfortable, as all the preaching is in Welsh.

4. Wesleyan Methodists – Unceasing Labours

Bala, July 8, 1795.

THINK not, dear Madam, that my prejudice against Methodism[6] is so great, as to render unsavoury to my palate so interesting an account of the success of the gospel through their instrumentality. I have been lately to Manchester and Liverpool, attended their preaching as often as I could, and perceived evidently the same divine energy accompanying the gospel there in their mouths, which has worked so effectually among the poor Welsh for these several years past. So that the gospel is preached and made effectual, I am satisfied. It is true I cannot view some points *exactly* in the same light as they do. But still I perceive, and I am satisfied, that the Lord is powerfully among them and blesses their labours. I am glad to find that your little vineyard at Buckingham is watered also. How delightful it is to read from the mouth of God himself such words as these: 'I the Lord do keep it; I will water it every moment: lest any hurt it, I will keep it night and day.'

... I have nearly dropped all my correspondents, except some occasion calls me to write to one or another of them. You may suppose that both my time and thoughts are much occupied, when you consider the multiplicity of concerns which must attend a large family, the extensive business in which my wife is engaged, and besides, I may add without boasting, 'the care of all the churches' in these parts. I feel and confess myself very insufficient for so extensive a sphere of action. But I have been by Providence brought into it without any design of my own; and now, as I find myself engaged in it, every other consideration must give way to the faithful discharge of the trust committed to me. Oh that I may be at last reckoned among the 'good and faithful' servants! I desire

---

[6] That is, Wesleyan Methodism.

to *labour*, that I may be accepted of him. I have reason to bless the Lord more than I can express, for his indulgence, and continual supports and supplies. I know what it is to be 'troubled on every side, yet not distressed; perplexed, but not in despair; persecuted, but not forsaken; cast down, but not destroyed.' Not only have I my own concerns, but also everybody's burden; and everybody's trials must be mine also: but still I do not complain. I see it is an honour and a high privilege to be thus employed by my Divine Master. I have but one desire, that of spending and being spent, till the good Lord, in infinite mercy, takes me to himself. 'The lines are fallen to me in pleasant places; yea, I have a goodly heritage.' I will bless the Lord who hath given me counsel.

5. Romaine's Death – Dress

Spa Fields, Aug. 14, 1795.

I THANK you for your kind letter. The account you give of Mr Ch—'s ministry is very pleasing. In the cloudy and dark day, when everything in providence looks threatening, and everything among the sons of men wears the appearance of distraction and dissension, it is very cheering to see that the gospel by one and another is almost universally preached over our land, and that there is also great reason to believe that it is on the whole much blessed. These are our good signs. The ship is in a storm; but the Lord has an *interest* in it, and will have a care over it, and bring it safe into harbour in the end. Some useful hands in the vessel, to be sure, are every now and then lost: but the great Pilot still remains: and I hear him say, 'Instead of thy fathers shall be thy children, whom thou mayest make princes in all the earth,' – so numerous shall they be, and so eminent in spiritual gifts and graces. You have heard, doubtless, that the great *Romaine* is dead, and that Mr *Goode* has succeeded to his Church, to the universal satisfaction and joy of all lovers of the gospel. Mr R's death was triumphant; and his memory stands high in the minds of all of every party in the religions world. He long continued in the firmament of the Church, a bright star, revolving in his appointed course with the Sun of righteousness full in view, continually receiving of his light and heat, and communicating them to others to the unspeakable benefit and comfort of their souls. May his mantle drop on his successor!

Your remarks on dress are very just. It would be very desirable to see simplicity taking the place of folly, and humility that of pride. Were we once convinced that holiness is our beauty, and that the graces of the Spirit are our brightest jewels, it would ennoble our minds and dignify our conduct; we should cheerfully cast away childish things and beautify ourselves with ornaments that are spiritual and heavenly. What a glorious change: the garments of salvation instead of our own filthy rags! 'Take away the filthy rags from him'; – gracious words! Instead of driving him and his filthy garments into destruction, he is saved, as a brand plucked out of the burning: and he is clothed with a change of raiment. What a dispensation of abounding grace is here! The sin destroyed and not the sinner! Not saved in his filthy raiment, but saved and washed and dressed gloriously in the robes of gospel righteousness. How shall we adore, wonder and praise, when we appear above, thus completely arrayed! We shall never cease to love and praise him who laid aside his glory, and took our sins and shame upon him, that we might be raised from the dunghill, from the dreadful ruins of the fall, to set us among the princes of his people and make us inherit the throne of glory. My prayer is, that he would strengthen us with might by his Spirit, in the inner man; that we may be enabled to live to him that died for us, and to be faithful unto death in unwearied attempts to promote his glory and hasten his kingdom.

To Mr R. D—, of Liverpool

The Honour of Promoting God's Cause

Bala, Feb. 27, 1810.

SINCE my last visit to Liverpool, it has occupied a place in my thoughts which it never had before. Your generous offer to forward the erection of a place of worship on a *broad basis* for preaching the gospel, was noble and unexpected. And as I find you continue still in the same mind, I hope something will be done soon. To mature the plan, a personal interview is requisite, and many points of bearing must be discussed. In the meantime I hope you and I shall be directed of the Lord in our proceedings, and that in simple dependence on him we shall be able to go on with courage as his providence may lead. To promote the furtherance of the gospel is a work of the highest honour and importance. A world without the gospel is not, for sinners, worth having. It is the grand instrument of God's appointment for their recovery: and there is no other means suitable and relevant: and none other will be owned of God. What a world this will be, when filled with the knowledge of the Lord through the gospel! This, we have sufficient ground to hope, will be fully accomplished, and that *speedily*. We live in a most favourable period to exert ourselves. I was on a fortnight's tour this month through Carmarthenshire, and I was much delighted with the prospect there. The fields are there white already to harvest. From one end to the other, all the young people are most delightfully engaged with the Bible. Satan's kingdom must fall; for soon I trust, he will have none to support it, in many parts of our country.

Whilst you and I are in the same vessel with the ransomed of the Lord, and I trust, of their number, whilst the ship cuts its way through the mighty deep with its precious cargo safe, under the guidance of a perfectly skilful pilot, I hope, my dear sir, we shall not he idle, but pull a little at some rope, whilst the wind fills her crowded sails, and she rides triumphantly through all storms towards the desired haven. We do not support the gospel, but the gospel supports us, and carries us through the great deep. The strength of the ship and the skill of the Pilot will prove our safety. I beg my most affectionate Christian regards to Mrs D—, and Mrs W—. I trust Mrs W— has gained much in her health and strength since I had the pleasure of seeing her. Mrs W—, I hope, is enabled to cast all her cares on the Lord, and trust him for soul, body and all. I find sometimes a most refreshing relief, when I am enabled to leave all my concerns with him for time and eternity. We need being strengthened in the faith to do this.

To Edward Morgan
(A Young Clergyman)

1. Guidance of Providence, etc.

Bala, March 23, 1808.

I TRUST you will be enabled to commit your ways to the Lord, without reserve, cheerfully willing that he should dispose of you for his service wheresoever his providence may lead you. No doubt but that according to his gracious and repeated promises of guidance to his people, who look up to him, 'he will instruct you and teach you in the way you should go,' Psa. 32:8. 'The fields are everywhere ripe: the harvest truly is plenteous; but the labourers are few.' I sincerely hope you will be a faithful and diligent labourer wherever you are stationed. Our time is short, and sinners are perishing all around us; and an idle Clergyman acts a very sinful and a very cruel part, and his responsibility is awful indeed! As to a *quiet* Bishop, which you wish for, if *he* is quiet, and you are active and useful, somebody will be unquiet, wherever you are, be assured of it. The gospel can succeed nowhere without opposition, because *it* proclaims war *first* against all the kingdom of darkness. You must count the cost, labour to be faithful, and leave the issue with the Lord. The Lord can make friends foes and foes friends, as he pleases. He deserves our *highest* confidence and our *best* services.

2. Present Faithfullness

Bala, Aug. 3, 1809.

Do not look forward much; be faithful today, as a man who may die before tomorrow. And if you should live, sinners are perishing all around you; and eight or nine years hence will be too late to speak to them. Be sure to study to have a conscience *void of offence* towards God, and that your heart should be *whole* with God. Our time is short, our work is important, our charge is awful, and our account must be soon given. Oh that it may be done with joy and not with grief! Be the *man of God* wherever you are: this will bring you peace in the end. I shall be anxious to hear of your success in the Lord's work. I feel perfectly indifferent whether you have £50 or £1,000 a year; but that you may be enabled to prove yourself a good and faithful servant, and that the Lord may address you as such in the day of account. I pray earnestly for this, both for your sake and for the Lord's glory.

3. Extempore Preaching – Davies's and Walker's Sermons – Old German Divines – Learning Hebrew

Bala, Feb. 27, 1811.

You must be the best judge whether you had better preach *extempore* or not, as you find liberty and ease in the work. If you cannot deliver your thoughts distinctly, clearly, accurately and fluently, I think you had better read, at least use notes. As to writing your sermons, however you may deliver them, I think there can be no demur about that: and always write every sermon, or whatever else you may write, with all the care and attention you can possibly command. A habit of writing slovenly and carelessly is a very lazy and a very bad one. It would be in every way useful to you to use yourself to accurate composition. It will increase your stock of ideas, and beget a habit of close and accurate mode of thinking and of arranging your ideas.

I do not remember the title of the publication of Baxter, from which Davies copied. But one was a sermon or a tract on Matthew 22:5, on making light of the gospel; and the other on the good part, Luke 10:42. As you have Davies's Sermons, you will see long quotations marked as such by inverted commas. He has taken Baxter's ideas in others very generally, which are not thus marked. Very few sermons of his are original as to matter. The dress is his own, and that not a very happy one often. He wants simplicity. I think Walker of Truro's 'Christian,' and 'Lectures,' would be serviceable and furnish you with very many evangelical and practical ideas, and point out to you a close and practical mode of preaching.

To Edward Morgan

As to your purchasing the works of the fathers you name, I should apprehend you had better defer it for the present, as they will prove expensive in your removals. When you are settled, if you happen to meet with them cheap, they can do no harm in your study, and may occasionally be consulted. Some of the old German and Dutch divines I judge preferable; such as: Jerome Zanchius, Musculus, Vitringa, Venema, Witsius, Cocceius, etc. I think Turretin's works would be very useful to you. It is an excellent body of divinity. Learn Hebrew by all means, and make yourself well acquainted with modern Biblical critics; such as Lowth, Blayney, Newcome on the Prophets, Campbell and Macknight on the New Testament, and others of a similar nature. I take in now Boothroyd's Biblia Hebraica, and approve of it. It contains a selection of various readings and different translations, with English critical notes. Such studies surely ought above all things to be pursued as tend to make the holy writings clear and familiar to those who are to elucidate them to others.

4. Liverpool Bible Society – Rev. J. Owen and Hughes

Liverpool, March 25, 1811.

THERE is a very great stir here about the Bible Society; and a very full meeting is expected. If you should be at the Manchester meeting, you may introduce yourself without ceremony to Mr Owen: but as his time is so much taken up with the business he is engaged in, I fear he will have hardly any time to speak to you. The whole weight of the concerns of the different meetings rests altogether upon him; so that every moment of his time is taken up. We all of us preached here three times each, yesterday, to very crowded audiences. I preached twice in English, and once in Welsh. Mr Owen preached in the churches to the Mayor and corporation; and Mr Hughes in different dissenting chapels. Today we are all big with expectation, waiting the hour of meeting. It will be well, if in all this bustle, we do not lose sight of the Lord. We are but poor worms at best; and without his concurring help and blessing our labour profiteth nothing.

... I had written so far at Liverpool with a view of posting it there, but in my great hurry I forgot it. The meeting at Liverpool was glorious; and in the issue, I hope, will prove very beneficial to that profligate place, as well as afford ample support to the parent Institution in London.

5. Activity – The Sinner's Encouragement

1811.

LET not trials drive you, nor imaginary prospects entice you; but follow Providence, and then you will walk safely. I fear we have mistaken notions about liveliness in religion. True liveliness is unwearied activity in spreading the knowledge of divine truths among ignorant and perishing sinners. I find it much easier to draw tears from their eyes than to stir them up from their sloth to vigorous activity and assiduity in the cause of religion.

I am sorry to hear of your dejection of mind. Look up, look up, all is well *there*. Come as a sinner, and you will find all in your favour – all, the door open, and every face smiling upon you. But if you attempt to come as a saint, and you are dubious whether you are so or not, you will come as an impostor and a hypocrite; and you will be detested. There can be no doubt that you are a sinner. Well then, come in your real character, and you will be welcome. Everything in the councils of heaven favours a *returning sinner*: election, particular redemption, vocation, justification, etc. – all, all are in his favour, and give him every encouragement he can want and God can give. But impostors are abhorred. And such is everyone who assumes a character which he is not sure belongs to him.

6. Directions for Studying, etc.

1812.

YOU say, you want time to read, write, and study. Doubtless you do. Get up at five o'clock every morning: never spend half an hour in smoking, idle talking, or lazy lounging; think when you walk for

To Edward Morgan

health, or ride; converse profitably with all you converse with; do these things and all is obtained that you want. I do not accuse you, by any means, of criminality in your conduct in these particulars; but only point out that you may have time enough for improvement in your present situation, by proper management. Your constitution, it appears to me, like my own, requires you to avoid all idleness and indulgence, and will bear great activity and vigilance without injuring your health. I find an hour in the morning more profitable than three in the evening. After a light supper you may go to bed immediately; which will properly prepare you to be up at 4 or 5 o'clock in the morning.

When you are at your studies, be sure that your hours there are not idly spent; but work with all the powers of your mind. Have always some work on the anvil that you may not lose time in thinking what you shall do. And when you think of what you shall take in hand, always fix upon something *useful*: and when you have fixed upon a subject, never give it up until you have finished it in the best manner you are able.

First of all think over the matter yourself – arrange it in your mind – enlarge upon it; and then consult authors who have written best on the subject. By this means you may correct your own ideas, or be more satisfied with them. Never be discouraged, or admit the thought, that you cannot go through anything you take in hand. If all appear darkness to you on the subject, earnestly apply to the Lord for the light of his Spirit, who *most assuredly* will be given to those that ask for him. When the mind is exhausted, wearied and blunted, it is useless to work then; for you must do the work over again that you compose in that state. Nothing refreshes the mind as well as the body more than seasonable and temperate sleep.

Conjoin also the active with the contemplative. You have the young, the aged, the poor, and the sick, to converse with about eternal things. We should never forget that sinners are perishing for lack of knowledge all around us: and all our time must not be spent in our studies, however profitably spent there. We profit ourselves by endeavouring to profit others. Some of the most luminous and profitable views I have ever had of divine things, I have obtained instantaneously by preaching, or by conversing with others about divine things.

Above all, pray earnestly and constantly for the teaching of God's Spirit; and avoid indulgence, sloth and idleness. Let every portion of your time be usefully and conscientiously spent. Our time is short, and life is uncertain. We are not debtors to the flesh; but we are debtors in an infinite degree to the dear Redeemer who lived and died for us. Let him be our pattern: and let us endeavour to be as diligent in setting forth his praises, as he was in redeeming our souls. He knew what it was to be hungry, thirsty, and weary, to be up late and early, and to be diligently going about doing good. He had flesh and blood as well as we, though none of our corruptions. We have an eternity to rest; let us be active here.

7. The Want of Activity in Ministers and Others

Bala, Oct. 15, 1812.

I SHOULD apprehend by your statement that the way is opened in providence for your going to S—d. Your description of the low state of religious knowledge among the inhabitants of M—d, and its environs, is very grievous, but by no means *singular*. I dare say you will find great ignorance at S—d, or wherever you may go. In my late excursion through Caernarvonshire I found on enquiry ten families without a Bible, and eighty poor children unable to purchase Bibles, and that in a district where the gospel has been preached since I have been in this country. And I am pretty certain that there are many districts in a similar or worse state.

Wherever you go, be particular in your enquiries, and active in endeavours to stir up, and to relieve the poor on this head. I am sadly grieved that we have been all these years such careless and slight labourers in the Lord's vineyard. I find it very difficult to stir up my brethren to proper activity in this cause. Many will give their money; but personal activity is not so easily commanded. However, I go on talking, and I find it accompanied with some effect in an increasing degree. In some instances the effects are pleasing and even astonishing. I wish I had a thousand tongues, and could be everywhere often. The Lord can stir up others and enable them to do ten times more than I have been enabled to do. Our time is short, and souls are hastening to eternity. We have not a moment to be idle, if we are in our right senses. Mind the work more than the income; and drive on with all your might. Next week I mean to set out for Glamorganshire, Monmouthshire, and Bristol. I go, as the spies, to examine into the state of those counties, and to see whether the Lord will give me an opportunity of doing any good there in any way. Pray for me.

8. Consciousness of Defects – Faith Described – Success of Sunday Schools

Bala, Sept. 16, 1813.

I AM happy to find by your Letter that you feel a desire to be active and diligent in the Lord's work. Our time is short, and if we do mean to do anything to promote it, it must be speedily and diligently. If his blessed cause does not prosper, the world answers no adequate end for its support. But it will and must prosper; and the world is supported for that very purpose: and all the works and designs carried on in it must be subservient to that grand design ultimately. I feel ashamed when I think how little I have done, compared with what I ought to have done – with what was wanted to be done. 'O God, be merciful to me a sinner,' is the language of my heart daily.

The great propitiation is the foundation of all my hopes. The last words of David were much upon my mind, with great comfort, in my late illness: 'he hath made with me an everlasting covenant, etc.' A Salvation in covenant, made by Jehovah and therefore '*well ordered* and *sure*,' appeared to me glorious. Everything is well ordered and sure – 'rhagderfynedig gyngor' (predetermined counsel). A salvation in covenant is but little known in these days, and therefore but little preached, but scouted and laughed at. Hence arise the prevailing notions about universal redemption, etc., etc., and a thousand other concomitant errors, which leave everything at random and in uncertainty. I hope the Lord will enable you and me more clearly to view a salvation in covenant – covenant of peace which cannot be moved; and then we shall preach it warmly to others; and our success will be certain.

You ask me some questions about faith. The difficulties which you state do not appear to me to be such. Last spring I gave our young people for their exercise, to find out all the names given to faith in the Scriptures. And they set about it, and laboured hard, and at last brought to me seventy-one names given to this grace in the Bible. They learnt all the Scriptures, and repeated them publicly twice in our chapel. I must confess I was most highly gratified and edified; and I believe, received more light upon this important subject than from all the authors I have ever read: and the effect still continues sweetly on my mind. I have printed fifteen heads of them with a little enlargement on each in my *Trysorfa*; and I mean to continue the subject till I have gone over the whole, Deo volente. They told us with appropriate proofs, that it was: believing God; believing in the Son of God; coming to Christ; receiving Christ; eating his flesh and drinking his blood; living upon him; building upon him; resting under his shadow; casting all our cares upon him; casting our burden upon him; trusting in him; committing our way unto the Lord; delighting in the Lord; counting all things but loss and dung to win Christ; resting in the Lord; drawing water out of the wells of salvation; taking hold of his strength; lifting up the eyes to God; looking in a glass; believing the word; understanding the word; receiving the word; seeing the glory of Christ; looking unto Christ; etc., etc. You can enlarge yourself, I cannot now: this is a sample of the seventy-one. Considering faith under all these appellations, the mist is scattered, and the object is clear.

The *Chester* Children performed well at the last annual meeting. I examined them in the New Hall (Union Hall), on Sunday evening, before the largest concourse of people I ever saw in those parts: and they answered *well* indeed. The work goes on with considerable success in several parts of our country. Yesterday I received the following pleasing account from Caernarvonshire: Gwnaeth yr Arglwydd beth tra rhyfedd yn ein gwlad er ys llai na blwyddyn. Chwanegwyd at yr Eglwys, rhwng dau gapel Clynnog, 130; yn Llanllyfni, ynghylch 90; rhwng Pen-y-graig a'r Ty-mawr (enwau dau gapel) tua 100; ac yn amryw barthau eraill o'r wlad, ryw gymaint. Y mae'r Ysgolion Sabothawl yn lluosog iawn o ysgolheigion; a'r ysgolfeistriaid, amryw o honynt, yn ddiwyd ac yn ffyddlon. Fel hyn yn rhyfedd ac yn rasol y mae Duw yn cofio am y Cymru tlodion. Ffrwyth yr Ysgolion Sabothawl yn bennaf yw y deffroadau cyffredinol hyn.[7]

9. Animation in Preaching – Zeal – Boldness

Bala, Jan. 18, 1814.

I NOW proceed to answer your important questions:

1. There may be *false*, I would rather say, *natural* or unholy animation in a carnal man, and also at times even in a spiritual man, when speaking publicly about divine things. A spiritual man knows the difference evidently in their different effects on his mind. There are holy effects and the workings of grace accompanying the one, and none the other, except self-complacency, pride, and self-sufficiency, which are very unholy effects. There is a vast difference between the free and ready exercise of gifts, natural and supernatural, in prayer and preaching, and the holy excitement of the several graces of the Spirit in those exercises: and to take the one without the other, and be satisfied with it, is most dangerous, and the readiest way to self-deception. For the sake of others I have been thankful for the free use of gifts, at the same time most deeply

---

[7] The Lord hath wrought a wonderful thing in our country, within less than a year. There have been added to the church, in the two chapels of *Clynnog*, 130; in *Llanllyfni*, about 90; in *Pen-y-graig* and *Ty-mawr* Chapels, about 100; and several in many other parts. The Sunday Schools are very full of Scholars; and the masters, many of them, are diligent and faithful. Thus wonderfully and graciously God is remembering the poor Welsh. These general awakenings are, for the most part, the fruits of the Sunday Schools.

grieved and humbled because God hid his gracious face from my own soul.

New ideas may affect a natural as well as a spiritual man, when thinking or speaking about divine things, through their novelty: and even a spiritual man may be differently affected at different times. *He* knows the difference, whilst the other knows nothing but natural effects, and therefore can perceive no difference, and is in a very perilous state. But observe, new and grand ideas about divine things may produce very suitable and holy effects, not by their novelty so much as by their truth, importance, and suitableness. Perhaps their novelty may have some effect upon the natural man; while at the same time their importance affects the spiritual or new man in a holy manner. Every proper idea about divine things is new to us at first. We have no *innate* ideas about the things of God. Perhaps we felt the effects very strong when we first received them: they may at the same time have a spiritual and holy effect upon us as long as we live. In this case it is not the novelty, but the excellence, the glory, the divinity, and the suitableness of them that produces the continued holy effects upon the mind.

There are some views of divine things to which I was a stranger during many years of profession, which are now most precious and present daily to my mind. They are like standing dishes on the table. And I am much grieved that I lived so long without them: and most thankful I am to God that by his Spirit he has ever brought me to see them. They were before in the divine record, but concealed from my view, till he opened my heart like that of Lydia.

I conclude therefore: first, that both good and unconverted men may be animated as to the natural man, without spirituality and holiness in their animation, or in their minds when animated; secondly, that it is a very common case, and much lamented by all the godly: and thirdly, that it is very pernicious in its effects on the unconverted, and very dangerous and delusive unless watched against carefully.

2. Your second question requires no particular reply, as the nature of the question contains the answer. No zeal, or boldness,

or confidence, can be *holy*, if not connected with humility and self-abhorrence, as there can be no holiness without humility and repentance for sin. I have never been more shocked by anything than by this carnal and irreverent boldness, or rather presumption, when men speak about divine truths, especially the decrees of God. It is insufferable to a humble and ingenuous mind that fears God. In our best frame, we are, the best of us, very far from what we ought to be: I have never been more tempted to despise the doctrines of grace, than when I have been so unfortunate as to hear them so treated.

3, Your third question, the answer to it is also clear. Speaking of the terrors of the Lord to sinners with firmness and at the same time without feeling compassion for them, shows the want of the fear of God and love to man in the speaker. We ought to weep over them as Jesus did over Jerusalem. The words in 2 Cor. 5:18-20, are particularly descriptive of the true ambassador of Christ, to whom the ministry of reconciliation is *given* – is *committed* – δόντος, θέμεος. 'We *beseech* – we *pray* you in Christ's stead – δεόμεθα ὑπὲρ Χριστοῦ, be ye reconciled to God.' As they *represent* Christ, they ought to be in that frame and temper of mind, in which Christ would be, if he in his own person were speaking. Knowing the terrors of the Lord, we *persuade* men. O my dear friend, our trifling with the souls of men about eternal concerns, is shameful – is most exceedingly sinful; it is beyond measure shocking! May God convince us of it, and make us able ministers.

10. Different Modes of Preaching, etc.

Bala, Feb. 2, 1814.

As to writing your sermons, I have not much to say. Mr Robinson, I believe, was an advocate for it: and he was a judicious man. Mr Walker, of Truro, never preached extempore, as I have been informed, and he was much blessed in his public ministry. I apprehend that much depends on the abilities of the speaker. I never could read my sermons, nor make use of skeletons, without being much embarrassed, even in my younger days. Mind that your matter be *thoroughly evangelical*, and set forth with plainness and zeal. Vent all the feelings you are excited with in a proper and decent manner. Never disgust your hearers; or else you cannot edify them. Never soar above their heads; or they cannot understand you. Be earnest about the salvation of your hearers; and the desire of doing them good will best direct you how to attain that end. If other writers' sermons are better than what you can compose, use them for the present: but do not leave off composing. *Study the Bible*, and compose something in divinity every day of your life.

I am nearly finishing the Bible, comparing the Welsh translation with the Originals; which I have found to be a very profitable work. This is always my morning work before breakfast; which I mean to follow as long as I live. I buy every new publication on *Biblical* criticism I hear of. GOOD on Job I am now going over, and I approve it much: and I have sent for his translation of the Song of Solomon.

11. Regeneration and Faith

Bala, May 3, 1814.

YOU seem to have puzzled yourself about the point you have written to me about: but I apprehend your perplexity arises from wrong ideas of cause and effect. The light in the understanding, and the holy bent of the will, are the effects of regeneration, and not regeneration itself. Faith is not regeneration, but the fruit and effect by which it is proved. By Christ *apprehending* our souls, by his word, through his Spirit, we are united to Christ. The effect of that act of Christ is the communication of the divine nature to the soul, which is regeneration. Then by faith we apprehend him by whom we are apprehended, Phil. 3:12, 13.

These are my simple ideas of this mysterious work: but fully to comprehend it we cannot. The embryo is formed by God in the womb, we are certain by its existence and all its appurtenances: but how it is formed is a secret to the greatest anatomist or philosopher in the world. It is a *mysterious, glorious, real,* and *gracious* work; in which God will be forever glorified. But that we should be unable *fully* to comprehend it, is no wonder. What work of God can we *fully* comprehend? If we are the subjects of this blessed work, we shall forever feel the effects, and bless God for his having graciously and effectually produced this great and most necessary change. The thing itself is clear and evident: but as to the *modus* – the manner how it is produced, we cannot fully comprehend. But I still venture humbly to assert, that it is by uniting the soul to Christ – ingrafting it into that true vine: and the consequence will be receiving out of his fullness all grace and all divine privileges to eternity. There can be no change, no holiness, no comfort, without that. Everything will forever wither and decay but what is one with Christ and proceeds from him.

12. No Abstruse Things in Sermons, etc.

Bala, May 28, 1814.

Do not bring any intricacies into your sermons or catechetical instructions. They will do your hearers no good; and it is only trifling with their souls. Let our instructions be clear, solid, and important. We should not so much aim at being ourselves great divines or making others so, as to be, and to make others, *real Christians*. The different appellations attributed in Scripture to regeneration, if properly understood and explained, will enable your people and children to obtain a tolerable knowledge of the important change wrought by the Holy Spirit in all that are saved. The names describe the thing; and by viewing it under its different appellations, we shall obtain a more enlarged and comprehensive view of the subject, than by considering it under one only. *Catechizing the children has taught me more divinity than any other means whatever.*

To Miss Mary Foulks, of Machynlleth

The Excellency of the Bible

Bala, March 31, 1807.

It gives me great joy to hear that my young friends at Machynlleth are perseveringly employed in learning the Bible. To say that is the Book of God, is recommendation enough. Nothing more can be said. If it be the Book of God, it must be a very wise book – very good – very profitable – and very useful. But we cannot be the better for it unless we *know* it. We must know it, to profit by it. And we cannot know its glorious and important contents, unless we '*seek* in it for knowledge as silver, and *search* for her as for hid treasures'; that is, unless we labour diligently for knowledge, as the miser does for riches. He never thinks he has enough, and deems no labour too great to obtain more. Oh what rich and inexhaustible mines there are in the Book of God! We must be fools indeed not to spend all our days in searching them.

The avidity with which the young people in all parts of the country learn the Bible is astonishing, and gives me the greatest joy of anything in the world. It is the Lord's doing, and it is marvellous in my eyes. It far exceeds my hopes and expectations. I could say years ago, I *wish* it; and I prayed for it, once in particular, *most* earnestly. But so great was my unbelief, that I never expected to see it, the appearance then being so very low and hopeless. But what hath God wrought since then! I am now anxious for its still further progress, till the whole country, and every individual in it, is filled with the knowledge of the Lord.

Now, my dear young friends, I hope you will be enabled to give up yourselves wholly to the Lord – to live to him through life. It is the only life worth living for. Determine never to be connected with any persons whatever, who will not prove an assistance to you in the Lord's work. If they should not be assistants, they will

To Miss Mary Foulks

prove beyond all doubt a very heavy clog. Pray the Lord daily to strengthen, assist, keep, and direct you in everything. He will hear your prayers, and will most assuredly grant your requests. May the God and Father of our Lord Jesus Christ be your God and portion forever.

To Miss Mary Hughes, of Liverpool

The Duty of Working for God

Bala, June 18, 1812.

I CONGRATULATE you, my dear Madam, on the high honour bestowed upon you by the Lord in engaging your attention to the success of this holy work, in this our benighted and sinful world, and that also, while you are young. Nature did not endow you, nor anyone else, with such a disposition of mind; quite the reverse. This is from the Lord the Spirit. And may he who implanted it at first, cause it to grow more and more, that you may continue to abound in the fruits of righteousness to the close of a long life. We live in a happy time. All are called forth to the Lord's harvest, and may find something to do, to help to bring it in. And we know, that our labour, neither is, nor shall be, in vain in the Lord. The night is far spent, and the dawning of a bright and long day is at hand. It is therefore very proper that we should all be awake, and put on the armour of light, that we may be ready for any work the Lord may call us to.

I see what I never entertained the most distant hope of seeing – I see the Lord's lines thickened with scores of young people at once in many parts. Oh may the Lord make them faithful soldiers all their days!

To Mrs E—, C—n

1. The Importance of Knowing God in Youth

Bala, August 21, 1808.

WE both feel anxious about you, and think and talk of you often. But our care availeth but little. The Lord's care is kind – unceasing – and effectual, and *he* careth for you. Nothing would rejoice me more than to hear, that the young branches of your family were taking a *decided* part on the Lord's side. The fashion of this world passeth away, and the fashion of the world we are hastening to, will abide forever, whatever that may be as to ourselves. I most earnestly wish to see them great and happy forever: the reverse of that is a thought too grievous to be borne for a moment. How kind was the Friend of sinners in coming into the world to rescue us from so great a misery! And does he not deserve our love, our service, and our confessing him before men? The moment he is *known*, hesitation will be forever at an end.

I have known a little of him now these forty years past; and I feel really more thankful every day, that he was pleased to lay his yoke upon me *when young*. Seeing it so great a privilege, I cannot but long that all others should partake of the same. I feel indignant at the thought, that Satan should have a moment's service from us, especially in the prime of life, when all our powers of body and mind are in their perfection. What gracious words are these: 'Take *my* yoke upon you'! I am ready to reply, and do so in heart, 'Lord, put it on.' The moment we have proved the *ease* of it, we shall never wish it off.

2. Consolation under Bereavements

Bala, March 13, 1810.

I CAN with truth say that I feel at all times interested in what concerns you and your comfort, and that of your family. I cannot of course be indifferent about you under the present awful dispensation. Though your mind must be agitated by a variety of sensations, acute and trying, yet I trust that the Lord will so support and direct you as to enable you in all things to conduct yourself with that propriety and decorum, which becomes a follower of Jesus, and shut the mouths of those who may be watching your footsteps – and thus to glorify your Father which is in heaven. You know who hath said, 'Counsel is mine, and sound wisdom; I am understanding, I have strength. I *lead* in the way of righteousness, in the midst of the paths of judgement.' I trust that you have access with confidence unto him, and that you are enabled to cast all your cares and burdens upon him. He most graciously requires this of you; and it is as much your privilege as your duty to comply with his gracious injunctions. 'Trust in the Lord – delight thyself in the Lord – commit thy ways unto the Lord – rest in the Lord – wait patiently for him,' – these are the most kind exhortations of our God and Father, pointing out to us the way of comfort and effectual relief under every possible circumstance in which we can be.

If the Lord spare your life, you may have trials to pass through, though of a different nature, yet equal to those you have already met with. How exhilarating the consideration, that you have the same powerful and faithful God to look to, who never can leave nor forsake those who trust in him. This chequered scene of vanity, sin and trouble, will be soon over; and if with Paul we can say, 'I have obtained mercy,' the prospect beyond these empty shadows, is substantial and glorious.

I should have been glad to have attended the funeral: but my work calls me another way. 'The Lord will remember his tender mercies and his loving kindnesses: for they have been ever of old.' The Lord does not expect that we shall ever be able to go on without help in *anything*: and he is 'a very present help in trouble' – 'Cymorth *hawdd* ei gael.'[8] I could do you no real good, were I with you; and you need no human help, if the Lord be present.

---

[8] This is the Welsh rendering, and means, 'Help *easy* to be found,' which is more literal than the English, נִמְצָא מְאֹד.

To Mrs E—

On my own part, I feel that I need him as much, yea, *more* than ever, and often find it difficult to rest in him; but I have no other resting-place – no other home but in him. In him I sometimes see all I want, and feel really thankful. Leaving you under his care, and committing you with all your various concerns to him, with very kind regards to each of your family, I am, my dear afflicted friend, your's affectionately and faithfully.

T. C.

To the Rev. Henry Grey, of Haddington, Scotland

1. Preaching Excursions – Progress of the Schools

Bala, September 26, 1812.

THOUGH we have often thought of the kind strangers who were so obliging as to spend a day with us, yet we have not hitherto been permitted to entertain one *unkind* thought of them. You have conferred an additional obligation upon us by your friendly letter giving us a detailed account of your journey, your safety, and your safe arrival at home to embrace your dear little ones, and also your friends. We feel in some degree thankful to the good Lord who hath preserved you safe through so long an excursion, and watched over your little ones in your absence. His wonders to the children of men are great: but what is too much for him to do who spared not his own Son, but delivered him up for us all? How shall he not with him freely give us all things? All things without him would prove but a beggarly portion; but with him they are delightful. The bridegroom far excels all his possessions: but with him his estate and kingdom are valuable.

We were glad to hear of your welfare at Caernarvon, by our friends from those who were at our annual meeting; and who were much pleased, and I trust edified, by the discourse you were pleased to favour them with. You have no occasion to distrust, but that hundreds understood you well. I am generally called upon to preach in English when I go there.

Since you left us we have also been on the alert. Our first journey was to Anglesey, to attend a large annual meeting there. The congregation amounted, at least, to *ten thousand* people, who heard in all *nine* discourses with great attention. After returning from there (preaching all the way going and returning, generally three times a day) and staying a few days at home, we set out again

To Rev. Mr Henry Grey

for Chester; where we stayed three Sundays, and then visited Liverpool, where I preached three nights, twice in Welsh and once in English. I preached in different parts of Cheshire during the weeks we were there, and all the way in going and returning. This was in the month of July. In August we set out for South Wales, where I attended two Associations; and Mrs Charles spent a week near the sea for the benefit of the sea air; which has proved very salutary to her. In two days we are to set out for Caernarvon to attend an annual meeting there, and mean to spend a fortnight in that county. Thus I have given you a general relation of our excursions since we had the pleasure of seeing you here. I take Mrs Charles with me as often as I can in summertime, as travelling proves very beneficial to her health.

The aspect of the country in general, as to the state of religion among its inhabitants, is upon the whole favourable. Schools flourish among young and old; and there are great awakenings in many places. I visited some of the same places in March last as I have now. I found in one place, that there are two hundred young people, who had joined the Church since then, and seventy had joined another society: and there was a general increase of the societies everywhere. No religious exercises are attended with a greater blessing than the instruction of the rising generation in the divine principles of our holy religion. This occupies much of my time and attention in all my travels. If I am enabled to stand, I have no relaxation from it. Through the Lord's goodness I am seldom fatigued in the day, though often in the evening exhausted.

I rejoice to hear that you have adopted our plan, in proposing some doctrine or duty to be proved and elucidated out of Scripture. I have no doubt but that they will find both pleasure and profit in that delightful exercise. Nothing has proved more profitable to our young people, after receiving instruction in our little catechism. Will you have the goodness to remember me very affectionately to your young people; and I shall be much obliged to them, if they will transcribe one of their exercises and send it me; and I promise that our young people shall return them the favour. And then we shall enjoy each other in the Lord this side heaven, and help each other on our way thither, to enjoy there that holy fellowship which will never end.

I have no doubt but that your Sacramental seasons are very solemn and profitable. I have often wished to attend one of them; but that is never likely to be the case. What a place heaven is! for there, I suppose, they all enjoy whatever is going on in all its confines. We shall there see everything as it is, and be in a suitable frame of mind to relish and enjoy all.

... My dear partner unites with me in very affectionate regards to Mrs Grey, and yourself: and if Providence ever should bring you this way again, I hope you will contrive to make a longer stay with us. I have read over your little pamphlet on Baptism with pleasure, We shall always be glad to hear from you. Pray for us.

2. Illness – Sunday Schools – Ministry – Innovation

1813.

BOTH my Sarah and myself are much obliged, and were highly gratified, by your favour, dated, I am ashamed to say, Feb. 10, 1813. I have often thought of you and Mrs Grey; and as often purposed to write to you; but the urgency of other calls and concerns, caused me to postpone it one time after another. Indeed some months ago I had begun a letter, which I was called off from before it was finished. We rejoice with you in the increase and prosperity of your family; and pray that the Lord's continued mercy may rest upon you and yours. My dear partner is much the same as when you saw her, only rather weaker, and not able to stir from the fireside but to bed, this severe weather. However the Lord's hand is very gently upon her, and we have loud calls daily for thankfullness.

Last summer I was so far affected by general debility (caused by too great exertion, said my doctors) as to be laid by for two months. I could neither preach, read, nor write, but lounged on the sofa, or lay upon the bed, most of the time. I am now through the Lord's goodness, tolerably recovered; but, still I am not so strong for work as heretofore. I look up to him, who can *renew strength*, for further supplies both for mind and body. Whilst I live, I *very much wish* I may be enabled to work. The work is most important and the labourers are comparatively but few. But the Lord of the harvest can send when he pleases, and as many as he pleases; only it is my comfort and privilege to work.

I am very much obliged to you for transcribing for me the passages your young people collected upon the subject given to them. Such exercises cannot fail of being profitable to them, if you can keep them to the work with constancy. Will you have the goodness to remember me very affectionately to all your young people. I love them all, and am very thankful that they have obeyed your exhortation to study and search the Scriptures more closely and particularly. I long to shake hands with them all: but as that is never likely to take place, let us pray for each other; and if we meet in heaven, we shall know and love one another forever, and never cease praising him who loved us and gave himself for us.

Our young people in different parts of the country are diligently pursuing the same work; and many points which they have compared have been printed, and three have been translated into English and printed; a few of which I would have sent to you, if the distance had not been so great, especially one composed by a poor girl in one of our Sunday Schools, on *Christ's Righteousness*: '1. By what names it is called in the Bible; 2. To what it is compared; 3. And what were the types of it under the old dispensation.' I gave the heads, and she herself, without any help, filled them up so excellently well, that I was requested to publish what she did for the sake of others.

The Sunday Schools flourish beyond any former examples: and adults, as well as children, flock to them in most parts of the country. Many *hundreds* of our young people from the schools have joined our churches or societies, in the course of the last year. When we admit any one into our societies, it gives them admission also to the Lord's table; and this we do, if upon examination there appear some hopeful signs of a work of grace upon their hearts. We have of late taken to the method of requesting, when the sermon is over, all to stay behind who wish to be spoken to particularly about the concerns of their souls in the way of conversation. This method hitherto has had a very good effect. Many stay behind, and speak freely to the minister about divine things, and sometimes with great effect.

We have no time to lose, and no method should be omitted that has a tendency to promote the concerns of eternity; which, as such, must be very important – souls perishing through want of knowledge, is most grievous to think of; and that, it may be, through *our negligence*. If I had now to begin the work of the ministry, I think I could do much more than I have done during the thirty-five years I have been in it. I had all to learn by painful experience. I thank God, who has in some degree succeeded my efforts from time to time. I have found it very useful to me never to be discouraged by difficulties in the way, or unfavourable appearances, but to make trial and to leave the issue to the Lord. Any attempt out of the usual way will cause a wonder and a talk at first; but it may be very beneficial in the end, and be highly approved of. Though I am no friend to innovations; yet when we do not succeed in the old track, we ought to seek out another path, which, we may be sure, will do no harm, and perhaps may be productive of important good.

PAPERS

Preface to the Rev. Mr Oliver's Hymn Book

Jan. 2, 1808.

... As one who sincerely wishes to be a helper of their joy, they will permit me to suggest the following hints:

1. Beware of a *contentious spirit*. Envyings, strife, and divisions, are evidences of a carnal and not a spiritual mind – of being babes and not men in Christ; and as such, having need of milk, being unskilful in the word of righteousness. A carnal mind is active and keen in perceiving the ignorances and differences of others: but a spiritual man sees and laments mostly his own ignorance, and his own great deficiencies. His language daily is that of the Apostle; 'Oh wretched man that I am, who shall deliver me from the body of this death?' We are best acquainted with our own defects. Overrating our own excellences, and undervaluing the good qualities of others, is a proof of a carnal mind. 'Let all bitterness, and wrath, and anger, and clamour, and evil speaking, be put away from you, with all malice: and be ye kind one to another, tenderhearted, forgiving one another, even as God for Christ's sake hath forgiven you.' Eph. 4:31, 32.

2. Beware of laying a *disproportionate stress upon circumstantials*, externals, and comparatively little things in religion, to the neglect of the grand and leading doctrines of the gospel. It is well to be minutely conscientious, and to have every pin and every nail in a building properly placed; but the building cannot subsist without the foundation, and the main pillars which support the superstructure. To be always busy about pins, nails, or some ornaments of the building, to the neglect of the grand supporters of the whole fabric,

[309]

is a proof of a little mind and of less grace; and that soul cannot thrive well. On this head I would recommend to your frequent perusal Mr W. Cradock's sermons on gospel liberty.

3. Have due respect to every truth which God has revealed in his word. Divine truths are one consistent whole; none of which can be spared without disfiguring the beauty and symmetry of the whole system, and injuring our own souls and the souls of others, by withholding from them a truth which they need for their spiritual improvement and comfort. It is a great mistake to suppose one part of the Bible to be legal, and another evangelical, as if the divine oracles contradicted themselves – far from it; they make one complete, united, and consistent system. Every truth beautifully fills its own place. Transpose it, and it becomes useless, yea, a pernicious error. Omit it, and a vacancy is left which nothing else can supply. If divine truths seem to us to militate against each other, the fault is in the medium through which we view them; and because we view them through a false medium, they appear contradictions to us, but are not so in themselves. We, as sinners, want them all; they were intended for our relief as such: and united together as a complete whole, they are a suitable and adequate remedy for all our miseries.

4. Beware of an *idle and fruitless profession* of religion. He that sees nothing to do for Christ and his cause, has reason to fear that he has never as yet truly believed in what Christ hath done for sinners. Be assured that an idle and barren profession will make but a very poor figure in the day of Christ. Every branch that beareth not fruit, he taketh away, and it is cast into the fire and burned. Herein is my Father glorified, saith Christ, that ye bear much fruit. The rising generation is a proper object of your care and attention; and they will repay well all your labours. Here every one will find something he can do, if in a proper frame of mind. If he be not capable of giving instruction, let him attend carefully the sabbath seminaries among you, to receive instruction, till, brought up in the nurture and admonition of the Lord, he is qualified, with a willing and cheerful mind, to assist in the instruction of those

who are perishing for lack of knowledge. An *idle* Christian can be no *real* Christian.

Remember, that it is not doing a work occasionally of a religious nature, that will denote an active disciple of Christ: but your whole heart and soul must be *wholly* engaged in it. It must be the *principal* business of your lives; it must be your aim and desire daily to live to him that died for us. Remember also, that a real *Christian* zeal is a very different thing from *party* zeal. The one labours to proselyte to a party, the other aims at profiting and saving the soul of the sinner, of whatever party he may be. We may be active and zealous for our party, as the Pharisees of old were, and have no zeal for Christ, Matt. 23:15. Though you meet with difficulties and discouragements, yet never think anything *impossible*. The work is God's, and all things are *possible* with him. If we see no fruit of our labours, that is no proof that our exertions are fruitless. Duty is ours, whatever the fruit may be.

An idle profession of the gospel is the *bane* and *curse* of the Christian world. Were all, who in this favoured isle profess the name of Christ, steadfast and immovable, always abounding in the work of the Lord, we should soon fill the whole kingdom, if not the whole world, with the savour of the knowledge of Christ.

Permit me to ask, Are your exertions equal to your ability? Our abilities consist in time, talents, and property. Are all these devoted cheerfully to the cause of religion? The Lord says of one, 'She hath done what *she could.*' This is what the Lord demands of us; and less we cannot offer, without being unfaithful to him. Let not carnal care, unprofitable talk, and idle visits, occupy those precious moments which might be most profitably spent in instructing, warning and comforting others, and furthering the concerns of their souls. It is no small change of mind that will bring a sinner, by nature an enemy to God, to be *sincerely*, *decidedly*, and *wholly* on the Lord's side, and against the opposite interest in whole and in part. He that is truly in earnest for the salvation of his own soul cannot be unconcerned for others whose salvation is equally important, and who have the same eternity before them. Let, my brethren, that mind be in you which was also in Christ Jesus, who came down from heaven and expired on the cross to save sinners. Can we approve ourselves as his real and faithful followers, if our days be spent in ease, negligence, and sloth? No, we are disciples only in name, but not in reality. Much may be done by zeal and faithful exertions, whilst sloth, ease, and negligence, ruin ourselves and others. Suffer the word of exhortation, and believe me, with great respect and affectionate regard, your friend and servant for Christ.

Sunday Schools

1. General Address, March, 1809

My dear Fellow Countrymen,

The account, from nearly every part of Wales, of the success and great usefullness of the *Sunday Schools*, is a cause of thankfullness and great joy. The faithful and diligent exertions of many, to teach the youth in their neighbourhood, are peculiarly praiseworthy, and a proof of unfeigned love to the cause of Christ and to the everlasting happiness of men. I hope that soon it will be felt to be a shame for anyone to say that he has true religion, without bringing forth good fruits as an evidence of it. The religious idlers, who always blame and slander those who are diligent in the work of the Lord, ought to be avoided, if they cannot be reformed, inasmuch as they are clearly the most useful instruments in the hand of the devil, to prevent the good work from going on.

The great avidity on the part of the youth to learn, is also very remarkable, and a cause of wonder and rejoicing. There are clear tokens that the Spirit of the Lord grants his aids, as to the strength of memory to retain, and quickness of mind to comprehend divine things, and their increasing diligence in searching the Scriptures. And to the great joy of their teachers, there are not only evident proofs of reformation in the manners and decent conduct of youths in many parts; but there are also lively convictions in many of them as to their state as lost sinners, and as to the need they have of being justified and sanctified, in the name of the Lord Jesus, and by the Spirit of our God. There are *hundreds* in Wales, whose minds are under the effectual working of these spiritual influences.

There have been held in South Wales, as a letter from a brother there shows, eight public meetings, to hear and examine the several schools in those parts where they were held. Six of them have also been held in North Wales. They have hitherto afforded the greatest satisfaction; and the effects have been clearly excellent. The order, seriousness, and sober decency of these meetings made it delightful to be in them. The importance of the subjects given to the children, the suitableness of the texts they had found out and learnt, to explain and confirm them, and their intelligence and readiness in repeating them, made the meetings exceedingly edifying. The subjects handled were such as the following: The being of God; the doctrine of the Trinity; the inspiration of the Scriptures; the prophecies respecting the coming of Christ and their accomplishment in him; the person of Christ as God-man; the person, titles and work of the Spirit; the corruption and renewal of the powers of man's soul; the necessity, nature, and effects of regeneration; the necessity, nature and effects of true faith; the privileges of believers; justification; redemption, that is, the necessity of it; the Redeemer, the price he gave, the redeemed and their privileges; the names given in Scripture to heaven and hell, with the names of the two roads which lead to these two places, and the names of the travellers of the two roads; the names given to the law, and the purpose of giving it; the names given to the gospel; the names given to Christ; the duties which belong to all in every situation; the sin of drunkenness; the sin of sloth and idleness; the directions of Scripture as to buying and selling, and managing our worldly business; covetousness and its sinfullness, etc. The texts of Scripture on these several points shall be given in this publication, when opportunity will permit. There are other materials which prevent their insertion in this number.

Though there be great cause of joy for the success of this useful and glorious work, yet there are many causes of great lamentation also. *One cause* of lamentation is that there are a great number of the Welsh, thousands if not hundreds of thousands, *who cannot read the word of God*, and make no effort and have no desire to learn it. Let anyone take the trouble to search and see the state of the country in this respect, and he will soon find how true is what I say. In many parts not one in ten can read in any language; and in other places, scarcely any are able to teach others; and there is a large number of people, from forty to seventy, in every part, who cannot read the word of God. These all have immortal souls, which must exist forever. Can it be thought, on just grounds, that they in this ignorance shall spend eternity in heaven? Can we think that they shall be there without knowing the way thither? Can any know the way without knowing the Bible? What reason have we to think that any love God without loving the word of God? And what ground have we to believe that any love God's word, and yet continue indifferent about learning to read it? The devil encourages many to believe that they *cannot* learn to read; and so they sleep carelessly in this ruinous darkness. Let them think seriously whether they shall stand before God in judgement, testifying that they cannot? Have they ever prayed for help to learn? Have they ever spent a week in the attempt to learn? It seems strange that they can learn almost everything that they attempt, except to read. There is an awful dread on my mind, that their idle excuses will not serve them before the great Judge. It is a wonder that the great God has given us a book to learn! It is a wonder (if everything were not so that is done by a sinner) that any man in the world should live and die contented without knowing what is in this book! The ignorance of those who hear the gospel in general, but cannot read, is very great. By examining I have found some not knowing how many the commandments are; others, not knowing anything particular of Christ, but having only heard of one of such a name having been in the world, without being able to say anything of the purpose for which he came, of what he did, or how he lived and died. I have met with others who did not remember to have ever heard of his name; and with others, who answered questions respecting him by saying, 'I don't know,' – 'I can't say anything of him.' I request all, particularly ministers, to examine people seriously, that they may perceive the great ignorance which prevails among us. Many hear without ever understanding the meaning of the words commonly used in preaching. I have myself asked some professors who have been a long time hearers, what was justification, regeneration, faith, repentance, etc., and I found that they understood no difference in those things, and that they were totally ignorant with respect to them all. It behoves us to tremble, lest we should be found at last unfaithful and superficial workers in the vineyard of Christ, without having ever felt much concern for the souls of men.

Another cause of great lamentation is the *neglect* and shameful *indifference* that is to be seen in many, who, alas! call themselves religious people, as to any help to bring forward this work. If all the religious people of Wales, of all denominations, were to devote themselves with all their might to the glorious work, there would soon be no ignorant man in the country. But it is much easier than this to live idly – to censure those who work – to dispute stoutly and conceitedly about small and circumstantial things in religion; to talk about things which distinguish the differing parties, etc. But is this the religion of the Bible? Can any man having the religion of the Bible, live idly and carelessly in the midst of a region full of ignorant neighbours, without ever making any attempt to save their souls from the great darkness in which they are? Alas! the blood of souls thus going to ruin for lack of knowledge, will cry against these ungodly idlers in the day of judgement. Awake to righteousness, and sin not by fruitless sloth and spiritual slumbers.

There are some who say nothing against the work, but perhaps praise it, and yet they will do nothing to help it forward. Some are too much of the gentleman, others too wise in their own eyes, and others without any leisure. But will these excuses do in the day of judgement? Thanks be to God, this is not the case with all. The appearance of many is delightful; and they seem like the true Christians in ancient times. Being active, diligent, skilful, laborious, faithful, they are cheerfully and unweariedly doing the work of the Lord, and are successful in turning the minds of many to God's word, and thereby to God himself. Go on, go on, be faithful unto death, and your labour shall not be in vain in the Lord.

There is great complaint, on the part of some, of their want of gifts to examine the children; and this is their excuse for neglect. I will ask these, have they ever had a deep concern for their souls?

Have they ever prayed God for gifts? Do they encourage those who have gifts? Are they not the chief hindrance to the work in their neighbourhood? It is strange that they can talk to children very aptly about everything, except the concerns of their souls! It is strange that their gifts fail here! Is not this a reason why they should seriously examine themselves whether God ever called them to the work of the ministry, as God hath not given them gifts? Has God ever said to anyone, 'Feed my lambs,' without bestowing on him gifts for the purpose? My mind overflows with reasons, but I shall not now add to these few considerations. May the Lord of the harvest send labourers into his harvest.

T. C.

2. A Letter to the Teachers and Scholars of a Sunday School at Blaenannerch, Cardiganshire

1809.

I RECEIVED your kind letter, and rejoiced to hear of your devotedness and success in the blessed and most necessary work which you have in hand; and I am thankful for the love you expressed towards me personally. In this, that is, in love, I firmly believe I am not your debtor. Since the time I had the privilege of hearing you publicly giving such suitable and excellent answers on the most fundamental truths of Christianity, you have not been absent from my kindest thoughts; and there has been ever since an earnest wish on my part for the continuance of your adherence to the noble work, and for your abundant success in it. It is not possible for me to doubt for a moment, but that a blessing shall descend like the dew from heaven upon you and others who are labouring to becoming acquainted with the divine truths of the Scriptures. Little will be our comfort, living or dying, without experiencing the consolations of the word of God. And how can any know what it contains, without being able to read it, and without diligently searching it, and meditating on it carefully and habitually?

Little children have as much need of knowing the Scriptures as grown-up people; and I judge it the greatest cruelty to withhold

God's word from them, and neglect to teach them in it. Is it not the worst of cruelties, to suffer them to go to eternity in a wretched state, without making known to them the Saviour of the lost – to face cold death when the affection of parents and kindest relatives will avail nothing, without making known to them Jesus, the faithful friend, who conquered death, who sticketh closer than a brother, who will come with us through death, and can hold up our heads above the deep waters, and bring us safe to the land of life? I have no name base enough, to give to this unkindness, of all the most cruel. There is no want of kindness to their bodies to be compared with this cruelty to their souls. The command of God is, to 'train them up in the way they should go,' and to 'teach' his truths to our children, Prov. 22:6; Deut. 6:7. And how can any answer God at last for the neglect of this? And how can they meet their children in judgement after having thus so dreadfully injured them? Will it do then to say that they had taught them everything else except this? Had they nothing but bodies and not immortal souls, this might be a sufficient reason. But it is not so: they have souls that must live as long as God himself. And what madness is it to be careful and to labour for their well-being and comforts during a few uncertain moments in this world, while they neglect everything that belongs to another world which is to endure forever.

My dear children, think and remember that you have immortal souls, and that you will exist forever in another world when this life shall come to an end. You have sinned against God, and thereby you have greatly displeased him. Yet so great is his goodness that he has, through grace only, prepared a way by which you may be reconciled to him, and delivered from sin – the vilest thing that can be. God has sent his son into the world to 'seek and to save that which was lost.' And he came willingly, and died for sinners to make an atonement for our sins. It is necessary that you should know this Saviour, come to him and believe in him. He has never rejected any, and never failed to save any. 'Him that cometh to me,' he says himself, were he a little child, 'I will in no wise cast out.' Oh

Sunday Schools

how kind are his words! He standeth in no need of us, but we stand in great need of him; and he is pleased to receive everyone that cometh to him, however unworthy he may be. The Bible (God's book is that) gives us full account what kind of being he is; and you may be well assured that he is such an one as the Bible describes him. God never disappointed nor deceived any. Make the Bible the chief friend of your life; and be very thankful to your teachers for teaching you to read and to understand what it contains; and pray that the Spirit of God may help you to understand it and to make proper use of it.

You have read, I have no doubt, the history of Lydia in Acts 16:14. This woman heard Paul preaching. Paul was an apostle of Jesus Christ and was a noted and very successful preacher. But yet Lydia did not understand nor notice what Paul said, until the Lord opened her heart. He must open your hearts too, else you will not understand nor take proper notice of the truth of God's word, any more than she did of what Paul said. You may know whether God has opened your hearts by what follows. If he has:

1. You see the need of the things which God speaks of in the Scriptures.

2. You see more value in them than in anything in this world.

3. You see the special need of rightly understanding them and of making a proper use of them.

4. You see the great danger of neglecting them and of living contrary to them.

5. You find a degree of delight in them, more than any delight that is to be had in vanity and worldly enjoyments.

6. You are longing and labouring continually to understand them better and more fully to enjoy them.

7. You carefully shun those things which hinder you from increasing in grace and the knowledge of God our Saviour.

8. Jesus Christ especially, of whom the whole Scriptures testify, is very precious to you, yea more precious than anything else.

9. Divine truths have impressed your minds, and the effects of them are seen in your lives. You cannot live like others who know

them not. The comforts and directions they give sweetly fill your minds; and they support, console and guide you. You long to be conformed to them, and not to walk after the course of this world. Farewell. I cannot do less than pray for you; and your success in the concerns of your souls will be one of my chief joys while I live.

I cannot finish this letter without addressing my dear brethren, the teachers of Sunday Schools, in an especial manner. Your success in the work is a proof of your faithfullness, diligence, and suitable gifts: there is therefore no need, were I able, to add many instructions to you in the employment. It will not yet be any harm for me to mention a few things that are on my mind:

1. Be careful *to place* the children *in a proper order* in the school. For this purpose it is necessary to divide them into suitable classes, and to place them in each class according to the degree of their information and knowledge. The divisions ought to be at least six:

The *first* is to contain those who learn the Alphabet and words of two or three letters; the *second*, those who spell words and read lessons of three and four letters; the *third*, those who spell, and who read words of one and two syllables; the *fourth*, those who spell, and who read words of three or more syllables; the *fifth*, those who spell, and who read in the New Testament; and the *sixth*, those who spell, and who read in the Bible.

It is peculiarly needful for the success of the schools, that these divisions should be made in them, and that the children should be moved from one to another as soon as they are fit; and that this promotion should be held forth to them as an encouragement to diligence and faithful exertion in learning. If there be not a sufficient number of teachers, the number of classes may be lessened. The removal of the scholar from one class to another should be public, before the whole school, after hearing his skill in what he has already learnt. *Twelve* children are sufficient for one teacher, if you have a sufficient number of teachers; otherwise fifteen or twenty may be placed under the care of each. The change from spelling to reading, and from reading to spelling, tends much to interest the children.

2. Beware of being negligent in *keeping your time*; and let your whole *conduct* before the children be *serious*, *decent*, and *dignified*. Say nothing and do nothing, but what you would wish the children to imitate. Show respect to one another by a kind greeting and good manners in every way, and teach such to the children. This is scriptural. Gen. 33; Lev. 19:32; Isaiah 3:5; Rom. 12:16; Phil. 2:3, 4.

3. Labour to make the children *understand* what you teach them, especially when you speak to them of things belonging to the concerns of their souls. Use scriptural expressions, and make them clear to the weakest mind, if you possibly can. Beware of using fine words, improper, not known by yourselves, and not affording any clear and particular idea to the children. Use no figurative words, such as *cleansing*, *healing*, without explaining them.

4. *Regard the Lord* and *not men* in your work. To have respect to him in the work will afford you comfort in it and strength to persevere. If it be a good work, it is God's work; and if it be a good work to teach children to know God and him whom he hath sent, Jesus Christ, to teach them to read the Bible is also a good work. *To train up one child, the poorest in the world, in the way of eternal life, is a greater privilege than to live a hundred years in the world, and to die the richest in it. There is no angel in heaven who would not think it a privilege to do this, were he to receive such a command from the Lord.* But it is not angels who have this privilege, but the meanest of us who has a heart to lay hold of it.

5. *Be not discouraged*, though you should not see great success at present attending your labour. Labour for God, and leave your work with God. The work of planting and watering is ours, but it is God that giveth the increase. His commands bind us, and his gracious promises encourage us to go on until death, faithfully and diligently, notwithstanding the ridicule and mockery of vain men, destitute of the fear of God.

Lastly, let all your *behaviour*, and your *treatment of the children*, show, that *the good of their souls is great in your view*, yea, infinitely greater than anything else in the world; and that you labour most willingly by prayer and by teaching to promote it. It would be easy to enlarge, but I must restrain myself. Farewell. I shall hasten to visit you with joy, when a convenience may be afforded. Pray for your poor brother and unworthy servant for Christ,

T. C.

3. Address to the Teachers of Sunday Schools

1811.

The success of your exertions in teaching the youth of the age, is much on my mind; and I look upon the work as of the greatest consequence to the improvement of our countrymen in general, in knowledge, religion, godliness, and morals. The good effects of your labour and faithfullness already appear most clearly in many parts of the country. I hope you will have help to persevere actively and cheerfully in the important work, until our country be filled with the knowledge of the Lord, and every decency of conduct and godliness.

For the success of your labour, there is one thing particular on my mind to mention to you. You well know, that the ordinances of the Lord Jesus have been appointed for the promotion of his great cause in the salvation of sinners; that is, *the preaching of his word – baptism – the Lord's supper –* and *prayer*. By these means, chiefly, he calls, feeds and comforts his people; and in the devotional use of them are we to look for the blessing of the Lord upon us. It is religious madness to expect a blessing in any other way than that which he has appointed. We should often remind one another of this, and also show to the children the nature and design of these ordinances, and the manner in which we should wait on God by faith in the use of them. None use them rightly, without acknowledging them to be divine ordinances, and expecting by faith a suitable blessing in them from God. They are not human rites, but divine ordinances; and they are also the only means appointed by God in the world to do good to the souls of sinners.

Baptism is not a civil or carnal rite, but an ordinance of the Lord; and there is a blessing to be had through the right use of it. It is a deplorable thing that it should be used in such a careless manner, as that scarcely anyone considers that it is a part of God's service, and that a peculiar blessing is to be had in the right use of it.

The neglect of youth in general as to the *Lord's supper*, in commemorating his death and the atonement he thereby made for sin, calls particularly for our notice. How can they meet him in judgement, after having lived all the days of their lives in such a shameful neglect? Cause them to consider this seriously. If they judge themselves unworthy, show them wherein this unworthiness consists. There is no sinner unworthy of the privilege, except the impenitent, and such as set no value on Christ and his sacrifice, that is, those who love their sins, resolve to live in them, and despise the most valuable thing in heaven and earth. True, some may eat and drink unworthily, not judging rightly of the Lord's body; but it is clear, that those who neglect to make a remembrance of him, do not judge rightly of his body; else they could not live in a neglect so slighting and ungrateful. I would not encourage them or any others to come to the Lord's table in an improper state as to their spirit and conduct; but I would earnestly exhort them to seek of God what may render them fit, instead of continuing to disobey a positive command of the Lord. That would be more likely to give them comfort at last, when going to appear before him in another world.

Remember to tell them also, that the *devil has his ordinances* as well as Christ, in this world: and by the means of these he also, in a like manner, maintains and advances the interest of his corrupt and ruinous kingdom. His ordinances are all the corrupting customs and practices of our country; such as, card-playing, dancing, wakes, feasts, revelling, drunkenness, etc. It has been peculiarly painful to me to hear that these foolish and mad practices, instead of reading the holy Bible, are common in some parts to this day, even on sabbath evenings, and continue to one or two o'clock in the morning. Enquire minutely about this in your different parts, and warn the children most seriously on the subject.

Man is a social being; but as the children of men are corrupt, it is very difficult for them to associate together, and the intercourse not to be corrupt. The grace of God alone can prevent this. But there are means for us to use, which by God's blessing may succeed in stemming the strong torrent of corruption.

There is one thing particular on my mind to mention here, that is, the common practice of letting children and young people go to fairs and markets, without any business or errand, but to be idle and to follow vanity. One fair often disorders and deranges a school for a quarter of a year. After bringing guilt and shame on themselves at the fair, they cannot for a long time after join in carrying on the work of the Lord. It is a foolish practice with parents to take their children to fairs as soon as they can walk: and when the boys begin to be idle and to fight, and the girls to be gadding, their parents begin to take some care of them, and to lament that they walk in the ways in which they were brought up by themselves. Rather let them show them the danger, vanity and sinfullness of such useless and corrupting habits and customs. Dinah was not the only girl who received the greatest injury by going out to see the damsels of the country; and that, no doubt, through the negligence of her parents, at least, of her mother. When I hear that a girl is gone to the fair merely to see its follies, I cannot but pity the sinful state of her mind, and tremble at the consequences.

As much as you can, show the children how vile, unseemly, dangerous and sinful are the ordinances of the devil; and on the other hand, show them how beautiful, desirable and blessed are the ordinances of God. It is a great pleasure to me to mention here, that the ordinances of Satan are entirely abolished in some parts of the country, and that going to fairs and such things are wholly given up. What has been done in some places may by the Lord's blessing be done in other parts. I must leave off here at present, intending to address you at another time on these and similar things. I am your sincere friend and unworthy servant,

T. C.

Minutes of Quarterly Meetings

1. Minutes of an Association at Llanrhwst

Jan. 1-2, 1795.

By a conference held with some of the brethren in the morning, it appeared:

1. That there is great injury in receiving wrong views of the fundamental principles of the gospel, which essentially appertain to the life of the soul and fellowship with the Lord: such as, the different character and design of the two covenants; faith in the Mediator; and the necessity of walking in the Spirit in order to obtain an evidence of our union with Christ. To regard faith as a strong belief as to the security of our state – and not a just and firm belief, according to the word, respecting Christ, our rock and refuge, our shelter and protection, who alone can preserve our souls – is an error which bears fruits that are very pernicious. To believe that our state is good and safe, without having the Lord as our special succour in the face of our misery, is one of the devices of Satan to lead astray and starve the souls of men. It is doubtless true, that he 'who hath begun a good work will perform it,' Phil. 1:6, but he is *performing* it, and not leaving it untouched, after having begun it, until the hour of death. Like a builder, having laid the foundation, he builds on that foundation, until he brings forth the topmost stone. What certainty have we that the work has been begun, and consequently will be completed, if the builder is not working at it, either cutting down timber, or hewing stones, or making some addition to the building? And what real certainty can we have of the security of our state, while our spirits are strangers to the nurture of the gospel, and fellowship with God, and the obedience of faith? It is not the certainty of faith, but the certainty of presumption. It appeared:

2. That great harm to our souls proceeds from a false view respecting the different character and design of the two covenants.

The covenant of works requires that we should be good and holy, that we may have communion with God and be acceptable before him: but the gospel discovers an open door for a sinner, as such, to come to God in Christ; 'In whom we have boldness and access with confidence by the faith of him,' Eph. 3:12. The gospel does not shut out the sinner, under any name, so that he cannot come to God through Christ; but it leaves him to be condemned to endless ruin for not coming, or neglecting to come, that he may be saved. 'Ye *will* not,' – not, ye *shall* not – 'come to me,' said Christ to the Jews, 'that ye might have life,' John 5:40. There is here an access – not, *after* having, but that we might have, life; not *after* having, but that we might have, the victory over our corruptions; not, *after* having, but that we might have, our spiritual healing and recovery. We find the godly crying to the Lord from the place where they were, that is, from 'the depths' – from 'the uttermost parts of the earth' – while fainting, when 'the sorrows of death compassed them and the floods of ungodly men made them afraid, etc.' If there be a foolish virgin, there is oil for such to be found in Christ. If there be a hypocrite, there is truth to be had for him instead of his hypocrisy. Prayer or calling upon the Lord in the state in which we may be, is what the Lord has appointed as means to bring quick, easy, and effectual deliverance to the weakest sinner in the most wretched condition. A mercy-seat, and a throne of grace, is Christ to such; to whom they can come 'boldly, that they may obtain mercy, and find grace to help in time of need,' Heb. 4:16. Hence we may see the great evil of a legal spirit, which keeps the sinner from the very place, where help to the soul can alone be had.

3. Confidence as to our union with Christ, and walking after the flesh, were considered to be two things wholly *inconsistent*. Walking after the flesh comprehends everything that belongs to our corrupt nature: such as walking according to sinful lusts and carnal affections, carnal imaginations, etc., etc. And to trust in man's own righteousness is called by the apostle 'trusting in the flesh,' Phil. 3:4. To be carnally-minded, and to walk after the flesh, are clear evidences of a man out of Christ. 'To be carnally minded

is death,' and he who is in Christ 'walks not after the flesh,' Rom. 8:1, 8, 9. 'To walk after the Spirit,' and 'to be spiritually minded,' are proofs of our union with Christ. 'To be spiritually minded is life and peace.' 'As many as are led by the Spirit of God, they are the sons of God.' The holy Spirit, as a guide to them, leads them into all truth; and that, not only as to their knowledge of the truth, but also as to their acquaintance with its power on their minds, and holy influence on their hearts. The fellowship of the Spirit thus with their minds, and his gracious operations directing them in the way according to the word, stirring them on and helping them to walk in it, will generate and nourish an assurance of hope as to their state and interest in Christ. What folly, then, is it to expect such a blessing while we are in a carnal and worldly spirit! And what benefit would it be, were it possible to possess it, while such a spirit prevails in us? Let us therefore seek, not for *one* gift of the Spirit, but for all his gracious gifts, and that in their due order. *They* who are led by the Spirit of God have the testimony that they are the children of God. And 'if ye be led of the Spirit, ye are not under the law.' But if you 'walk in the Spirit,' you will 'not fulfil the lusts of the flesh.' It is not the best sign of anyone's state, that he is continually trying to believe it good and blessed, and yet having no great care about the frame of his spirit, nor any great concern for the disorder in which it frequently is. There is not here but a small proof of any particular hatred to sin, or of any particular love to God and his commandments.

4. Notice was also taken of another fault observed in some as to the state of their souls, as dishonourable to God, as it is injurious to themselves. They spend much of their time in making disheartening complaints as to their unhappy frames of mind, without making much or any believing exertions and active strivings, joined with humble, patient, and longing expectations, for the remedy needful for them. There is a remedy, or there is not. If there is not, it is useless to complain or think of it. But if there is, as it is most true that there is, to make discouraging complaints is not what is suitable under such a circumstance, but to rise as the

prodigal did, and go to God that we may obtain the remedy. The fruit of a legal spirit is the one; and a pretty clear proof it is that the man has never been truly convinced and humbled on account of his sin, nor awakened to see the danger of his state: but the other is one of the chief fruits of the spirit of the gospel: it is faith sailing against wind and tide – the world of unbelief and the tide of corruptions – laying hold on the free promises of God to a sinner as a sinner.

In the afternoon meeting, a conversation was held with the Leaders (Elders) of the society at Ll—. Many exhortations were given them to take the lead in spiritual experience as to the things of God, in private communion with God, in manifesting an evangelical spirit, meek, gentle, faithful and diligent, and in a consistent walk, that they might be examples to believers 'in word, in conversation, in charity, in spirit, in faith, in purity,' 1 Tim. 4:12.

Observations were also made on the danger there is to those who employ their gifts in the Church in *prayer* or in some other way, to feel satisfied with their fluency in prayer, and with the degree of pleasure and delight which always accompany the free use of every gift, without stretching forward for an access to God through Christ. To see God by faith in prayer will cause our words to be few. Our distance from him, and losing sight of him, is what makes us talkative. To heap together swelling or unmeaning words before God when we pray is detestable. When faith is at work in prayer:

1. There is a prostration of soul before God, and a consciousness of our nothingness, and also of his infinite greatness.

2. There is a wrestling effort for a blessing. There is a sense of need and unworthiness; yet not without some measure of precious dependence on the word of promise, as a firm ground for expecting the blessing.

3. The soul sometimes takes delight in abhorring itself before God, and repenting in dust and ashes: it stands before God like Abraham, until it becomes dust and ashes, all vileness before him. Gen. 18:27.

4. The soul, at other times, is *giving* rather than *asking*. While looking, before the throne, on divine things, in a divine light, the soul breaks out, and pours itself out before God, in thankfullness rather than in supplications: the sacrifice of praise burns ardently, and sends forth a sweet perfume. The Spirit of God fills the soul with high thoughts of Christ's dignity, love and completeness, until it pours out itself in strains of gratitude and admiration.

However it may be with us, let us by no means rest satisfied, without the drawing nigh of the soul to God in prayer. It is certain, that the flesh with every lust and corruption, and the devil in all his devices, set themselves against this spiritual approach to God. The devil knows, that it is impossible for a sinner to draw nigh to God, without being benefitted: and he knows too, that the semblance of performances without God in them, will do no good to any. Therefore, if he cannot restrain us from duties, he will strive to keep us, as to the performance of them, in the outer court, without coming within the veil to the mercy seat, where the glory of God dwells. But the Spirit of the Lord is able to 'help our infirmities,' and strengthen us to overcome these inveterate enemies.

There is the same danger also in *hearing* and in *preaching*. There is no greater delight to those who have a taste for such things, than to listen to the melody of evangelic eloquence, under the gales of the Holy Spirit, 'when the Lord God blows the trumpet and goes with whirlwinds of the south,' Zech. 9:14. It must yet be observed, that a person may receive a high degree of delight in preaching or in hearing the word, under the exercise of such gifts, without much communion with the Lord through the word preached, or any permanent good from it. *Spiritual* use or habitude will form a judgement in these things, so that we shall be able 'to discern both good and evil,' Heb. 5:14. Let us be thankful for the dew and the sweet gales; but let us seek, gather, and feed on, the *manna* in the dew. Christ, in and through the word, and the pleasant gales, is the substance which wisdom enables those who love him to enjoy.

The meeting was attended with comfort and edification. A great many assembled to hear with great avidity. It is pleasant to work when we are 'workers together with God.' The joy of the labourers is to see the Lord of the harvest himself in the field.

The last year is to be noticed as a year of particular success as to religion in Wales. 'The paths' of the Lord in the preaching of his word, 'dropped fatness,' and he has 'crowned the year with his goodness,' Psa. 65:11. There are nearly *two thousand*, throughout Wales, added to the several churches. God has wonderfully prospered the free schools and Sunday schools throughout the country. The youth in many instances are turning to the Lord. The preachers have become more numerous, and evangelic gifts have increased. Yet, *not to us*. In the midst of the greatest success, is the greatest need of watchfullness. May the keeper of Israel keep us. 'Except the Lord keep the city, the watchman waketh but in vain'; the watchman, not asleep, but awake and watching, and yet for all that, in vain, except the *Lord keeps* the city, Psa. 127:1.

2. Minutes of an Association at Machynlleth

April 15-16, 1795.

In the conferences the first morning there appeared much brotherly kindness and love, seriousness and fidelity in the brethren towards one another. They exhorted each other to unceasing attention to the work of holding communion with the Lord, privately, and in their public labours. Two special hindrances to this were noticed: a *legal spirit*, keeping the soul at a distance from God under a sense of guilt and unworthiness; and a *disordered spirit and fruitless efforts*, these *two* things together, disheartening and enfeebling the mind.

To oppose these things, it would be well for us to have a right view of the great Mediator between God and men, and of his satisfactory merit, which renders an unworthy sinner acceptable before God. These were the thoughts which encouraged David, *in the depths*, to entertain a firm hope of deliverance. 'If thou, Lord, shouldest mark iniquities, O Lord, who shall stand? But there is forgiveness with thee, that thou mayest be feared,' Psa. 130:3, 4.

Not only forgiveness, but also divine assistances, are extended in the gospel for remedying our state, however bad it may be. The Lord heals all infirmities, as well as forgiving all iniquities. It is a mistake very injurious to us to set our *feelings* of comfort, or of no comfort, as our ground and rule in our communion with God, instead of the *word* of truth. The invitation of Christ to those who labour and are heavy-laden, is a sufficient ground for them to come to him, though every feeling of their own, and every effort of the enemy, are opposed to this. The gospel reveals a way to God, under the heaviest mountains of guilt, and every confusion of mind, for substantial comfort and sufficient remedy.

Another thing which hinders communion with God, and that most certain, wherever it may be, is a *dishonest mind*, concealing secret idols in the heart, without confessing them and falling out with them earnestly and with holy jealousy. Christ and Belial, Christ and the world, Christ and secret corruption that is fostered, cannot dwell together, any more than the Ark and Dagon, or light and darkness. Such spiritual deceptions are an abomination to the Lord, and a bad sign of man's state, Psa. 32:2. There is a nobleness, and an amiable princely honesty, in the spirit of the gospel, so that it humbles itself before God, and confesses against itself its sins unto the Lord, unfeignedly seeking to be delivered from them.

As to spiritual efforts, if not evangelic, they are lifeless, careless and momentary: such there are, but they spring from a *legal* spirit. These are not successful, and soon vanish away. But there are efforts of a different kind, and more excellent in their effects. *Faith* will strive against all discouragements; she will knock at a closed door, knowing that the keys belong to Jesus; she will fight even under the feet of her enemies; she will hope when she is being killed; and will cry, 'I shall come out,' when in the furnace of affliction. Faith is careful, is diligent, and unyielding under all repulses, like the woman of Canaan, Matt. 15:22. While *legal* diligence brings no advantage, and is soon wearied, driving in a barren and unproductive course, the Holy Spirit, as the Comforter and Succourer of his people, leads them unto *all truth*; and he enables them to experience the peculiar efficacy of these truths in their souls, to their comfort and sanctification, and their self-abasement and support.

It was remarked on these considerations, that they who continue without growing in their souls, afford a cause of doubt as to their *spiritual change*, whether they have ever been renewed by a spiritual regeneration. There may be some workings on the natural man without any substantial change. It was noticed, that this was a subject worthy of the deepest consideration; and all were requested to allow it a suitable place in their thoughts, that it might be handled more largely and particularly in the afternoon.

In the afternoon meeting the subject mentioned in the morning came to be considered and inquired into more at large, that is, the difference between *evanescent workings* on men's minds, and the *real change* in the nature and radical principle of the soul by the Spirit; or between the natural state at the best, and a gracious state in its lowest degree of spiritual life.

It is beyond a doubt clear from Scripture, that men may experience some powerful influences, and possess high and exalted gifts, without having a new nature, a real, saving change. As to influences, see Heb. 6:4, 5. The things mentioned there, are not the things which accompany salvation; for these are 'the better things,' ver. 9, better in their nature and effects, and permanent in their duration. With respect to spiritual gifts, see 1 Cor. 13. The gifts mentioned there, without love, leave men, as to their spiritual state, *nothing*. As to usefullness in the church, see Matt. 7:21, 22. Those mentioned there had prophesied *in his name*, cast out devils *in his name*, wrought miracles *in his name*, ate and drank before him, Luke 13:26: and yet they departed not from their sins, and never knew Christ in truth by a spiritual intercourse with him. This subject is most worthy of our minutest attention: but it is a knot very difficult to be untied; it is therefore necessary to be attentive and cautious. The remarks were the following.

1. When there is a real influence of the Spirit changing the heart of the sinner, there is a *death* which takes place. There is then what

the apostle calls being 'dead to the law,' 'crucified to the world,' 'mortifying the deeds of the body by the Spirit,' not leaving the law for a few discontented hours, but *dying* to it, not quarrelling sometimes with the works of the body, and corruptions of the heart, but *mortifying* them, by the Spirit. This spiritual death is what the others know nothing of. On the contrary, the workings on them die away, and leave them alive in their old state and in their sins. They and their sins are alive; and their sins have received no deadly stroke.

2. Where there is a real change, there is also a *new life*. 'You hath he quickened,' or 'to you hath he given life' – 'he that hath the Son hath life' – being 'dead to the law by the body of Christ,' they are 'married to another, even to him who is raised from the dead, that they might bring forth fruit unto God.' The holy Spirit hath regenerated them; and there is in them what is born of the Spirit, which Christ calls, '*spirit,*' John 3:6. There is in them a *seed* remaining. This divine nature is called by Paul, 'the law of the mind.' There are two *contrary* natures in these, contending continually with each other; the one is to be mortified, and the other to be quickened and fostered. The others, notwithstanding all, are without this oil in their vessels.

3. There is also a *reconciling of the mind to God*. The man has been brought down, made gentle, and tamed. The enmity is being killed, and contention ceases. He has been brought, as it were, to himself; and God and his law are viewed by him as just and glorious, the plan of salvation wholly pleases him, and Christ is chosen and received as he is set forth in the glass of the word. In this respect also the others are deficient; this reconciliation and peace with heaven are wholly unknown to them.

4. The saving work is *remedial*; it mends the state of man, and does not leave him, after all, a *worker of iniquity*. Many figurative expressions are employed in Scripture to show this in a very extensive way, such as: healing diseases, opening the eyes of the blind, cleansing the unclean, taking away filthy garments, clothing with change of raiment, emptying and fructifying the wilderness,

making it blossom and rejoice, Isaiah 35, making fruitless trees fruitful, taming wild beasts, and changing their nature, Isaiah 11. Many other similar comparisons are to be found often in the Scripture which exhibit, at the same time, the dreadful and wretched state of the sinner by nature, and also the wonderfully restorative effects of the Spirit in his change. But the others are different as to this healing of their souls; or, if they seem to possess it, it is only superficial and in appearance. They are as to the Spirit, and radical bent of their minds, the same; the law of sin is ruling in them. This difference is set forth very clearly in the parable of the sower. The seed falls on three sorts of ground, where notwithstanding all the symptoms of a fruitful crop in the early appearances of two of them, the whole withers and becomes fruitless, because the soil is bad, not having been fallowed nor cleaned. But there is a fourth sort of ground called good ground; there the seed obtains depth of soil, takes root and brings forth fruit unto perfection. There is 'the honest and good heart,' which by the healing treatment of the Spirit has been renewed and restored to health.

5. There is a *permanency* in a saving work. The Holy Spirit, the gift of the Father and the heavenly Comforter, 'abideth there forever.' There is a continuance in his operations. He is cleansing them from day to day, that they may bring forth more fruit, and watering them every moment, and is in them a fountain of water springing up to everlasting life. Notwithstanding all opposition, a 'seed remaining,' is the new principle in their souls. Continuing convictions are their convictions; and continuing comforts are their comforts. Faith, hope, and love *remain* in spite of all storms; and life eternal will be their end. But at some season or another, at death or before that awful hour of nature's dissolution, the lamps of the others will go out, and be quenched forever.

6. Where there is a really spiritual work on the sinner's soul, the *walking* of that man (the fruit of his union with Christ) will be after the Spirit, and not after the flesh. His union is evident by his walk. 'He shall be as a tree planted by the waters, and that spreadeth out her roots by the river, and shall not see when heat

cometh; but her leaf shall be green, and shall not be careful in the year of drought, neither shall cease from yielding fruit,' Jer. 17:8. The authority of God and his truth exercise dominion in the conscience; there is a solemn regard in the mind to the rule of the word; and a renewal of strength is afforded to run, according to this rule, without fainting, and to walk without being wearied. The others are inconstant in all their ways, without the real fear of God in their hearts; without a right and clear view of the holy ways of the gospel, and without a guide to direct them, except their own changeable tempers, or the corruption which for the present holds the sceptre in his hand. Something unbecoming and unsuitable is in their appearance at best; and often their steps are polluted and wretched; 'destruction and misery are in their ways, and the way of peace have they not known.'

7. Jesus Christ, as he is exhibited in his word, not only cheers the minds of those who have experienced a real change, and at times gladdens them (as may be the case in some respects with others) but he is as it were, their *living*. He is *all* to the life of their souls. They hunger for him, and feed themselves on him; his *flesh* is *meat indeed*, and his *blood* is *drink indeed*, to their wearied souls. They drink of this river and lift up their heads. He is to them all in all. He is in their view a sufficient and an eternal substance: he is 'all their salvation and all their desire.' But Christ is to the others, they know not justly what; someone rather common, without whom they can generally live very well, but one needed too, at times, in some *great strait*. If there should appear in them some zeal, as if they wished to exalt Christ, this springs not from any precious view they have of him, but from a cursed wish to exhibit their own gifts and talents. His gifts are better than himself in their esteem; and to show their fine clothing of gifts, and their own selves, is more in their view than to show Christ, the author of every gift and giver of all grace.

Before separating at this time, all the brethren were exhorted to notice particularly the breaches, which, it was feared, were widening among us, and to endeavour to repair them: –

1. Respecting *family religion*, it was remarked, that there were signs of decay and neglect with regard to it too common. It was enjoined on those who teach others in the church, while conversing with their brethren on the state of their souls, to enquire minutely respecting their conduct and religious exercises, and to exhort them to be attentive, watchful and diligent in performing them, that they might be lights in the world, and seasoning-salt in their families and neighbourhood.

2. Of the *Sabbath* it was noticed with a degree of sorrow and lamentation, that more liberty was taken by religious people now to talk on this day of unsuitable and unprofitable things, than there was some years ago by our fathers. Instead of meditating on the word, and examining ourselves, the war, foreign and home news, or some worldly business, fill our minds, and form the substance of our conversation even on the Sabbath. The transgression and the despising of *one* commandment leads to the disregard of *every* commandment: and the man who can live in the constant practice of transgressing *one*, may by degrees be led to trample underfoot *all* the commandments. All were earnestly requested to endeavour faithfully to effect a reform in this respect, in the fear of the Lord.

3. Under the present *difficult circumstances of the kingdom*, the danger was stated, and a caution was given, lest we should be found, as the world in general, complaining of the instruments and second causes, without considering seriously, and penitently, the crying sins, which have justly caused the Lord to threaten us with his scourges. This is very perilous, and a sign of a hardness of heart, ripening for judgement. Whensoever, and howsoever (if in the way of his judgements) our Lord may come, let us be sober, faithful and wise, looking for his coming, with our loins girt, and 'our lamps burning.' Let us be awake, let us be ready, that when he comes and knocks, we may immediately open to him, Luke 12:35, 36.

4. A brief notice was also taken, particularly, of *our obligations to obey the powers that be*. The command of the Lord is clear, and positive on this subject, 'Let *every* soul be subject unto the higher

powers: the powers that *be*, are ordained of God,' Rom. 13:1. The example of Christ, meekly and readily paying tribute, clearly shows the course which we are to take as his followers. He showed respect, by a willing obedience, to a government, which he knew would unjustly put him to death. It is not the spirit of a prickly, pecking, and bitter politician, who puts down all as fools and offenders except himself, that we observe in our meek Saviour. Our Lord was not a slanderer of dignities; nor does it become any one of his followers to be so. This is one of the many ways which Satan has, to bring reproach on the holy ways of God, and to starve and corrupt the souls of men. To settle the affairs of government, without ever being called to such a work, and to neglect things of the greatest moment, which belong to us and our families, is a great folly, and one of the snares of the devil, in which he catches depraved and changeable men at his will. A kind warning was given to all to shun such ruinous courses; and that they should willingly pay 'tribute to whom tribute is due, custom to whom custom, fear to whom fear, honour to whom honour.'

We experienced abundant proofs of the kindness of the Lord in this meeting. The private conference was profitable and edifying; and the public preaching was very glorious and powerful: and we parted at this time, as on many former occasions, in love, peace and joy in the Holy Ghost. The Lord be praised.

3. Minutes of an Association at Bala

June 15-16, 1795.

In the conference held the first morning, some few remarks were made on the following subjects.

1. On the necessity of genuine faith in the *truth of God's word*, for the life of godliness, and for every branch of that life; and also on the subject, that a belief in the truth of the word produces in us an unfailing expectation as to the entire fulfilment of every part of it. It is not possible ever to annihilate or to change one iota or one tittle of the word, until all be accomplished. No event or any circumstance can happen, different from, or contrary to, what the

word declares. As the mighty and wise God, who orders all things, *has said*, so he *will do*. What he has eternally pre-ordained has been made known to us in the divine word; and 'he is of one mind, and who can turn him?' Job 23:13. To give an example: if he has said, 'Whosoever exalteth himself shall be abased; and he that humbleth himself shall be exalted,' Luke 14:11; God is true, and so it will be, most certainly, with respect to each of the persons described in the passage. There is a power and authority in the word to pull down the one, and to raise up the other. Notwithstanding all that the power and cunning of men and devils may do to withstand it, the word shall be accomplished. Let us bear this in mind that according to our *faith* in the truth of the word will be our *submission* and *obedience* to it, our *dependence* on it, and our *comforts* from it.

2. On faith in the truth of the word, not only as it produces *assent* in the mind, but also as it works *conformity* of heart and life to the truth. There is in the believing soul an obedience *from the heart* to the form of doctrine that is believed, Rom. 6:17. The Holy Spirit impresses, by means of faith in the truth, the *image* of the truth on the spirit of the believer, *forms* and fashions him according to the word, and leads him, if we may so speak, to the Spirit, to the path and region of the truth. The Holy Spirit *engrafts* the word, James 1:21; and thus faith receives it into the heart, so that he takes root and lodges there, and changes it to his own holy nature. Immoveable faith in the truth and divinity of the holy word is the working of a power above all the powers of corrupt nature: it is 'the exceeding greatness of God's power,' working in the soul of the sinner; and exceedingly great are the effects which proceed from it. To believe on the Son of God is to live on him; and that enables us to live *with* him and *to* him, and from the heart to reject everything else in his stead. To believe the promise is to welcome it with the greatest joy, to embrace it with cordial endearment, to live and rely on it, and on the mighty and faithful promiser who has made it.

3. It was also remarked, that it was a very easy thing, though very dangerous, and injurious in its consequences, for religious people, through gradual and secret defections, to slide from the *spiritual*

working of faith, to the *assent of the natural mind* and conscience to the truth. The mind by common light can comprehend many a part of the divine word, and the conscience may consent, judging rightly respecting it; yet, after all, the soul lays no hold on it, and carries on no fellowship with God. This is the case, it is to be much feared, with many a professor, once flourishing, but now withering, notwithstanding his profession, in a state of estrangement from God, being asleep, having nothing but a natural perception of the gospel, without partaking substantially of its blessings, and living spiritually upon them. Such meddling with the gospel will do good to none, while the veil remains on the mind. To 'behold,' through divine revelation, 'with open face, the glory of the Lord,' is the only way to change us 'into the same image,' 2 Cor. 3:18.

In the afternoon one of the Brethren said that there were *three* things on his mind which he wished to offer to our serious consideration, as subjects of self-examination:

1. Does our doctrine in public and private *correspond* with the word – no branch or part of truth being left out – no extremes on any side – no truth being without the notice it deserves, and without being set forth in its glory and usefullness? There is to every truth a place and purposes peculiar to itself; and we are causing a loss to the souls of men by leaving out one truth in our instructions. The Holy Spirit leads into *all* truth; and as far as we are under his guidance, we must be seeking to regard and set forth all divine truths in their own places and to their own purposes. Do we therefore, 'with reverence and godly fear,' speak of the great God in the glory of *all* his perfections? Is the unchangeable rectitude and purity of his holy law set forth frequently by us? Are we endeavouring to show what God in his Son is to a lost sinner, and what is the extent, depth, and freeness of the grace of the gospel? Are we setting forth *unceasingly* the divine glory of the person of the Mediator, the sufficiency of his sacrifice, the completeness and dignity of his offices, etc.? Is our doctrine full of the *divinity* of the person and work of the Holy Spirit? Do we show particularly *what* is his work on the souls of his people, and the

indispensable necessity of experiencing it; and what are the fruits of the Spirit, which proceed from our union with Christ? Further, does our doctrine regard and exhibit, according to the minuteness of the Bible, what we ought to be towards God as to graces and duties, as to the state of our spirits inwardly and of our conduct outwardly? Is *every* grace shown in its beauty and value and in its proper place? Is *every* duty mentioned, with every important and *evangelic* motive necessary to its due performance? The graces are necessary for the right performance of duties; and in the serious performance of the duties it is that the Holy Spirit fosters and strengthens graces. Graces will never flourish in that man who is neglectful of duties; and without the operation of graces, duties will be dead and formal.

2. Is the *impress* and *image* of our doctrines on our own spirits? To exhort others to show mercy, and to live in a spirit contrary to such a thing – to preach the duty of forgiveness and to entertain an unforgiving spirit – to recommend humility, and to be arrogantly proud – these surely are things very unseemly and detestable. The chief teacher, Christ Jesus, is the example set before us. He exhibited perfectly through his whole life, the glorious doctrines which he preached. He was *practically*, what the whole Bible is *doctrinally*. In him was seen the holy law, walking the earth with feet of dust, without any deviation or halting in one of his steps. In him the spirit of the gospel flourished in all the perfection of gracious sympathy and meekness. Such as he was, it behoves us his followers to be. He has 'left us an example, that we should follow his steps,' 1 Pet. 2: 21. 'Let this mind be in you, which was also in Christ Jesus,' Phil. 2:5. Pure doctrine and a corrupt spirit will not long stand together. It is most certain, that if the doctrine will not mend and improve our spirits, the doctrine itself will not continue long without being corrupted. Though it be *earthen* vessels that have the treasures of the gospel in them, yet let us remember, that they are not to be *filthy* vessels. 'If a man,' says the apostle, 'purge himself from these, he shall be a vessel unto honour, sanctified and meet for the master's use, and prepared unto every good work,' 2 Tim. 2:21.

3. What are we in our conduct, and as to *religious exercises*? While conversing on this point, the opportunity was taken to inquire what had been done in the several counties with regard to the subject mentioned in the Association at *Machynlleth* (see page 332) and whether the Monthly Meetings had been active in repairing these breaches. It was answered in the *affirmative*, especially with respect to *family duties*. This subject was felt much, in a peculiar manner, by those that were present at Machynlleth. In this spirit it was that they returned to their friends at home: and inquiry was made in the Monthly Meetings of every county, and in the particular meetings of every church. Though the breaches were more and wider than it was thought, yet much cause of joy and thankfullness was found in the faithfullness of hundreds, and for the abounding grace bestowed on them. The happy effects of the gospel had been seen in the conduct of a *large* number of the poor sinners of our country. Sixty years ago it would have been difficult to find a single family calling upon God in North Wales: but now, by the grace of heaven, there are hundreds of families worshipping God in every county. It is probable that the mentioning of the subject was a happy thing, and may be the means of multiplying praying families in our country.

Some *questions* were asked about family duties:

1. What is the duty of men-servants in prayerless families? (i) Humbly to request the head of the family to set up prayer in his family. (ii) If he refuses, then to ask leave for him, the servant, to read and pray with the family; and let him endeavour by every kindness and faithfullness to persuade him to consent.

2. Ought a maid-servant to do the same? Yes, if possessed of suitable gifts, and there be no man in the family willing to take the lead in the worship of God.

3. What discipline is to be exercised on those among us who neglect to worship God in their families? To exhort them to do so with all faithfullness, and to show them the great danger of such shameful and ungodly neglect, their want of faithfullness to the souls under their care, and the account they must give to God of their stewardship as heads of families. If they doubt the

suitableness of their gifts to take the lead in prayer, let them use *forms*, until they attain a gift to pray with propriety without them.

4. What if they continue perversely in this neglect, notwithstanding every exhortation to reform? We cannot view it as too severe a measure, that such, after *one or two admonitions*, should be cut off from the Church. But it is probable that *such neglecters* are not often to be found, but who have other faults clinging to them, which at once unfit them for taking the lead in holy duties, and divest them also of the privilege of being Church members.

One of the brethren said, that he was in some doubt on this head: is the neglect of duties a fault which justly cuts off a man from Church fellowship? It was answered: That the defect of gifts does not require such a discipline, because no *certain* decision can be made on a point that is not *evident*; but that a wilful and continued neglect of enjoined duties, is a *public* disobedience and rebellion against God. Another brother asked, Is there a positive command in the Bible with respect to family prayer? It was answered,

1. Though there is no command in so many words, yet that there is enough to show that it is the duty of everyone who has a serious mind and a tender conscience. It is commanded that 'men should pray everywhere," 1 Tim. 2:8; and if so, it is most certain that men ought to pray with their families. Again, 'If any provide not for his own, and especially for those of his own house, he hath denied the faith, and is worse than an infidel,' 1 Tim. 5:8. And if it be sinful to make no provision for their bodies, we may certainly say, that it is more sinful not to provide for their souls. And again, 'And these words which I command thee this day, shall be in thine heart: and thou shalt teach them diligently to thy children, and shalt talk of them when thou sittest in thine house, and when thou walkest by the way, and when thou liest down, and when thou risest up,' Deut. 6:6, 7. And is not prayer *with* our children, as well as for them, one of the means for 'bringing them up in the nurture and admonition of the Lord?' Eph. 6:4.

2. It was judged too, that what may be gathered unerringly from Scripture, is Scripture; and that the religious examples of the

godly bind us in the same manner as a positive command. David consecrated his house, (title of Psalm 30) and how could he do so except by prayer? Abraham, Joshua, Job, Daniel, Cornelius, Priscilla and Aquila, are mentioned with honour and praise in Scripture, for their faithfullness and attention in the performance of this duty. Gen. 18:19; Josh. 24; Job 15; Dan. 6:10; Acts 10:2; Rom. 16:3-5; 1 Cor. 16:19; Col. 4:15; Philemon 2. The wrath of God is to be poured down on 'the families that call not upon the name of the Lord,' Jer. 10:25. If the word *families* is to be taken here in the largest sense, that is, of a nation that sprung from the same root, that does not leave the individual or the smallest family exempt from the denounced wrath: rather, the one contains the other; and this threatening is a black cloud over every family which call not on the name of the Lord. It was therefore decided, without a dissentient voice: *That to read the word of God and use family prayer, is a duty, enjoined to be practised daily, and that we are to expect thereby a blessing to ourselves and our families.* We separated this time again in peace, confessing that it was good for us to be there. Praise to the Trinity. Amen.

4. Minutes of an Association at Llanfair

April 11-12, 1796.
Our intercourse was in the first meeting, peculiarly delightful and profitable, to the increase of love and spiritual edification. We conversed, first, on our spiritual experience as Christians, and secondly, on our ministerial office as preachers.

It was observed briefly on the *first* head, that it is very necessary, and indeed indispensable, to live and walk in the spirit of the gospel, in order to be fit and useful in any work in the Lord's house. The wisdom of man and the spirit of the world are not meet for God's house, or for any spiritual work in it. The strength of self and of the flesh will do nothing in the place of the Spirit's strength and power; nor natural kindness instead of the tender fostering spirit of the gospel; nor legal severity, instead of evangelic faithfullness. It is only while we live with God and in the spirit of

God, that we shall prosper in his holy work. On the *second* subject the three following observations were made:

1. As ministers are called *ambassadors*, it is necessary that they should be *well acquainted* with the message they bring from God to men. They cannot deliver intelligibly what they do not understand themselves. They must be well acquainted with God's plan in reconciling the world to himself and in saving sinners, before they can make it known to others. Ignorance of the chief articles of the Christian religion wholly unfits a person for the work of the ministry. God never called the blind to be a leader to the blind. This is the enemy's work, that he may lead the guide and the guided both into the ditch. Such leaders are called by Christ, 'fools and blind'; and he pronounces upon them the most dreadful woes. Such blind leaders may be very active, encompassing sea and land to make one proselyte, and after proselyting him, making him twofold more the child of hell than themselves. These are the messengers of Satan, and not the messengers of God; and the children of hell are those they beget; and the image of hell is on them. These blind guides are the chief officers of the devil: to his dark kingdom they belong, and not to the bright kingdom of Christ. *His* officers are light in the Lord; stars in his right hand; candles lighted and put on candlesticks, to give light to all in the house. Though they spend themselves, they yet lighten a dark world, and show to its inhabitants the way of life.

2. They ought also to possess a suitable measure of spiritual gifts, to deliver their message in a becoming and intelligent manner. There is no small difference between the gifts which the Holy Spirit bestows on the officers of the Church: but the lowest are intelligible, suitable and becoming. Every gift is meet for edification. They are all given for the edifying of the body of Christ. They are therefore fit to answer this purpose, in a measure more or less. It is not natural gifts that we have chiefly in view; but more especially *spiritual* gifts, for the edifying of the body of Christ, Eph. 4:11, 12; not elegance of language, nor an eloquent and fluent tongue; but rather a gift and skill, derived from *spiritual* experience, rightly to

divide the word of truth, and to apply it to the souls of men, to their edification.

3. It is further necessary, in order to be *ambassadors*, that they should have been *called* to the office by Christ, the great head of the Church. Their knowledge, their gifts, or their desire for the office, are not sufficient; but they must have been *sent*. 'How shall they preach, except they be sent?' Rom. 10:15. To become preachers, they must have their mission from God; otherwise, according to the apostle's judgement, they cannot preach. How shall they preach? What hinders them? The want of being sent. See, you may say, there are here many qualifications. Very true: but the *sending* is wanting, and therefore they cannot preach.

The apostle says of true ambassadors, that God had 'committed to them the word of reconciliation.' The word of reconciliation, that is, the gospel, has been committed to them, not only for their own use, but ministerially, to be delivered unto others. The Holy Spirit, in thus committing the word of reconciliation to the ambassadors of Christ, not only endows them with suitable and edifying gifts, but also produces in them a ready mind, and makes them feel a constraint and a necessity to preach, such as we find in the prophet Isaiah, when the live coal touched his lips; in the Apostles at the day of Pentecost, in Paul, etc. There are different degrees of this feeling, according to the greatness of the work which God has for each: but the lowest degree is the same in its nature as the highest.

It was here observed that strong impulses are not *always* proofs of a mission from God. There may be in one a strong wish for the holy office, springing from wrong motives, without any mission from the Almighty.

1. 'Some preach Christ' says the Apostle, 'of contention, not sincerely; of envy and strife, not of good will, not of love.' We see that there was wanting in these 'good will,' εὐδοκία a word that signifies sometimes the free and eternal love of God to his elect, but in this place, their love to him. The two are in their nature the same; and the one springs from the other, as the stream from the fountain. This is the love which the Spirit sheds abroad

in the hearts of his people, and which constrains them in a manner wonderfully sweet and supernatural, to live to him who died for them. But these envious preachers are destitute of this excellent spirit. They are also wanting as to purity – 'not purely' (so according to the Welsh translation). They are pure as to doctrine; for the Apostle rejoices on this account, that *Christ was preached* by them; but they are not pure as to their spirit and conduct. The impurity is the *envy* and *contention* that were working in their hearts, which moved and powerfully led them to the work. A sorry motive, truly, to take in hand a work so glorious!

2. 'Filthy *lucre*' also, and *worldly lusts*, are to others strong motives to undertake this holy work. What they have in view is not the glory of God or the good of immortal souls, but profit, or some worldly advantages. Filthy indeed! Profaning the temple of God! Under many a guise is this wolf to be found: for he can change and disguise himself, as circumstances and occasions may require. But under every guise he may be known by this one mark, *No gain, no work*. Gain or lucre are the weights which make the clock to go and strike. Take away the weights, and it stops at once. To make merchandise of this holy office, or make it the means of worldly gain, for filthy lucre's sake, is a heinous sin. They who thus make it, feed themselves instead of feeding the flock, and rule the flock with oppression and cruelty. Such men the prophet calls '*greedy dogs*, which can never have enough, all looking to their own way, everyone for his gain from his quarter, dumb dogs who cannot bark, sleeping, lying down, loving to slumber,' Isaiah 56:10, 11. It is not of a ready mind, and for the glory of the Lord, that they do what they do in the work, but for filthy lucre's sake. Were it not for gain, lying down, sleeping, and slumbering, would most shamefully be the case with them still. But the Lord speaks thus of such graceless shepherds: 'Behold I am against the shepherds; and I will require the flock at their hands, and cause them to cease from feeding my flock; neither shall the shepherds feed themselves anymore,' Ezek. 34:10. 'Woe to the idle shepherd that leaveth the flock: the sword shall be on his arm, and on his right eye: his arm

shall be clean dried up, and his right eye shall be utterly darkened,' Zech. 11:17.

3. There is another thing, noticed by the apostle, which has a strong influence on many, that is, the love of *dominion* and pre-eminence, 1 Pet. 5:2, 3. It is not the good of the flock, but their own honour, that they chiefly regard. Self must be exalted, though God's inheritance be trodden underfoot, and their own brethren be haughtily treated. Against such a spirit Christ gave a warning to his disciples, 'The kings of the Gentiles exercise lordship over them; and they that exercise authority upon them are called benefactors: but *ye shall not be so*,' Luke 22:25, 26. 'One is your Master, even Christ; and all ye are brethren'; and the 'greatest among you shall be your servant.' It is the mark of hypocrites and blind leaders, to 'love the uppermost rooms at feasts, and the chief seats in synagogues, and greetings in the markets, and to be called of men, Rabbi, Rabbi,' Matt. 23.

No doubt, such motives as the above, work strongly, the one or the other, in false teachers. But to Satan's kingdom they belong; they are the moving wheels of his vile government. Other views and other designs, altogether different, yea, spiritual, pure, and evangelic impulses, wrought by the Holy Spirit, move, influence and constrain the true messengers of Christ. The baptism by fire, the touching of the live coal, the constraining of the love of Christ: these make his ministers a flame of fire, or living angels, to fly through the midst of heaven, carrying with them the everlasting gospel. They are fiery themselves, and set others on fire. They tread underfoot, gain ease and honour, and thousands of such vanities; and through honour and dishonour, through praise and dispraise, they spend and are spent in the cause of Christ, and for the good of immortal souls. The fire of God is in their hearts, the authority of Christ in their words, and his image in their conduct. Their chief work in this world is to 'take heed to the ministry which they have received in the Lord, that they may fulfil it,' Col. 4:17.

It belongs not to us to judge the hearts of men; but when we observe clear proofs that the above motives bear rule in anyone in his ministry and conduct, there is reason to fear that he is not a messenger of Christ's sending; and therefore the unseemly fruit of his ministry will be, to corrupt and not to edify the Church. If the eye be single, the motives pure and right, the whole body will be light. But if the eye be evil, the motives corrupt, the whole body will be dark, Matt. 6:22; Luke 11:34.

In the second private meeting, some conversation was had with some of the old leaders of the Societies of the county, with respect to their experiences, their hopes and fears, their discouragements and encouragements. In this converse, an occasion was found to notice the indispensable necessity of walking with God, and of living a spiritual life, in order to retain an assurance of hope as to our eternal state. Presumptuous sins corrupt and wound the conscience, weaken our strength, and bring a cloud on the soul, estrange us from God, and generate doubts and dreadful fears. Such also are the effects of secret sins, except there be godly sorrow on their account, and a cleansing of them by a renewed application of the blood of Christ to the soul. On this account David cried, 'Cleanse thou me from secret faults: keep back thy servant also from presumptuous sins,' Psalm 19:12, 13. To bear witness *with* our spirit is what the Holy Spirit does. He first renews our spirit, and raises him on his feet as a witness; and then he bears a joint-witness or testimony, according to his own will, at the time and in the degree he pleases. It will be of no avail for men in a state of declension to expect a sure testimony as to their eternal condition. A *restoration* is what we need *first*; we ought therefore to labour and strive by earnest prayer to him who is able to renew us. It is by believing and loving, or by the exercise of faith and love, and not without this, that we can be brought to *know* that we truly believe and sincerely love the Lord. The spirit of adoption, and nothing else without it, will bring a clear satisfaction to the mind, that we are the children or the adopted of God. It is madness to expect a clear testimony as to our eternal safety, while we live in a spirit of backsliding from God and lead a careless life. This is one of the devices of Satan to lead astray souls to their great hurt, if not to their eternal ruin. It is an awful contradiction, to profess confidence as to our being in the ways of God, and our conduct showing, it may be, that we walk not a single step in them!

It was also observed, that it is a bad sign of a man's state, that he is continually looking for the witnessing of the Spirit, or for what he so calls, and yet negligent and unwatchful as to his spirit and conduct. The devil is content that we should comfort ourselves in anything we please, if it be only that we live without the remedy and the holy nourishment which the gospel has provided for our souls. But true confidence is what proceeds from the restorative influence of the Holy Spirit. He first restores the straying soul to the way eternal, sets his feet on the rock, and directs his going: then he puts in his heart a hopeful satisfaction as to his safety, and in 'his mouth a new song, even praise unto our God,' Psalm 40:2, 3. Those were very sure as to their safety, whom we find boldly crying out, 'Lord, Lord, open unto us.' As if they said, 'See, *we* are here; how strange is it that the door is closed, and *we* here! Dost thou know that *we* are here?' 'Yes,' as if our Lord had said, 'I know that you are there; but who has ever seen you associating with me in your spirits, and walking, as to your conduct, in my holy ways while in the world? You have lived without oil in your lamps, without God's Spirit and his holy influences on your hearts. I *know you not*, depart from me ye workers of iniquity,' Matt. 25:11, 12; 7:23. We cannot think, according to the Bible, that the seal of the Holy Spirit is put on an empty soul and a corrupt life, or that the witness of the Spirit is given, but to those who are led by the Spirit, and who live according to the Spirit. The confidence that we are children, and the obedience of children, and the nurture of children, *go together inseparably*. 'Come out from among them, and be ye separate, saith the Lord, and touch not the unclean thing; and I will receive you; and I will be a Father unto you, and ye shall be my sons and daughters, saith the Lord Almighty,' 2 Cor. 6:17, 18.

The Holy Spirit is the Spirit of truth. He is so in one respect, because he shows to man what he in truth really is, and not what he is not. If a man's spirit be worldly and carnal, he convinces him and shows him that his spirit is so. If his spirit is holy and evangelic, the divine Spirit will shine on his own work, and will give satisfaction in a degree more or less, that he is the worker, and that the work is his.

It is a very unseemly thing, to observe men professing religion, yet withering in their souls, and still seeking to retain confidence as to their spiritual safety. It is grievous to see some, notwithstanding the withering state of their souls, apparently whole and thoughtless, instead of lamenting and sorrowing for their lukewarmness and disordered state of mind, and intreating the Lord for restoration, who is able to confirm his inheritance when it is weary, and make his people 'fat and flourishing' in their old age. May the Lord give us a right understanding in all things.

5. Minutes of an Association at Bala

June 13-14, 1797.

A CONVERSATION was held at the private meeting, the first morning, with some of the brethren of the county. One brother, advanced in years, gave some account of the beginning of his religion, and of his experience in general during his life afterwards. The Lord first began to work on his feelings, as he often found some delight to his mind in hearing and praying. But after a time he lost these tender feelings, and corruptions raised their heads, working strongly and effectually. Upon this his mind became much distressed; and he felt great concern and trouble about his state. In the midst of this distress, arising from a view of his own sinfullness and misery, the Lord manifested to him the fitness of Christ as a Saviour, and the indispensable necessity of believing in him for salvation. This manifestation of Christ wrought a peculiar change in his mind, which has endured in its fruits to this day. He perceived that there was neither justification nor sanctification for a sinner but in him, and that everything that a sinner wants is in him abundantly, and to be had freely. He testified that he continues to feel a degree of peace in his soul and trust in the Lord, arising from the view he had of Christ according to the testimony of his word concerning him, though he enjoyed but little of the 'joy unspeakable and full of glory,' mentioned by the apostle. He said that he saw himself vile, unclean, and very detestable, that he was longing to know Christ and the worth of his sacrifice more, and that he had special reasons to lament his want of earnest striving to walk with God in spiritual-mindedness and self-denial; but, notwithstanding all, that he was acquainted with some degree of reliance in his soul on the sacrifice of Christ, and that this produced a corresponding degree of comfort to his mind.

From what this aged brother said of himself, an occasion was taken to notice briefly the difference between some feelings arising from pleasing influences on a man's mind, and the real discovery of Christ to the soul by the Holy Spirit. That the one can be without the other is evident from Scripture. The hearers, signified by the seed on stony places, prove this most clearly. Immediately with joy they received the word; yet soon after, through the fiery heat of persecution, they withdrew, withered and vanished.

1. There is no real discovery of Christ made to any, without previous conviction of sin, and self-abasement on its account in true repentance, Matt. 9:12. There may be strong workings on the affections of men without this.

2. The mind of him, who has a spiritual discovery of Christ by faith, is changed and renewed. 'The natural man receiveth not the things of the Spirit of God,' 1 Cor. 2:14. A real view of the glory of Christ in the gospel changes the soul into the same image: but there may be temporary and evanescent workings on the feelings, without any holy change in the mind.

3. When there is a real acquaintance with Christ, there is an union between Christ and the soul. The soul has a beloved, and Christ is he; and it rejects everything else in comparison with him, and cleaves to him only. Everything is counted but dung and loss, on account of the excellence of Christ. There is a choosing of him, and a surrender of one's self to him forever. There are none in so much danger of deceiving themselves, as those who are satisfied

with feeling strong impressions now and then, and yet without a renewal in the mind.

While conversing with another, he was asked whether he ever saw that *unbelief* was a sin. It was not asked whether he had seen that an unbelieving state was a lost state; but whether he had seen that unbelief in every respect is a sin against God, besides its being injurious and uncomfortable to himself? Yea, and more sinful than any other sin? And if so, had he known what it was to humble himself penitently before God on its account? It was observed that little was heard in prayers generally of confessions made of unbelief as a sin against God; and that there was reason to fear, that few viewed it really as a sin, and repented of it. One must be convinced of it as a sin, before he can be penitent on its account: and it is the peculiar work of the Holy Spirit to convince man of this sin. It was asked, what are we to understand by unbelief? The answer was that it is not to believe God speaking in his word as to everything, especially as to his testimony respecting his Son. Not to believe God:

1. *Dishonours* God greatly. 'He that believeth not God hath made him a liar,' 1 John 5:10. The danger of an unbelieving state is greater in our view than the sinfullness of the offence. But what dishonour is it to God to count him unworthy of being believed? It is a great dishonour to him, not to consider seriously what he speaks to us; but it is yet a greater dishonour, after having considered it, not to believe it, and not to act in a manner suitable to such a belief in every way. We should judge him to have but a poor opinion of us, who should not count us worthy of being believed, or take no notice of what we might say; but this is the dishonour which the God who is infinitely worthy of being believed, receives continually at our hands.

2. Unbelief is a sin which *provokes* God greatly. 'How long,' says God, of Israel, 'will this people provoke me? and how long will it be ere they believe me?' Num. 14:11.

3. No sin produces *worse effects* on the souls of men than this. It is the nurture and strength of every other sin: such as perverseness, disobedience, murmuring, carnal lusts, etc., as we clearly observe

in the history of the Israelites in the wilderness, who were not able to enter into rest in Canaan, because of their unbelief, Heb. 3:19. It hinders every spiritual blessing from coming to the soul. The gospel, the word of life, is not profitable to any without being mixed with faith in them that hear it, Heb. 4:2.

4. God *threatens the heaviest judgements* on its account: it must therefore exceed everything else in its sinfullness, Matt. 11:24. God never threatens nor punishes any, more than their offence deserves! And if he threatens to punish unbelief in an awful manner, it must be a very great sin.

5. It is a sin which *opposes* more peculiarly than any other the whole plan of salvation. It makes no account of infinite love in its most glorious manifestations, regards the wisest and the most gracious plan as folly, and cleaves to rebellion against God, when a full deliverance from it is freely proclaimed. It departs from the living God, treads underfoot the Son of God, counts the blood of the everlasting covenant an unholy thing, and does despite to the Spirit of grace, Heb. 10:29. This was the sin which appeared first on the earth, and opened the door for every other sin to enter in. 'Yea,' said the serpent, 'hath God said, ye shall not eat of every tree of the garden?' Then God was not believed, and sin came into the world, and death by sin. This sin killed the Israelites in the wilderness, after they escaped from Pharaoh, walked through the sea, and were kept alive under the awful thunders of Sinai. This closed up the hearts of men from receiving Christ, restrained the wonder-working hand of Christ himself, and hindered saving blessings to the souls of men. It is still putting man in the place of God, the folly of man in the place of God's wisdom, the strength of man in the place of God's strength, and man's filthy garments in the place of Christ's Divine Righteousness. It is in effect casting God from his government, Christ from his mediation, and the Spirit from his work. The language of unbelief always is, 'man can work,' or 'God cannot or will not.' It was observed:

1. That though the godly are delivered from an unbelieving state, yet unbelief is working in them strongly and continually, as

a sin ready to beset them to their great hurt, and that instead of being less, it is more sinful in them than in others. But in whom is true repentance on its account to be found? Who, feeling a pain within, confesses his sin before God with a godly sorrow? Do we deem it a small matter to make God a liar, by acting towards him, as if he were so?

2. It was observed, that a real belief of the word, brings a man, as to the state of his mind, to a compliance with the word in everything, that is, in his intercourse with God as to salvation, in his conduct towards men, in his worldly transactions; in all he walks according to this rule. He trembleth at the word, and dreads proceeding in any way contrary to it.

3. It was also mentioned, that none really believe without feeling the difficulty of believing. To believe is the gift of God and the work of God, wrought in the soul of man by the mighty working of the Holy Spirit. To believe is not a carnal consent to divine truths: that is a dead faith, which receives nothing from God, and does nothing for him. Men believe by the mighty power of the Holy Spirit working in their souls, enabling them to lay hold on the truth of the promise, in the face of every corruption and misery. It is to believe, like Abraham, against every ground of hope in ourselves, on the ground of God's promises, who is faithful and able to fulfil what he has promised. The translation of the soul accompanies true believing. The soul, like Sarah, barren, receives strength to conceive: from being afar off from God, it is brought to great nearness to him; from a state of enmity, it is brought to a reconciliation with God; from flesh and self, it is brought to live and walk with God.

While considering these things, all were exhorted to a self-examination with respect to every truth – do I really believe it – is my spirit according to the truth – is it according to the path of truth that I desire to live, and hope to prosper – is it in the truths of God that I seek for light, guidance, strength and consolation, while I live in the world – is there in me real and continued repentance on account of my unbelief? A peculiar blessing accompanied the handling of this subject, and many confessed, that they clearly perceived that their unbelief was the lamentable cause of all their languor, deadness and misery.

We parted in love and peace, longing for the opportunity of meeting again. Twelve of the Brethren preached during the meeting, in a savoury and edifying manner; and there were pleasing tokens, that the dew of heaven was poured down on the numerous assembly that attended.

THE END.

THE FIRST MAJOR BIOGRAPHY OF THE WELSH CALVINISTIC
METHODIST LEADER SINCE 1908!

Thomas Charles of Bala
John Aaron

ISBN: 978 1 80040 095 5, cloth-bound, 400pp. approx.

Thomas Jones, Denbigh, and Thomas Charles were the two most discerning theologians of the last [19th] century; indeed they were the greatest [Welsh] theologians from 1790 to the present day.

R. M. JONES

Perhaps no man was the means of bringing more blessing to his native land [than Thomas Charles], and yet no books on his life have been available for a long time.

IAIN H. MURRAY

Only four biographies of Thomas Charles have ever been published, and none, in English or Welsh, since 1908. Not one is currently in print and this has been the situation for over a hundred years. The 1908 *Life* by D. E. Jenkins is a massive three-volume work of 1,927 pages: it is a gold-mine of letters, documents, and facts but is utterly unreadable as a biography. In all its pages there is not one discussion of Charles's theological position.

John Aaron's new biography (2021) is an accurate and readable account of Thomas Charles's life, presented against the backcloth of his day and age, and in the light of his extensive network of correspondents, both Welsh and English. The author describes and gauges Charles's strengths and weaknesses, and discusses briefly his scholarship and theology, particularly as expressed in his very popular catechism, *Yr Hyfforddwr* (*The Instructor*) – published in 1807 and going through eighty editions before 1900 – and his *magnum opus*, the 944-page *Geiriadur Ysgrythyrol* (*Scriptural Dictionary*), published in parts from 1805 to 1811.

This volume is a valuable companion to *Thomas Charles's Spiritual Counsels*.

The Banner of Truth Trust originated in 1957 in London. The founders believed that much of the best literature of historic Christianity had been allowed to fall into oblivion and that, under God, its recovery could well lead not only to a strengthening of the church, but to true revival.

Interdenominational in vision, this publishing work is now international, and our lists include a number of contemporary authors, together with classics from the past. The translation of these books into many languages is encouraged.

A monthly magazine, *The Banner of Truth*, is also published, and further information about this, and all our other publications, may be found on our website, banneroftruth.org, or by contacting the offices below:

Head Office:
3 Murrayfield Road
Edinburgh
EH12 6EL
United Kingdom
Email: info@banneroftruth.co.uk

North America Office:
PO Box 621
Carlisle, PA 17013
United States of America
Email: info@banneroftruth.org

Looking from Bala, across Llyn Tegid, towards the Aran peaks.